The Popularization of Malthus in Early Nineteenth-Century England

The Popularization of Malthus in Early Nineteenth-Century England

Martineau, Cobbett and the Pauper Press

JAMES P. HUZEL

Routledge
Taylor & Francis Group

LONDON AND NEW YORK

First published 2006 by Ashgate Publishing

2 Park Square, Milton Park, Abingdon, Oxon OX14 4RN
711 Third Avenue, New York, NY 10017, USA

Routledge is an imprint of the Taylor & Francis Group, an informa business

First issued in paperback 2017

British Library Cataloguing in Publication Data
Huzel, James P.
 The Popularization of Malthus in Early Nineteenth Century England:
 Martineau, Cobbett and the Pauper Press. – (Modern Economic and Social
 History)
 1. Malthus, T.R. (Thomas Robert), 1766–1834 – Influence. 2. Malthus, T.R.
 (Thomas Robert), 1766–1834. 3. Cobbett, William, 1763–1835.
 4. Demography – Great Britain – History – 19th century. 5. Malthusianism.
 I. Title
 304.6'092

US Library of Congress Cataloging in Publication Data
Huzel, James P.
 The Popularization of Malthus in Early Nineteenth Century England:
 Martineau, Cobbett and the Pauper Press / James P. Huzel.
   p.   cm. – (Modern Economic and Social History)
 Includes index.
 1. Malthus, T.R. (Thomas Robert), 1766–1834. 2. Malthusianism. 3. Press –
 England – History – 19th century. I. Title. II. Modern Economic and Social
 History.
 HB863.H88 2006
 330.15'3–dc22   2005049430

ISBN 978-0-7546-5427-8 (hbk)
ISBN 978-1-138-26302-4 (pbk)

Typeset in 10/12 Sabon by IML Typographers, Birkenhead, Merseyside

Contents

CONTENTS

List of illustrations

Modern Economic and Social History Series
General Editor's Preface

Economic and social history has been a flourishing subject of scholarly study during recent decades. Not only has the volume of literature increased enormously but the range of interest in time, space and subject matter has broadened considerably so that today there are many sub-branches of the subject which have developed considerable status in their own right.

One of the aims of this new series is to encourage the publication of scholarly monographs on any aspect of modern economic and social history. The geographical coverage is world-wide and contributions on non-British themes will be especially welcome. While emphasis will be placed on work embodying original research, it is also intended that the series should provide the opportunity to publish studies of a more general and thematic nature which offer a reappraisal or critical analysis of major issues of debate.

Derek H. Aldcroft
University of Leicester

Preface

'The First Dr. Death gets new respect' ran a bold heading for a major article on Malthus in *The Globe and Mail*, one of Canada's national newspapers (14 November 1998). A short time later *The New York Times* devoted several pages to the subject of global population and world resources that included a piece headed '**Why Malthus Was Mistaken**' (19 September 1999). Several letters to the editor followed. It is obvious, then, that two hundred years after he first published his *Essay on the Principle of Population* (1798) Malthus remains very much with us in the popular press. What is more surprising, however, is that the myths surrounding his theory and motivations still persist as tenaciously as they did in his own time. Although his popular critics in the early nineteenth century never actually referred to him as 'Dr Death', they nevertheless viewed him as a cruel and heartless apologist for the landed elite who advocated death by starvation for the poor. Malthus, they believed, argued that surplus population – a product of reckless childbearing among the labouring classes encouraged by welfare subsidies – would, and more important, *should* be alleviated by famine and disease. They even viewed him as a promoter of infanticide and abortion. His recommendation that all relief to the impoverished should be abolished in order to curb excess population growth only furthered the popular image of a political economist so evil and callous as to make Charles Dickens's Scrooge look like a philanthropist.

Yet the endurance of such misrepresentation and the vitriolic press he received is perhaps not so astounding. I must confess that when I first read Malthus almost four decades ago my reaction was deeply hostile. His prescriptions seemed unduly harsh and prejudiced against the poverty-stricken labourers of England. His pessimism, moreover, was equally disturbing. To describe the poor as 'unhappy persons who, in the great lottery of life, have drawn a blank' was hardly satisfying to a young and admittedly idealistic graduate student. Since then, I have assigned the first *Essay* as prescribed reading for undergraduates in a course entitled 'Population in History' which I designed in the early 1970s and taught for over three decades. Most students – no background reading or lectures were given – reacted negatively to his ideas. Only on reading selections from his later works did they adopt a more balanced view of his writing.

My views on Malthus have altered considerably over the years with the realization that one must read far beyond his first *Essay* of 1798 and even his second *Essay* of 1803 to fully comprehend his theories and intentions. Indeed, the misinterpretations of his work and much of the antagonism towards him were, and continue to be, largely based on a reading of the first *Essay* and selected portions from the second. A total perspective gained from reading the entire body of his writings paints a very different picture of the man. Far from advocating the demise of the 'lower orders', Malthus honestly sought solutions that would improve their position in society and became increasingly optimistic about such a possibility. He never, of course, supported infanticide or abortion. Nor was he a mere lackey of the ruling classes. Indeed, he often spoke against the interests of the landed aristocracy.

What impressed me about Malthus was his ability to alter his views on issues in light of shifting economic and social realities. Equally impressive is the fact that he was no doctrinaire follower of the accepted tenets of political economy and was prepared, often at great personal cost, to take positions counter to free market principles and Ricardian orthodoxy. Although I still have strong disagreements with many of his views, my respect for his intellectual depth and sincerity has grown significantly.

In any case, whether one thinks Malthus right or wrong has little to do with what follows. My purpose is neither to bash Malthus nor to exalt him but rather to delineate and, as far as possible, to explain the dissemination of and reaction to his ideas in the popular press of his time. I further intend to draw conclusions regarding the overall influence of his writings. In doing so, I have taken the liberty of quoting extensively from both his supporters and detractors. Only through such exposition – what some of my colleagues refer to as the 'Full Monty' approach – can the true texture of this early nineteenth-century discourse be understood. Only in this manner can one fully comprehend what, for contemporaries, was truly at stake and the passion with which they defended and promoted their interests.

I would like to thank the University of British Columbia for Humanities and Social Sciences Research Grants that funded some of the research upon which this study is based. My thanks also go to Louise Robert for her valuable research assistance. I am also indebted to Ian Dyck for reading and commenting on the chapter dealing with William Cobbett. My late friend and colleague Murray Greenwood and James Winter of the University of British Columbia read significant portions of the manuscript. I thank them for their editorial and critical advice. My deepest gratitude, however, is to my wife Gail not only for her research, editing and word processing of the manuscript but also for her constant encouragement and faith in the project. Without her prodding –

sometimes mild, sometimes not so mild – the work would never have come to fruition.

James P. Huzel,
The University of British Columbia, 2005

A note on the text

All quotations in the text and endnotes are verbatim and thus retain the original spelling, grammar and punctuation. Emphasis of words, phrases or sentences is not mine unless specified as 'my emphasis'. Abbreviations have been used only in the endnotes: *PR* denotes *Political Register*; *PMG* denotes *The Poor Man's Guardian*.

This book is dedicated to Gail with love and thanks

Introduction: significance and agenda

E. J. Hobsbawm, in his *Industry and Empire*, remarked that the New Poor Law of 1834 'created more embittered unhappiness than any other statute of modern British history'.[1] This legislation denied outdoor relief to able-bodied males and their families, offering instead the discipline of the workhouse where the sexes would be segregated and conditions made 'less-eligible' – worse off – than those of the poorest independent labourer. The landed interest of England, in conjunction with the newly enfranchised middle classes, thus enacted perhaps the most significant social and economic reform of the nineteenth century. The application of such principles finally destroyed what William Godwin, a contemporary adversary of Malthus, referred to as 'the old received notions of morality'[2] – a 'moral economy' in the vernacular of modern historians – which recognized the *right* of the destitute to relief under provisions of the Old Poor Law (my emphasis). Henceforth, the individual, especially the male head of the household, would be totally responsible for his livelihood and that of his wife and children or else suffer pain and humiliation inside the workhouse. The New Poor Law thus established the most critical component in the emergence of a new and revolutionary capitalist market economy: a national labour market where individuals, no longer entitled to monetary relief, would be compelled to earn wages unsupplemented by Poor Law payments. 'Not until 1834', Karl Polanyi astutely observed over half a century ago, 'was a competitive labor market established in England; hence industrial capitalism as a social system cannot be said to have existed before that date.... It is no exaggeration to say that the social history of the nineteenth century was determined by the logic of the market system proper after it was released by the Poor Law Reform Act of 1834.'[3]

Some recent scholars have given Malthus a central role in the creation of the New Poor Law, viewing him as one of the most influential thinkers in the rise of liberal capitalism. Although debate continues about his specific influence, few would deny that from his first publication in 1798 to his death in 1834 he shaped the entire discourse on the poor and became the beacon against which all proposals for solving the growing problem of poverty in early industrial society had to be measured. Even though he was eventually overshadowed in the realm of political economy by figures such as David Ricardo and John Ramsay McCulloch, his views on population and poverty held sway throughout his lifetime and far beyond. The term 'Malthusian' became embedded in the language of the early nineteenth century and Malthus became one of the most controversial writers of his age.

The publication of Malthus's first work – *An Essay on the Principle of Population* – in 1798 could not have been more timely.[4] Poverty had been rapidly increasing in England and expenditure on poor relief had reached unprecedented levels, generating an intense public debate on the subject of pauperism.[5] The 'moral economy' both in theory and practice was under increasing assault from an accelerating market economy and its attendant justifications emanating especially from the individualism of Adam Smith.

Malthus's anonymous 1798 *Essay* immediately attracted widespread public attention. His fundamental thesis that population growth among the lower orders was outstripping the food supply and creating mass misery ran counter to prevailing Mercantilist theories that viewed a growing and bountiful population as an economic benefit. His proposals regarding the Old Poor Law garnered even more notice. Monetary allowances to the poor, both single and married, paid out of the poor rates to the unemployed or to those whose wages were insufficient to provide adequate subsistence, he argued, were an incentive to earlier marriages and larger families. A vicious circle thereby ensued among the labouring poor: welfare subsidies leading to earlier marriage resulting in more unsupportable children, increasing poverty and increased Poor Law expenditure. The remedy for such improvidence lay in the total abolition of the Poor Laws and denial of any legal entitlement to relief. The principle of 'benevolence', Malthus contended, should be replaced by the individualistic precept of 'self-love.'[6] Able-bodied individuals, especially males, would now be fully responsible for their material survival. Even such drastic measures, however, would not eliminate misery. Malthus concluded his *Essay* with a pessimism which boldly contradicted Enlightenment assumptions of human progress. Indeed, the *Essay* launched specific critiques of optimistic thinkers such as Adam Smith, the Marquis de Condorcet and William Godwin.

Although Malthus gained many influential adherents to his principles especially in Whig circles and eventually even among the gentry and aristocracy – support which ensured the legislative triumph of his ideas – what stands out is the hostile, indeed extremely vituperative, response he provoked and the broad spectrum from which such intense opposition originated. Tory paternalists, Romantics, Enlightenment thinkers and advocates for working-class justice assaulted Malthus throughout his lifetime with a venom rarely witnessed by historians.

The primary aim of the present work is to substantiate a claim made by J. R. Poynter in his now-classic book entitled *Society and Pauperism*: 'Whatever the intrinsic interest or possible influence of Bentham's writings on poverty and indigence, it must be admitted that for every reference to him in later discussion of the Poor Law, there were twenty to Malthus. If we judge influence by fame, then Malthus's contribution to shaping opinion on pauperism was incomparable.'[7] Many significant expositions, of course, have emerged in support of Poynter's hypothesis in the more than three decades since he wrote. Donald Winch's *Riches and Poverty* explores with great finesse the intellectual impact of Malthus's ideas.[8] Not only does he analyse theoretical differences between Malthus and Smith, and Malthus and Ricardo, he also provides a detailed treatment of the extremely hostile attack launched by early Romantics such as William Hazlitt, Robert Southey, the Lake Poets and Samuel Taylor Coleridge. Mitchell Dean's *The Constitution of Poverty* explores Malthus's prominent role in the early nineteenth-century debate on poverty.[9] Like Gertrude Himmelfarb in *The Idea of Poverty*,[10] he gives Malthus paramount influence in the creation of the New Poor Law of 1834.

In terms of Malthus's impact on specific social groups, Peter Mandler and Boyd Hilton have made important contributions to our understanding of how Malthusian ideas permeated the mental world of influential sections of the aristocracy and gentry in the decades before 1834.[11] Not only, insists Mandler, had many in the ruling elite read Malthus but also they gained increasing influence on the numerous parliamentary committees investigating poverty in the post-1815 period culminating in their dominance as assistant commissioners for the *1834 Poor Law Report* which provided the rationale for the legislative Bill of that year.[12] Boyd Hilton stresses the rise of Christian versions of political economy that eventually established a 'moral hegemony over public life' in the early nineteenth century, especially among liberal elements within the Tory party.[13] Winch argues that Malthus played a significant role in promulgating such views.[14] The integration between Malthus's Christian theology and his political economy has also been a theme in the writings of A. M. C. Waterman, John Pullen and E. N. Santurri.[15] Such analysis helps explain why Malthus eventually gained the support of the Anglican establishment. Mandler argues that such adherence permeated down the social scale to the level of the country parson.[16]

Although such a rich body of work has enlightened our historical understanding of Malthus's influence, little discussion has taken place regarding his impact at a more popular level. No study, for example, has been undertaken to consider the ways in which his message was translated to a wider middle- and especially working-class audience in an attempt to convert them to the Malthusian cause. Likewise, no serious treatment has been devoted to the popularization of his ideas among the working class and the highly critical reaction which ensued. The analysis which follows attempts to remedy this situation, arguing that Malthus's contribution to shaping public opinion was indeed incomparable and penetrated well below elite levels of intellectual discussion and policy making.

The obvious choice for an examination of attempts to favourably popularize Malthus was Harriet Martineau. The most fervent admirer of his ideas on population and poverty, she wrote *Illustrations of Political Economy* between 1832 and 1834.[17] This work, consisting of twenty-five didactic tales, sought to convey the key principles of political economy in fictional form. Many of her stories contained specifically Malthusian themes. Martineau had no doubt regarding her intended audience. She believed her serialized work was 'craved by the popular mind'[18] and thus aimed her work at a mass public comprising the middle and especially the working class. She achieved a level of sales that astonished even her publisher Charles Fox. In the same years she also published *Poor Laws and Paupers Illustrated* in four volumes comprising similar tales dealing specifically with poverty and Poor Law administration.[19] These works, although frequently cited, have received scant analytical attention from historians with the exception of a chapter in a recent work by Caroline Roberts entitled *The Woman and The Hour*.[20]

Regarding the diffusion of and hostile reaction to Malthus's ideas among the working class, the writings of William Cobbett provide the best focus of analysis. Cobbett was Malthus's single most determined adversary in the early nineteenth century. He achieved even greater mass circulation than Martineau, especially in his radical journal *Political Register* and the twopenny tracts he published which often reprinted articles from his journal. Determined to reach not only urban but also rural labourers both literate and semi-literate – those who could not read would have his works read aloud to them – he deliberately tailored his style and content to the lower orders. His message was also transmitted through the vast number of speeches he gave throughout England. With an invective rivalling the best of nineteenth-century authors, Cobbett fuelled detestation of Malthus and anyone who espoused his principles, especially Harriett Martineau. He died fighting the New Poor Law with every ounce of energy he could muster and was thoroughly convinced of its Malthusian origins.

Although numerous works have appeared on Cobbett, little attention has been paid to his critique of Malthus. Two brief but somewhat inadequate articles appeared in the 1950s.[21] George Spater's two-volume study of Cobbett in 1982 relegates discussion of Cobbett and Malthus to a short Appendix.[22] Gertrude Himmelfarb does devote a chapter to Cobbett in her *The Idea of Poverty* (1984). To be sure, she makes frequent reference to Malthus but views Cobbett's attack on him as mainly based on personal animosity devoid of serious content.[23] More recently Ian Dyck's admirable *William Cobbett and Rural Popular Culture* provides important insights but does not provide detailed discussion of the prominent role Malthus played within the framework of Cobbett's thought.[24] The latest biography of Cobbett by Anthony Burton devotes only two pages to Malthus but quite rightly stresses the passion in Cobbett's writing that 'smokes off the page'.[25]

Cobbett, of course, was but one – the main one to be sure – of a chorus of voices attacking Malthus from a radical perspective. A third focus, then, of the popular reaction to Malthus concerns the wider working-class press, often referred to as the 'unstamped' or 'pauper press', which burgeoned in the pre-1834 period and reached a wide audience. Although works by Patricia Hollis and Joel Wiener explore the ideology of this vast body of popular literature, once again almost no emphasis is placed on the significant anti-Malthusian sentiment expounded by a wide range of radical editors.[26] Himmelfarb devotes a chapter in her *Idea of Poverty* entitled 'The Poor Man's Guardian: The New Radicalism' to the pauper press but deals with only one – albeit a significant one – among hundreds of papers. Malthus receives no mention.[27]

Many of these writers drew heavily on Cobbett's critique of Malthus which provides further testimony to the widespread influence of his radical thought. Others in the pauper press took Cobbett's analysis to new levels expounding more sophisticated ideological platforms and attacking Malthus from directions Cobbett publicly abhorred. The best example of the latter was the advocacy, especially by Richard Carlile, of contraceptive birth control as a solution to the Malthusian dilemma. He explicitly stated the specific technical methods by which fertility could be curtailed and also argued that such means should be utilized by both unmarried and married females. He further shocked Cobbett and the vast majority of English society by proposing that sexual intercourse regardless of marital status was absolutely necessary to the health and happiness of all individuals. Indeed, the first public debate on birth control in English history took place within the pages of the early nineteenth-century working-class press.

Although the main purpose of this work is to support Poynter's thesis concerning Malthus's dominant influence on conceptions of poverty, a broader aim is to give Malthus the prominence he deserves in the widest possible historical sense. To be sure, the significance of his writings has been accelerating since 1980 when a major International Conference on Historical Demography convened in Paris with the title *Malthus Past and*

Present. Participants from 61 countries presented over 160 simultaneously translated papers to more than 500 participants on all aspects of his thought and influence.[28] In 1998, on the bicentennial of the publication of Malthus's first *Essay*, the journal *History of Political Economy* published a 'Minisymposium: Malthus at 200' with contributions from major scholars in the field.[29] In the intervening years numerous works appeared culminating in two seminal books by Donald Winch and Samuel Hollander which, contends A. M. C. Waterman, 'at last canonized' Malthus in the fields of intellectual history and the history of economic analysis respectively.[30]

Nearly one-half of Winch's *Riches and Poverty* deals with 'Robert Malthus as Political Moralist'.[31] Such emphasis towers over the relatively insignificant weight he gives to the likes of Jeremy Bentham, James and J. S. Mill, John Ramsay McCulloch and especially David Ricardo. Winch is intent on rectifying the neglect of Malthus relative to Ricardo in previous works and is convinced that 'one can no more understand Ricardo without Malthus than one can understand either without Smith.'[32] Nor, he claims, can one interpret the transformation of Smith's science of political economy in the early nineteenth century without comprehending Malthus's Christian beliefs and natural theology.[33]

If Winch's reappraisal has given Malthus his rightful place in the realm of intellectual history, Samuel Hollander's mammoth *The Economics of Thomas Robert Malthus* does so in the realm of economic analysis providing us with the most thorough monograph to date of Malthus as an economist. As Waterman succinctly points out, Hollander's most important achievement 'consists in dispelling once and for all the idea that Malthus was not really a theoretician of the same order – and of at least as much historic importance – as Ricardo'.[34] He thus places Malthus fully alongside Smith and Ricardo as a major figure in the history of political economy. The present work seeks to complement recent writings on Malthus by according prime significance to Malthus's thought; not to be sure, in the fields of Winch and Hollander but rather in the realm of mass popular opinion.

The reappraisal of Malthus over the last quarter century has enriched our comprehension of Malthus in other significant ways. A number of myths surrounding Malthus that began in his own time and continued well into our own have finally been dispelled. Many of these misconceptions were fuelled by Karl Marx's invective well after Malthus's death. According to Marx, Malthus was a superficial plagiarist whose works did not 'contain a single sentence thought out by himself'.[35] More seriously, he was 'a professional sycophant of the landed aristocracy, whose rents, sinecures, extravagance, heartlessness etc., he justified from the economic point of view.'[36] He was, furthermore, not '*a man of science but ... a bought advocate ... a shameless sycophant of the ruling classes*.[37] It is true that Malthus relied on a substantial body of contemporary works but, contrary to Marx, he gave their authors full credit and developed original theories of his own.[38] Hollander among others has found, moreover, the accusation that Malthus was a mere propagandist for the landed aristocracy utterly lacking in substance.[39]

Additional interpretations of Malthus have been found wanting. Although he advocated delay of marriage he never proposed laws specifying minimum ages for matrimony. He was not anti-natalist but rather sought to bring population into balance with the food supply.[40] He did not wish misery upon the poor nor did he sanction the starvation of adults and children as a method of limiting population. In his later works he developed an increasing optimism that the lower orders would benefit significantly in material terms. He deeply resented accusations that he was hard-hearted. He sought solutions to seemingly insurmountable problems with what his contemporary Robert Torrens described as 'a spirit of candour and love of truth',[41] an opinion echoed by both Francis Horner and David Ricardo who disagreed with Malthus on many substantial issues. Ricardo referred to Malthus's 'honest conscientious opinions'.[42]

Another important service that some recent scholarship has provided is to clarify our interpretation of Malthus's writings by considering the entire body of his work rather than treating specific treatises in isolation. Although the latter practice still prevails, the strength of Winch and Hollander lies in their ability to analyse the *total* Malthus (my emphasis).[43] Such interpretation has been greatly facilitated by the painstaking work of Patricia James and John Pullen who have produced variora editions of Malthus's 1803 *Essay* and his *Principles of Political Economy* (1820) respectively and by E. A. Wrigley's and David Souden's publication of Malthus's remaining works in eight volumes.[44]

If Malthus was one of the most infamous writers of the early nineteenth century, he was clearly one of the most misunderstood. Such misunderstandings, which persist to the present day, stem from manifold roots. D. E. C. Eversley remarked of Malthus that no writer of his fame had greater facility in nullifying in a footnote what had previously taken six or seven pages to explain.[45] Hollander, indeed, has pointed out serious inconsistencies in Malthus's economic theory.[46] Others abound. At times, for example, Malthus categorically stated that the Old Poor Law encouraged early marriage and at others seemed to doubt this was the case.[47] At times he wrote as if moral restraint – delay of marriage while maintaining absolute celibacy – was the only viable solution to overpopulation among the poor while in other instances he relied on prudential restraint, the practice of delaying marriage with occasional premarital lapses. In addition, as Hollander points out, Malthus 'left himself wide open for misunderstanding because of his love of paradox, argument, and provocation as well as a certain carelessness in his use of terms'.[48]

Another source of confusion originates from the fact that Malthus, often in the face of stern censure from his fellow political economists and at great personal cost, changed his mind on many of his key assumptions.[49] As Winch argues, Malthus was committed to observation and experiment.[50] Such pragmatism led him to alter his views in light of current economic circumstances. In the post-Napoleonic depression following 1815, for example, he violated free market principles in favour of state-sponsored public works to ease unemployment and distress. His rejection of Say's law, even on a temporary basis, was seen as a 'profound heresy' on the part of orthodox Ricardians.[51]

Over the years Malthus changed position in many other crucial areas. Earlier works stressed agriculture over manufacturing as the route to economic betterment. He later viewed such sectors as equal contributors. In the 1798 *Essay* he recommended the abolition of primogeniture while later supporting it.[52] Even though the 6th edition of his *Essay* in 1826 (the last during his lifetime) continued to advocate the abolition of the Old Poor Law, his final public statement on the matter in 1830 entitled *A Summary View of the Principle of Population* allowed that under certain circumstances parochial relief might constitute a net benefit.[53] Overall, Malthus became more optimistic as the years wore on. He abandoned the stark pessimism of the 1798 *Essay* and foresaw increased improvement in the lot of the labouring poor.

If Malthus was at times inconsistent and changed his views on fundamental issues there nevertheless is a further source of misunderstanding that has little or nothing to do with the writer himself. As Winch observes, Malthus was an author 'who has suffered more than most from systemic misreadings some of them bordering on the deliberate'.[54] Many of Malthus's contemporary critics, especially Cobbett and editors of the working-class press, constantly harped on the more sensational passages especially from the 1803 *Essay* even though Malthus had removed them from later editions and had altered his position significantly. Romantic critics were guilty of similar misinterpretations, often attacking Malthus not for what he said but for public opinions his writings supposedly encouraged. Most of his opponents simply selected segments from his work that would be most suitable in denigrating him and clearly did not read later editions of the *Essay* or his *Principles of Political Economy*.[55] Many of his supporters, Martineau included, likewise misread him and took his theories to extremes. Lest one thinks that modern scholarship is immune to such distortions, John Pullen reminds us of the 'precipitate attempt to simplify and generalize' in some current Malthus studies, stemming from taking too narrow a focus on particular writings to the neglect of others.[56]

Even though the work of Waterman, Pullen, Winch, Hollander and others have avoided the pitfalls of prior misreadings, Malthus, like many influential writers, still remains difficult to interpret. It is no surprise, then, that significant areas of debate still remain. To what extent is the approach of Winch (from the perspective of Intellectual History) compatible with that of Hollander (from the vantage point of the History of Economic Analysis)? Should these methodologies be viewed as competing alternatives?[57] What is the significance of theology within Malthus's overall framework and what specific role did the writings of William Paley play?[58] Did Malthus, in the end, abandon his support for the Corn Laws?[59] Did he, in the final analysis, favour emigration as a solution to overpopulation?[60] Such questions will no doubt gain increased attention from Malthus scholars.

Given the complexities of Malthus's writings and the persistent misinterpretations of his work, I find it important at the outset to clarify his ideas and intentions. Chapter 1, therefore, provides an overview of Malthus's life, thought and influence. Only by tracing the many changes in his views over successive editions of his *Essay on the Principle of Population* and in his *Principles of Political Economy* as well as in the many pamphlets, articles and tracts that he wrote can one determine which Malthus, if any, his popular supporters and detractors had read and the degree to which they deliberately misinterpreted him to serve their own ideological interests. Also included is a discussion of the debate concerning Malthus's influence on the New Poor Law of 1834. Contemporary historians are divided on this issue. Although this new social policy was clearly a combination of complex forces – social, economic and intellectual – I contend that Malthus played a prominent, if indirect, role in its emergence and enactment. If Malthus had a profound influence on popular opinion concerning poverty he also had a significant impact on the practical legislative reforms which eventually governed treatment of the poor. I hope, in addition, that this first chapter will offer a suitable introduction for those readers not entirely familiar with his writings and provide an overall context for the book as a whole.

Chapter 2 considers Malthus's most fervent admirer and popularizer – Harriet Martineau. I undertake a detailed examination of the pro-Malthusian content in her *Illustrations of Political Economy* (twenty-five stories published between 1832 and 1834 which achieved astonishing levels of sales) and her *Poor Laws and Paupers Illustrated* (1833–34). In addition, I address a number of key issues of interpretation. Was Martineau merely a 'female Malthusian' as her critics charged? Why, moreover, was she the focus of such belligerent criticism especially when other female writers such as Jane Marcet, who also fictionalized Malthusian principles of political economy, emerged unscathed and, in fact, highly praised? I express here strong disagreement with Caroline Robert's recent views on this issue in her book entitled *The Woman and the Hour*.[61] A final concern is the extent to which Martineau's project backfired. Did her work, which often took Malthus to extremes, foster increased detestation of Malthus rather than win over converts to his cause?

Chapter 3 examines the vituperative, not to mention voluminous and widely read, writings of William Cobbett against his arch-enemy 'Parson Malthus'. His literary output assumed an impressive variety of forms: articles in his popular radical journal *Political Register* which were often cheaply reprinted in his *Twopenny Trash*, books, pamphlets, sermons, travel observations, advice manuals, open letters to the public and even a play entitled *Surplus Population: A Comedy in Three Acts*. I argue that Malthus played a far more dominant role within the body of Cobbett's thought than once assumed. His attacks on Malthus were far more than mere personal, emotional outbursts devoid of intellectual content. Although he often misread Malthus, he nevertheless brought a wealth of social, legal and economic evidence against proposals to deny relief to the poor and restrict their numbers. In the process, he developed original definitions of the nature of property rights, natural law, the social compact and civil liberty while at the same time fuelling detestation of Malthus and Martineau among the working class.

Chapter 4 turns to the wider working-class press – often termed the 'Pauper Press' – which grew prolifically in the early nineteenth century. Well over two hundred such radical papers were published, many illegally, in London alone between 1817 and 1836, the vast majority between 1830 and 1836. Over two dozen of the most important and widely read of these were selected for analysis. They include the writings of a cross-section of the most influential radical editors and publishers – Thomas Wooler, Richard Carlile, Henry Hetherington and Bronterre O'Brien among others. Although often beset with internecine disputes, these writers were virtually unified in their opposition to Malthus, often echoing the criticisms levelled by Cobbett. Even those who accepted Malthus's premise of overpopulation rejected his solutions. They argued, for example, that delaying marriage by practicing moral restraint (that is, celibacy) was unfeasible. In proposing their own remedies for poverty, many went beyond what Patricia Hollis has termed the 'old ideology' of Cobbett – which focused on 'Old Corruption' – and developed a 'new ideology' based on the economic and social inequities of a class system. Others, against widely prevailing views to the contrary, advocated voluntary birth control as the way out of the Malthusian dilemma of overpopulation.

A concluding chapter draws together the major themes of my study. The degree to which Malthus was popularized both for and against must place him among the most important thinkers of early nineteenth-century England. No individual had greater influence on reshaping conceptions of poverty and reframing solutions to pauperism. To be sure, his critics, vocal as they were, could not halt the tide of an emerging market economy whose principles culminated in the New Poor Law of 1834. True to Malthus, the new Act denied outdoor relief to the able-bodied, thrusting responsibility for the livelihood of the poor on their own shoulders, and offering only the humiliation of the workhouse as a final bulwark against destitution. Thus was finally established a competitive labour market where wages, unfettered by Poor Law subsidies, could freely seek their level. Nevertheless, the reaction of Cobbett and the wider working-class press against Malthus and his advocate Martineau reveal the passion with which the rights of the poor were defended in a last-gasp attempt to forestall a fully fledged market economy. Such efforts, of course, were in vain. In associating Malthus's name and that of Martineau and other Malthusians with the New Poor Law, however, they had grasped a defining element in early nineteenth-century social and intellectual change.

Endnotes

1. E. J. Hobsbawn, *Industry and Empire: An Economic History of Britain Since 1750* (London: Weidenfeld and Nicolson, 1968), 194.
2. From William Godwin, *Of Population* (1820) cited in *An Essay on the Principle of Population* ed. Philip Appleman (New York: W. W. Norton, 1976), 145. Hereafter cited as *Essay 1798*. For the concept of the 'moral economy' see E. P. Thompson, *Customs in Common: Studies in Traditional Popular Culture* (New York: The New Press, 1993), Chapters IV and V.
3. Karl Polanyi, *The Great Transformation: The Political and Economic Origins of Our Time* 2nd edn (Boston: Beacon Press, 2001), 87. This work was originally published in 1944. Recent research suggests that Polanyi, and to some extent, Hobsbawm overestimated the speed and geographic extent to which the New Poor Law was implemented. Outdoor allowances continued in some areas after 1834 and implementation was subject to local variation. Nevertheless, relief expenditure per head of population declined dramatically after 1834 as did the percentage of the population receiving relief. Anti-Poor Law riots were widespread in south-east England and in Wales. Working-class hostility was also strong in the north. More important, the workhouses became a place of dread in the eyes of the poor who viewed them as prisons in which they would be tormented or even poisoned. See James P. Huzel, 'The Labourer and the Poor Law,

1750–1850' in *The Agrarian History of England and Wales, 1750–1850*, vol. VI, ed. G.E. Mingay (Cambridge: Cambridge University Press, 1989), 792–810 (hereafter cited as 'Labourer and Poor Law') and Anthony Brundage, *The English Poor Laws 1700–1930* (New York: Palgrave, 2002), 74–81. For opposition in the north see Nicholas C. Edsall, *The Anti-Poor Law Movement, 1834–44* (Manchester: Manchester University Press, 1971).

4.   Appleman, *Essay 1798*.

5.   Between 1750 and 1800 poor expenditure in England and Wales quadrupled. See Huzel, 'Labourer and Poor Law,' 761–2 especially Fig. 8.2.

6.   Appleman, *Essay 1798*, 75.

7.   J. R. Poynter, *Society and Pauperism: English Ideas on Poor Relief, 1795–1834* (London: Routledge and Kegan Paul, 1969), 109.

8.   Donald Winch, *Riches and Poverty: An Intellectual History of Political Economy in Britain, 1750–1834* (Cambridge: Cambridge University Press, 1996). Hereafter cited as *Riches and Poverty*.

9.   Mitchell Dean, *The Constitution of Poverty: Toward a Genealogy of Liberal Governance* (London: Routledge, 1991). Hereafter cited as *Constitution of Poverty*.

10.   Gertrude Himmelfarb, *The Idea of Poverty: England in the Early Industrial Age* (London: Faber and Faber, 1985). Hereafter cited as *Idea of Poverty*.

11.   See Peter Mandler, 'The Making of the New Poor Law Redivivus', *Past and Present*, no. 117 (November 1987): 131–57. See also his contribution to 'Debate: The Making of the New Poor Law Redivivus', *Past and Present*, no. 127 (November 1990): 194–201. For Boyd Hilton see *The Age of Atonement: The Influence of Evangelicalism on Social and Economic Thought* 1795–1865 (Oxford: Oxford University Press, 1988). Hereafter cited as *Age of Atonement*.

12.   See Mandler, 'Debate: The Making of the New Poor Law Redivivus': 198.

13.   Cited in ibid., 199.

14.   See Winch, *Riches and Poverty*, 24.

15.   See A. M. C. Waterman, 'Malthus as a Theologian: The "First Essay" and the Relation between Political Economy and Christian Theology' in *Malthus Past and Present*, eds J. Dupâquier, A. Chamoux and E. Grebnik (London: Academic Press, 1983), 195–209 and *Revolution, Economics and Religion: Christian Political Economy 1798–1833* (Cambridge: Cambridge University Press, 1991). See also J. M. Pullen, 'Malthus's Theological Ideas and Their Influence on his Principles of Population', *History of Political Economy* 13, no.1 (Spring 1981): 39–54 and E. N. Santurri, 'Theodicy and Social Policy in Malthus's Thought', *Journal of the History of Ideas* 43 (Apr.–June 1982): 315–20.

16.   Mandler, 'Debate: The Making of the New Poor Law Redivivus': 199.

17.   Harriet Martineau, *Illustrations of Political Economy*, 9 vols. (London: Charles Fox, 1834).

18.   Cited in Caroline Roberts, *The Woman and the Hour: Harriet Martineau and Victorian Ideologies* (Toronto: University of Toronto Press, 2002), 10. Hereafter cited as *Woman and the Hour*.

19.   Harriet Martineau, *Poor Laws and Paupers Illustrated*, 4 vols. (London: Charles Fox, 1833–34).

20. Roberts, *Woman and The Hour*.

21. See Herman Ausubel, 'William Cobbett and Malthusianism', *Journal of the History of Ideas* 13 (1952): 250–56 and Charles H. Kegel, 'William Cobbett and Malthusianism', *Journal of the History of Ideas* 19 (June 1958): 348–62.

22. George Spater, *William Cobbett: The Poor Man's Friend*, 2 vols. (Cambridge: Cambridge University Press, 1992).

23. Himmelfarb, *Idea of Poverty*, ch.IX, 207–29,

24. Ian Dyck, *William Cobbett and Rural Popular Culture* (Cambridge: Cambridge University Press, 1992).

25. Anthony Burton, *William Cobbett: Englishman: A Biography* (London, Aurum Press, 1997), 174.

26. See Patricia Hollis, *The Pauper Press: A Study in Working-Class Radicalism of the 1830s* (Oxford: Oxford University Press, 1970) and Joel H. Wiener, *The War of the Unstamped: The Movement to Repeal the British Newspaper Tax, 1830–1836* (Ithaca, NY: Cornell University Press, 1969).

27. Himmelfarb, *Idea of Poverty*, ch. X, 230–52.

28. Major papers from the conference are published in J. Dupâquier et al., *Malthus Past and Present*.

29. See 'Minisymposium: Malthus at 200' in *History of Political Economy* 30, no. 2 (Summer 1998): 289–363. The contributors were Neil De Marchi, A. M. C. Waterman, Samuel Hollander, John Pullen and Donald Winch. Hereafter cited as 'Minisymposium'.

30. Winch, *Riches and Poverty* and Samuel Hollander, *The Economics of Thomas Robert Malthus* (Toronto: University of Toronto Press, 1997).

31. Winch, *Riches and Poverty*. See Part III, 221–405.

32. Ibid., 411

33. Ibid., 411.

34. Waterman, 'Minisymposium': 324.

35. *Marx and Engels on the Population Bomb*, ed. Ronald Meek (Berkeley: Ramparts Press, 1971), 88, from *Capital*, vol. 1, 1867.

36. Ibid., 129 from *Theories of Surplus Value*, vol. 2 1861–63.

37. Ibid., 137 from *Theories of Surplus Value*, vol. 2 1861–63.

38. See Winch, *Riches and Poverty*, 233.

39. Hollander, *The Economics of Thomas Robert Malthus*, 855–6 and 908–9. See also Waterman, 'Minisymposium': 318.

40. *Malthus Past and Present*, eds J. Dupâquier et. al., viii.

41. For Torrens's statement see Hollander, *The Economics of Robert Thomas Malthus*, 886.

42. For Horner's and Ricardo's views see Winch, *Riches and Poverty*, 336 and 336n. 37.

43. See Pullen, 'Minisymposium': 349. It should be pointed out, however, that J. J. Spengler as early as 1945 in 'Malthus's Total Population Theory: A Restatement and Reappraisal,' *Canadian Journal of Economics and Political Science* 11, no. 83 (1945): 234–64 took a total view of Malthus's work. His article was neglected until recently.

44. T. R. Malthus, *An Essay on the Principle of Population: or a View of its past and present Effects on Human Happiness; with an Enquiry into our Prospects respecting the future Removal or Mitigation of the Evils which it occasions: The version published in 1803, with the variora of 1806, 1807,*

1817, and 1826, 2 vols., ed. Patricia James (Cambridge: Cambridge University Press, 1989), *T. R. Malthus: Principles of Political Economy: Variorum Edition*, 2 vols., ed. John Pullen (Cambridge: Cambridge University Press, 1989), *The Works of Thomas Robert Malthus*, 8 vols., eds E. A. Wrigley and David Souden (London: William Pickering, 1986). See also *T. R. Malthus: The Unpublished Papers in the Collection of Kanto Gakuen University*, vol 1, eds John Pullen and Trevor Hughes Parry (Cambridge: Cambridge University Press, 1997). (Volume II is planned for publication in the near future.)

45. D. E. C. Eversley, *Social Theories of Fertility and the Malthusian Debate* (Oxford: Clarendon Press, 1959), 107.

46. Hollander, *The Economics of Thomas Robert Malthus*, 950.

47. See James P. Huzel, 'Malthus, the Poor Law, and Population in Early Nineteenth-Century England', *Economic History Review*, 2nd Ser. XXII, no. 3 (1969): 430–32.

48. Hollander, *The Economics of Thomas Robert Malthus*, 950.

49. For Malthus's rejection by the Political Economy Club see Patricia James, *Population Malthus: His Life and Times* (London: Routledge and Kegan Paul, 1979), 361–2. Younger members of the club met without Malthus upon the death of Ricardo in 1823 to discuss the Ricardo Memorial Lectures, which were eventually given to Malthus's rival John McCulloch.

50. Winch, *Riches and Poverty*, 232.

51. For a discussion of Malthus's opposition to Jean-Baptiste Say's free market principles and his disagreement with Ricardo see ibid., 358–62.

52. Ibid., 269.

53. Ibid., 321.

54. Winch, 'Minisymposium': 354.

55. See Winch, *Riches and Poverty*, 306–8 where he specifically charges Southey and Hazlitt with such bias.

56. Pullen, 'Minisymposium': 349.

57. De Marchi, 'Minisymposium': 290.

58. Boyd Hilton disagrees with Winch's interpretation of Paley's role. See his review of *Riches and Poverty* in *Times Literary Supplement* (16 August 1996): 9.

59. Hollander takes this position. Pullen and Winch disagree. See Chapter 1 for a more detailed discussion.

60. Hollander takes this view. See Chapter 1 for further discussion of this issue.

61. Caroline Roberts, *Woman and the Hour*.

CHAPTER ONE

Thomas Robert Malthus: an overview of his life, thought and influence

The early years and the 1798 *Essay*

Thomas Robert Malthus was born with a cleft palate and a harelip on 13 February 1766 at a small country house called the Rookery in Wotton, Surrey. He was the sixth child and second son of Daniel Malthus and his wife Henrietta who gave birth to her last child, a daughter, five years later. Robert – he was never called Thomas and often signed his letters T. R. Malthus or T. Robt Malthus – keenly felt the influence of his father throughout his entire education. Daniel had inherited enough money earned through family connections in law and medicine to establish an affluent gentry family and lived comfortably as a cultivated gentleman in different locations in the Home Counties. He occupied much of his time pursuing the classics, contemporary philosophy and botany, becoming a friend and fervent admirer of Jean-Jacques Rousseau who, with David Hume, visited the Rookery a few weeks after Robert's birth.[1] Daniel took responsibility for his son's early education and then sent him, at age twelve, to the Revd Richard Graves at Claverton Rectory near Bath. In 1782, when Robert was sixteen, his father entrusted him to the radical Unitarian Gilbert Wakefield: first at the Dissenting Academy at Warrington established for the sons of Protestant Dissenters and then at Wakefield's home at Bramcote near Nottingham. Wakefield had been a fellow at Jesus College, Cambridge, and in 1784 Malthus took up residence there and began his undergraduate studies. His first tutor was William Frend, a Unitarian, pacifist and advocate of religious toleration who was later barred from the college for his Dissenting views. In 1788 Malthus graduated as 'Ninth Wrangler' – the University's ninth best mathematician of the year. Despite his disability, he won prizes for declamations in Latin and English and he was soon ordained a minister of the Church of England, taking an appointment as curate at Okewood in Surrey in 1789. In 1793 he became a non-resident fellow of Jesus College. For an entire decade after graduation he lived with his parents and two unmarried sisters.

Malthus, then, in the years prior to his literary career had been exposed to a number of tough-minded, unorthodox and contentious thinkers – traits that emerged strongly in his own writings. His father's influence, perhaps, was ultimately the most significant. Daniel always kept in close touch with Robert throughout his education. His correspondence with his son reveals an intense interest in the course of his studies and a loving concern for his welfare. A typical exchange occurred in 1783. On 20 November, Robert, then seventeen, wrote to his father from Bramcote:

> I mention'd to Mr. Wakefield the Greek Historians: he says, that to read either of them through separately (Thucydides for instance) would take up a very long time, & after all, make you acquainted only with the style & matter of one Author; that therefore he thinks, the best way to proceed, is to select the most celebrated pieces from each, & work those through well, by which means you become acquainted with their different styles, & gain a more thorough knowledge of the language.
>
> I am at present reading a funeral eulogy from Thucydides, whose manner of writing is so short & concise, that I find it very difficult to get on. After tea I read Horace & Cicero alternately. Mr. Wakefield wishes me to go on a little in Geometry at the same time as the Algebra, so as to be able to understand some of Sir Isaac Newtons Principia.[2]

Daniel replied on 27 November:

> Nothing can give me greater pleasure than the account you send me of your present situation: it is everything I could have desired according to my own tastes & real opinions; & I have no doubt you will find you are laying a foundation for the happiness of your future life. Believe me, my dear boy, that I would not have any part of it disagreeable to you; & therefore it is a double satisfaction to me that you pass your present time as you like to do.... I think Mr. Wakefield has made the best determination with regard to the manner of making yourself acquainted with the Greek Historians; as indeed I have no doubt he will in every plan of study which he may suggest – at the same time perhaps it might not be disagreeable to you to read an English or French translation of them as your amusing books – if a passage occurs which strikes you you may refer to the Greek – it would be proper to begin with Herodotus, & I think I have one.
>
> It will be much for your advantage to go on with your geometry, when you begin to have some notion of algebra. It has been said that even Sir Isaac Newton himself regretted his too great preference of Algebraical solution; but however this be it is certain the flights of Algebra may be better regulated by the sober Geometrician. Dr Berkeleys father, in the early part of his life, enterd into a controversy upon this subject.[3]

They discussed a wide range of issues including contemporary politics on which they often disagreed. Writing again to Daniel from Brancote on 16

March 1784, Robert expressed grave doubts about William Pitt:

> Mr. Fox, & his party have, it seems, at last given up the struggle, & by the account of the papers Mr. Pitt is quite elated with his success. I really think he will ruin himself, & will not be able to stand it after all, for the rest of the ministry, I believe have but very little ability. He will never be so great a man, as if he had shewn a little more condescention & less ambition. It appears almost ridiculous so young a man should hold the two highest offices in the State.[4]

His father replied on 7 April:

> Thank you for your politicks; but I am not of your mind with regard to young ministers. They may have a little honesty, & a little of the fine enthusiasm caught from Athens Lacedaemon & Rome, which Sr Robert Walpole used to say cost him a year or two to rid some obstinate boys of. I am afraid that in 'face Romuli' old men buy their political experience with the loss of too many virtues.[5]

Weightier arguments ensued in the Malthus household when Robert returned home after graduation. One such debate concerned William Godwin's vision of utopia. Daniel, although in disagreement, was so impressed by Robert's rejection of Godwin's views on the perfectibility of mankind that he urged his son in 1798 to publish anonymously *An Essay on the Principle of Population, as it affects the Future Improvement of Society, with Remarks on the Speculations of Mr. Godwin, M. Condorcet, and Other Writers.* Godwin in *An Enquiry into Political Justice* (1796) had envisioned a future utopian society: the elimination of private property would ensure equality for all; mind would triumph over the body and the passion between the sexes would disappear; humans would cease to propagate and immortality would prevail. In such a society, he stated: 'There will be no war, no crimes, no administration of justice, as it is called, and no government. Every man will seek with ineffable ardour, the good of all.'[6] The Marquis de Condorcet, an ardent French revolutionary, had expressed similarly utopian views in his *Esquisse d'un Tableau Historique des Progrès de l'Esprit Humain* (*Sketch for a Historical View of the Progress of the Human Mind*) published posthumously in 1795 after his imprisonment by Robespierre and subsequent death. In his future world of unbounded technological improvement where all inequalities of class and gender would disappear, population would be controlled by contraception. As Donald Winch points out, Condorcet, unlike Godwin, envisioned future equality '*within a society based on commerce and private property*'. Elimination of laws favouring the privileged along with social insurance schemes (both private and public) would lead to equality of wealth, education and social status.[7] Malthus devoted a third of his *Essay* to a refutation of these two thinkers. In addition, even though he revered Adam Smith and accepted many of his principles, he devoted a chapter to disputing his claim in *The Wealth of Nations* (1776) that the abundance generated by the 'unseen hand' of the market would necessarily benefit the lower classes. Even though Malthus's thought bore some resemblance to Enlightenment thinking, his first *Essay* launched perhaps the most devastating assault on the foundation of this intellectual movement – its unqualified optimism.[8]

In the first seven of the nineteen chapters of the *Essay* Malthus constructed his population theory, which laid the foundation for his conclusions about the nature of society and its potential improvement. Employing a deductive method of reasoning, he stated in Chapter 1: 'I think I may fairly make two postula. First, That food is necessary to the existence of man. Secondly, That the passion between the sexes is necessary and will remain nearly in its present state.'[9] He then succinctly summed up his theory:

> Assuming, then, my postula as granted, I say that the power of population is indefinitely greater than the power in the earth to produce subsistence for man. Population, when unchecked, increases in a geometrical ratio. Subsistence increases only in an arithmetical ratio. A slight acquaintance with numbers will shew the immensity of the first power in comparison of the second. By that law of our nature which makes food necessary to the life of man, the effects of these two unequal powers must be kept equal. This implies a strong and constantly operating check on population from the difficulty of subsistence. This difficulty must fall somewhere and must necessarily be severely felt by a large portion of mankind.[10]

Malthus thus claimed he had discovered a 'great' and universal law of nature that had profound implications for the lot of mankind. The potential geometric increase of population ('1,2,4,8,16,32,64,128,256, 512 etc.'), he argued, constantly had to be kept in line with the inferior arithmetic ('1,2,3,4,5,6,7,8,9,10 etc.') ability to increase the food supply.[11]

The specific nature of these inevitable checks became Malthus's central concern and fell into two broad categories. 'Preventive' checks, which prevailed 'in some degree' among all ranks of society, inhibited new additions to the population and included delay of marriage, all forms of sexual intercourse which did not result in procreation – contraceptive use and homosexuality – and abortion. The 'positive' checks, which operated chiefly among the poor, reduced population after it had come into existence. Here Malthus referred to famine, disease, war and infanticide. All such checks, he maintained, stemmed ultimately from lack of subsistence.

Thus far, Malthus's theory and the language in which it was couched

sounded almost Newtonian. Indeed, Malthus had studied Newton at
Cambridge and all his life kept his well-used 1726 edition of Sir Isaac
Newton's *Principia Mathematica*, referring near the end of the *Essay* to
'the immortal mind of a Newton'.[12] If the latter set out to discover the
natural laws of the universe, so Malthus viewed his project as
accomplishing a similar task for human society. Yet by concluding that
all checks, both 'preventive' and 'positive', ultimately resolved into 'vice'
and 'misery', he boldly injected a set of Christian moral values into his
argument.

Malthus argued that all forms of the preventive checks led eventually
to unacceptable forms of 'vice', continually 'involving both sexes in
inextricable unhappiness'.[13] Thus, even delay of marriage, given the
constant passions between the sexes, would lead to premarital
intercourse. He rejected Condorcet's advocacy of birth control,
describing such behaviour as 'promiscuous concubinage' which would
'destroy that virtue and purity of manners which the advocates of
equality and of the perfectibility of man profess to be the end and object
of their views.'[14] Malthus thus opposed contraception as a viable
solution to overpopulation, even within marriage. In adopting this stance
he reflected the dominant mores of his time. A number of his critics –
especially Francis Place, Richard Carlile and John Stuart Mill –
advocated birth control as an escape from the Malthusian dilemma.
Godwin had no qualms about such forms of voluntary family limitation,
and also advocated abortion and infanticide as preferable alternatives to
starvation. These arguments, however, shocked most contemporaries
and posed no serious threat to Malthus's views in terms of public
opinion.

The conclusion that the life of humankind could only be one of
perpetual vice and misery was a pessimistic one indeed. It was certainly
the case, Malthus contended, that short-run increases in the food supply
could temporarily ease the situation of the lower orders. The pendulum,
however, would rapidly swing back. The mass of the labouring
population would satisfy their natural wants by marrying earlier. The
geometric power of population increase would soon take over, outstripping the means of subsistence at the same time as lowering wages in
an over-supplied labour market. Misery, especially in the form of
starvation and disease, once again would ensue.

Many of these ideas, of course, were far from original. In 1761 Robert
Wallace had written *Various Prospects of Mankind, Nature, and
Providence* warning that human population would increase 'so
prodigiously ... that the earth would at last be overstocked, and become
unable to support its numerous inhabitants'.[15] Other writers had
discussed the concepts of checks to population growth and had employed

ratios pertaining to population and the food supply. Karl Marx labelled the first *Essay* as 'nothing more than a schoolboyish, superficial plagiary of De Foe, Sir James Stewart, Townsend, Franklin and Wallace etc.' containing not 'a single sentence thought out by himself'.[16] Such charges, however, possessed more venom than substance. Malthus, in fact, acknowledged all of these writers and critiqued many of them. The first *Essay* was distinct, moreover, in the systematic manner in which he constructed his theory and the way in which he employed it to justify specific social institutions such as marriage and private property.

That the natural laws of population led to perpetual vice and misery Malthus viewed as the 'great' and 'insurmountable' difficulty 'in the way to the perfectibility of society'.[17] This clearly dispelled any notion of a future utopia. He went much further, however, especially in critiquing Godwin's notion that the abolition of private property and marriage would create an equal and benevolent society.[18] With provisions guaranteed and no restraints on marriage, Malthus argued, 'unshackled intercourse' would destroy any preventive check and lead to 'early attachments'.[19] In turn, population increase would become so rapid that any 'spirit of benevolence, cherished and invigorated by plenty, is repressed by the chilling breath of want'.[20] 'The mighty law of self-preservation,' he continued, would lead to virtual anarchy. Some would hoard food, leaving others to starve. Eventually the institutions of marriage and private property would be re-established 'as the best, though inadequate, remedy for the evils which were pressing'.[21] Society, 'from the inevitable laws of nature', would return to 'a plan not essentially different from that which prevails in every known State at present; I mean a society divided into a class of proprietors, and a class of labourers, and with self-love the main-spring of the great machine'.[22] Inequality would be inherent and irremediable. 'Some human beings,' especially those unable to support large families, 'must suffer from want. These are the unhappy persons who, in the great lottery of life, have drawn a blank.'[23] The metaphor of the lottery, which Malthus used again in later editions of his *Essay*, effectively conveyed not only his pessimism but also his intense fatalism especially with regard to the lower orders. No effort of the human will, it seemed, could propel the masses out of their misery.

Many contemporaries replied that those in want should be provided subsistence by the state. Indeed, such relief had been given since the sixteenth century and especially since the enactment of the Old Poor Law under Elizabeth I in 1601. Such laws originally intended to care for the aged and infirm, to provide apprenticeships for destitute children and to supply work for unemployed able-bodied adults. By the time Malthus published his first *Essay* in 1798, however, the provision of outdoor relief in cash or kind to able-bodied workers was becoming widespread in reaction to increased poverty in the countryside. In 1795 such relief reached its climax when justices of the peace in the village of Speen, Berkshire, established a form of outdoor poor relief geared to both the size of family and the price of bread. Under this 'Speenhamland' system, unemployed individuals or those in receipt of wages below subsistence would receive weekly monetary payments from their parish according to a detailed scale. Costs were covered by poor rates levied on occupiers of land who were mainly farmers. The larger a labourer's family and the higher the price of bread, the greater sum he would receive. Settlement in a parish guaranteed a legal entitlement to relief.[24]

In terms of social reform, the most significant aspect of Malthus's *Essay* was his argument that the Poor Laws be totally abolished. He claimed that Prime Minister William Pitt's Poor Bill, which attempted to pass legislation sanctioning liberal outdoor relief on a national scale 'possessed in a high degree the great and radical defect of all systems of the kind, that of tending to increase population without increasing the means for its support, and thus to depress the condition of those that are not supported by parishes, and, consequently to create more poor'.[25] Once again he powerfully brought to bear his population theory in defense of his position. The Old Poor Law, although based on benevolence, nevertheless destroyed the 'preventive' check. Encouraged by parish relief, 'men are thus allured to marry with little or no prospect of being able to maintain a family in independence.'[26] Such early and more frequent marriages, moreover, led to a rapid increase in the population of the labouring classes, causing the supply of labour to exceed demand and, in turn, lowering wages. Increased population put greater pressure on the food supply, thus raising prices. Individual actions, then, had dire social consequences. In addition, Malthus continued, the Poor Laws encouraged 'idleness' and 'dissipation' which provided a 'strong and immediate check to productive industry'.[27]

There was a clear assumption here that the lower orders were irrational by nature. Governed essentially by their passions 'they seldom think of the future' and especially their ability to support an increasing number of offspring. Preferring 'leisure' and 'drunkenness' to 'industry' and 'sobriety', they were in constant need of a 'stimulus' to work. Abolishing the Poor Laws and viewing dependent poverty as 'disgraceful' was just the measure needed to provide 'the goad of necessity'. The problem of indolence was to occupy Malthus throughout his life. He did advocate country workhouses for those in 'extreme distress' but the fare here would be hard and those able to do so would be 'obliged to work'. One must stress, however, that even abolishing the Poor Laws and providing such 'asylums' would not completely eliminate the inevitable misery of the lower orders which Malthus viewed as 'an evil so deeply seated that no human ingenuity can reach it'.[28]

In the last two chapters Malthus tempered such pessimism by discussing what some historians refer to as the 'theology of scarcity'.[29] In an attempt to reconcile the evils resulting from his natural law of population with the existence of a benevolent and omniscient God, he claimed: 'Evil exists in the world not to create despair but activity. We are not patiently to submit to it, but to exert ourselves to avoid it.'[30] Only through such activity – in the face of scarcity created by the Supreme Being – would the 'Mind' awaken and thus allow man to rise above his 'inert' and 'sluggish' nature.[31] The last sentence of the *Essay* read as follows:

> It is not only the interest but the duty of every individual to use his utmost efforts to remove evil from himself and from as large a circle as he can influence, and the more he exercises himself in this duty, the more wisely he directs his efforts, and the more successful these efforts are, the more he will probably improve and exalt his own mind and the more completely does he appear to fulfil the will of his Creator.[32]

Mitchell Dean contends that Malthus's theodicy was simply a 'Christian apologia' for the abolition of the Poor Laws and the reinforcement of the work ethic.[33] Samuel Hollander views Malthus's theology as 'extraneous to analysis and without influence on the theory of policy'[34] and furthermore sees his work as imbued with an 'implicit secular utilitarianism approaching Benthamism'.[35] An important group of intellectual historians, however, offer convincing arguments that Malthus's theology must be viewed as integral to the body of his thought. A. M. C. Waterman points out that '"science" and "theology" in eighteenth-century Britain were so closely intertwined as to be almost a single discipline', especially at Cambridge where Malthus's training in divinity involved the study of Newton who believed that his studies of 'nature' had proved the divine attributes.[36] J. M. Pullen argues that Malthus's theological views were so central to his philosophy that the principle of population cannot be adequately analysed without reference to them.[37] Donald Winch describes Malthus as a 'theological utilitarian' heavily indebted to William Paley and thus rejects Hollander's secular view.[38] Malthus, he asserts, played a key role in furthering 'evangelical economics'.[39] From this perspective the separation of Malthus the 'moralist' from Malthus the 'scientist' is a false dichotomy. Malthus was a Christian political economist viewing human experience within a divine plan. Winch, neatly sums up: '"Parson Malthus", as William Cobbett and Marx called him, with disobliging intent, was not Ricardo or John Stuart Mill wearing a dog collar merely for fashion or convenience.'[40]

The *Essay* made an impact rarely seen in publications by unknown writers. Knowledge of the work and its author spread rapidly. Malthus wrote to a friend in November 1800 that the *Essay* was 'now nowhere to be bought'.[41] Favorable notices appeared in the *Analytical Review* and the *New Annual Register*. The newly formed Whig journal, *The Edinburgh Review*, immediately sided with Malthus. William Pitt, moreover, withdrew his Poor Bill in reaction, some maintain, to Malthus's arguments against the Poor Law.[42] Although many in the Church of England had grave doubts concerning his notion of a God creating inherent evil and his rejection of the biblical injunction to 'go forth and multiply', Malthus's arguments were quickly recognized as formidable.

The success of the *Essay* was partly due to the clarity and forcefulness of Malthus's first-person prose and his mathematical ratios, which lent an aura of authority to the work even though he never fully proved them. More important, perhaps, was the timing of his publication. High bread prices, food riots, increasing numbers of poor seeking relief and rising poor rates in the 1790s were forcing contemporaries to examine and define the problem of poverty as never before. Malthus's position that the Poor Laws only exacerbated the condition of the poor was bound to appeal to those sections of society increasingly imbued with notions of a market economy where individuals, unaided by the state, would assume individual responsibility for their condition. Indeed, the moral economy had been under threat long before Malthus wrote. The *Essay* thus appeared at a critical point of transition in English society.[43]

Prior to publishing the much-revised and expanded second edition of his *Essay* in 1803, and partly as preparation for it, Malthus travelled extensively in Europe. In 1799 he toured Scandinavia and St Petersburg with university friends, keeping a detailed diary replete with social observations, many of which he published almost verbatim in later editions of the *Essay*.[44] In early 1800 both his father and mother died. Malthus, unfortunately, left no autobiography and one knows little of his personal reaction to the death of his parents. He did write to *The Monthly Magazine*, however, correcting errors in his father's obituary and describing him as a 'singular' man of 'fine understanding and genius'.[45] In 1802 he visited France and Switzerland with a large family party including his cousin and future wife Harriet Eckersall. In addition, he read widely to further develop his population theory. In between his tours he published an anonymous pamphlet entitled *An Investigation of the Cause of the Present High Price of Provisions* (1800). This was the first of several pamphlets Malthus wrote intending to influence government policy. Returning to a crucial theme of the first *Essay*, he argued that the current and dramatic increases in food prices were due not to manipulators of the market but to liberal Poor Law allowances which put excessive pressure on the food supply by allowing the labouring poor to continue to purchase wheat in spite of extraordinarily high prices. Malthus claimed, soon after the pamphlet was published, that his reasoning had been adopted by a government report, which recommended the poor eat substitutes for wheat.[46]

Ascendancy: 1803–17

In 1803 Malthus published the second and much enlarged edition of his 1798 work in two volumes with a new title: *An Essay on the Principle of Population: or A View of its past and present Effects on Human Happiness; With an Inquiry into our Prospects respecting the future Removal or Mitigation of the evils which it occasions*.[47] His extensive readings and travels allowed him to introduce vast amounts of new data, much of it statistical in nature, in proof of his concept of checks to population. The first half of the *Essay* (Books 1 and 2), in fact, was one vast exercise in comparative demographic ethnology, spanning the entire known world in ancient and modern times with considerable emphasis on the states of contemporary Europe.

More significantly for his theory as a whole, Malthus introduced a new preventive check that entailed neither vice nor misery and would 'soften some of the harshest conclusions of the first essay'.[48] This additional check Malthus termed 'moral restraint' defined as 'the restraint from marriage which is not followed by irregular gratifications'.[49] The only viable method of controlling the potential geometric increase of population was for individuals to delay marriage – practicing 'strict chastity'[50] in the meantime – until they could support their offspring.[51] Malthus, on Christian grounds, continued to reject any form of contraception either within or outside wedlock as vice, arguing that such 'promiscuous intercourse' would 'weaken the best affections of the heart, and ... degrade the female character'.[52] Since children would come naturally once couples wedded and expressed their natural passions, great emphasis was placed on later age at marriage. Moral restraint, then, was the only vice-free mode of behaviour, which would promote 'any essential and permanent amelioration in the condition of the lower classes of people'.[53] Such behaviour, by controlling the numbers of labourers, would decrease the supply of labour, thus raising wages. In addition, the 'period of delayed gratification' would allow a single man to save income and acquire 'habits of sobriety, industry, and economy' which would allow him to marry without 'fear of its consequences'.[54] With wages now sufficient to maintain 'with decency a large family' and with some savings for contingencies, all 'squalid poverty would be removed from society'.[55]

These were indeed optimistic expectations, which stand in stark contrast to the determinism of the first *Essay*. Returning to the metaphor of the lottery, Malthus now claimed that society would 'consist of fewer blanks and more prizes'. Individuals were no longer bound by fate to a life of misery. Their own prudential actions would allow them to escape the evils resulting from the laws of nature. Yet how could he justify such a position in light of his earlier contention that the poor were irrational beings, lacking in foresight, and bound by the constant passions between the sexes? Malthus proposed that if the poor were not rational they could be made so through education. A system of state-sponsored parochial schools of the kind Adam Smith had earlier proposed would train 'the rising generation in habits of sobriety, industry, independence and prudence, and in a proper discharge of their religious duties'.[56] The curriculum would also include grounding in the basic principles of political economy.[57] The central message that would be 'brought home to their comprehensions', however, was 'that they are themselves the cause of their own poverty; that the means of redress are in their own hands, and in the hands of no other persons whatever; that the society in which they live, and the government which presides over it, are totally without power in this respect'.[58] As Mitchell Dean points out, Malthus had now prescribed an entirely new 'form of life' for the poor; one where the male, as 'breadwinner', would be totally responsible upon marriage for the fate of his wife and children.[59] Deborah Valenze comments further that in bifurcating the roles of 'mother-as-nurturer and father-as-provider' he presented 'one of the clearest and earliest expositions of the nineteenth-century notion of separate spheres'.[60] In doing so, he both reflected and encouraged a new middle-class ideology of domesticity, which he applied unrealistically to the labouring classes where women's work was vital to family survival.[61]

Malthus's model of family life and formation was predicated on the assumption that no state-sponsored relief would be available to individuals. He thus returned to the subject of the Poor Laws. In perhaps his most infamous passage, he employed the powerful metaphor of 'nature's mighty feast':

> A man who is born into a world already possessed, if he cannot get subsistence from his parents on whom he has a just demand, and if the society do not want his labour, has no claim of right to the smallest portion of food, and, in fact, has no business to be where he is. At nature's mighty feast there is no vacant cover for him. She tells him to be gone, and will quickly execute her own orders, if he does not work upon the compassion of some of her guests. If these guests get up and make room for him, other intruders immediately appear

demanding the same favour. The report of a provision for all that come fills the hall with numerous claimants. The order and harmony of the feast is disturbed, the plenty that before reigned is changed into scarcity; and the happiness of the guests is destroyed by the spectacle of misery and dependence in every part of the hall, and by the clamorous importunity of those who are justly enraged at not finding the provision which they had been taught to expect. The great mistress of the feast, who, wishing that all her guests should have plenty, and knowing that she could not provide for unlimited numbers, humanely refused to admit fresh comers when her table was already full.[62]

Malthus then denied the poor any legal entitlement to parish assistance and proposed a 'gradual abolition' of the Poor Laws. He advocated a new law that would deny relief to any legitimate child born one year after enactment and to any illegitimate child after two years. It would then be the 'obligation on every man to support his children'.[63] Even a deserted child would not be entitled to relief. Such an infant, he argued, was 'comparatively speaking, of no value to the society, as others will immediately supply its place'.[64] If the rising generation starved because of imprudent marriages they were doomed to do so by the 'laws of nature, which are the laws of God'.[65] Stressing once again the patriarchal responsibility of the male to support his family, he claimed 'that the sins of the fathers should be visited upon the children'.[66] Even the county workhouses he advocated in 1798 were not mentioned. Private charity, to be sure, would still exist. Malthus argued, however, that such benevolence 'should be administered very sparingly'.[67]

Although Malthus continued to refer to the 'laws of God', some historians argue that his theology underwent a significant change. In the second *Essay* he eliminated the last two chapters of the 1798 edition where he attempted to reconcile evil with divine intent. His unorthodox position clearly did not sit well with critics in the Church of England, some of whom were his friends. As a result, contends A. M. C. Waterman, Malthus came to embrace the more orthodox position of William Paley: that this world was a state of trial or probation providing challenges to improve one's behaviour. This shift in theodicy allowed the introduction of moral restraint as a solution.[68]

Malthus did not wish misery for the poor, although many of his critics argued that his prescriptions were specifically designed to do so. The conclusion of the 1803 *Essay*, with its qualified optimism, is very different in tone and substance from that of the original work. Malthus claimed that his principle of population by no means precluded a 'gradual and progressive improvement in human society'.[69] Although 'a class of proprietors and a class of labourers' will always remain, he now held out hope that rational individuals exerting themselves to better their conditions would alter the 'proportion' which such classes 'bear to each other'.[70] There is a flicker here, though shrouded in qualifications, of the improvement in living standards he foresaw more clearly in his later works.

If the 1798 *Essay* had made a profound impact, that of 1803 caused an uproar! A flood of venomous criticism emerged, much of it seizing upon the 'nature's mighty feast' metaphor. One anonymous letter-writer in the December 1804 issue of *The Monthly Magazine* claimed that nature's table was not full and railed against the injustice that 'the rich man's horses have a better right to be fed than the poor man's children'.[71] The Revd Robert Ingram condemned Malthus's hardheartedness in allowing children 'who come into the world through no fault of their own' to perish through want.[72] Others raised severe doubts about whether the Old Poor Law, in fact, promoted population growth by encouraging early marriage. Malthus never proved such a contention and some modern historians have suggested this to be unlikely.[73] Even Malthus himself seemed to contradict himself when he claimed in the 1803 *Essay* that relief was so often 'scanty' and 'capricious' that it deterred many of the 'more thinking' members of the peasantry from marrying to gain parish assistance.[74] Some critics quite logically argued that urging moral restraint, given the inequality of social institutions, was tantamount to telling the poor not to breed at all, thus condemning them to a life of celibacy. What guarantees, after all, did they have of future economic security?

Moreover, as Donald Winch points out, Malthus became 'the single most common figure whom those we now think of as the first generation of romantics, the Lake poets and some of their admirers, loved to hate'.[75] Robert Southey, Samuel Taylor Coleridge, William Wordsworth and William Hazlitt, among others, mercilessly attacked Malthus to the point where, 'for tactical purposes at least', both Southey and Hazlitt felt it necessary to apologize if only in a mocking manner.[76] Southey, the prolific Tory writer of verse and prose, for example, claimed in *The Annual Review* of 1804:

> The folly and wickedness of this book have provoked us into a tone of contemptuous indignation; in affixing these terms to the book, let it not be supposed that any general condemnation of the author is implied, grievously as he has erred in this particular instance. Mr. Malthus is said to be a man of mild and unoffending manners, patient research, and exemplary conduct. This character he may still maintain; but as a political philosopher, the farthing candle of his fame must stink and go out.[77]

Southey was proved wrong. Harold A. Boner claims that by 1806 Malthus 'could now afford the luxury of ignoring his critics' which 'were so far making little headway against the tide of his influence'.[78] In that year Malthus published the third edition of the *Essay* in two volumes that included important statistical revisions and the addition of an Appendix replying to some of the book's opponents. Others critics, he claimed, 'were so full of illiberal declamation, and entirely destitute of argument, as to be evidently beneath notice'.[79] Southey, no doubt, fell in this category. In the revised text Malthus paradoxically maintained his abolitionist stance regarding the Poor Laws while at the same time arguing that their tendency to encourage reckless marriages was counteracted – even more than previously thought – by landlords tearing down cottages to lessen the burden on the poor rates. Such actions, he argued, explained why the Poor Law had been in existence for so long without creating intolerable population pressure.[80]

In addition, Malthus – in response to a barrage of public condemnation – withdrew the 'nature's mighty feast' passage and never included this metaphor in subsequent editions of the *Essay*. He also toned down somewhat his harsh assessment of poor infants. Instead of being of 'no value to the society' they became of 'little value'[81] – a concession hardly sufficient to satisfy those critics who labelled him as hard-hearted.

More important, Malthus placed much greater emphasis on the net benefits of 'prudential restraint' or what David Levy has termed 'immoral restraint'[82] – a delay in age at marriage with 'irregular gratification'. To be sure, this concept appeared in the 1798 *Essay* as a preventive check especially regarding the middle and upper classes. Since such behaviour, however, led to vice, Malthus did not view it as a viable solution. Even though he introduced the ideal method of 'moral restraint' in the 1803 *Essay*, he nevertheless expressed strong reservations concerning its practical application:

> Judging merely from the light of nature, if we feel convinced of the misery arising from a redundant population on the one hand, and of the evils and unhappiness, particularly to the female sex, arising from promiscuous intercourse, on the other, I do not see how it is possible for any person, who acknowledges the principle of utility as the great foundation of morals, to escape the conclusion that moral restraint, till we are in a condition to support a family, is the strict line of duty; and when revelation is taken into the question, this duty undoubtedly receives very powerful confirmation. At the same time, I believe that few of my readers can be less sanguine in their expectations of any great change in the general conduct of men on this subject than I am.[83]

In the Appendix to the 1806 *Essay* Malthus made his position far more explicit. Replying to Arthur Young's criticism and again emphasizing the principle of moral utility he stated:

Mr. Young has asserted that I have made perfect chastity in the single state absolutely necessary to the success of my plan; but this surely is a misrepresentation. Perfect virtue is indeed absolutely necessary to enable man to avoid *all* the moral and physical evils that depend upon his own conduct; but whoever expected perfect virtue upon earth? I have said what I conceive to be strictly true, that it is our duty to defer marriage till we can feed our children, and that it is also our duty not to indulge ourselves in vicious gratifications; but I have never said that I expected either, much less both, of these duties to be completely fulfilled. In this, and a number of other cases, it may happen, that the violation of one of two duties will enable a man to perform the other with greater facility; but if they be really both duties, and both practicable, no power *on earth* can absolve a man from the guilt of violating either. This can only be done by that God who can weigh the crime against the temptation, and will temper justice with mercy. The moralist is still bound to inculcate the practice of both duties, and each individual must be left to act under the temptations to which he is exposed as his conscience shall dictate. Whatever I may have said in drawing a picture *professedly* visionary, for the sake of illustration, in the practical application of my principles I have taken man as he is, with all his imperfections on his head. And thus viewing him, and knowing that some checks to the population must exist, I have not the slightest hesitation in saying that the prudential check to marriage is better than premature mortality. And in this decision I feel myself completely justified by experience.[84]

The moral costs of prudential restraint were clearly less onerous than death occasioned by poverty and destitution.

In the interval between the second and third editions Malthus was instituted as rector of Walesby in Lancashire, an absentee living he retained for the rest of his life. Soon after, on 12 April 1804, the 'love-sick' Malthus married his pretty and athletic cousin Harriet Eckersall and – no longer a bachelor – forfeited his fellowship at Jesus College. Robert and Harriet's first and only son Henry was born eight months later on 16 December 1804, leading Patricia James, the author of his definitive biography, to speculate on the 'ribald comments that must have been made'.[85] In a letter written on the day of the birth, Malthus claimed that Henry was premature: Harriet, he said, had been 'brought to bed ... before her time'.[86] On 10 July 1805 Malthus was appointed Professor of General History, Politics, Commerce and Finance at the East India College in Hertfordshire that trained future civil servants for duty in India. Malthus later described himself as Professor of History and Political Economy – a position he retained until his death – and was the first to hold such a title in England. In his lectures he so constantly harped on the theme of increasing population that his students fondly called him 'old Pop'.[87] On 5 July 1806 his first daughter, Emily, was born followed by his last child, Lucy, in December 1807.

Signs of Malthus's growing influence, especially in Parliament, marked the year 1807. Samuel Whitbread introduced a very detailed bill in the House of Commons to amend the Poor Laws. In an attempt to ward off opposition from Malthusians, Whitbread praised Malthus's principles as a whole and even recommended a national system of free education. He rejected, however, Malthus's proposal to abolish relief, arguing that such a measure was so hard-hearted it would lead to a revolt of the poor. Malthus felt compelled to enter the political fray once again, deeply hurt, he claimed, by this kind of accusation made in such a high place.[88] In addition, he disagreed vehemently with Whitbread's proposal to empower parish authorities to build cottages for couples that married. In the resulting pamphlet, written as a public letter entitled *A Letter to Samuel Whitbread, Esq., M.P. on his Proposed Bill for the Amendment of the Poor Laws*, Malthus strongly denied the charges that he lacked sympathy for the poor. His proposals, he claimed, would lead to 'the general and permanent improvement of their condition'.[89] He again expressed his reservations about whether or not the Poor Laws actually encouraged early marriages. He had no doubt, however, that providing habitations for the newly married poor would drastically undermine the preventive check and lead to population growth so rapid as to render the condition of the labourers 'absolutely hopeless'.[90] He had earlier used similar arguments against Arthur Young's proposal to supply the poor with enough land to grow potatoes and feed one or two cows. This clearly articulated pamphlet, again written in the first person, went through two editions in 1807 and testifies to Malthus's impact on public policy. The Malthusians won the day and Whitbread's bill was defeated in the House. The *Essay*, in the meantime, went into its fourth edition with minor revisions.

Between 1808 and 1813 Malthus's publications were mainly confined to the pages of *The Edinburgh Review* that had consistently supported his abolitionist stance. He published four review articles during this period, two on the condition of Ireland (July 1808 and April 1809) and an additional two on monetary issues (February 1811 and August 1811).[91] Ireland's very rapid increase in population and the consequent misery and vice that ensued, he argued, were due to reliance on prolific potato cultivation which allowed large families to subsist on very small plots of land thus encouraging earlier and more frequent marriages. Unlike many of his contemporaries, Malthus spoke in favour of Catholic emancipation and increased civil liberties for the Irish. Pullen, in fact, contends that Malthus was 'imbued with the spirit of religious toleration characteristic of the Enlightenment'.[92] He firmly adhered to an economic policy of *laissez-faire*, arguing strongly against mercantilist trade policies and any government interference with Irish wages or rents. Ireland had no Poor Law and, as expected, Malthus later vehemently opposed the introduction of such laws into the country.

The 1811 articles indicate Malthus's growing concern with issues of political economy. While agreeing with David Ricardo – he began his lengthy correspondence with this eminent political economist on 16 June 1811 – that inflation followed from the over-issue of paper money, he developed a more complex analysis which stressed the varying demand for different types of products. Ricardo, according to Malthus, was too theoretical in his approach and ignored the many empirical realities involved. This initial critique by Malthus set the tone for the amicable debates between the two, both public and private, which lasted until Ricardo's death in 1823. Malthus later remarked of his friend: 'I never loved anybody out of my own family so much.'[93]

Malthus continued lecturing at the East India College, which moved to its new site at Haileybury, Hertfordshire, in 1809. Increasingly, he became involved in affairs both within and outside the college. In his 1813 pamphlet entitled *A Letter to the Right Honourable Lord Grenville* he defended the college against attacks made by Grenville in the House of Lords. Once again in first-person letter format, he produced a very calculated response justifying the institution's competitive examinations, its disciplinary procedures and its broad-based curriculum that included political economy.[94] Partly as result of Malthus's *Letter*, the college was granted statutory recognition in 1813. In addition to dealing with college matters, Malthus became involved in a number of important organizations: the Bible Society, where he advocated cooperation with dissenters, Lancaster's committee for educating poor children, and worker's savings banks.

In 1814 and 1815 Malthus again entered the public arena in order to influence government policy. Parliamentary discussions were about to commence on revisions to the existing Corn Laws that regulated the import and export of wheat. Malthus's stand on this issue placed him in the center of another major controversy that was to have drastic consequences for his stature as a political economist. David Ricardo, supported by James Mill and John Ramsay McCulloch, argued the orthodox position of political economists. The Corn Laws should be abolished in the interests of free trade. The unrestricted flow of wheat into Britain would lower food prices and wages, thus expanding profits in the manufacturing sector. In 1814 Malthus published his *Observations on the Effects of the Corn Laws*, a pamphlet which tried to be impartial by stating both the advantages and disadvantages of government intervention in the food supply.[95] By 1815, however, he came out firmly in favour of restricting the importation of foreign corn. In his *Grounds of an Opinion on the Policy of Restricting the Importation of Foreign Corn*

(1815), he displayed an agrarian bias which had prevailed in much of his previous work: the critical importance of the food supply as against the production of manufactured goods.[96] Government restriction of imports, he argued, would render Britain independent of the vagaries of foreign exporters such as France, especially in time of war. The resulting higher domestic price of wheat would provide incentives for landlords and farmers to expand cultivation and would also protect investments already made. Malthus again had his way. In 1815 Parliament approved a new set of Corn Laws whereby no wheat could enter the country unless prices rose to 80s. a quarter or higher – exactly the policy he had advocated in his pamphlet.

But such influence came at immense personal cost. His support of government intervention was unpardonable heresy for a genuine *laissez-faire* Whig of his day. To advocate state-sponsored education was at least consistent with Adam Smith's position. To suggest tampering with food prices, however, was viewed by free market advocates as the grossest violation of the principles of economic liberty. The voice of the Whig establishment, *The Edinburgh Review*, refused to publish any further articles by Malthus on political economy, allowing him only one other publication and restricting him to the subject of population. His support of the Corn Laws, and thus higher wheat prices, moreover, provided even more fuel for his opponents to label him an advocate of the landed interest and an enemy of the poor who wished to starve them out. Malthus maintained in the *Grounds of an Opinion* that he was free from 'all interested motives'.[97]

Contemporary scholars such as Hollander and Winch have accepted Malthus's statement at face value. The former contends that Malthus 'was no sycophantic apologist of the landlord class', citing his critical view of 'feudal' society and his statement in the 1817 *Essay*: 'it was by the growth of capital in all the employments to which it was directed that the pernicious power of the landlords was destroyed, and their dependent followers were turned into merchants, manufacturers, tradesmen, farmers, and independent labourers; – a change of prodigious advantage to the great body of society, including the labouring classes.'[98] Winch points out that both Francis Horner and David Ricardo, strong advocates of abolishing the Corn Laws, 'went out of their way to defend Malthus's reputation for candour on this subject'.[99] Malthus's critics, however, would never be convinced of such claims.

Indeed, a further torrent of criticism surfaced between the years 1815 and 1817. In spite of mounting opposition, however, Malthus continued to gain widespread and influential support for his views on the poor. John Bird Sumner, holder of numerous clerical offices, later a member of the Poor Law Commission of 1834 and Archbishop of Canterbury, produced his *Treatise on the Records of Creation ... and the Consistency of the Principle of Population with the Goodness of the Deity* (1816) in clear support of the theological implications of Malthus's population principle. Malthus later praised this work highly. Malthusian views were now gaining hold among respectable clergymen. If *The Edinburgh Review* had rejected Malthus, the Tory *Quarterly Review* swung over to his side in 1817. More important, Parliament established a Malthusian-inspired committee early in 1817 to consider the Poor Laws. As one supporter of the committee in the House of Commons remarked of Malthus: 'With the latter gentleman I perfectly agree, thinking that nothing less than a total change of system can cure the evil.'[100] Such an intense hold had abolitionist views taken among all sections of the ruling classes that Mitchell Dean argues that Malthus in less than two decades had placed the 'fundamental reorganization of the Poor Laws' on philanthropic, intellectual and parliamentary agendas.[101] The year 1817, he claims, witnessed the 'hegemony of abolitionism'.[102] The committee eventually concluded that although abolition was the obvious solution, such action was impracticable at least for the moment. The system would have to be propped up until it could be radically altered, a task finally accomplished by the New Poor Law of 1834.

Shifting positions: 1817–21

In June 1817 Malthus produced his fifth and penultimate edition of the *Essay* in three volumes. The revisions to this edition were the most substantial he had made since 1803. He rewrote six chapters, added four new ones (two of these on the poor) and provided a new Appendix where he again replied to his critics. In addition, he replaced the chapter on Godwin with one disputing the cooperative views of Robert Owen, much to the former's chagrin. Malthus continued to press for abolition of the Poor Laws but placed even stronger emphasis on 'the gradual and very gradual' nature of this measure, stressing it would not effect 'any individuals at present alive', only applying to the new generation of children born one or two years after the enactment of new laws.[103] Moral restraint, inculcated through education, still remained the only viable solution to overpopulation and poverty although Malthus again stated that it did 'not prevail much among the male part of society' and that 'delay of the marriage union from prudential considerations, without references to consequences' was 'the most powerful of the checks which in modern Europe keep down the population to the level of the means of subsistence'.[104] Malthus denied charges made by his critics that he had actually proposed laws prohibiting the poor from marrying. Individuals, he claimed, were at perfect liberty to do so but must suffer the consequences if they found themselves in want. Against those advocating contraception, he replied that his opposition to such practices rested on more than Christian moral grounds: 'If it were possible for each married couple to limit by wish the number of their children, there is certainly reason to fear that the indolence of the human race would be very greatly increased; and that neither the population of individual countries, nor of the whole earth, would ever reach its natural and proper extent.'[105] Malthus advocated the notion of an optimum population that forms an important part of the vocabulary of modern demographic analysis. Indeed, it is often forgotten that Malthus feared underpopulation, although clearly his main preoccupation ran in the opposite direction.

Malthus also clarified his position on emigration as a potential solution to pauperism – a subject raised in earlier editions of the *Essay*. In the 1803 *Essay* he claimed that 'no plans of emigration ... can prevent the continued action of a great check to population in some form or other' and that 'emigration is perfectly inadequate' for the purpose 'of making room for an unrestricted increase of population'. He nevertheless was prepared to admit that as a 'partial and temporary expedient' it should not be prevented by government.[106] In the 1817 *Essay*, aware of the acute distress following the end of the Napoleonic wars, he argued more positively that emigration 'was well worthy the attention of government, both as a matter of humanity and policy'.[107] He emphasized once again, however, that such a solution be temporary. 'Emigration,' he stressed, 'if it could be freely used, has been shown to be a resource which could not be of long duration. It cannot therefore under any circumstances be considered as an adequate remedy.'[108] Malthus, of course, feared that in the long run the vacuum created by the exodus of labour would soon be filled.

Hollander may be correct in contending – on the basis of Malthus's support in 1830 for Wilmot-Horton's scheme regarding government-sponsored emigration – that Patricia James was wrong to assert that he 'was no great enthusiast for emigration'. In arguing the contrary, however, Hollander overstates his case.[109] In a letter on 15 February 1830, Malthus chastised Wilmot-Horton's rashness in categorically denying 'that the removal of a redundant population would have a tendency to stimulate the increase of the remainder' and again stressed that a plan of emigration could only apply 'in certain circumstances of a country'.[110] Malthus's support for government-sponsored emigration was qualified. Such a policy would at best provide temporary relief in times of distress.

On one issue Malthus had no doubts. Under no circumstances should emigration be forced. 'It would surely be unjust,' he asserted in 1806, 'to oblige people to leave their country and kindred against their inclinations.'[111] Malthus, in fact, had great sympathy for those who felt an attachment to their 'native soil' and to their parents, kin, friends and companions – those 'cords', as he termed them, 'which nature has wound in close and intricate folds round the human heart'.[112]

The 1817 *Essay*, however, went beyond such points of clarification. On two significant issues Malthus radically altered his previous views. Recognizing the severity of post-Napoleonic distress and unemployment, he recommended state-sponsored public works 'to carry the sufferers through to better times'.[113] Such employment would involve the construction of roads, bridges, canals and 'almost every sort of labour upon the land.'[114] Poverty, he argued, could be caused by the 'want of demand' in both the agricultural and manufacturing sectors thus warranting state intervention. To be sure, Malthus viewed such measures as short-term solutions in times of crisis. In the long run, he maintained, individuals would be held solely responsible for their own livelihoods.

A second major shift concerned his views on the relationship between agricultural and industrial interests. In earlier editions of the *Essay*, Malthus claimed that all nations – and the mass of the labouring poor within them – relying on industrial labour to increase their wealth would fare much worse than those building a sound agrarian economy. He now contended that it was 'the union of the agricultural and commercial systems, and not either of them taken separately, that is calculated to produce the greatest national prosperity'.[115] Malthus thus became more optimistic about such balanced growth and its potential benefits. The labourer, he said, 'with a small family ... may be better lodged and clothed, and better able to command the decencies and comforts of life'.[116] Malthus continued to support the Corn Laws. Such restrictions, he argued, were not prejudicial to a balance between the agricultural and commercial classes.

Following the publication of the fifth edition of the *Essay*, Malthus made a brief summer visit to Ireland. On 5 March 1818 he was elected a Fellow of the Royal Society. Most of his energies, however, between 1817 and 1820 were devoted to preparing the most important work of his mature years. In April 1820, at the age of 54, he published his *Principles of Political Economy Considered with a View to their Practical Application*. The book stemmed partly from Malthus's desire to refute David Ricardo's *Principles of Political Economy* published in 1817. He also viewed the work as transmitting the tradition of Adam Smith as he interpreted it. Even though Malthus substantially disagreed with many of Smith's views, he had contemplated producing an edition of *The Wealth of Nations* as early as 1804 and had devoted numerous lectures at the East India College to aspects of Smithian political economy. In the introduction to the *Principles*, he claimed Smith's work was 'still of the very highest value'.[117] Malthus, however, clearly stated a broader aim that emphasized his empirical method: 'to prepare the general rules of political economy for practical application, by a frequent reference to experience'.[118]

The book was essentially a collection of dissertations disputing points raised by Ricardo, Jean-Baptiste Say and others. Robert Torrens, a fellow political economist and critic of both Ricardo and Malthus, aptly described the work as 'a chaos of original but unconnected elements'.[119] Original it certainly was. Malthus, grounded in empiricism, attacked many of the central tenets of classical political economy. Expanding on ideas from his 1817 *Essay*, he refused to accept Say's law that supply and demand in the market economy would naturally self-adjust.[120] General gluts – what might now be called depressions – could occur, he argued, mainly through deficiencies in effective demand. Problems of demand thus took precedence over questions of supply, with Malthus devoting almost a third of his book to the former. Ricardo and all orthodox political economists, believing that supply would automatically generate demand, thought Malthus was attempting to solve an imaginary problem.

Malthus went on to commit the further unorthodoxy of claiming that increasing levels of unproductive labour and consumption would lead to economic recovery. Near the end of the *Principles* he summed up his position:

> And altogether I should say, that the employment of the poor in roads and public works, and a tendency among landlords and persons of property to build, to improve and beautify their grounds, and to employ workmen and menial servants are the means most within our power and most directly calculated to remedy the evils arising from that disturbance in the balance of production and consumption.[121]

The notion that such labour – unproductive in the sense that it produced no goods for sale in the market or the capacity to produce such goods – could lead to future production and economic prosperity was greeted with near-derision by Ricardo and others. Malthus received a similar reception to his contention that unproductive consumption – which did not translate savings into investment with a view to future profit – would lead to equally beneficial results.[122]

What implications did Malthus's demand-side economics have for the labouring poor? One must reiterate that Malthus, in essence, was responding to the post-1815 depression. The provision of public works was thus a short-term corrective to a failure in the national demand for labour, even though other types of unproductive consumption – what

Malthus later referred to more positively as 'personal services' – might be necessary to continuously prop up demand and ensure more stable growth. For the long run, he continued to advocate abolition of the Poor Laws, especially the 'baneful system of regularly maintaining the children of the poor out of the rates'.[123] He repeated the familiar theme that 'the progress of population might be very rapid' under such a system because of the encouragement it 'might offer to marriage'.[124]

The *Principles,* however, provide testimony to Malthus's increasing optimism in his later works. He foresaw an 'increased degree of prudence' among the labouring classes encouraged by the progress of education, general improvement and 'a greater consumption among the working producers'.[125] The labourers, he contended, were 'really the arbiters of their own destiny'.[126] Higher real wages in a country like England, which enjoyed civil and political liberty, need not translate into increasing population. Under such conditions the lower classes would increasingly opt to purchase the 'comforts and conveniences of life' in preference to early marriage and large families. The availability of such goods provided by the manufacturing sector would provide, in turn, a growing incentive to prudential and industrious habits. Malthus had come a long way from the first *Essay* of 1798 where the mass of labourers in 'the great lottery of life' had drawn a 'blank'! Winch, in fact, credits Malthus for perceiving the conditions necessary for the embourgeoisement of the working classes.[127] Some nine months after his *Principles* appeared, Malthus wrote to his publisher John Murray hoping that 'the principles which I have laid down, will be found so comfortable with experience that they will gradually prevail like those of the *Essay on Population.*'[128] The last fourteen years of his life were not to see this hope fulfilled.

The later years: 1821–34

Between 1821 and 1834 Malthus published no fewer than ten pieces, while working continuously on a second edition of his *Principles* that was published posthumously in 1836. This was certainly a substantial literary contribution, especially given his increasing obligations to both professional and family life. In addition to his continuing duties at the East India College, he became a founder and life-long member of the Political Economy Club whose monthly meetings and debates he regularly attended along with such prominent figures as David Ricardo, James Mill and J. R. McCulloch. In 1824 he became a member of the Athenaeum Club as well as one of the ten Royal Associates of the Royal Society of Literature where he later presented papers. His energies were also increasingly occupied by family worries and his own ill health. In 1821 he lost his beloved older brother Sydenham, his sister Charlotte, two nephews, and his cousin Henry Dalton, the patron of his living at Walesby. In 1825 he suffered the loss of his youngest child Lucy who died at the age of 17. His only son Henry fell ill in 1827 and 1828. Such events eventually took their toll on Malthus. In 1829 he contemplated retirement from the college and in December 1830 he retreated to St. Leonards, Hastings, a well-known resort for invalids and convalescents.

His declining stature as a political economist no doubt added to his anxieties. Such fortune was not due to any lack of effort on his part. Of the ten publications in his later years, six dealt with issues of political economy. The most substantial of these were *The Measure of Value* (1823)[129] and *Definitions in Political Economy* (1827).[130] Two articles appeared in the *Quarterly Review* of April 1823 and January 1824 reviewing works by Thomas Tooke and J. R. McCulloch respectively.[131] In addition, two lectures on value, which Malthus read to the Royal Society of Literature in 1825 and 1827, were published in its transactions.[132]

While his concept of rent – originally presented in a pamphlet entitled *The Nature and Progress of Rent* (1815), expanded upon in Chapter III of the *Principles* and discussed in his *Definitions* – became the basis of Ricardian theory, many critics, both contemporary and modern, have found much that was either confusing, contradictory or tautological in these later works.[133] *The Measure of Value*, for example, was perhaps the least convincing of Malthus's publications.[134] That both Ricardo and McCulloch eclipsed him in the field of political economy, however, had deeper reasons. Malthus's continued support of the Corn Laws and critiques of Say's Law had rendered him so suspect among his younger peers that they met without him at the Political Economy Club a month after the sudden death of Ricardo on 11 September 1823, to discuss the Ricardo Memorial Lectures. John Lewis Mallet, who attended, claimed the group agreed that although Malthus 'had a considerable name ... he entertained opinions on many points, and those some of the most important, which are generally considered as unsound'.[135] The 34-year-old McCulloch was selected to give the lectures. Malthus also later made the unfortunate mistake of launching an uncharacteristically polemical attack on McCulloch in *Definitions*, provoking a cruel and cutting reply. In *The Scotsman* of 10 March 1827, the latter questioned Malthus's 'qualifications for the office of Dictator in the Economical Republic'.[136] Malthus's ideas on political economy were virtually ignored in his later years.

In 1826, the sixth edition of his *Essay* – the last during his life – was published. Although Malthus retained with minor revisions the views expressed in the 1817 *Essay*, Hollander maintains that a significant shift occurred in his position on the Corn Laws. A lengthy new footnote added in Book III to the chapter entitled 'Of Corn Laws. Restrictions upon Importation', he argues, indicates a rejection of agricultural protection, a disavowal, he claims, which took place as early as 1824 in Malthus's *Quarterly Review* article on 'Political Economy'. Deletions made in the posthumous second edition of the *Principles* (1836) and correspondence with Nassau Senior (1829), Thomas Chalmers (1832) and Jane Marcet (1833), he maintains, provide further evidence of Malthus's recantation.[137] John Pullen, however, raises serious doubts concerning Hollander's evidence and interpretation, contending that Malthus remained consistent in viewing the Corn Laws as an '*exception* to the *principle* of free trade'.[138] (Pullen's emphasis). Regardless of where one stands on this debate it is clear that Malthus never publicly renounced his views on the Corn Laws in unambiguous terms. His protectionist arguments remained prominent in both the *Essay* and the *Principles*. Those contemporaries, then, who viewed him as an advocate of the Corn Laws – for good or ill – cannot be faulted for adopting this position.

Two years prior to the publication of the 1826 *Essay*, Malthus wrote an article entitled 'Population' which appeared in the *Encyclopaedia Britannica* (1824).[139] This concise piece was published with some deletions and revisions as *A Summary View of the Principle of Population* in 1830 and may be considered the final restatement of his population theory.[140] Malthus effectively utilized new statistical materials from the 1821 Census to bolster his renewed optimism regarding prudential restraint, claiming there were 'the best reasons for believing that in no other country of the same extent is there to be found so great a portion of late marriages, or so great a proportion of persons remaining unmarried, as in Great Britain'.[141]

Civil and political liberty, Malthus contended, would continue to encourage such behaviour. He had emphasized these liberties as early as 1803 when he devoted an entire chapter of the *Essay* (Book iv, Chapter vi) to the subject, adding a further chapter in the 1817 *Essay*. In his *Summary View* he argued that civil liberty – which would allow 'free scope' to 'industrious exertions' and guaranty security of property – could not be permanently secured without political liberty which would 'teach the lower classes of society to respect themselves, by obliging the higher classes to respect them'.[142] Malthus firmly opposed radical proposals for universal male suffrage and possessed a deep mistrust of the '*vox populi*'.[143] Although he supported government by landed aristocracy, Winch describes him as a 'moderate Whig anxious to preserve the middle ground between extra-parliamentary radical discontent and executive tyranny'.[144] Malthus favoured gradual reform that could involve adjustments in the balance of power within the constitution.[145] During his lifetime he never publicly declared his position on the 1832 Reform Bill. In a footnote added to the 1836 posthumous edition of his *Principles*, however, he gave lukewarm support to the enfranchisement of the middle classes.[146] One must reiterate, however, that for Malthus 'the principal cause of want and unhappiness is unconnected with government and totally beyond its power to remove.'[147] To be sure, the state provision of primary education would promote the development of prudence and foresight among the poor and civil and political liberty.[148] Ultimate responsibility, however, rested with the individual. In the conclusion of his *Summary View* Malthus placed such duties in the wider context of his theology:

> *Lastly*, It will be acknowledged, that in a state of probation, those laws seem best to accord with the views of a benevolent Creator, which, while they furnish the difficulties and temptations which form the essence of such a state, are of such a nature as to reward those who overcome them, with happiness in this life as well as in the next. But the law of population answers particularly to this description. Each individual has, to a great degree, the power of avoiding the evil consequences to himself and society resulting from it, by the practice of a virtue dictated to him by the light of nature, and sanctioned by revealed religion. And, as there can be no question that this virtue tends greatly to improve the condition, and increase the comforts both of the individuals who practise it, and through them, of the whole society, the ways of God to man with regard to this great law are completely vindicated.[149]

He continued to deny 'the right of full support to all that might be born', claiming that a concession of this nature was 'absolutely incompatible with the right of property' and that poor relief would encourage earlier marriage, increasing numbers of poor and mass destitution.[150] He did, however, qualify his abolitionist stance by allowing that where prudential habits prevailed among the poor – where relief was considered discreditable and 'few or none marry with a certain prospect of being obliged to have recourse to it – those who were really in distress might be adequately assisted.'[151]

Malthus had earlier made such qualifications both privately and publicly. In an 1822 letter to the Reverend Thomas Chalmers, a Scottish divine and ardent supporter, he admitted that an improved administration of the Poor Laws along with 'education and moral superintendence' would be more feasible than outright abolition.[152] In 1827, testifying to the House of Commons Select Committee on Emigration, he was asked if parochial assistance that was 'rigidly and invariably limited to the support of the aged and infirm, or of children, and universally denied to able-bodied men who have no opportunity of working ... would be prejudicial to the country?', Malthus replied 'Perhaps not'.[153] In reply to the next question asking whether a Poor Law administered under such strict limitations 'might not be inexpedient', he responded: 'it would be a great improvement, as compared to the present mode of administration.'[154] Malthus, however, maintained his abolitionist – albeit gradual – stand in the last edition of the *Essay* (1826) published during his lifetime. His qualifications thus remained relatively obscure and the public rightly categorized him as siding with abolition.

Anti-Malthusian criticism mounted in the 1820s and especially the early 1830s as Parliament considered passage of the New Poor Law. In 1820 William Godwin published *Of Population* disputing Malthus's ratios and insisting that poverty was the result of social conditions and institutions, and not the product of natural and immutable laws of population.[155] Malthus replied with untypical invective in *The Edinburgh Review* of July 1821: the book, he exclaimed, was 'the poorest and most old-womanish performance that has fallen from the pen of any writer of name, since we first commenced our critical career'.[156] The theme of unequal distribution of resources was reiterated in the writings of many of Malthus's critics, especially in the widely circulated working-class press. This barrage of criticism was accompanied by a smaller core of individuals such as Francis Place and Richard Carlile who took the radical stance of advocating contraception as the solution to the Malthusian dilemma.[157]

Despite such opposition, the dominance of Malthusian ideology persisted, leading Samuel Taylor Coleridge to remark in 1832: 'Is it not lamentable – is it not even marvelous – that the monstrous practical sophism of Malthus should have gotten complete possession of the leading men of the kingdom.'[158] Even though Malthus's economics remained suspect among political economists, his advocacy of the abolition of the Poor Laws and any right to relief was accepted as orthodoxy by Ricardo and others.[159] The reformed Parliament of 1832 allowed entry to middle-class members imbued with Malthusian principles. Even the country gentry were becoming increasingly saturated with Malthusian views.[160] Malthus's ideas, moreover, were popularized on a much greater scale in the early 1830s than before, especially in the moral tales of his admirer Harriet Martineau.[161]

The Poor Law Amendment Act, following on the heels of a massive Royal Commission on the Poor Laws in 1832, became law on 14 August 1834 after passing through both houses of Parliament with relative ease. Second reading in the House of Commons, much to the government's exhilaration, passed by a resounding vote of 319 to 20.[162] In its third reading, the Act was subject to more opposition but passed 187 to 50 in a thin house.[163] More resistance was encountered in the House of Lords but only on certain key clauses, especially concerning bastardy where the onus for the support of illegitimate children was placed on the mother. Affiliation actions against putative fathers were not entirely eliminated but became virtually impossible since they had to be brought before quarter sessions. In its third reading, although the Act passed by a comfortable margin, the bastardy clauses were only narrowly approved by a vote of 93 to 82.[164]

The New Poor Law contained a number of significant changes some of which had been foreshadowed under the Old Poor Law in local experiments conducted in the 1820s and early 1830s – especially the curtailing of outdoor relief and the abolition of child allowances. Three permanent commissioners to be located in London were appointed with the task of drawing up national regulations regarding poor relief and overseeing the construction of workhouses over the entire country. Outdoor relief was denied to the able-bodied. Such individuals would now be offered the workhouse where the situation would render them 'less eligible', that is, in a state materially and psychologically worse than the poorest of the independent poor. The sexes would be segregated. Inmates would be subject to a meagre diet, strict supervision, hard work and harsh discipline. Such conditions would force work-shy, indolent labourers back into the market where jobs were supposedly available. Boards of Guardians elected by rate-payers would organize and preside over poor relief.[165]

Historians have been intensely divided over the complex set of forces leading to the eventual passage of the New Poor Law, some denying or entirely ignoring the influence of Malthus. Anthony Brundage, for example, plays down the role of theorists such as Jeremy Bentham and gives no weight to Malthus.[166] The New Poor Law, he argues, 'represented an administrative system "of the landlords, by the landlords and for the landlords"' who sought to reorganize social control in the 1830s.[167] David Eastwood and Peter Dunkley, on the other hand, place considerable emphasis on the role of Benthamite rather than Malthusian bureaucrats. Eastwood, in fact, views Bentham as an 'uncle to the Poor Law Amendment Act'.[168] W. D. Grampp, while conceding that two provisions of the New Poor Law were clearly Malthusian in content, that is, the abolition of family allowances and the segregation of the sexes within the workhouse to prevent procreation, denies that Malthus had any fundamental influence. Nassau Senior and Edwin Chadwick who headed the Royal Commission did not believe, according to Grampp, that England had a surplus population problem. The New Poor Law, moreover, did not legally deny the right to relief as Malthus had strongly advocated. Most important, Malthus was never consulted regarding the changes being made.[169]

Other historians are prepared to give Malthus a prominent role. Mitchell Dean disputes Grampp's claims, arguing that Senior's views were closer to Malthus's than assumed and that even though the New Poor Law did not deny the right to relief in principle it rendered such provision 'practically non-existent'.[170] The main objectives of the New Poor Law, he claims, remained 'starkly Malthusian even if its administrative means were fabricated from other sources'.[171] The *1834 Poor Law Report,* which summed up the findings of the Royal Commission, moreover, was laden with Malthusian language:

> We have seen that one of the objects attempted by the present administration of the Poor Laws is to repeal *pro tanto* that law of nature by which the effects of each man's improvidence or misconduct are borne by himself and his family. The effect of that attempt has been to repeal *pro tanto* the law by which each man and his family enjoy the benefit of his own prudence and virtue.[172]

One of the main aims of the new regime, the report asserted, was 'the diminution of improvident and wretched marriages; thus arresting the increase in population'.[173] By abolishing outdoor relief to able-bodied men and their families, the New Poor Law, Dean argues, revealed its Malthusian purpose of 'making the ... independent labourer the sole responsible agent of the welfare of *his* wife and children'.[174] The breadwinner model thus lay at the core of the new administration's assumptions.

In addition, both Gertrude Himmelfarb and Anne Digby would concur with Dean that for decades prior to 1834 Malthusianism structured the 'philanthropic debate over relief and articulate discourse more generally'.[175] Malthus, according to Himmelfarb, defined the problem of poverty, giving it 'a centrality it had not had before' and making it 'dramatically, urgently, insistently problematic'.[176] Malthus's ideas, claims Digby, 'were of central intellectual significance in shaping the debate over poor-law policy for nearly 40 years before the decisive reform of 1834'.[177] The New Poor Law, she adds, was a 'Malthusian measure because it reflected moral and reformist elements that were central to Malthus's later prescriptions for a practicable social policy'.[178]

Perhaps the most balanced and persuasive arguments are presented by Peter Mandler, especially if one accepts the proposition – as one must – that it would be simplistic to attribute the New Poor Law to a single factor or thinker.[179] He sees a constellation of forces – social, economic and intellectual – crystallizing in the 1830s which fuelled the drive for Poor Law reform. Like Brundage, he argues that the landlords and country gentry played a crucial role.[180] Contrary to Brundage, however, he allows that intellectual influences were critical to the process, especially the Noetics (reasoners) movement at Oxford imbued with

Christian political economy and individualism – what Boyd Hilton refers to as 'the rage of Christian economics' – which appealed in particular to liberal Tories.[181] Such intellectuals were inspired by and owed a great debt to Malthus who, as Winch points out, 'played a key role in making this vision possible'.[182] According to Mandler, these Christian and liberal Tory thinkers conveyed the political economy of Malthus to the elite among the landowning classes who found it increasingly necessary to revamp the Poor Laws. By 1830, he contends, this elite 'was not only familiar with but absolutely saturated by Christian versions of political economy'.[183] Such ideas, moreover, influenced a much broader spectrum of the landed classes. The country gentry, he maintains, 'had been stuffed with Malthusian views for decades 'integrating market logic into their way of thinking' and eventually consolidating 'their own position as the lynchpin of the English governing class'.[184]

Contemporaries who favoured the New Poor Law consistently praised Malthus. Those opposed severely castigated him. Both groups were not far off the mark. Although Malthus did not directly intervene in the debate over the New Poor Law and was not involved in its passage, his influence – though indirect and only one among a myriad of factors – was nevertheless highly significant. If, moreover, Karl Polanyi is correct in asserting that the New Poor Law eliminated subsidized wages and created a competitive labour market thus establishing a fully-fledged market economy for the first time in history, then Malthus's importance runs much deeper.[185] Although no doctrinaire advocate of *laissez-faire*, his definition of individual responsibility within a society devoid of relief for the able-bodied poor became the cornerstone of a new market society that, Polanyi contends, determined the social history of nineteenth-century England.[186] Only by emphasizing the impact of Malthusian ideas can one fully explain why the ruling elite abnegated its paternal role towards the less fortunate in society. To be sure, this was a long drawn-out process. Its acceleration in the early nineteenth century, however, cannot be adequately analysed without reference to Malthus. If Smith and Ricardo among others laid the groundwork for a capitalist economic system, it was Malthus who brought it to fruition. Bentham may have been an 'uncle' to the New Poor Law. Malthus was its father.

Malthus died at the age of 68 at Bath on 29 December 1834, four months after passage of the New Poor Law. The bitter criticism he endured in his later years was allayed, no doubt, by the honours he received. In 1833 he was elected to both the Academy of Sciences of France and the Royal Academy of Berlin. In the same year John Linnell painted his portrait. In February 1834 he became a founding member of the Royal Statistical Society. He was buried at Bath Abbey on 6 January 1835.

Endnotes

1. Patricia James, *Population Malthus: His Life and Times* (London: Routledge and Kegan Paul, 1979), 11. Most of the biographical information on Malthus is drawn from this biography. Hereafter cited as *Population Malthus*.

2. *T.R. Malthus: The Unpublished Papers in the Collection of Kanto Gakuen University*, vol. I, eds John Pullen and Trevor Hughes Parry (Cambridge: Cambridge University Press, 1997), 11. Hereafter cited as *Unpublished Papers*. Errors in spelling, which were frequent, especially in Robert Malthus's letters, have not been corrected.

3. Ibid., 12–13.

4. Ibid., 20.

5. Ibid., 22 and 22 n.122.'Face Romuli' translated from the Latin means 'the lower classes of Rome'.

6. Quoted by James, *Population Malthus*, 59–60.

7. For a fuller discussion of Condorcet see Donald Winch, *Riches and Poverty: An Intellectual History of Political Economy in Britain, 1750–1834* (Cambridge: Cambridge University Press, 1996), 259–61. Hereafter cited as *Riches and Poverty*. The phrase quoted is from 259.

8. For parallels between Malthus and the French Enlightenment see John Pullen, 'Thomas Robert Malthus (1766–1834)', *University of New England School of Economics Working Paper Series in Economics*, no. 2001–2002 (Jan. 2001):12. Pullen relies mainly on Malthus's work from 1803 onwards and stresses themes such as religious toleration, utilitarianism and natural law.

9. *An Essay on the Principle of Population: Thomas Robert Malthus*, ed. Phillip Appleman (New York: W.W. Norton, 1976), 19. All subsequent citations from the first *Essay of 1798* are from this edition. Hereafter cited as *Essay 1798*.

10. Ibid., 20.

11. Ibid., 23.

12. Ibid., 120.

13. Ibid., 35.

14. Ibid., 60.

15. Quoted by James, *Population Malthus*, 59.

16. Quoted from Marx's *Capital* (1867) in Appleman, *Essay 1798*, 159–60. Samuel Hollander points out that Malthus made no claims to originality in employing the formal ratios. See Samuel Hollander, *The Economics of Thomas Robert Malthus* (Toronto: University of Toronto Press, 1997), 18 n.3

17. Quoted from Appleman, *Essay 1798*, 20.

18. For a further discussion of Malthus's reaction to Godwin see Winch, *Riches and Poverty*, 249–87. Winch argues that both Malthus and Godwin did agree 'that human dignity and happiness were strongly connected with the absence of relations of paternalistic dependence, and with self-exertion and the exercise of discretionary foresight in conducting personal affairs.' (256). Malthus disagreed most strongly, however, with Godwin's contention that social, economic and political institutions were the sources of society's evils. The complete abolition of such institutions – that is, marriage and private property – Malthus argued, would not

produce Godwin's perfect world but would, in fact, retard the progress of civilization (256–7).

19. Appleman, *Essay 1798*, 70.
20. Ibid., 70.
21. Ibid., 72.
22. Ibid., 75.
23. Ibid., 74.
24. There is a voluminous literature on the Old Poor Law and its impact. For a brief introduction see James P. Huzel, 'The Labourer and The Poor Law, 1750–1850' in *The Agrarian History of England and Wales, 1750–1850*, vol. VI, ed. G. E. Mingay (Cambridge: Cambridge University Press, 1989), 755–810. For a recent bibliography see Anthony Brundage, *The English Poor Laws 1700–1930* (New York: Palgrave, 2002), 170–79. Hereafter cited as *English Poor Laws*. Although the extent to which the Speenhamland system spread across the country was no doubt over-emphasized by contemporaries, outdoor relief in general had increased markedly in the latter decades of the eighteenth century.
25. Appleman, *Essay 1798*, 42–3.
26. Ibid., 40.
27. Ibid., 41, 42 and 38.
28. All quotations in this paragraph are from ibid., 40 and 43. Samuel Hollander contends, however, that such statements by Malthus are misleading in the sense that poverty and misery were irremediable only in the absence of prudence and that Malthus from the outset recommended delay of marriage in spite of the 'vicious' consequences. Malthus, however, gave very little emphasis to such a possibility in the 1798 *Essay*. See Hollander, *The Economics of Thomas Robert Malthus*, 886 and 925.
29. See Mitchell Dean, *The Constitution of Poverty: Toward a Genealogy of Liberal Governance* (London: Routledge, 1991), 89. The phrase was first coined by D.C. LeMahieu, 'Malthus and the Theology of Scarcity', *Journal of the History of Ideas* 40 (July-September 1979): 467–74. Dean is hereafter cited as *Constitution of Poverty*.
30. Appleman, *Essay 1798*, 130.
31. Ibid., 130.
32. Ibid., 130.
33. Dean, *Constitution of Poverty*, 90.
34. See Samuel Hollander, 'An Invited Comment on "Reappraisal of Malthus the Economist, 1933–97" by A. M. C. Waterman', *History of Political Economy* 30, no. 2 (Summer 1998): 338. This contribution is part of the 'Minisymposium: Malthus at 200' held in this journal. Hereafter cited as 'Minisymposium'. Hollander, Neil De Marchi, A. M. C. Waterman, J. M. Pullen and Donald Winch contributed. Hollander does, however, accept the significance of political morality for Malthus's economics (339).
35. For a discussion of Hollander's position see Donald Winch, *Riches and Poverty*, 243.
36. A. M. C.Waterman, 'Reappraisal of "Malthus the Economist", 1933–97' in 'Minisymposium': 308. See also A. M. C. Waterman, 'Malthus as a Theologian: The "First Essay" and the Relation between Political Economy and Christian Theology' in *Malthus Past and Present*, eds J. Dupâquier, A. Fauve-Chamoux and E. Grebnik (London: Academic Press, 1983), 195–209 hereafter cited as 'Political Economy and Christian

cultural reasons for the romantic attack', he concludes that the Nature/
Culture borderline opened up by Malthus aroused powerful feelings in
those 'who regarded any confusion of the world of man with that
discovered by Newton, and later by Darwin, as anathema. Naturalism
entailed for such critics an abandonment of moral judgement; it could
never be what it was for Malthus, a basis for improving such judgments.'
See ibid., 420–21.

78. Boner, *Hungry Generations*, 55.
79. Cited in ibid., 55.
80. James, *Malthus Variora*, II: 190 and 190 n.19. Although Malthus made
     this argument in 1803, he presented it in greater detail in 1806.
81. Ibid., 141 n. 16.
82. Cited in Hollander, *The Economics of Thomas Robert Malthus*, 887.
83. James, *Malthus Variora*, II: 104.
84. Ibid., 221–2. Hollander points out that Malthus had drawn similar
     conclusions in the 1803 *Essay*. My point here is that Malthus's statement
     in 1806 is clearer and more explicit. See Hollander, *The Economics of
     Thomas Robert Malthus*, 888–9.
85. James, *Population Malthus*, 165.
86. Ibid., 166.
87. Ibid., 323.
88. Whitbread wrote a lengthy letter to Malthus on 5 April 1807 claiming that
     he 'had not imputed' to Malthus 'anything like "hardness of heart"' and
     that he had clearly stated his belief in the 'most benevolent intentions' of
     the author of the *Essay on the Principle of Population*. He also defended
     his proposal to tax personal property and empower parishes to build
     cottages 'to a very limited amount'. See Pullen, *Unpublished Papers*,
     80–85.
89. T. R. Malthus, *A Letter to Samuel Whitbread, Esq. M.P. on his Proposed
     Bill for the Amendment of the Poor Laws* (1807), reprinted in *The
     Pamphlets of Thomas Robert Malthus* (New York: Augustus M. Kelly,
     1970), 36. The letter is also reprinted *The Works of Thomas Robert
     Malthus*, 8 vols, eds E. A. Wrigley and David Souden (London: William
     Pickering, 1986), 4: 5–19. Hereafter cited as *Works of Malthus*.
90. *The Pamphlets of Thomas Robert Malthus*, 40.
91. These articles are collected in Bernard Semmel, ed., *Occasional Papers of
     T. R. Malthus: On Ireland, Population, and Political Economy, from
     Contemporary Journals, written anonymously and hitherto uncollected*
     (New York: Burt Franklin, 1963), 31–142. Hereafter cited as *Occasional
     Papers*. These pieces are also reprinted in Wrigley and Souden, *Works of
     Malthus*, 4: 23–67 and 7: 21–82.
92. See Pullen, 'Thomas Robert Malthus (1766–1834)': 5.
93. Quoted in *T. R. Malthus: Principles of Political Economy: Variorum
     Edition*, 2 vols, ed. John Pullen (Cambridge: Cambridge University Press,
     1989) I: xxi. Hereafter cited as Pullen, *Variorum* with volume I or II
     specified.
94. *A Letter to the Rt. Hon. Lord Grenville, Occasioned by Some
     Observations of his Lordship on the East India Company's Establishment
     for the Education of their Civil Servants* (1813) reprinted in *The
     Pamphlets of Thomas Robert Malthus*, 57–89. Also reprinted in Wrigley
     and Souden, *Works of Malthus*, 4: 73–92.

95. Reprinted in *The Pamphlets of Thomas Robert Malthus*, 91–131 and also in Wrigley and Souden, *Works of Malthus*, 7: 87–109.
96. Reprinted in *The Pamphlets of Thomas Robert Malthus*, 133–73 and also in Wrigley and Souden, *Works of Malthus*, 7: 151–74.
97. *The Pamphlets of Thomas Robert Malthus*, 138.
98. See Hollander, *The Economics of Thomas Robert Malthus*, 908–909. Hollander also discusses Malthus's 'marked impatience with the pretensions of landlords in 1823 when they proposed to adjust contracts to their own benefit and at the expense of the fundholders', ibid., 855–6. He also points out that Robert Torrens, in spite of labelling Malthus inconsistent and contradictory, felt that such qualities nevertheless reflected 'a spirit of candour and a love of truth', ibid., 1002 n.4.
99. Winch, *Riches and Poverty*, 336. Ricardo referred to Malthus's 'honest, conscientious opinions' on the Corn Laws.
100. Quoted in Boner, *Hungry Generations*, 82–3.
101. Dean, *Constitution of Poverty*, 95.
102. Ibid., 95.
103. James, *Malthus Variora*, I: 374.
104. Ibid., 304–305.
105. Ibid., II: 235.
106. Ibid., II: 87 and I: 346.
107. Ibid., I: 347.
108. Ibid., II: 237.
109. Hollander, *The Economics of Thomas Robert Malthus*, 903. Hollander's conclusions are based on letters Malthus wrote to Wilmot-Horton on 22 February and 9 June 1830.
110. Pullen, *Unpublished Papers*, 103–104. The letter quoted is in fact a draft of a letter sent on 15 February 1815. The final version is in the Catton Collection, Derbyshire Record Office.
111. James, *Malthus Variora*, II: 220 n.31.
112. Ibid., I: 344.
113. Ibid., 368.
114. Ibid., 369.
115. Ibid., II: 48.
116. Quoted in G. Gilbert, 'Economic Growth and the Poor in Malthus's *Essay on Population*', *History of Political Economy* 12 (Spring 1980): 92.
117. Pullen, *Variorum*, I: 5.
118. Ibid., 21.
119. James, *Population Malthus*, 293–4.
120. For further discussion of Malthus's heretical position against Say, see Winch, *Riches and Poverty*, 358–9.
121. Pullen, *Variorum*, I: 512.
122. For a fuller discussion of Malthus's views on unproductive labour and consumption see Winch, *Riches and Poverty*, 363–5. As Winch points out, Malthus tried to avoid the negative implications of the term 'unproductive' especially regarding the expenditure of the landowning classes by using the term 'personal services'.
123. Pullen, *Variorum*, I: 288.
124. Ibid., 259.
125. Ibid., 475.
126. Ibid., 306.

127. See Donald Winch, *Malthus* (Oxford: Oxford University Press, 1987), 65.

128. Pullen, *Variorum*, I: xxxiv.

129. T. R. Malthus, *The Measure of Value Stated and Illustrated, with an Application of it to the Alterations in the Value of the English Currency Since 1790* (London: John Murray, 1823). Reprinted in Wrigley and Souden, *Works of Malthus*, 7: 179–220.

130. T. R. Malthus, *Definitions in Political Economy, Preceded by an Inquiry into the Rules which Ought to Guide Political Economists in the Definition and Uses of their Terms; with Remarks on the Deviation from these Rules in their Writings* (London: John Murray, 1827). Reprinted in Wrigley and Souden, *Works of Malthus*, 8: 5–120.

131. T. R. Malthus,'Tooke on High and Low Prices', *Quarterly Review*, XXIX, no. lx (April 1823): 214–39 and T. R. Malthus, 'Political Economy', *Quarterly Review*, XXX, no. lx (January 1824): 297–334. These articles are reprinted in Semmel, *Occasional Papers*, 145–208 and in Wrigley and Souden, *Works of Malthus*, 7: 225–97.

132. T. R. Malthus, 'On the Measure of the Conditions Necessary to the Supply of Commodities', *Transactions of the Royal Society of Literature* I, part 1 (1825–29): 171–80. and T. R. Malthus, 'On the meaning which is most usually and most correctly attached to the term "Value of a Commodity"', *Transactions of the Royal Society of Literature*, I part 2 (1825–29): 74–81. Reprinted in Wrigley and Souden, *Works of Malthus*, 7: 301–23.

133. T. R. Malthus, *An Inquiry into the Nature and Progress of Rent and the Principles by which it is Regulated* (London: John Murray, 1815) reprinted in *The Pamphlets of Thomas Robert Malthus*, 175–225 and in Wrigley and Souden, *Works of Malthus*, 7: 115–45.

134. For a detailed discussion and critique of Malthus's treatment of rent and value, see Hollander, *The Economics of Thomas Robert Malthus*, chapters 3 and 7, especially 112–13 and 350.

135. James, *Population Malthus*, 361–2.

136. Quoted in ibid., 411.

137. See Samuel Hollander, 'Malthus's Abandonment of Agriculture Protectionism: A Discovery in the History of Economic Thought', *American Economic Review* 82 (June 1992): 650–59 and 'More on Malthus and Agriculture Protection', *History of Political Economy* 27 (Fall 1995): 531–8 and *The Economics of Thomas Robert Malthus*, 846–56, and 1002.

138. See John Pullen, 'Malthus on Agricultural Protection: An Alternative View', *History of Political Economy* 27 (Fall 1995): 528. I would favour Pullen's arguments as does Winch. See Winch, *Riches and Poverty*, 335 n.36.

139. 'Population' in *Supplement to the Fourth, Fifth and Sixth Editions of the Encyclopaedia Britannica*, 6 vols, ed. M. Napier (London: Hurst Robinson, 1824), 307–33 and in Wrigley and Souden, *Works of Malthus*, 4: 179–243.

140. See. T. R. Malthus, *A Summary View on the Principle of Population* (1830) reprinted in *Introduction to Malthus*, ed. D. V. Glass (London: Watts and Co., 1953), 115–81. All further references to this work are from this source. Hereafter cited as *Summary View*.

141. Ibid., 137.

142. Ibid., 156.

143. James, *Malthus Variora,* II: 135 and 124. From the 1803 *Essay.*
144. Winch, *Riches and Poverty,* 339. See also Hollander, *The Economics of Thomas Robert Malthus,* 906 especially n.26.
145. See Winch, *Riches and Poverty,* 341.
146. See ibid., 345–6.
147. James, *Malthus Variora,* II: 132 from the 1803 *Essay.* In 1806 Malthus replaced 'is unconnected with government' with 'is only indirectly connected with government'. See ibid., 132 n.19.
148. For Malthus's discussion of education see Malthus, *Summary View,* 156–7.
149. Ibid., 181.
150. Ibid., 177–8.
151. Ibid., 178.
152. James, *Population Malthus,* 450.
153. See *Irish University Press Series of British Parliamentary Papers. Emigration 2. First, Second and Third Reports from the Select Committee on Emigration from the United Kingdom with Minutes of Evidence, Appendix and Index* (1827), Question 3255.
154. Ibid., Question 3256.
155. William Godwin, *Of Population. An Enquiry concerning the Power of Increase in the Numbers of Mankind, being an Answer to Mr. Malthus's Essay on that Subject* (London, 1820).
156. See *Edinburgh Review,* XXXV, no. lxx (July 1821): 362–77. Reprinted in Semmel, *Occasional Papers,* 127–42. The article consists of a review of Godwin's book. Also reprinted in Wrigley and Souden, *Works of Malthus,* 4: 161–76. The quotation from Malthus may be found in Semmel, 127 or Wrigley and Souden, 161.
157. For the critique of the Romantics see Winch, *Riches and Poverty,* especially chapter 11, 288–322. For an analysis of the attack on Malthus by William Cobbett and the wider working-class press see Chapters 3 and 4 which follow.
158. Quoted in Boner, *Hungry Generations,* 123.
159. J. R. McCulloch, however, eventually abandoned his support for the Malthus-Ricardo position on the Poor Laws. See Winch, *Riches and Poverty,* 376.
160. See Peter Mandler, 'The Making of the New Poor Law Redivivus', *Past and Present* 117 (November 1987): 131–57. Hereafter cited as 'Making of the New Poor Law'.
161. For an analysis of Martineau's writings see Chapter 2 which follows.
162. Anthony Brundage, *The Making of the New Poor Law: The Politics of Inquiry, Enactment and Implementation* (New Brunswick, NJ: Rutgers University Press, 1978), 56. Hereafter cited as *The New Poor Law.*
163. Ibid., 67.
164. Ibid., 72.
165. Like the Old Poor Law, the literature on the New is voluminous. Many debates on the impact of the new law are still ongoing. A major one, of course, is whether its principles were actually carried out in practice. For an excellent, brief, recent introduction to such issues see Brundage, *The English Poor Laws,* especially Chapter 4. See 170–79 for his comprehensive bibliography.
166. Brundage, *The New Poor Law,* 182–3. See, however Brundage, *The*

English Poor Laws, 32–6 where greater weight is given to both Malthus and Bentham.

167. See Brundage's contribution to 'Debate: The Making of the New Poor Law Redivivus', *Past and Present*, no. 127 (May 1990): 183. Hereafter cited as 'Debate: New Poor Law'. Brundage is quoting Peter Mandler's agreement with his thesis. See Mandler, 'Making of the New Poor Law': 132. See also Brundage, *The New Poor Law*, 182.

168. See David Eastwood, 'Rethinking the Debates on the Poor Law in Early Nineteenth-Century England', *Utilitas* 6, no. 1 (May 1994): 115–16. See also Peter Dunkley, 'Whigs and Paupers: The Reform of the English Poor Laws, 1830–1834', *Journal of British Studies*, XX, no. 2 (1981): 124–49 and 'Paternalism, the Magistracy and Poor Relief in England, 1795–1834', *International Review of Social History* XXIV, no. 3 (1979): 371–97 and *The Crisis of the Old Poor Law in England, 1795–1834* (New York: Garland Publishing, 1982).

169. W. D. Grampp, 'Malthus and his Contemporaries', *History of Political Economy* 6 (Fall 1974): 36–7. For evidence that Malthus agreed with the segregation of the sexes within the workhouse see ibid., n.55.

170. Dean, *Constitution of Poverty*, 103.

171. Ibid, 104.

172. Cited in ibid., 104

173. Cited in ibid., 105.

174. Cited in ibid.

175. Ibid., 97.

176. Gertrude Himmelfarb, *The Idea of Poverty: England in the Early Industrial Age* (London: Faber and Faber, 1985), 126.

177. Anne Digby, 'Malthus and the Reform of the Poor Law' in *Malthus Past and Present*, eds J. Dupâquier et. al., 194.

178. Ibid., 106.

179. See Winch, *Riches and Poverty*, 232.

180. Mandler, 'Making of the New Poor Law': 156–7. See also 148–9 where agricultural depression and the Swing Riots of the early 1830s are given prominence in making Poor Law reform more urgent.

181. See Mandler's contribution to 'Debate: New Poor Law': 198–9 and also Peter Mandler, 'Tories and Paupers: Christian Political Economy and the Making of the New Poor Law', *Historical Journal* 33, no. 3 (1990): 84 n.20 where Mandler includes as Noetics not only those in and around Oriel College in the 1820s – that is, Edward Copleston, Richard Whately, Nassau Senior, and John Davison – but also those who shared their views of political economy. See also Boyd Hilton, *The Age of Atonement: The Influence of Evangelicalism on Social and Economic Thought 1795–1865* (Oxford: Oxford University Press, 1988).

182. Mandler, 'Tories and Paupers': 92 and Winch, *Riches and Poverty*, 24.

183. Mandler, 'Debate: New Poor Law': 198.

184. Mandler, 'Making of the New Poor Law':151 and 157.

185. See Karl Polanyi, *The Great Transformation: The Political and Economic Origins of Our Time*, 2nd edn (Boston: Beacon Press, 2001), 87. This work was originally published in 1944.

186. Ibid., 87.

CHAPTER TWO

Harriet Martineau: the female Malthusian?

> Malthus, whose speech was hopelessly imperfect, from defect in the palate. I dreaded meeting him when invited by a friend of his who made my acquaintance on purpose .... I could not decline such an invitation as this: but when I considered my own deafness, and his inability to pronounce half the consonants in the alphabet, and his hare-lip which must prevent my offering him my tube, I feared we should make a terrible business of it. I was delightfully wrong. His first sentence, – slow and gentle with the vowels sonorous, whatever might become of the consonants, – set me at ease completely. I soon found that the vowels are in fact all that I ever hear. His worst letter was *l*: and when I had no difficulty with his question, – 'Would not you like to have a look at the Lakes of Killarney?' I had nothing more to fear. It really gratified him that I heard him better than any body else; and whenever we met at dinner, I somehow found myself beside him, with my best ear next him; and then I heard all he said to every body at the table.
>
> (Harriet Martineau on first meeting Malthus in 1832)[1]

It is not surprising that Malthus was highly amused when Harriet Martineau informed him, twenty years after the fact, that she was 'sick of his name' before she was fifteen without ever having read any of his work.[2] For by 1834, Martineau, now in her thirties, had become not only a fervent admirer and close friend of the eminent political economist but also the most widely read popularizer of his ideas on population and the Poor Laws. In February 1832 she published the first of twenty-five tales in a series entitled *Illustrations of Political Economy* that appeared in monthly installments over the next two years.[3] The 1500 copies of the first story, 'Life in the Wilds', sold out in ten days, astonishing her publisher Charles Fox who later estimated monthly sales of the tales at 10,000 copies reaching 144,000 immediate readers.[4] According to one biographer these 'simple little stories had a positively miraculous success'[5] and catapulted a virtually unknown young woman from Norwich to instant fame. Soon moving to London, Martineau found herself 'lionized' in literary circles.[6] While continuing her initial series on Political Economy, Lord Chancellor Brougham urged her to publish another group of tales entitled *Poor Laws and Paupers Illustrated* in four volumes during 1833 and 1834.[7]

Martineau, unlike earlier popularizers of political economy, aimed her work at the 'mass of the people'. Jane Marcet, who published *Conversations on Political Economy* in 1816, restricted her readership to 'young persons of either sex' in the middling and upper classes. James Mill in his *Elements of Political Economy* (1821) wrote his work as a 'primer for students of the subject'.[8] Martineau, however, in her preface to the *Illustrations* claimed that 'Political Economy should be understood by all' and made clear who her intended audience was: 'We do not dedicate our series to any particular class of society, because we are sure that all classes bear an equal relation to the science, and we much fear that it is as little familiar to the bulk of one as of another.'[9]

The degree to which Martineau's readership transcended class boundaries is, of course, debatable. The historian, R. K. Webb, quite rightly points out that the eighteen pence charge for each monthly instalment over a two-year period 'was a heavy outlay to expect from a working-man'.[10] Even though the libraries of Mechanics' Institutes purchased the series, he is convinced that 'circulation was almost entirely middle class.'[11] Gillian Thomas, however, argues that because Martineau's 'didacticism' was 'unusually open and straightforward, shot through with naive enthusiasm rather than high-handed sermonizing', she did indeed reach many working-class readers.[12] In addition, the often vitriolic criticism of Martineau in worker's papers such as *The Poor Man's Guardian* spread her views far beyond the middle class. 'The sheer quantity of readers', as Gertrude Himmelfarb points out, 'was impressive.'[13]

Martineau's purpose was to convey 'the principles of Political Economy'[14] in a series of self-contained didactic stories that followed a set format: each presented a specific social problem and a final resolution based on theoretical postulates. With regard to such theories, she made no claim whatsoever to originality. In the preface, for example, to the last number of the *Illustrations* entitled 'The Moral of Many Fables' she stated:

> Great men must have their hewers of wood and their drawers of water, and scientific discoverers must be followed by those who will popularize their discoveries. When the woodsman finds it necessary to explain that the forest is not of his planting, I may begin to particularize my obligations to Smith and Malthus and others of their high order.[15]

It is significant that Martineau mentioned Malthus by name in this passage. Although her work drew on the theories of many political economists – Smith (mentioned above), James Mill and David Ricardo among others – Malthus's *Essay on the Principle of Population* was central to her entire framework. In her autobiography she made her debt to him even more explicit: 'It was my business, in illustrating Political

Economy, to exemplify Malthus's doctrine among the rest. It was that doctrine "pure and simple", as it came from his virtuous and benevolent mind, that I presented.'[16]

In her *History of England during the Thirty Years' Peace 1816–1846* (1849) she emphasized the critical importance of his theory: 'it was he who first placed clearly and by elaborate statement before society the all-important fact which lies at the bottom of the poverty of society – that the number of consumers naturally presses upon the means of subsistence.'[17]

If Martineau's enthusiasm in spreading Malthusian principles to a wider public is clear, the degree to which she succeeded is another matter. Is it possible, in spite of huge sales, that Martineau may have done more harm than good to the popular image of Malthus? William Otter, who published a *Memoir of Robert Malthus* in 1836, claimed that his friend's reputation had 'in many instances suffered more from the headlong zeal of his followers and imitators than from the mistakes and even malice of his enemies'.[18] Patricia James, in her definitive biography of Malthus, suggests that the moral tales of Martineau 'must have helped to diffuse detestation of Malthus as well as of the workhouse'.[19]

In assessing James's contention one must thoroughly analyse the Malthusian content of Martineau's stories. Was she a pure Malthusian, as her contemporary critics claimed, or did she deviate significantly from his theories? Second, one must examine the critical reception of *Illustrations of Political Economy* and *Poor Laws and Paupers Illustrated*. Historians and literary critics, in the main, have tended to underestimate the volume of hostile reaction to her works.[20] Why was she so frequently attacked and, in particular, why was such venomous criticism based on gender? In addition, since Martineau was not the only female writer popularizing notions of political economy, why was she singled out for such harsh treatment and not writers like Jane Marcet?

A disciple of Malthus

Seven of the twenty-five tales comprising the *Illustrations of Political Economy*: 'Weal and Woe in Garveloch', 'Cousin Marshall', 'Ireland', 'Homes Abroad', 'For Each and For All', 'The Moral of Many Fables' and 'A Manchester Strike' – dealt explicitly with Malthusian themes, while all four of the stories in *Poor Laws and Paupers Illustrated* – 'The Parish', 'The Hamlets', 'The Town' and 'The Land's End' – treated issues surrounding pauperism and its solutions. A perusal of this body of work reveals that, with some significant exceptions, Martineau adhered to the structure and logic of Malthusian theory about the causes of population increase, the harmful results of unchecked population growth, and the means by which individuals could bring such growth under control.

The tales, for example, are replete with references to the unequal ratio of population increase when compared to the food supply. 'Weal and Woe in Garveloch', a story set in the island fishing village of Garveloch in Scotland, portrays a classic Malthusian crisis of subsistence. Angus, the prudent fisherman and spokesman for Malthus, says to his wife Ella:

> Still, as the number of people doubles itself for ever, while the produce of the land does not, the people must increase faster than the produce. If corn produced corn without being wedded to the soil, the rate of increase might be the same with that of the human race. Then two sacks of barley might grow out of one, and two more again out of each of those two – proceeding from one to two, four, eight, sixteen, thirty-two, sixty-four, and so on.[21]

He later makes the Malthusian comparison between population growth in the old and new world, telling Ella: 'In some of the best settlements I saw in America, the increase of capital and of people went on at a rate that would scarcely be believed in an old country.'[22] In the last of the tales in *Illustrations*, 'The Moral of Many Fables', which summarizes the key principles of political economy, Martineau almost quotes Malthus verbatim: 'The increase of population is necessarily limited by the means of subsistence. Since successive portions of capital yield a less and less return, and the human species produce at a constantly accelerated rate, there is a perpetual tendency in population to press upon the means of subsistence.'[23]

If Malthus's ratios are clearly articulated, so too is his notion that such patterns are the product of natural law. In 'For Each and For All', Martineau's anti-Owenite tale, Lord F—— points out to his wife Letitia that only 'by giving the eternal laws of society fair play, and not by attempting to subvert them' will 'man … be better served as the world grows older.'[24] Angus in 'Weal and Woe in Garveloch', again speaking to Ella, claims that 'human laws have little influence in this case, while the natural laws which regulate the production of life and of capital are seldom suffered to act unchecked.'[25] Martineau, in her last tale of the *Illustrations*, succinctly states: 'The laws of nature are too strong for kings.'[26]

Like Malthus, Martineau frequently asserts that the fundamental cause of rapid population increase is early and improvident marriage, especially when induced by the generous provisions of the Old Poor Law – the poor deliberately marrying young and having children in order to receive poor relief. In 'Cousin Marshall', the anti-Poor Law tale, she makes detailed reference to what historians refer to as the Speenhamland scale adopted in the county of Berkshire in 1795, which geared relief to the size of pauper families and the price of bread. Having been informed of this practice by Mr Burke, surgeon to the workhouse infirmary, his sister Louisa replies: 'Paupers will spend and marry faster than their betters as long as this system lasts.'[27] Later in the story, Jane, an orphan who eventually becomes pregnant while in service, informs her cousin Mrs Marshall that the pauper father of the child has deserted her. Martineau, as narrator, comments on Jane's attitude:

> She laid much of the blame on the workhouse, where it was a common boast among the women how early they had got married, being so far better off than honester people that they need not trouble themselves about what became of themselves and their children, since the parish was bound to find them. It was considered a kind of enterprise among the paupers to cheat their superiors and to get the girls early married ... Jane's leading idea was the glory of getting married at sixteen.[28]

She returns to the theme of early marriage in 'Homes Abroad' – a tale dealing with emigration – where she notes that newly erected cottages in a Kent parish have been occupied by 'reckless youths with their younger wives, who depended on the parish to help out the insufficient resources of their labour'.[29] Again, in 'The Parish', the first story in *Poor Laws and Paupers Illustrated*, the following dialogue occurs between Mr Donkin (the overseer), farmer Goldby and widow Brand:

> 'You have taken pay for three children, I think,' said the overseer to the widow. 'You have managed to live on this and your own allowance and the little you earned.'
> 'Just managed, sir. With one more child I should have been pretty comfortable.'
> 'The devil you would,' cried Goldby. 'So you and your neighbours have children to be made comfortable out of our pockets.'[30]

Later, in her non-fictional *History of England during the Thirty Years' Peace*, she claims that the Old Poor Law had 'become public spoil' upon which 'ignorant boys and girls married'.[31]

The results of such rapid population increase among the improvident poor follow a strictly Malthusian pattern in Martineau's fiction. The classic checks of 'misery' and 'vice', for example, permeate her work. In 'The Moral of Many Fables', she claims that 'the over-pressure of the people upon its food' is 'painfully kept down by the death of its infants and its aged, and of those who have grown sickly through want by the agency of famine and pestilence'.[32] Mr Burke, in *Cousin Marshall*, informs his sister Louisa:

> Not only do numbers increase very rapidly; but from their increasing beyond the means of comfortable subsistence, the people are subject to a multitude of diseases arising from hardship alone. It would

make your heart ache if I were to tell you how large a proportion of my Dispensary patients are children born puny from the destitution of their parents, or weakly boys and girls, stunted by bad nursing, or women who want rest and warmth more than medicine, or men whom I can never cure until they are provided with better food.[33]

If misery in the form of starvation and disease result from overpopulation among the poor, so too does vice. In 'Weal and Woe in Garveloch', Magistrate Mackenzie tells Angus: 'I should find it difficult to assert that any set of vices could be more to be dreaded than those which arise from extreme poverty.'[34] Angus concurs, claiming 'such poverty to be the hot-bed of *all* vices'.[35] Martineau (closely adhering to Malthus) sums up her views in 'The Moral of Many Fables': 'The ultimate checks by which population is kept down to the level of subsistence, are vice and misery.'[36]

A further important effect of rapid population growth is diminishing returns in agriculture as more and more inferior land is cultivated, a concept central in Malthus's thought. In 'Weal and Woe in Garveloch', Angus predicts that even in a newly settled country like America such a phenomenon will inevitably occur:

And still ... the produce will fall behind more and more, as every improvement, every outlay of capital yields a less return. Then they will be in the condition of an old country, like England, where many are but half fed, where the imprudent must see their children pine in hunger, or waste under disease till they are ready to be carried off by the first attack of illness.[37]

Martineau reiterates this theme in 'The Moral of Many Fables': 'These principles are two: – That, owing to the inequality of soils (the ultimate capital of society), the natural tendency of capital is to yield a perpetually diminishing return; –and that the consumers of capital increase at a perpetually accelerated rate.'[38] She further adds that such principles 'serve as a key to all the mysteries relating to the distribution of wealth'.[39]

Malthus, of course, predicted that an unrestrained population expanding with the support of the Poor Laws would eventually create a situation where the 'great body of the community' would be 'a collection of paupers'.[40] Martineau faithfully echoes this dismal forecast throughout her works. In 'Cousin Marshall', Mr Burke says to his friend Mr Effingham: 'Thus is our pauper list swelled, year by year. It grows at both ends. Paupers multiply their own numbers as fast as they can, and rate-payers sink down into rate-receivers.'[41] Earlier in the tale, he warns his sister Louisa that England will 'become a vast congregation of paupers'.[42] In 'Ireland', Alexander, the son of Mr Rosso the Protestant landlord, opposes the introduction of a Poor Law in Ireland claiming it would 'swallow up all we have gained and effectively prevent the further progress to improvement'.[43]

Indeed, the central theme of 'The Parish' is that of the hard-working independent labourer driven by low wages and unemployment onto poor relief. Ashley, the prototype of the prudent worker, cannot find a job because farmers are hiring paupers whose wages are subsidized by the parish. A widower with children to support, he finds his savings dwindling and exclaims despairingly: 'I know they will soon make a pauper out of me.' He later remarks, 'all will become paupers and nothing will be left.'[44] Dr Warrener, the rector, contrasting the 'honest poor' with their 'pauper neighbours' sees the Poor Law 'transforming the one race into the other'.[45] Martineau, as narrator, at one point states: 'where the principle and practice of giving parish support to idlers is once allowed, there is every prospect of the substance of all who are not paupers being consumed unproductively to the destruction of the whole society where such consumption is permitted.'[46]

Not content merely to illustrate the catastrophic problems resulting from the Malthusian dilemma, Martineau consistently discusses solutions, strongly rejecting some, and wholeheartedly prescribing others. Although she displays important differences with Malthus, the core of her argument conforms to and, at times, takes his line of reasoning to absurd extremes.

To begin with, in pure Malthusian fashion, she rules out any form of institutional redistribution of wealth as a panacea for England's ills. In 'For Each and For All', she attacks Owenite socialism – a critique that closely parallels Malthus's rejection of Owen's theories in the 1817 edition of *An Essay on the Principle of Population*.[47] Joel, the church sexton, remarks to Letitia:

> But how would co-operation mend the matter? However the total produce is divided, it still goes on lessening, while numbers increase …. Co-operation, equalization, and all those things, cannot make all lands equally fertile, they cannot make capital grow as numbers grow; and unless they could do those things, they can make no permanent provision for unlimited numbers; they cannot prevent the decline of profits, whether those profits are taken by individuals, or thrown into the common stock.[48]

Lord F—— again reverts back to natural law. Of man he states: 'His nature involves inequality of powers; and this decree of Providence can never be set aside, or its operation neutralized by any decree of man that the fruits of those powers shall be equally divided.'[49]

The key demographic mechanism, which worked against attempts to equalize wealth, was the encouragement to early marriage that caused such growth in numbers as to reduce the population to starvation. Joel predicts in typically Malthusian fashion: 'Then would ensue a scramble; if anything should be left, competition would come into play again.'[50] Thus private property is absolutely essential to prevent excessive population growth. As Martineau sums it up: 'but for the barriers of individual rights of property, the tide of population would flow in with an overwhelming force.'[51]

For similar reasons, Martineau rejects the idea that the provision of cottages for the poor could be a viable means of curing pauperism. Like Malthus, she raises the spectre of overwhelming population increase under such an arrangement. In 'Cousin Marshall', Mr Burke is asked by his friend Effingham what he thinks of the 'cottage system' and replies: 'It will not bear the test. Under no system does population increase more rapidly; – witness Ireland.'[52] 'The Parish' repeats the theme of early marriage. Mr Bloggs says to Mr Donkin, the overseer of the poor: 'Cottages do not stand empty long where there are young people of the parish ready to marry.'[53]

The positive solution that Martineau most consistently advocates, often to extremes, is the classic Malthusian preventive check of moral restraint, that is, delay of marriage, while practicing strict chastity, until individuals are in a position to support their offspring. In 'Ireland', Mr Orme, the Protestant clergyman, praises the 'old Scotch practice of accumulating a stock of linen for bed and board, which could scarcely be consumed in a lifetime'. Such behaviour, he claims, 'proved an important check upon population. Young people had to wait two or three years before they married ... . Those who thus began their married life were never known to become paupers.'[54] Mr Jackson, the curate in 'Homes Abroad', vows to use his 'pastoral influence in inducing the young folks to delay the publication of their banns till they have secured something besides a bare shelter to begin with'.[55] In the summary to 'Cousin Marshall', Martineau makes a statement that some critics later misinterpreted as advocating the practice of voluntary birth control: 'A parent has a considerable influence over the subsistence-fund of his family, and an absolute control over the numbers to be supported by that fund.'[56]

It is 'Weal and Woe in Garveloch', however, where moral restraint is pushed to limits that go beyond Malthus. For, in all probability, not even Martineau's mentor would have found believable the absolute selflessness of Ronald, the cooper, in delaying marriage. Ronald had formed an early love attachment to a maiden named Katie, only to lose her to his friend Cuthbert. After becoming widowed upon Cuthbert's death at sea, Katie is left to raise four children. Ronald still pines for her but gives up so completely on marriage that the widow wonders if she has done something to put him off. Her friend and neighbour, Ella, however, sets her straight: 'We have not the power of increasing food as fast as our numbers may increase; but we have the power of limiting our numbers to agree with the supply of food. This is the gentle check which is put into our own hands; and if we will not use it we must not repine if harsher checks follow.'[57] She explains Ronald's refusal to marry thus: 'It is not for himself only, but for you and your children, and for us and for society, that he thinks and acts as he does.'[58] Katie comments on how hard it must be for Ronald 'to deny himself because his neighbours are imprudent'. Ella simply replies how 'sweet' it is for 'him to help us in our need'.[59] Malthus, of course, never recommended life-long celibacy and although he argued that if workers limited their numbers their wages would increase, Ronald's complete denial of marriage for the wider social good would have surely strained his credulity.[60]

In strict conformity with Malthusian doctrine, however, Martineau makes it clear that 'moral restraint' on its own could not provide an effective solution. Institutional measures, both negative and positive, would be required to make delay of marriage feasible. In the *Illustrations of Political Economy* she advocates, for example, the total abolition of the Poor Laws, later – in *Poor Laws and Pauper Illustrated* – modifying her position in support of the New Poor Law of 1834. In addition, she consistently rejects any universal right to relief and denies the principle of benevolence, which traditionally governed the treatment of poverty under the Old Poor Law. On the other hand, she strongly advocates state-sponsored education for the lower orders and supports Benefits and Savings Clubs for the poor.

Her initial stance on the Old Poor Law as revealed in the *Illustrations* is totally Malthusian. Only the complete elimination of this system would restore the independence of the lower classes. The knowledge that their children would receive no support from parish funds would induce them to postpone marriage. In 'Cousin Marshall', Mr Burke, when asked by his friend Effingham in what specific manner he would eliminate the Poor Law, replies almost in Malthus's own words:

> The best plan, in my opinion, yet proposed, is this: – to enact that no child born from any marriage taking place within a year from the date of the law, and no illegitimate child born within two years from the same date, shall ever be entitled to parish assistance. This regulation should be made known, and its purpose explained universally; and this, if properly done, might, I think, prevent violence, and save a vast amount of future distress. The people should be called together, either in their places of worship or elsewhere, in such a manner as to attract the whole population to listen, and the case should be explained to them by their pastors or others. It is so plain a case, and so capable of illustration, that I see no great difficulty in making the most ignorant comprehend it.[61]

In conversation with his sister Louisa, Burke denies the very principle upon which the Old Poor Law was based; namely, the right to assistance from the state:

> Some assert the right of every individual born into any community to
> a maintenance from the state; regarding the state and its members as
> holding the relation of parent and children. This seems to me
> altogether a fallacy; – originating in benevolent feelings, no doubt,
> but supported only by a false analogy. The state cannot control the
> number of its members, nor increase, at its will, the subsistence-fund;
> and, therefore, if it engaged to support all the members that might be
> born to it, it would engage for more than it might have the power to
> perform.[62]

In 'Ireland', Mr Rosso, the Protestant landlord, strongly advocates the
annihilation of the 'English pauper system' and opposes any *right* to
assistance' which offers a 'premium to improvidence' and renders the
poor 'more reckless'.[63]

Closely intertwined with notions of rights to relief is the general
principle of benevolence, encompassing those 'benevolent feelings'
mentioned by Mr Burke. Indeed, Burke elaborates to his sister Louisa in
great detail on this theme: 'The failure of British benevolence', he tells his
sister Louisa, 'vast as it is in amount, has hitherto been complete.'[64] He
later warns against letting 'kindly emotions run in the ruts of ancient
institutions!'.[65] So convinced are both Burke and his sister of their
principles, they carry them out in practice. The former gives up his
voluntary involvement in the Dispensary and Lying-in hospitals, while
Louisa refuses to give alms to beggars or to sanction gifts of clothing to
children. Moreover, she declines subscribing or yielding her services to
soup and blanket charities.[66] Burke even rejects alms-houses for the aged:
'Only consider the numbers of young people that marry under the
expectation of getting their helpless parents maintained by the public!'
'Working men', he claims 'should support their parents' just as 'they
should support their children'.[67] Martineau in the summary section
concluding 'Cousin Marshall' makes her position clear. She states:

> The small unproductive consumption occasioned by the relief of
> sudden accidents and rare infirmities is necessary, and may be
> justifiably provided for by charity, since such charity does not tend to
> the increase of numbers; but, with this exception, all arbitrary
> distribution of the necessaries of life is injurious to society, whether
> in the form of private almsgiving, public charitable institutions, or a
> legal pauper-system.[68]

By severely limiting relief, Martineau, employing one of Malthus's most
infamous metaphors, believed she would further the process of ridding
the poor 'of all deadly struggle or pining desire for a due share of the
bounties of nature's mighty feast'.[69]

If Martineau gives great weight to such negative measures in
establishing the context within which moral restraint could function, she
places even stronger emphasis on positive inducements, in particular,

state-funded education. Like Malthus, she argues that in the absence of poor relief and widespread private charity, education would be the crucial vehicle encouraging the lower orders to become prudent and rational. In her *Autobiography* she claims that she advocated 'above all, education without limit'.[70] Earlier in her *History of England during the Thirty Years' Peace* she states: 'it must be a consideration of the first moment so to educate the rising generation, and so to arrange the inducements of their life, as to train them to prudence for their own comfort, and humanity towards their children.'[71]

Her fiction is replete with references to the beneficial effects education would have on the poor in reducing their numbers and improving their standard of living. In 'The Three Ages', a tale dealing with the proper boundaries of government expenditure, she vociferously complains about the vast amounts spent on defence when compared to the paltry sums given to public education. She proposes that education be given top priority in funding.[72] In 'Ireland', Martineau appears as narrator during a discussion between Father Glenny, the Catholic priest, and Mr Orme, the Protestant clergyman: 'both gentlemen decided that the only method by which the permanent prosperity of the people could be secured was the general diffusion of such knowledge as would make them judges of their own condition and controllers of their own destinies.' They both agree, moreover, that 'an impartial plan of general education be framed by government'.[73] Mr Burke, in 'Cousin Marshall', having emphasized to his sister Louisa the paramount importance of limiting population, proposes free education for the masses: 'Schools should be multiplied and improved without any other limit than the number and capabilities of the people.'[74] Martineau, as usual, states her views succinctly in 'The Moral of Many Fables':

> The number of consumers must be proportioned to the subsistence-fund. To this end, encouragements to the increase of population should be withdrawn, and every sanction given to the preventive check; *i.e.* charity must be directed to the enlightenment of the mind instead of to the relief of bodily wants.[75]

In addition to state-sponsored education, she recommends other Malthusian remedies of a voluntary nature. In 'Cousin Marshall', Effingham remarks to Mr Burke: 'But Friendly Societies and Benefit Clubs will bear your test. They tend to the increases of capital, and by encouraging prudence, to the limitation of numbers.'[76] Marshall himself, 'a slow and dull, though steady workman' earning moderate wages, would have sunk into poverty had he not been a member of a Benefit club.[77] Ashley, the prototype of the independent labourer in 'The Parish', attempts to revive the local benefit club,[78] while in 'The Hamlets' individuals establish a savings bank to the advantage of the parishioners.[79]

Divergence from her mentor

The above analysis reveals Martineau's adherence to the essential elements of Malthus's principles; nevertheless, she was far from a pure Malthusian. Many historians and literary analysts have stressed – as she would have been the first to admit – her theoretical reliance on Adam Smith, Jeremy Bentham, James Mill, David Ricardo and Edward Gibbon Wakefield, all of whom had important differences with Malthus.[80] Martineau diverged from her mentor in four important areas: her changing views on the Old Poor Law, her assessment of the role of emigration in counteracting population increase, her rejection of the Corn Laws and her overall optimism concerning the future improvement of society.

Even though Malthus during the 1820s wavered in private over his stance on the Old Poor Law, he remained an abolitionist in public as successive editions of his *Essay* indicate.[81] Martineau, on the other hand, moved quickly towards reform. She had been given advance copies of some of the materials being prepared by the Poor Law Commission prior to writing *Poor Laws and Paupers Illustrated* in 1833 and 1834. These tales clearly reflect the commission's recommendations for the enactment of a New Poor Law, not surprising in light of the fact that Lord Brougham, who as Lord Chancellor was the most influential proponent of an amended Poor Law, had suggested the idea to Martineau in the first place.[82] The four stories advocated the three core guidelines of the New Poor Law: the elimination of outdoor relief in favour of the workhouse, the principle of less eligibility (that is, that inmates inside the house should live at a standard below that of the independent labourer), and the creation of a central board to ensure uniformity of administration.

In 'The Parish', the rector, Dr Warrener, in a lengthy conversation with the overseer Mr Donkin and other parishioners, refers to several categories of paupers who should be denied outdoor relief and sent to the workhouse: 'widows who, with their children are able to work ... unmarried mothers and their children ... vagrants ... apprentices, who having obtained a settlement by apprenticeship, threaten to bring pauper wives from other parishes ... servants who make the parish pay for their imprudent marriages' and finally all 'able-bodied labourers'.[83] In 'The Hamlets', the reforming overseer Mr Barry refuses outdoor relief to anyone able-bodied regardless of age or circumstance. Thus Widow Dyer and her children are denied such assistance even though her husband and son died at sea.[84]

Inside the workhouse, conditions should be inferior to those outside. Mr Barry, speaking of persons inside, succinctly states the principle of less eligibility: 'You will always bear in mind the rule that they are to have whatever comes below the limit of what is enjoyed by the independent labourers who help to support them.'[85] Mr Orger, the efficient assistant overseer in 'The Town', proposes a uniformity of diet and clothes in every workhouse and insists that pauper women work as nurses in the infirmary.[86] Martineau best sums up conditions inside the workhouse in her *History of England during the Thirty Years' Peace*. Reflecting upon the New Poor Law fifteen years after its enactment, she stresses not only work but also segregation:

> One condition was, that the able-bodied should work – should do a certain amount of work for every meal. They might go out after the expiration of twenty-four hours; but while in the house they must work. The men, women, and children must be separate; and the able-bodied and infirm. The separation of the men and women – husbands and wives among others – was absolutely necessary to common decency, in an establishment like a workhouse; and that of husbands and wives was required by every consideration of justice to the state, which could not rear a race of paupers within the workhouse, to the prevention of virtuous marriage without. That the aged and infirm should be separated from the able-bodied was necessary to their own quiet and comfort. Their diet included indulgences which others could not have; and the turbulence of sturdy paupers was no fit spectacle for them. That the children should be segregated was necessary to their moral safety and educational training.[87]

Having denied outdoor relief to paupers in exchange for their confinement in the workhouse under principles of less eligibility, Martineau finally proposes a centralized administration of the entire system with power concentrated in London. As the vicar in 'The Town' states:

> Whenever a blessed society of three or four wise men in London shall be appointed to superintend, and their country agents to administer without fear or favour, so that our poor shall cease to be an object of barter and sale, I may hope to do some little good among those who want it most.[88]

Mr Orger, the assistant overseer, concurs claiming a 'central board' would ensure 'impartial management' while 'district boards acting through salaried offices, and responsible to a central board' would administer newly created unions of parishes in the counties.[89]

If Martineau diverges from Malthus on the issue of the Poor Laws her position on emigration marks an even greater divide. Malthus viewed emigration as at most a 'weak' or 'slight palliative' to the problem of overpopulation claiming, in the 1803 *Essay*, 'no plans of emigration ... can prevent the continued action of a great check to population in some form or other' and further stating that such measures could not 'under any circumstances be considered as an adequate remedy'.[90] In contrast, Martineau – heavily influenced by Edward Gibbon Wakefield – wholeheartedly endorses government sponsored movements of paupers out of the country.[91]

In 'Homes Abroad', the curate Mr Jackson elaborates in great detail on a plan for parish-funded emigration. Speaking to Frank, a young labourer and potential emigrant, he advocates sending young men and women of marriageable age in 'equal proportions' so that the colonies instead of England would receive their descendants:

> If, instead of sending out people of all ages, we were to select those who become marriageable, one-sixth of that number, or about 133,000 persons emigrating annually, would prevent our population increasing; and this might be done at an expense not exceeding a fourth of the sum annually raised for poor-rate, sending half to America and half to Australia.[92]

Frank concurs claiming 'it would relieve the country of its over-fullness at once.'[93] He eventually emigrates successfully to Van Diemen's Land and receives a letter from Mr Jackson who has decided to emigrate there himself. Reflecting Wakefield's theory of social balance in emigré colonies, Jackson writes:

> Wherever colonization has succeeded best, the emigrating party has been composed of specimens of every rank and class; so that no one felt stripped of the blessings of the mother-country, but rather that he moved away in the midst of an entire though small society. If gentlemen go to one place, and labourers to another, the settlement is sure to pine.[94]

He later states that the best mode of 'emigration is to send out a company as a swarm of bees goes forth, – under proper leaders, and in a state of organization'.[95]

If emigration would solve England's overpopulation, it would be even more beneficial to Ireland. Advocating Irish migration to Van Diemen's Land, Martineau remarks:

> Why should not a bridge be built across this wide sea with the capital which is now unproductively expended on the maintenance of these paupers? Why should not the charity which *cannot* in Ireland give assistance to one without taking it from another be employed in a way which gives support to many, to the benefit of many more? Whatever funds are judiciously employed on emigration are used as if to bring to a junction with the over-peopled country a rich region, into which a hungry multitude may be poured, to the relief of the old, and the great advantage of the new land.[96]

In 'Ireland', the Protestant Landlord Mr Rosso rejects the introduction of Poor Laws in favour of planned emigration 'carefully providing a settlement in Canada or Australia for every family'.[97] In the summary section of this tale Martineau concludes: 'Population should be reduced … by well-conducted schemes of emigration.'[98]

Perhaps the greatest departure from Malthusian theory is Martineau's stance on the Corn Laws. Malthus, at great risk to his reputation as a political economist, publicly supported government controls on the import of corn. Martineau, however, takes a more orthodox Ricardian position in favour of repeal.[99] 'Very little can be done to improve the condition of the people', she claims in 'The Moral of Many Fables', 'till the Corn Laws are repealed' and refers to the 'evils of a restricted trade in corn'.[100] She thus advocates a 'liberal commercial system which shall obviate the necessity of bringing poor soils into cultivation'.[101] In 'For Each and For All', Lord F—— says to his wife Letitia: 'Of course, we must change our system; not, however, by discouraging competition, or abolishing private property, but by removing all artificial restrictions upon food.'[102] So convinced is Letitia that 'she sighed for the time when an unrestricted provision of food (unrestricted by state-laws) should check the rise of rents.'[103] Martineau, of course, later writes stories on behalf of the Anti-Corn Law League to support the movement against protectionism.[104]

Martineau's expansive optimism is the final major difference with Malthus. Although Malthus became increasingly optimistic in his later writings, especially in *The Principles of Political Economy* (1820) – where he envisioned the increasing spread of prudential restraint and an improved standard of living for the working classes – he never exhibited Martineau's unbounded and simplistic faith in human progress and social harmony.[105] In 'The Moral of Many Fables', for example, she claims, 'it seems absolute impiety to doubt man's perpetual progression.' She further asserts that even English artisans 'have made a vast approach … towards participating in the most perfect conceivable condition of society'.[106] The last lines of the entire series comprising the *Illustrations* reads like Jeremy Bentham:

> Therefore shall the heaven-born spirit be trusted while revealing and announcing at one the means and the end – *the employment of all powers and all materials, the natural recompense of all action, and the consequent accomplishment of the happiness of the greatest number, if not of all.*[107]

More specifically, Martineau is convinced of significant improvements in the lot of the working classes stating that 'probably no day passes in which my readers do not hear or say something about the wonderful improvements in art, the variety of new conveniences, and the spread downwards of luxuries to which the wealthy were formerly believed to have exclusive title.'[108] Such comforts spreading to an increasingly 'enlightened multitude' will encourage the poor to 'fall into our way of thinking, and prefer a home of comfort, earned by forethought and self-denial to herding together in a state of reckless pauperism'.[109]

The basis of Martineau's optimism, as Valerie Pichanick points out, lies in her adherence to Adam Smith's identity of interests premise.[110] An increased standard of living through the exercise of moral restraint allowing labour to curtail its numbers and increase its wages will lead to social harmony since the 'interests of the two classes of producers, Labourers and Capitalists, are therefore the same; the prosperity of both depending on the accumulation of Capital.'[111] As Lord F—— says to Letitia in 'For Each and For All': 'If there were food enough for our people, their occupations and interests, be they as various as the minds that adopt them, would assist and promote each other from end to end of society …. Where there is plenty there will be a harmony.'[112] In 'The Moral of Many Fables' she reiterates this theme:

> When the labouring class fully comprehends the extent of the power which it holds, – a power of obtaining not only its own terms from the capitalists, but all the necessaries and comforts of life, and with them the ease and dignity which become free-born men, they will turn their other power of combination to better purposes than those of annoyance and injury.[113]

Hostile reception

Clearly then, Martineau did not simply adhere blindly to Malthus's ideas. Critical reaction to her work ranged from ecstatic to lukewarm to vitriolic. What is significant for our purposes, however, is that her severest critics seized mainly – in most cases solely – on the Malthusian themes in her fiction. They did not recognize or, more likely, refused to recognize the profound differences with her mentor and instead directed their venom at her insistence on limiting population and her rejection of the Old Poor Law in favour of the New. Such criticism, often based on gender, not only provides important insights into contemporary attitudes to birth control but also reveals a new wave of hostility to Malthus. Even though he did not enter the debate on the 1834 Poor Law and did not publicly support it, he was tarnished as one of its progenitors. Malthus was thus subject to much abusive criticism on his own account. Thanks to Martineau's popularization of his views (especially in working-class and Tory circles) he became even more despised. Never was he so unpopular than in the last two years of his life prior to his death in 1834.

To be sure, Martineau had her enthusiastic supporters. Her hometown *Norwich Mercury* referred to her 'delicacy of perception' and urged that

'The Hill and the Valley', the first tale of *Illustrations*, be disseminated throughout the country 'not only among those who can read, but even among those who have not yet enjoyed the good effects of the schoolmaster, in order that they may hear and read this cheap and unpretending volume, which while it teaches how to spread around the greatest good to the greatest number, inculcates a morality which must lead to the best results'.[114] *The Spectator* excitedly dubbed her a 'benefactor of her species'.[115] John Stuart Mill in *The Monthly Repository* of May 1834, gave her a kind review.[116]

Other reviewers were lukewarm, seeing much that was objectionable in her writings but nevertheless bestowing considerable praise. The *New Monthly Review*, for example, concluded:

> Miss Martineau's talents, and the value of her works, are indisputable. She has arrived at that point of excellence where we begin to estimate the value and adjudge the station of the writer. The greatest and most consummate order of perfect intellect, is that in which the imaginative and the reasoning faculties are combined, – each carried to its height: – the one inspired, the other regulated, by its companion; and though we cannot of course attribute to Miss Martineau these faculties in their greatest extent, we can yet congratulate her on no inconsiderable portion of them united with no common felicity.[117]

The prominent Whig periodical, *The Edinburgh Review*, claimed that 'the public has already significantly expressed its delight at her remarkable performances.' William Empson, the reviewer, also stated that 'she has already made, by a previously undreamed-of route, a brilliant progress towards the rescue of her beloved science – the science of Adam Smith – from the cloud which some persons have thought was gathering over its condition and its fate.'[118]

On the whole, historians have given sufficient emphasis to the positive reaction to Martineau. The diverse, abundant, often cruel critique of her work however – with the exception of Caroline Roberts – has been severely underestimated. From the radical press to Tory and even Whig periodicals, Martineau was attacked for her Malthusian views. Even working-class newspapers that originally supported her ideas turned strongly against her when she rejected Owen in favour of Malthus.

A case in point was *The Poor Man's Guardian*, a weekly newspaper published between 1831 and 1835. Selling for 1d. per copy, this paper was one of the most influential publications of the radical working-class unstamped press. Initially describing Martineau's early stories in her *Illustrations* as 'excellent',[119] it turned hostile in reaction to 'Weal and Woe in Garveloch' and 'For Each and For All'. In 1834 it cynically remarked: 'News for Miss Martineau – *The Portland Courier* (an

American Paper) says that the young ladies of that town have formed an anti-matrimonial society!'[120] Later in the same year it labelled Martineau 'the anti-propagation lady' and immediately proceeded to castigate the Revd Malthus who 'had £100 given him as a present by the late King (the father, undoubted, of a host of bastard children)'.[121] On 10 January 1835 under the heading 'SCRAPS FROM COBBETT', extracted from his Political Register, it cited Cobbett's reference to the New Poor Law as 'the Mother Martineau bill'.[122]

Other radical working-class papers consistently opposed Martineau. *The Working Man's Friend and Political Magazine*, another unstamped weekly, published a letter in 1832 containing a fictitious exchange between John Bull (a poor labourer) and a Whig:

> 'I don't believe you', said poor Johnny: 'you only wish to put me into a workhouse.' 'Read Malthus and Martineau,' said the Whig: 'the *fewer* labourers, the *more* wealth.' 'Aye, the more wealth for the idlers, because the less worry,' said poor John Bull. 'But I am a working man.'[123]

The People's Conservative and Trades' Union Gazette on 17 May 1834 declared the proposed New Poor Law Bill a violation of 'the chartered rights of the poor' and then printed an extract from *The True Sun* which stated:

> At some of the parish meetings held to deliberate on this Whig measure, Miss Martineau we perceive has been alluded to as its author. Miss Martineau is a woman of genius but her philosophy is very false. The Whig Bill might very rationally be supposed to emanate from her budget, did we not know Lord Brougham to be quack enough to concoct fifty such measures, without foreign aid of any sort.[124]

In attacking Lord Brougham's speech supporting the New Poor Law in the House of Lords, *The True Sun* later lumped Martineau with Malthus. Claiming that Brougham 'repeats by rote the lessons which Mr MALTHUS has taught him', it continued: 'He is a noisy echo of the Malthusian system … he would appear to reverberate even an echo of that system, which Miss Martineau has in later times supplied.'[125]

Established Tory periodicals, moreover, were equally unkind. *Fraser's Magazine*, in a review of 'Cousin Marshall', castigated Martineau for advocating abolition of the Old Poor Law and totally rejected her Malthusian views:

> Then, we must tell her, in the plainest terms, that THE EVIL of which she stands in so much dread, is WHOLLY THE CREATURE OF HER OWN IMAGINATION; aided, probably, by the absurd exaggerations of Malthus, Chalmers, and others. This supposed evil is the growth of pauperism, the decline of the wealth of the nation,

the gradual absorption of property in the support of the poor, ending, of course, in universal poverty and distress at the last. This is the ever-recurring burden of her song.[126]

'She adopts', the reviewer continued, 'most implicitly the Malthusian fancy, that people always breed up to food, and the more food the more children; whereas the truth is exactly the reverse.'[127] *The New Monthly Magazine* that was prepared to praise Martineau nevertheless found serious fault in her fiction:

> Were Miss Martineau viewed only as a political economist, her merits would shrink into an exceedingly small compass; for though, as we before said, it is a great merit to popularize known truths, the merit is that of a writer, not a philosopher. Miss Martineau has not added a single new truth to the science; and it is only the most generally acknowledged axioms which she has ventured to embody in her tales; – this, indeed, with obvious wisdom; for if she had illustrated the more equivocal and less settled principles, the merit of the illustration would have become exceedingly questionable.[128]

From a literary standpoint, the reviewer – Edward Bulwer-Lytton – found 'Weal and Woe in Garveloch' totally unrealistic. 'In the most barbarous spot of earth', he claimed, 'half-starved fishermen take the most astonishing views on the theory of population.' That Angus, in particular, could 'utter the intricate doctrines of a Malthus in the elegant simplicity of a Hume' was especially unbelievable.[129]

In addition, even Whig periodicals such as *The Edinburgh Review* saw faults in Martineau: 'A certain proportion of absurdity, though small in quantity, and unimportant in quality, will, with many, discredit and leaven any amount of truth; and must destroy, with all, that feeling of security, which is a great part of a pupil's pleasure, and which is in some degree his right.'[130] William Empson, the reviewer, found the character Ronald – the epitome of moral restraint and self-sacrifice in 'Weal and Woe in Garveloch' – particularly absurd:

> Still, (we ask on the part of single gentlemen,) if Ronald is not to marry, who is? Are the burden and drudgery of population to be thrown on the thoughtless only? Are the charms of domestic life to be given by preference to those who will feel them least? Has society an interest in assigning over the monopoly of the bringing up of families to that portion of the community who will assuredly bring them up ill?[131]

Empson also found Martineau's restriction of charity to 'sudden accidents and rare infirmities'[132] highly objectionable:

> Is her doctrine, or at least her illustration of it, quite correct? The true doctrinal principle, most pursued, does not insist on our excluding from public charity Dispensaries for the sick, supported by

subscription, or wither the discriminating hand of private benevolence when stretched out for any distress which is not as entirely pure accident, as the fact of being born blind, or subsequent loss of sight. It is a great fault to overstate a case, and to go on tightening an argument until its cord inevitably snaps. Nature has not subjected either the feelings of the rich, or the necessities of the poor, to so severe a trial.[133]

Martineau was particularly upset by the reaction of the highly influential *Times*, a newspaper that, she claimed, changed its position at the last moment and vociferously opposed the New Poor Law. She labelled the paper dishonest and unduly influenced by country justices of a paternalist bent.[134] *The Times*, indeed, could be as vituperative as the radical press. On 13 May 1834 it referred to the 'accursed heresy pervading all the trash of Malthus, Martineau, and their disciples – the heresy that poverty is a crime'.[135] The following miscellaneous item was included in its 10 October 1834 edition:

> COMFORT FOR MISS MARTINEAU – (Extract from a private letter.) Before I close, I cannot forbear telling you a fact that will make William laugh. The wife of a lodgekeeper to Major B—, of T— hill, about 12 miles from here, had 11 children at a birth, which were all put in a sleve, but they died. I hear it was laughable to see the father, as every account came to him of each increase, till when they came to the 11th, he rushed into the lake, swearing he'd drown himself, and crowds of country people running after him, they succeeded in saving him. She was before this mother of six children. This only happened the other day, and incredible as it may appear, is positively true. – Dublin Freeman's Journal.[136]

If Martineau was castigated by both the established and radical press on the basis of her Malthusian views, she was also subject to extremely malicious attacks based on her gender. It was bad enough to disseminate the ideas of the detestable Malthus. It was even worse, in the eyes of her critics, that such sentiments should stem from a woman's pen. Martineau, indeed, was highly conscious of her purpose as a female author. In a letter to Francis Place in 1832 she claimed: 'I want to be doing something with the pen, since no other means of action in politics are in a woman's power.'[137] She was likewise aware of the potential dangers of writing about Malthusian issues. Her prescience is revealed by the following entry she made in her autobiography:

> When the course of my exposition brought me to the Population subject, I, with my youthful and provincial mode of thought and feeling, – brought up too amidst the prudery which is found in its great force in our middle class, – could not but be sensible that I risked much in writing and publishing on a subject which was not universally treated in the pure, benevolent, and scientific spirit of Malthus himself. I felt that the subject was one of science, and

therefore perfectly easy to treat in itself; but I was aware that some evil associations had gathered about it, – though I did not know what they were. While writing 'Weal and Woe in Garveloch,' the perspiration many a time streamed down my face, though I knew there was not a line in it which might not be read aloud in any family. The misery arose from my seeing how the simplest statements and reasonings might and probably would be perverted.[138]

In the scathing remarks of *The Quarterly Review* in 1833 her worst fears were realized. Written by the economist George Poulett Scrope, this review of her *Illustrations* constituted, as one contemporary put it, 'the filthiest thing that had passed through the press for a quarter of a century'.[139] Martineau claimed that the 'insulting' remarks were 'interlarded' by John Wilson Croker and by John Gibson Lockhart. Croker, indeed, had declared at a dinner party his intention of 'tomahawking Miss Martineau in the *Quarterly*'.[140]

Although Martineau, like Malthus, never supported voluntary family limitation and advocated only delay of marriage, *The Quarterly Review* clearly implied otherwise. Quoting a passage from 'Cousin Marshall', the reviewer added the following emphasis: 'A parent has a considerable influence over the subsistence-fund of his family, and an *absolute control over the numbers to be supported by that fund.*' Asking whether 'the young lady picked up this piece of information in her conferences with the Lord Chancellor', he then labelled Martineau 'a *female Malthusian.* A *woman* who thinks child-bearing a *crime against society*! An *unmarried woman* who declaims against *marriage*!! A *young woman* who deprecates charity and a provision for the *poor*!!!'[141] The reviewer had earlier remarked that it was 'quite impossible not to be shocked, nay disgusted, with many of the unfeminine and mischievous doctrines on the principles of social welfare, of which these tales are made the vehicle'.[142] Again referring to her age and marital status he claimed:

> A little ignorance on these ticklish topics is perhaps not unbecoming a young unmarried lady. But before such a person undertook to write books in favour of 'the preventive check,' she should have informed herself somewhat more accurately upon the laws of human propagation. Poor innocent! She has been puzzling over Mr. Malthus's arithmetical and geometrical ratios, for knowledge which she should have obtained by a simple question or two of her mamma.[143]

Initially, Martineau was extremely upset by such criticism and referred in her *Autobiography* to 'the low-minded and foul-mouthed creatures who could use their education and position as gentlemen "to destroy" a woman whom they knew to be innocent of even comprehending their imputation.' She claimed, however, that such 'hostile reviewing' soon toughened her resolve. 'I stood', she said, 'unharmed, and somewhat enlightened and strengthened.'[144] Later, in conversation with Malthus, she recounted:

> I asked Mr. Malthus one day whether he had suffered in spirits from the abuse lavished on him. 'Only just at first,' he answered. – 'I wonder whether it ever kept you awake a minute.' – 'Never after the first fortnight,' was his reply. The spectacle of the good man in his daily life, in contrast with the representations of him in the periodical literature of the time, impressed upon me, more forcibly than anything in my own experience, the everlasting fact that the reformers of morality, personal and social, are always subject at the outset to the imputation of immorality from those interested in the continuance of corruption.[145]

Martineau would need all the resolve she could muster against the torrent of abuse heaped upon her. *Fraser's Magazine* was as venomous as *The Quarterly Review*. Referring to 'Cousin Marshall' the reviewer remarked: 'What a frightful delusion is this, called, by its admirers, Political Economy, which can lead a young lady to put forth a book like this! – a book written by a *young woman* against marriage!' The tale, he claimed, was nothing but 'a tissue of reasonings, which would disgrace the third class of any ladies' boarding-school of decent character, in these days of improved female education'.[146] 'The young lady', moreover, had made 'the grand mistake' of theorizing, 'instead of consulting facts and human nature'.[147]

Cobbett's Magazine questioned not only her originality but also her authorship:

> Miss MARTINEAU never wrote all, by a great deal, of those tracts on 'Political Economy' which profess to be hers. We do not know this by any of the ordinary means of ascertaining fact. But, we are morally convinced, nevertheless, that a very considerable part of her economical vagaries have been prepared for the press by persons of the other sex, and that, if she even understood their tendency, she had not, at least, any hand in concocting them.[148]

'That this lady', the reviewer continued, 'has had *men* along with her, is clear. Men, very likely, who would not venture to put their own names to that in print which they have advised her to adopt as her own.'[149] Claiming that her discussion of population was 'too repugnant to nature for us to believe that it was ever put on paper by one of her sex', he advised the author thus:

> Let us, however (though without any hopes of effecting a perfect cure), tender our advice to this lady, and to all others that may be seized in the same way. She should choose subjects more becoming a female student, and more fit for a woman to discuss. Is *domestic economy* so perfect, that Miss MARTINEAU'S talents could not find something to improve in it? Norfolk dumplings, for instance; is there

no room for reform in these? If there is, and Miss MARTINEAU be truly patriotic, we think she might do her country more good in a dissertation upon dumplings than by sending forth an epitome of *Malthus on Population*.[150]

The pauper press joined in the denunciation. *The Poor Man's Guardian* in its 16 August 1834 edition delivered the most personal of attacks referring to 'Miss Martineau' as 'the anti-propagation lady a single sight of whom would repel all fears of surplus population as regards himself, her aspects being as repulsive as her doctrines'.[151] In a later edition, the paper included an extract from William Cobbett's *Political Register* which stated: 'Mother Martineau is a poor gossiping creature, vain of talking nonsense, because it appears to her to be something new, and because it gets her something in the way of pelf at the same time.'[152] *The People's Conservative and Reformer* on 7 June 1834 prefaced an extract from another paper with the following:

> We proceed to give some examples from the Devizes Gazette (29th inst.) of what the Malthusians and Martineaus call 'overfed and lazy pauperism.' We copy the extract verbatim, and we do so the more readily, because it appears in a paper of whose libels on the agricultural labourers we have oft made angry mention, and which has lately been made the vehicle of much of that revolting stuff, with which growling Malthusians and mumping old devils of maids have pestered the public under the names of 'moral restraint' – 'preventive checks' and all that damnation sort of thing.[153]

Even William Empson, who in the *Edinburgh Review* gave considerable praise to Martineau, felt she was possessed by an 'intellectual fever' which he trusted would eventually be subdued by her 'own peremptory and self-controlling reason'.[154] 'A young lady', he remarked, 'can scarcely possess the experimental knowledge of mankind without which a confident imagination must occasionally run wild in the paradise of its own conceptions.'[155] Although Empson congratulated Martineau and other 'popular priestesses' such as Jane Marcet and Maria Edgeworth, he restricted their function within the realm of political economy to educating women about the proper roles they should play in local community life. To be sure, Empson conceived a bridge between domestic economy and Political Economy but by no means rejected the notion of separate spheres. He opened his review with the following:

> WOMEN have long reigned supreme over both the learning and practice of domestic economy. They are the proper legislators for, as well as ministers of, the interior. But the province of Political Economy, although it may begin with home, is so vast and complicated, that these two departments cannot have much in common beyond the approximation of a name. There is one point of view, however, in which women may be said to have an honourable

and preeminent interest in this latter subject. If they do not rejoice with those that rejoice more than we do, they far surpass us in the nobler office of mourning with those who mourn. The science, therefore, may properly be recommended to them from its intimate connexion with the protection and comfort of the poor. This recommendation is by no means inconsistent with a horror of the Amazons of politics. The less women usually meddle with any thing which can be called public life out of their village, we are sure the better for all parties.[156]

What is obvious is that Martineau's critics concentrated on her espousal of Malthus's ideas and neglected the areas of important disagreement with her mentor. They ignored her obvious, and often self-acknowledged, debt to other prominent writers: Smith, Bentham, James Mill, Ricardo and Wakefield. This in itself is not surprising. Malthus himself was subject to similar vituperative attacks from a wide variety of circles: Romantics, Tories, working-class radicals, and even his fellow political economists. Few of these critics engaged Malthus head on. In the heat of the moment they seized upon statements in his earlier works and ignored the subtle shifts and often complete *volte-faces* that occurred in subsequent editions and writings. In a similar vein, Martineau's enemies refused to see the non-Malthusian content in her writings and instead focused purely on issues pertaining to population and the Poor Laws.

Gender bias: Martineau and Marcet compared

What does need explanation, however, is the intense gender bias contained in the anti-Malthusian critique of Martineau. The fact that she was a woman entering the male domain of Political Economy will clearly not suffice. Martineau was not the first woman to write on such issues. Nor was she the first to avow Malthusian principles. Other female authors such as Jane Marcet, dealing with similar themes, did not receive the same venomous outpouring of hostility.[157]

Jane Marcet in 1816 published *Conversations on Political Economy, in which the Elements of that Science are Familiarly Explained*. Although this work did not attract the volume of readers that Martineau's *Illustrations* did in the 1830s, it soon became and remained her most famous book, going through seven editions in the next twenty years.[158] *Conversations* was the first attempt to popularize political economy, pre-dating James Mill's *Elements of Political Economy* by four years. Martineau, in fact, explicitly acknowledged this work as the inspiration for her own stories. As Pichanick points out, she read *Conversations* in 1827 and 'influenced by Mrs. Marcet's arguments, derived the idea of teaching the principles of political economy by narrative illustration'.[159]

In 1833, Marcet published *John Hopkins's Notions of Political Economy*.[160] Like Martineau, she drew on a wide range of political economists, mentioning Smith, Malthus, Say and Sismondi by name.[161] Malthusian theories received considerable emphasis in both of these works.

Conversations consists of twenty-one dialogues between Mrs B., the teacher, and her pupil Caroline. Conversation IX 'On Wages and Population' and Conversation X 'On the Condition of the Poor' contain the most explicit treatment of Malthus's ideas regarding the nature and causes of population increase, the disastrous results of overpopulation and the means of limiting the future growth in numbers. *John Hopkins's Notions* presents nine stories dealing with John Hopkins, a poor labourer supporting a huge family on minimal wages. Two of these – 'Population, etc.; or, The Old World' and 'The Poor's Rate; or, The Treacherous Friend' – deal directly with Malthusian themes.[162]

Although Marcet does not cite Malthus's specific ratios concerning population growth and the food supply she is in no doubt as to the superior power of the former. Mrs B. in *Conversations* says to Caroline:

> But it often happens that as soon as the labouring classes find their condition improved, whether by diminution of numbers, or augmentation of capital, which may spring up from some new source of industry, marriages again increase, a greater number of children are reared, and population once more outstrips the means of subsistence; so that the condition of the poor, after a temporary improvement, is again reduced to its former wretchedness.[163]

John Hopkins, in 'Population, etc.; or, The Old World', when asked why Old England is so poor, replies to his young son Tom: 'The fault lies in there being more people here than there is food to maintain, clothes to cover, or houses to lodge them. There's your mother there has had sixteen children; and God knows we have never had wherewithal to bring up half that number.'[164]

The natural tendency of population to outstrip subsistence, moreover, is fuelled by the encouragement of early marriage created by the Poor Laws. Mrs B. explains to a bewildered Caroline:

> The certainty that the parish is bound to succour their wants, renders the poor less apprehensive of indigence than if they were convinced that they must suffer all the wretchedness it entails. When a young man marries without having the means of supporting his family by his labour, and without having saved some little provision against accidents or sickness, he depends upon the parish as a never-failing resource. A profligate man knows that if he spends his wages at the public-house instead of providing for his family, his wife and children can at worst but go to the poor-house.[165]

In 'The Poor's Rate; or, The Treacherous Friend', Marcet elaborates more forcefully on this theme. John Hopkins, who is eventually forced to apply for parish relief, is told by Farmer Stubbs: 'You yourself own you would not have married so early, had you not reckoned on the parish. Others would not either: families would have been smaller; labourers would have been fewer; they would more easily have got employment; ay, and have been better paid too.'[166] Stubbs later explains the disastrous effects of the Poor Laws in Berkshire where married men with children were paid higher than single men. Wages, moreover, were geared to the price of bread and subsidized by the poor rate:

> Why, when the regulation was first made, it did well enough, for a while. But no sooner did the young lads find that a married man got double wages, and more, too, if he had several children, than their heads were all agog after getting wives; for you know it is natural enough they should fancy the girls, when they get the money to boot. My uncle says, that he remembers the time when a decent young man never thought of a wife till he had put by forty or fifty pounds; and some, much more: but now, instead of working hard to save up the money, and getting habits of industry before they marry, they take a wife in order to get the money without working for it, and so begin life with habits of indolence. Why, the magistrates might just as well have gone about driving the young couples into church, as you would sheep into a fold.[167]

The consequences of such 'imprudence of the lower orders' is the classic Malthusian positive check of misery.[168] Mrs B. states: 'Increase of population therefore under such circumstances cannot be permanent; its progress will be checked by distress and disease, and this I apprehend to be one of the causes of the reduced state of the poor in this country.'[169] Caroline concurs, claiming, 'this then must be the cause of the misery which generally prevails amongst the poor.'[170] Even charity bestowed by the church has a similar result. Quoting Townsend in his travels through Spain, Mrs B. says to Caroline:

> Leon, destitute of commerce, is supported by the church. Beggars abound in every street, all fed by the convents and at the bishop's palace. Here they get their breakfast, there they dine. Beside food at St. Marca's, they receive every other day, the men a farthing, the women and children half as much. On this provision they live, they marry, and they perpetuate a miserable race.[171]

In Marcet's later work, John Hopkins refers to the death of one of his children and says to his wife: 'but if it had not been a poor weakly thing, it might have got through the measles as well as the rest of them. Why, to be sure, none of them died of starvation; but who knows but that they might all have lived, had they been reared in plenty?'[172]

Not unexpectedly, moral restraint is viewed as the only viable solution to overpopulation. As Mrs B. informs Caroline: 'It is evident, therefore, that a labourer ought not to marry unless his wages are adequate to the maintenance of a family; or unless he has, like your gardener, some little provision in store to make up the deficiency.'[173] Indeed, Thomas the gardener, like Martineau's Ronald, is seen as a paragon of Malthusian behaviour:

> Were all men as considerate as your gardener Thomas, and did they not marry till they had secured a provision for a family, or could earn a sufficiency to maintain it; in short, were children not brought into the world until there was bread to feed them, the distress which you have just been describing would be unknown, excepting in cases of unforeseen misfortunes, or unless produced by idleness or vice.[174]

In 'Population', John Hopkins, full of regrets about marrying too young and having had such 'a swarm of brats', exclaims to his wife: 'If you and I had not married till the time of life Fairburn and his wife did, we should not have been troubled with such a monstrous family.'[175] He later assumes full responsibility for his imprudent action:

> When God has given us hands to labour with, and heads with common sense to teach us what we ought to do, we have no reason to complain, and it is our own fault if we do not guard against poverty by prudence and saving. We ought not to have married so young, and then we should not have been troubled with so large a family. But what is done can't be undone, only it should serve as a warning against another time.[176]

So convinced is Hopkins of the error of his ways, he plots to prevent the marriage of his son George (twenty-two years of age) with Betsy Bloomfield (nineteen) by ordering his wife to get Betsy 'a service as soon as you can'.[177]

In pure Malthusian fashion Marcet argues that such delay in marriage could not possibly occur without the abolition of the Poor Laws. Echoing Malthus of the 1803 *Essay*, she claims that such abolition should be gradual. Mrs B. hopes that it will be possible 'in the course of time to abolish the poor rates'.[178] Farmer Stubbs is more specific. He suggests the following to John Hopkins's wife:

> ... but suppose a law was made that no child born after three or four years from this time should be entitled to parish relief, why, that would give time for people to think of the consequences; large families would thus be discouraged; and when those who receive relief from the parish died off in the course of nature, why, the poor's rate would die of a natural death too; for if there was none to want it, it would not be raised; so the landholders would get their own again, the labourers higher wages and plenty of work, and the world would jog on merrily.[179]

Like Malthus, Marcet also proposes positive measures to induce the prudence necessary for moral restraint. Education, of course, is given great emphasis. The *Conversations* contain numerous references to the 'instruction of the poor'. Marcet's position is best summed up when Mrs B. lectures to Caroline:

> ... but I would endeavour to give the rising generation such an education as would render them not only moral and religious, but industrious, frugal, and provident. In proportion as the mind is informed, we are able to calculate the consequences of our actions: it is the infant and the savage who live only for the present moment; those whom instruction has taught to think, reflect upon the past and look forward to the future. Education gives rise to prudence, not only by enlarging our understandings, but by softening our feelings, by humanizing the heart, and promoting amiable affections. The rude and inconsiderate peasant marries without either foreseeing or caring for the miseries he may entail on his wife and children; but he who has been taught to value the comforts and decencies of life, will not heedlessly involve himself and all that is dear to him in poverty, and its long train of miseries.[180]

Marcet also advocates Benefit Clubs and Saving Banks. Mrs B. praises such institutions to the extreme:

> But independently of schools and the various institutions for the education of youth, there is an establishment among the lower classes which is peculiarly calculated to inculcate lessons of prudence and economy. I mean the Benefit Clubs, or Friendly Societies; the members of which, by contributing a small stipend monthly, accumulate a fund which furnishes them relief and aid in times of sickness or distress. These associations have spread throughout the country, and their good effects are rendered evident by comparing the condition of such of the labouring classes as belong to them with those of the same district who have no resource in times of distress, but parochial relief or private charity.[181]

She later says of Saving Banks:

> An institution has within a short time been established in Scotland, and is, I understand, now rapidly spreading in England, which is likely to prove still more advantageous to the lower classes than the benefit clubs. 'The object of this institution,' says the *Edinburgh Review*, No. 49., 'is to open to the lower orders a place of deposit for their small savings, with the allowance of reasonable monthly interest, and with full liberty of withdrawing their money, at any time, either in whole or in part – an accommodation which it is impracticable for the ordinary banks to furnish. Such an establishment has been called a *Saving Bank*.[182]

In 'The Poor's Rate', Farmer Stubbs claims that John Hopkins could have avoided the shame of accepting poor relief. He informs Mrs Hopkins that if her 'husband had been a prudent man, and had belonged to the benefit club, he might have got relief when his children were sick, without going to the parish.'[183]

Marcet, however, does diverge from Malthusian views on a number of significant issues. Like Martineau, for example, she supports emigration as a corrective to the surplus population of the poor. In 'Emigration; or, A New World', John Hopkins tells his wife that for those incapable of maintaining themselves at home 'it's better to seek your fortune abroad, than to be half starved, or go to the parish.'[184] He earlier remarks: 'America, they say, is too large by half for the folks that live in it; and ship loads of people go over there, because there's a scarcity of hands, and wages run high. They go such lengths as to say, that the more children you have there, the better you are off.'[185] He later claims that Van Dieman's Land is a 'Paradise for fine weather, beautiful prospects, and abundance of all things – fish, flesh, and fowl, besides fruit and garden-stuff'.[186] Hopkins, moreover, is in favour of state-sponsored emigration. 'They say,' he claims, 'that sometimes the government, or the parish, will lend a helping hand, and pay their passage, or supply them with the needful, to prevent their becoming a burthen upon the parish.'[187]

In addition, Marcet, like Martineau, favours the abolition of the Corn Laws. In 'The Corn Trades; or The Price of Bread', John Hopkins defends his views supporting a free trade in corn against Farmer Stubbs. At the end of this tale Hopkins sums up his position when questioned by Stubbs as to whether he continues to believe that the 'Misery of the poor came from there being too many people'. Hopkins replies:

> And so I do still so long as you will not let us have bread to eat, cheap and plenty; that is, as cheap as we might get it if the corn trade were free. If there's too many people, it's not for want of room to live in, and stir about as much as they will; but there's too many people, because there's not food enough for all. Let us be free to have corn from all parts as cheap as it is to be had, and then, mayhap, there may be enough for all. There never can be too many people when there's wherewithal to maintain them; there cannot be too many happy people: but when they are pinched for food, and suffer in body and mind, they can do no good to themselves or to others either, and the country would be all the better without them.[188]

Finally, Marcet adheres as strongly as Martineau to Smith's identity of interests theory and its optimistic assumptions. In 'The Poor's Rate; or The Treacherous Friend', Hopkins is persuaded by Farmer Stubbs of the necessity to gradually abolish the Poor Laws. His wife, not nearly so convinced, says of Stubbs: 'I can't abide to hear him talk in so hard-hearted a manner.' John replies: 'Ay, but the matter is much more to the point than the manner; and I do agree with him, that if we understood it rightly, the interest of the rich and poor might go hand in hand, like a loving man and wife, who, though they may fall out now and then, jog on together till death parts them.'[189]

In spite of the fact that Marcet diverged from Malthusian theory, in the final analysis she was as much inspired by Malthus as was Martineau. Marcet's emphasis, in particular, on moral restraint – the basis from which so much of the vicious criticism of Martineau emanated – was equally as prominent. Yet Marcet received no such disparagement either in the review journals or the wider press. Even in 1833 when *The Quarterly Review* savagely attacked Martineau, Marcet emerged unscathed. She was not even mentioned and her *John Hopkins's Notions of Political Economy*, published in 1833, was never reviewed in this journal. It was not that Marcet went unnoticed. *The Edinburgh Review* heaped praises on her since *Conversations on Political Economy* had been published in 1816. In 1819, for example, one reviewer remarked: 'We know one female, at least, fully competent to instruct the members of our present Cabinet in Political Economy.' He referred to Marcet's work as an 'admirable little book' which had rendered the principles of Smith, Say, Malthus, and Ricardo 'familiar to every schoolgirl'.[190] In April 1833, *The Edinburgh Review* reviewed both Martineau's *Illustrations of Political Economy* and Marcet's *John Hopkins's Notions of Political Economy* in the same article. Comparing the two authors, the reviewer, William Empson, concluded: 'Mrs. Marcet has less of imagination and of poetry about her. But we feel, while with her, that we are in the hands of a more judicious reasoner, and a surer guide.'[191]

It is not surprising that Marcet received accolades from political economists in general and the Whig *Edinburgh Review* in particular. After all, Martineau herself, although not rated as highly, was nevertheless given relatively high commendation in similar circles.[192] More puzzling is the fact that the Tory and working-class press, which so venomously attacked Martineau as a Malthusian and a woman, left Marcet – as much influenced by Malthus – alone.

Such differential treatment becomes highly relevant in light of Caroline Roberts's recent explanation of the intensely hostile criticism unleashed on Martineau.[193] She contends that Martineau feminized male discourse on Political Economy through the use of the narrative form, thus demystifying the upper-class male language through which such principles were conveyed. Not only did she overturn the hierarchy of masculine/feminine discourse but also may have collapsed this distinction altogether. By popularizing Malthus, claims Roberts, Martineau was, in essence, 'destabilizing' the domestic ideal so central to the separation of public and private spheres.[194] After all, as her critic John Ham pointed out, would not delay of marriage on the part of males leave more single females unemployed and more likely to seek an occupation and income in the public sphere? Would not more single women remain un-protected?[195] Malthus's advocacy of the preventive check of moral restraint and Martineau's support of such behaviour thus 'challenged prevailing ideologies of the middle class'.[196] Roberts further argues that Martineau's readers 'feared an attack on their society's organization'.[197]

There are problems with such explanations. Did Malthusian views actually constitute an assault on the domestic ideal that emphasized patriarchal roles and the necessity of separate spheres? Based on a closer reading of Malthus, Mitchell Dean and Deborah Valenze think not.[198] They take the opposite view. Dean contends that Malthus, in fact, advocated the 'breadwinner' model of family life where the husband – no longer entitled to parish relief – would be totally responsible for the well-being of his wife and children.[199] Valenze is convinced that Malthus, by distinctly separating the roles of 'mother-as-nurturer' and 'father-as-provider', presented 'one of the clearest and earliest expositions of the nineteenth-century notion of separate spheres'.[200] Far from threatening the middle-class ideology of domesticity he, in fact, justified it and wished to impose this on the working class. In promoting moral restraint, Malthus did not seek to challenge family roles but merely sought a solution to the misery of the poor resulting from youthful marriage. He never advocated the employment of women outside the domestic sphere nor did he think this would result from delayed marriage. Certainly, neither he nor Martineau opposed childbearing or, as Croker, wrongly implied, supported voluntary birth control within marriage.

In addition, Roberts pays insufficient attention to Malthus's abolitionist views on the Old Poor Law. It is no coincidence that Martineau's most venomous critics berated her for opposing – in her *Illustrations* – the right to relief for the poor and for proposing 'mischievous doctrines on the principles of social welfare'.[201] Such criticism had more to do with Malthusian attacks on the Old Poor Law than with fear of threats to the domestic ideal, patriarchal authority or the separation of spheres.

More important, Roberts's theory cannot explain the question at hand; namely, why Martineau was singled out for such hostile criticism while Marcet emerged unscathed. After all, Marcet's popularization of political economy also broke the boundaries of male discourse by employing the narrative form in *John Hopkins's Notions of Political Economy* (1833) and the dialogue format in *Conversations on Political Economy* (1816). Her support of delayed marriage through moral restraint was just as pronounced as Martineau's as was her adherence to broader Malthusian theory. If one accepts Roberts's interpretation, Marcet's work should have constituted a challenge, similar to Martineau's, against prevailing ideologies of the middle class and should have provoked equally hostile reactions among critics. Yet clearly this was not the case.

A number of explanations for such differential treatment suggest themselves. The first concerns the level of readership. As J. R. Shackleton points out, Marcet's *Conversations on Political Economy* first published in 1816 was 'her most popular book, selling tens of thousands and going through seven editions'.[202] Valerie Pichanick, however, argues that its appeal was nevertheless limited to young people of the middle and upper classes.[203] Martineau's *Illustrations of Political Economy* most certainly reached a wider mass readership. More important, no doubt, than the number of copies sold or the number of readers – which are at best guesstimates – is the timing of publication. Both Martineau's *Illustration of Political Economy* (1832–34) and her *Poor Laws and Paupers Illustrated* (1833–34) were published in years when the debate on the Old Poor Law prior to its amendment in 1834 had reached an apogee. To be sure, Marcet's *John Hopkins's Notions of Political Economy* went to print in 1833 but never achieved the widespread readership or the acclaim of her earlier work. Martineau's higher profile in the early 1830s rendered her more susceptible to criticism especially given the intense hostility, in many quarters, to Malthusian theory.

Another factor was even more critical. Martineau, unlike Marcet, strongly favoured the New Poor Law and became directly involved in the campaign to support its passage. Late in 1832, Lord Brougham convinced her to write the pauper tales claiming that 'his hope of reforming the existing Poor Laws would be doubled if she would undertake this task.'[204] William Johnson Fox, editor of *The Monthly Repository*, had cautioned Martineau in a review article that her association with Brougham would be viewed as a political alliance with Whiggism and would make her 'a less efficient, because less trusted, national instructor'.[205] The tales, of course, were published in 1833 and 1834 under commission by the Society for the Diffusion of Useful Knowledge. One-quarter of Martineau's fees were to be paid by Brougham himself – that is, £25 pounds of the £100 paid for each tale.[206]

Fox's warning turned out to be prophetic, even though Martineau denied any association with the Whigs, declined affiliation with any political party and fell out with Brougham when he refused to pay his share for the stories. Her tales, used in the campaign for the amendment of the Old Poor Law provoked the Tory and working class press to tarnish her with the same brush as Malthus and Brougham who had become the twin villains of the new political economy. *The Quarterly Review* reviewing the *Report from His Majesty's Commissioners for Inquiring into the Administration and Practical Operation of the Poor Laws* claimed that the Commissioners shared 'the opinion of Miss

Martineau, and her disciple, Lord Brougham, that the principle of the poor-law is faulty, and that such an institution has been, and can only be, productive of unmixed evil'.[207] The earlier savage attack by Croker in the same journal, of course, made specific reference to Martineau picking up information 'in her conferences with the Lord Chancellor'.[208] *The Times,* in addition, only turned against Martineau when it came out in opposition to the New Poor Law. *Cobbett's Magazine* claimed that Miss Martineau had been gallanted 'to the elbow of ministers of state' and concluded its review of her *Illustrations of Political Economy* by harshly condemning her association with the SDUK and making a veiled reference to Brougham:

> If any 'radical change' be necessary, all we mean by our present observations is, to protest against its being attempted by measures tending to do further injury to whose wants are the greatest. It is said that Miss MARTINEAU has been patronised by the 'Society for the Diffusion of Useful Knowledge.' And if such be the fact, we give this authoress joy on the event. The endeavours to degrade the poor and to deny them their rights, which have appeared in publications under her name, are worthy of a Society who have Humbug for their Minerva, we are quite ashamed to say who for their *magnus Apollo.*[209]

Marcet, of course, steered clear of any support for the New Poor Law and did not involve herself in the campaign for its enactment. *John Hopkins's Notions of Political Economy* did not waver in its Malthusian view of the Old Poor Law, that is, gradual abolition. No mention is made of a new workhouse system, nor is less eligibility under a centralized administration advocated. By not entering the heated debate on the New Poor Law she rendered herself immune from the harsh criticism directed at Martineau on this issue.

Yet the more difficult question still remains as to why Martineau, unlike Marcet, was subject to such virulent abuse on the basis of gender. To be sure, such attacks may have been part and parcel of hostility towards women who were perceived as moving from the domestic sphere into the realm of politics. But perhaps one can delve deeper. A number of historians, for example, have emphasized Martineau's radicalism. Although her promulgation of women's rights and enfranchisement did not fully emerge until the late 1830s – she was to become a leading feminist in the latter half of the nineteenth century – R. K. Webb stresses the degree to which many of the tales in her *Illustrations of Political Economy* attacked 'entrenched interests and inherited prejudices'.[210] 'Demarara', for example indicted slavery while 'Cinnamon and Pearls' and 'A Tale of the Tyne' launched an assault against colonial monopoly and privileged trading corporations respectively. He argues that

Martineau's purpose went far beyond instructing workers on the new political economy and draws a direct comparison with Marcet:

> If the series were directed solely to the task of convincing the lower classes of the inevitability of the bourgeois industrial order and social morality, if its effect were intended to be entirely conservative, preponderant attention would hardly have been given to the present abuses of the system, and something more on the hygienic order of Mrs. Marcet's fairy tales would have resulted. In the coupled purpose of the series, the radical outweighs the conservative; the clearing away is the greater task; and in the very association of the two appeals is reflected her confidence in the amenability to reason, in the educability, of the audience she was addressing. She could afford to be bold, she told Place, because she had nothing to lose which could stand in comparison with her regard for the people – and she meant it.[211]

Marcet, herself, was initially highly supportive of Martineau's earlier tales in the *Illustrations of Political Economy*, at one point saying proudly to Harriet that Louis Phillipe of France had ordered copies of each story for all members of his family as had the Czar of Russia. She was deeply shocked, however, when Martineau's twelfth tale – 'French Wines and Politics' – appeared, saying to her: 'I thought I had told you that the King of the French read all your stories, and made his family read them: and now you have been writing about Egalité; and they will never read you again.'[212] Martineau comments in her *Autobiography*:

> My good friend could not see how I could hope to be presented at the Tuilleries after this: and I could only say that it had never entered my head to wish it. I tried to turn the conversation to account by impressing on my anxious friend the hopelessness of all attempts to induce me to alter my stories from such considerations as she urged. I wrote with a view to the people, and especially the suffering of them; and the crowned heads must, for once, take their chance for their feelings.[213]

She then recounts how the Russian Czar and the Emperor of Austria ordered every copy of her tales to be burnt or deported and how she was banned from entering both countries.[214]

Marcet's concern about access to European courts certainly reflects a desire for respectability in high social circles (which was absent in Martineau) and possibly shielded her from malicious criticism especially in the Tory press. Harriet certainly had no great love for the blue-stocking set. As she points out in her *Autobiography*:

> Some people may be disposed to turn round upon me with the charge of giving blue-stocking parties. I believe that to blue-stocking people my soirées might have that appearance, because they looked through blue spectacles: but I can confidently say that, not only were my parties as diverse in quality as I could make them, – always including many who were not literary; but I took particular care that no one

was in any way shown off, but all treated with equal respect as guests. My rooms were too small for personages who required space for display: and such were not therefore invited .... Nor had I a place for rouged and made up old ladies who paraded literary flirtations in the style of half a century ago.[215]

If Martineau's radical liberal values possibly played an indirect role in encouraging attacks on her gender could her age and marital status also be important? Much of the anti-Malthusian invective levelled at her from all quarters dwelt on the fact that she was young and unmarried. Indeed, Martineau was thirty-one years of age when she published her *Illustrations on Political Economy* and never married during her lifetime. Marcet, on the other hand, was forty-seven when *Conversations on Political Economy* went to press in 1816 and sixty-four years old when she wrote *John Hopkins's Notions of Political Economy* in 1833. In addition, she was married in 1799 at the age of thirty to Dr John Marcet, a highly respected medical doctor who published papers and delivered lectures on medicine and chemistry. If the sensitive subject of moral restraint was to be broached by a woman in the early nineteenth century better she have the experience that comes with age and marriage.[216]

Beyond the comparative issue concerning the reception of Marcet and Martineau lays the question raised at the beginning of this chapter; namely, Patricia James's contention that Martineau helped foster the detestation of Malthus. Although we can never be sure just how many middle-class readers thought, like William Empson of *The Edinburgh Review*, that her tales took moral restraint to absurd lengths, she probably gained numerous converts to Malthusian views among these groups. What is more significant, however, is the reaction of the Tory and especially working-class press. If Malthus was coming under increasing criticism during the debate concerning the introduction of the New Poor Law, Martineau's bold entrance into the fray heightened the venom against his ideas. The influential *Times* turned against Martineau and increased its attacks on Malthus. In addition, the most widely read and most powerful working-class paper of the 1830s, *The Poor Man's Guardian*, turned vast numbers of the lower orders against both Martineau and Malthus. Other working-class papers joined in the chorus of abuse. Malthus, ironically, in the last years of his life never joined the debate and, in any case, did not publicly support the New Poor Law. In ill health, he watched from the sidelines as a torrent of criticism, often grossly misplaced, was heaped upon him. Martineau, although upset by her critics, at least could savour the victory. In the summer of 1834, the New Poor Law sailed through the House of Commons virtually unopposed. The vituperation of both conservatives and radicals could not stem the tide of the new political economy.

Endnotes

1. Harriet Martineau, *Harriet Martineau's Autobiography*, 3 vols. (London: Smith, Elder and Co., 1877), 1: 327–8 (hereafter cited as *Autobiography*). See also Patricia James, *Population Malthus: His Life and Times* (London: Routledge and Kegan Paul, 1979), 3 (hereafter cited as *Malthus*).
2. *Autobiography*, 1: 71 and James, *Malthus*, 346.
3. Harriet Martineau, *Illustrations of Political Economy*, 9 vols (London: Charles Fox, 1834). Hereafter cited as *Illustrations*.
4. See Valerie Kossew Pichanick, *Harriet Martineau: The Woman and Her Work* (Ann Arbor: University of Michigan Press, 1980), 52 (hereafter cited as *Harriet Martineau*) and R. K. Webb, *Harriet Martineau: A Radical Victorian* (London: Heinemann, 1960), 113 (hereafter cited as *Radical Victorian*). Compare these sales with John Stuart Mill's *Principles of Political Economy* (1848) which sold only 3,000 copies in four years. See Pichanick, *Harriet Martineau*, 50.
5. Vera Wheately, *The Life and Work of Harriet Martineau* (London: Secker and Warburg, 1957), 96 (hereafter cited as *Life and Work of Martineau)*.
6. Gillian Thomas, 'Harriet Martineau' in *Victorian Prose Writers Before 1867*, vol. 55, *Dictionary of Literary Biography*, ed. William B. Thesing (Detroit, MI, Washington, DC, London: Bruccoli, Clark, Layman, 1987), 172. Vera Wheately claims that Martineau's reputation increased by 'leaps and bounds' to the point that 'she could not walk in public places without being stared at and pointed out as the authoress of *Illustrations of Political Economy*'. Wheately, *Life and Work of Martineau*, 96.
7. Harriet Martineau, *Poor Laws and Paupers Illustrated*, 4 vols. (London: Charles Fox, 1833–34). Hereafter cited as *Poor Laws*.
8. Jane Marcet, *Conversations on Political Economy; In Which the Elements of that Science are Familiarly Explained* (Philadelphia, PA: Moses Thomas, 1817), vi (hereafter cited as *Conversations*). James Mill is quoted in Pichanick, *Harriet Martineau*, 51.
9. Martineau, *Illustrations*, 1: xvi and xiv. Martineau believed her series was 'craved by the popular mind'. Cited in Caroline Roberts, *The Woman and the Hour: Harriet Martineau and Victorian Ideologies* (Toronto: University of Toronto Press, 2002), 10. Hereafter cited as *Woman and the Hour*.
10. Webb, *Radical Victorian*, 123.
11. Ibid., 124.
12. Gillian Thomas, *Harriet Martineau* (Boston: Twayne Publishers, 1985), 89.
13. Gertrude Himmelfarb, *The Idea of Poverty: England in the Early Industrial Age* (London and Boston, MA: Faber and Faber, 1984), 169 (hereafter cited as *The Idea of Poverty*).
14. Martineau, *Illustrations*, 'The Moral of Many Fables', 9: v.
15. Ibid., vi.
16. *Autobiography*, 1: 210.
17. Harriet Martineau, *A History of England During the Thirty Years' Peace A.D. 1816 – 1846*, 4 vols (London: George Bell and Sons, 1877), 4: 78 (hereafter cited as *History of the Peace*).
18. Quoted in James, *Malthus*, 451. See also Donald Winch, *Riches and Poverty: An Intellectual History of Political Economy in Britain,*

1750–1834 (Cambridge: Cambridge University Press, 1996), 419–20 where he claims that Marcet and Martineau created a public image of Malthus based on a misunderstanding of his work.

19. James, Malthus, 451.
20. See for example, Dorothy Lampen Thomson, *Adam Smith's Daughters* (New York: Exposition Press, 1973), chapter 2, 29–42. Angus McClaren briefly mentions the anti-Malthusian attacks on Martineau. See Angus McClaren, *Birth Control in Nineteenth-Century England* (New York: Holmes and Meirers Publishers, 1978), 62. Shelagh Hunter, *Harriet Martineau: The Poetics of Moralism* (Aldershot: Scolar Press, 1995), 44–48 and Deborah Anna Logan, *The Hour and the Woman: Harriet Martineau's 'Somewhat Remarkable' Life* (DeKalb, IL: Northern Illinois University Press, 2002), 137–40 also provide brief discussion. Hunter's work is hereafter cited as *Harriet Martineau*. For a recent, important analysis of the significance of Martineau's critical reception see Roberts, *Woman and the Hour*, Chapter 1, 10–25.
21. Martineau, *Illustrations*, 'Weal and Woe in Garveloch', 2: 42.
22. Ibid., 49
23. Ibid., 'The Moral of Many Fables', 9: 35.
24. Ibid., 'For Each and For All', 4: 60.
25. Ibid., 'Weal and Woe in Garveloch', 2: 48.
26. Ibid., 'The Moral of Many Fables', 9: 38.
27. Ibid., 'Cousin Marshall,' 3: 52.
28. Ibid., 96.
29. Ibid., 'Homes Abroad', 4: 3.
30. Martineau, *Poor Laws*, 'The Parish', 1: 6. For other references to early marriage in Martineau's fictional works see ibid., 33 and Martineau, *Illustrations*, 'Weal and Woe in Garveloch', 2: 43–4 and 96, 'Cousin Marshall', 3: 53, 'Ireland', 3: 106.
31. Martineau, *History of the Peace*, 2: 500.
32. Martineau, *Illustrations*, 'The Moral of Many Fables', 9: 37–8.
33. Ibid., 'Cousin Marshall', 3: 38.
34. Ibid., 'Weal and Woe in Garveloch', 2: 119.
35. Ibid., 120. By vice, Mr Mackenzie and Angus are referring to property crime and fraud in addition to malicious speech, envy and violence among the poor. They do not, like Malthus, refer to voluntary limitation of births. Ibid., 118.
36. Ibid., 'The Moral of Many Fables', 9: 33.
37. Ibid., 'Weal and Woe in Garveloch', 2: 49–50.
38. Ibid., 'The Moral of Many Fables', 9: 33.
39. Ibid.
40. T. R. Malthus, *An Essay on the Principle of Population; or a View of its past and present Effects on Human Happiness; with an inquiry into our Prospects, respecting the future Removal or Mitigation of the Evils which it occasions: The version published in 1803, with the variora of 1806, 1807, 1817, and 1826*, 2 vols, ed. Patricia James (Cambridge: Cambridge University Press, 1989), I: 374. His comments are contained in the 1803 edition (hereafter cited as *Malthus Variora* with vol. I or II specified).
41. Martineau, *Illustrations*, 'Cousin Marshall', 3: 111.
42. Ibid., 49.
43. Ibid., 'Ireland', 3: 56.

44. Martineau, *Poor Laws,* 'The Parish', 1: 30 and 199.
45. Ibid., 122.
46. Ibid., 94.
47. James, *Malthus Variora*, II: 175–8.
48. Martineau, *Illustrations*, 'For Each and For All', 4: 82.
49. Ibid., 59.
50. Ibid., 42.
51. Ibid., 'The Moral of Many Fables', 9: 41.
52. Ibid., 'Cousin Marshall', 3: 114–15.
53. Martineau, *Poor Laws*, 'The Parish', 1: 9.
54. Martineau, *Illustrations*, 'Ireland', 3: 106–107.
55. Ibid., 'Homes Abroad', 4: 35.
56. Ibid., 'Cousin Marshall', 3: 131.
57. Ibid., 'Weal and Woe in Garveloch', 2: 97.
58. Ibid., 94.
59. Ibid., 95.
60. R. K. Webb comments: 'Moderation is hardly an outstanding character-istic of the tales. At many points she goes beyond her mentors.' See R. K. Webb, *Radical Victorian*, 118. J. R. Shackleton claims that Malthus was 'very pleased' with 'Weal and Woe in Garveloch' but provides no specific evidence for this claim. See J. R. Shackleton, 'Two Early Female Economists: Jane Marcet and Harriet Martineau,' 'Research Working Paper, The Polytechnic of Central London', no. 35 (October 1988): 19. Hereafter cited as 'Two Early Female Economists'. In a letter to Jane Marcet written on 22 January 1833 Malthus, however, referred to 'Miss Martineau's Tales which are justly so much admired.' He nevertheless thought Marcet's stories contained in her 1833 publication entitled *John Hopkins's Notions on Political Economy* were 'in many respects better suited to the labouring classes'. See Bette A. Polkinghorn, 'An Unpublished Letter from Malthus to Jane Marcet, January 22, 1833', *American Economic Review* 76 (September 1986): 845 (hereafter cited as 'Unpublished Letter from Malthus').
61. Martineau, *Illustrations*, 'Cousin Marshall', 3: 119.
62. Ibid., 45–6.
63. Ibid., 'Ireland', 3: 53 and 57.
64. Ibid., 'Cousin Marshall', 3: 39.
65. Ibid., 44.
66. Ibid., 45 and 44.
67. Ibid., 42.
68. Ibid., 130.
69. Ibid., 'The Moral of Many Fables', 9: 39. The metaphor of nature's mighty feast was used by Malthus in the 1803 edition of the *Essay*. See James, *Malthus Varoria*, II: 127–8.
70. *Autobiography*, 1: 210.
71. Martineau, *History of the Peace*, 4: 79.
72. Martineau, *Illustrations*, 'The Three Ages', 8: 114–15. She ranks priorities for government spending in the following order: Education, Public Works, Government and Legislation, Law and Justice, Diplomacy, Defence and Dignity of the Sovereign. Ibid., 115.
73. Ibid., 'Ireland', 3: 116–17.
74. Ibid., 'Cousin Marshall', 3: 40–41. At times Martineau proposes a small

user fee. In 'The Hamlets', a school in Hurst charged two pence a week. Martineau claims the poor thought 'more highly of education the more completely it was disconnected with public and private charity'. See Martineau, *Poor Laws*, 'The Hamlets', 2: 161. Burke in 'Cousin Marshall' suggests a means test claiming he 'would have all those pay something for the education of their children who can; but let all be educated whether they pay or not.' Martineau, *Illustrations*, 'Cousin Marshall', 3: 41.

75. Ibid., 'The Moral of Many Fables', 9: 70.
76. Ibid., 'Cousin Marshall', 3: 116.
77. Ibid., 73–4.
78. Martineau, *The Poor Laws*, 'The Parish', 1: 192.
79. Ibid., 'The Hamlets', 2: 159.
80. See Webb, *Radical Victorian*, 116; Pichanick, *Harriet Martineau*, 55 and 65, and Valerie Sanders, *Reason Over Passion: Harriet Martineau and the Victorian Novel* (Brighton: Harvester Press, 1986), 1.
81. See James P. Huzel, 'Thomas Robert Malthus (1766–1834)', in *British Reform Writers, 1789–1832*, vol. 158, *Dictionary of Literary Biography*, eds Gary Kelly and Edd Applegate (Detroit, MI, Washington, DC, and London: Bruccoli, Clark, Layman, 1996), 208 and James, *Malthus*, 450. See also Chapter 1 above.
82. See Himmelfarb, *The Idea of Poverty*, 170. Martineau also supports the New Poor Law, especially the principle of less eligibility, in the last story of her *Illustrations*. See Martineau, *Illustrations*, 'The Moral of Many Fables', 9: 66.
83. Martineau, *Poor Laws*, 'The Parish', 1: 210–13.
84. Ibid., 'The Hamlets', 2: 95.
85. Ibid., 63.
86. Ibid., 'The Town', 3: 90 and 94.
87. Martineau, *History of the Peace*, 2: 504.
88. Martineau, *Poor Laws*, 'The Town', 3: 113.
89. Ibid., 90.
90. See James, *Malthus Variora*, II: 87 and 237. Samuel Hollander argues that Malthus, in the final analysis, favoured emigration. Malthus remained highly ambiguous on this issue. He advocated government-sponsored emigration only as a temporary measure and certainly never supported forced emigration. See my discussion in Chapter 1.
91. See Pichanick, *Harriet Martineau*, 65–6 for the influence of Wakefield.
92. Martineau, *Illustrations*, 'Homes Abroad', 4: 14.
93. Ibid., 13.
94. Ibid., 124.
95. Ibid.
96. Ibid., 76.
97. Ibid., 'Ireland', 3: 59.
98. Ibid., 136.
99. As Pichanick points out, however, in 'Sowers and Reapers' she departs from strict Ricardian analysis 'by including the landlords among the casualties of corn protection'. See Pichanick, *Harriet Martineau*, 56. Ricardo, of course, argued that the Corn Laws benefited the landed interest. Martineau reasoned that the cultivation of inferior soils would beggar tenant farmers and that the landlords would lose rents. For evidence that Malthus, at least privately, qualified his support of the Corn

Laws in the last years of his life, see Samuel Hollander's arguments in Chapter 1.

100. Martineau, *Illustrations*, 'The Moral of Many Fables', 9: 118 and 117.
101. Ibid., 42.
102. Ibid., 'For Each and For All', 4: 40.
103. Ibid., 44.
104. See Thomas, *Harriet Martineau*, 88 for reference to *Forest and Game Law Tales* (1845) and *Dawn Island* (1845).
105. See Huzel, 'Thomas Robert Malthus (1766–1834)', 206 and Donald Winch, *Malthus* (Oxford: Oxford University Press, 1987), 65, where he argues that Malthus by 1820 had envisioned the embourgeoisement of the working classes.
106. Martineau, 'The Moral of Many Fables', 9: 140 and 143.
107. Ibid., 144.
108. Ibid., 131.
109. Ibid., 132 and 83.
110. Pichanick, *Harriet Martineau*, 56–7.
111. Martineau, *Illustrations*, 'The Hill and The Valley: A Tale', 1: 140. Also cited in Pichanick, *Harriet Martineau*, 56.
112. Martineau, *Illustrations*, 'For Each and For All', 4: 37.
113. Ibid., 'The Moral of Many Fables', 9: 52–3.
114. Cited in Webb, *Radical Victorian*, 120 and 122.
115. Ibid., 120.
116. Mill claimed that the *Illustrations* 'as an exposition of the leading principles of what now constitutes the science ... possesses considerable merit'. Although he disagreed with Martineau's 'unqualified condemnation of the principle of the poor-laws,' he wished her 'numerous readers and a favourable reception.' See *Monthly Repository* 7 (January 1833): 321–2. See also Pichanick, *Harriet Martineau*, 70. Martineau also received a favourable review in *Tait's Edinburgh Magazine* written by a woman, Christian Isobel Johnstone, novelist, editor and co-owner of Tait's. See Hunter, *Harriet Martineau*, 46–7 and 225, n. 108.
117. *New Monthly Review* 37 (January–February 1833): 151.
118. *Edinburgh Review* LVII (April 1833): 3 and 2 [William Empson: Wellesley Index]. For additional positive reactions by Empson and others see Roberts, *Woman and the Hour*, 17–18.
119. Cited in Webb, *Radical Victorian*, 123, from *The Poor Man's Guardian* (5 May 1832). Hereafter cited as *PMG*.
120. Cited in Webb, *Radical Victorian*, 123 from *PMG*. (22 February 1834). Webb argues that Martineau's emphasis on the equality of human rights initially impressed the *PMG*. Webb, *Radical Victorian*, 123.
121. *PMG* (16 August 1834).
122. Ibid. (10 January 1835).
123. *Working Man's Friend and Political Magazine*, no. 4 (12 January 1832).
124. *People's Conservative and Trades Union Gazette* (17 May 1834).
125. *True Sun* (22 July 1834).
126. *Fraser's Magazine* 6 (August–December 1832): 405. See also *Fraser's Magazine* 7 (April 1833): 499 where the following statements are made: 'We would beg our correspondent not to indulge in language which looks too much like the *Malthus* and *Martineau* slang; such as, "the people of England are now saddled with an encumbrance of eight million and a half

per annum, without any equivalent decrease of pauper wretchedness."
Such language as this, rather gives countenance to the false and wicked
delusion spread by the economists, that the poor-laws are an actual *curse*,
instead of being, as they really are, a *blessing* – the very stay of the country,
and the only cement which could possibly, in the present condition of the
labouring classes, preserve us from a dissolution of all the bonds of
civilised society.'

127. Ibid., 405.
128. *New Monthly Magazine* 37 (January–February 1833): 147.
129. Ibid., 149.
130. *Edinburgh Review* LVII (April 1833): 39.
131. Ibid., 27.
132. See n. 68 above.
133. *Edinburgh Review* LVII (April 1833): 31.
134. See Martineau, *History of the Peace*, 2: 508–509. For a discussion of the
origins of *The Times*'s opposition to the New Poor Law see Himmelfarb,
The Idea of Poverty, 178–80. John Walters, the proprietor, was a Justice
of the Peace in Berkshire who had been attacked by Edwin Chadwick in
the preliminary report to the New Poor Law. Walter favoured the right of
the poor to relief. Thomas Barnes, the editor, disliked Lord Chancellor
Brougham and three members of the Royal Commission on the Poor Laws
– Nassau Senior, Walter Coulson and Blomfield, Bishop of London.
135. *Times* (13 May 1834).
136. Ibid. (10 October 1834).
137. Webb, *Radical Victorian*, 114. Letter written 12 May 1832.
138. Martineau, *Autobiography*, 1: 200.
139. A comment made by an unnamed friend to Martineau after the printer had
informed him of the nature of the review. See Ibid., 205.
140. See Pichanick, *Harriet Martineau*, 65, and Martineau, *Autobiography*, 1:
205.
141. The reference to the Lord Chancellor deprecates Martineau's relationship
with Lord Brougham. See *Quarterly Review* XLIX(April 1833): 151
[George Poulett Scrope and John Wilson Croker: Wellesley Index].
142. Ibid., 136.
143. Ibid., 141. For a defence of Martineau against *The Quarterly Review* see
The Monthly Repository 7 (January 1833): 314–23.
144. Martineau, *Autobiography*, 1: 206.
145. Ibid., 211.
146. *Fraser's Magazine* 6 (August-December 1832): 403. It is puzzling that
Martineau did not react to this review since it appeared before the hostile
comments in the *Quarterly Review* of April 1833.
147. Ibid., 413. See also *Fraser's Magazine* 8 (November 1833): 576 where it
was stated that Martineau was 'certain of applause from those whose
praise is ruin, and of the regret of all who feel respect for the female sex,
and sorrow for perverted talent, or, at least industry; doomed to wither in
the cold approbation of the political economist'. A portrait of Martineau
was reproduced and the claim made that she even looked pro-Malthusian:
'Here is Miss Harriet in the full enjoyment of economical philosophy; her
tea-things, her ink-bottle, her skillet, her scuttle, her chair, are all of the
Utilitarian model; and the cat, on whom she bestows her kindest caresses,
is a cat who has been trained to the utmost propriety of manners by that

process of instructions which we should think the most efficient on all such occasions', ibid., 577. A later issue of the magazine presented in eight stanzas 'An Ode to Miss Harriet Martineau' referring to her as Harry Martineau. One stanza read: 'Her political economy / Is as true as Deuteronomy; / And the monster of Distress she sticks a dart in O! / Yet still he stalks about, / And makes a mighty rout, / But that we hope's my eye and Harry Martineau!' Immediately following the ode it was hoped that Martineau 'will yet see the error of her ways, and comport herself as a female-woman ought to do'. See *Fraser's Magazine* 9 (May 1834): 623.

148. *Cobbett's Magazine* 1 (April 1833): 214–15. This publication was produced by John and James Cobbett not William Cobbett.

149. Ibid., 215.

150. Ibid.

151. *PMG* (16 August 1834).

152. Ibid. (10 January 1835). 'Pelf' refers to money gained in an unprincipled manner.

153. *People's Conservative and Reformer* (7 June 1834).

154. *Edinburgh Review* LVII (April 1833): 11.

155. Ibid., 10.

156. Ibid., 1.

157. Maria Edgeworth, the novelist and educationalist (1767–1849), was considered by William Empson as one of the three 'popular priestesses' of Political Economy along with Martineau and Marcet. She did not deal, however, with Malthusian issues. For comparative purposes, only Marcet will be considered. See *Edinburgh Review* LVII (April 1833): 2.

158. See Marcet, *Conversations*.

159. Pichanick, *Harriet Martineau*, 50.

160. Jane Marcet, *John Hopkins's Notions of Political Economy* (London: Longman, Rees, Orme et al., 1833). Hereafter cited as *John Hopkins*. Marcet also published *Rich and Poor* in 1851 that contains thirteen lessons by Mr B presented to his students in a village school. Interestingly, Marcet makes no reference to Malthus or the Poor Law in this later work. See Jane Marcet, *Rich and Poor* (London: Longman, Brown, Green, and Longmans, 1851). Malthus was highly impressed by *John Hopkins*. In a letter to Marcet written on 22 January 1833 he said: 'I have read John Hopkins's Notions on Political Economy with great interest and satisfaction, and am decidedly of opinion that they are calculated to be very useful. They are in many respects better suited to the labouring classes than Miss Martineau's Tales that are justly so much admired. I am strongly therefore inclined to advise you to publish them in as cheap a form as you can, for general circulation, and to give away. We shall be happy to purchase a dozen of them to distribute to the Cottagers in our neighborhood. I think your doctrines very sound, and what is a more essential point, you have explained them with great plainness and clearness.' See Polkinghorn, 'Unpublished Letter from Malthus': 845.

161. Marcet, *Conversations*, vii.

162. See also 'Emigration; or, A New World' and 'The Corn Trade; or, The Price of Bread' that deal with emigration and the Corn Laws (hereafter cited as 'Emigration and Corn Trade'). For a content analysis of *John Hopkins* see Bette Polkinghorn, 'Political Economy Disguised as Fanciful Fables', *Eastern Economic Journal* 8 (April 1982): 145–56 (hereafter cited

as 'Political Economy Disguised'). Polkinghorn, although recognizing that Marcet drew heavily on the works of Malthus, offers no specific analysis of Malthusian themes.

163. Marcet, *Conversations*, 123.
164. Marcet, *John Hopkins*, 'Population, etc; or, The Old World', 66 (hereafter cited as 'Population').
165. Marcet, *Conversations*, 137.
166. Marcet, *John Hopkins*, 'The Poor's Rate; or, The Treacherous Friend', 107 (hereafter cited as 'Poor's Rate').
167. Ibid., 112. Marcet is no doubt referring to the Speenhamland system introduced in Berkshire in 1795.
168. Ibid., 115.
169. Marcet, *Conversations*, 122 and 118.
170. Ibid., 124.
171. Ibid., 141.
172. Marcet, *John Hopkins*, 'Population', 77. Marcet also refers to the Malthusian check of vice quoting Townsend: 'But the misfortune is, that undistinguished benevolence offers a premium to indolence, prodigality, and vice.' See Marcet, *Conversations*, 141.
173. Ibid., 104.
174. Ibid., 125.
175. Marcet, *John Hopkins*, 'Population', 68–9.
176. Ibid., 75.
177. Ibid., 78.
178. Marcet, *Conversations*, 137.
179. Marcet, *John Hopkins*, 'Poor's Rate', 118–19.
180. Marcet, *Conversations*, 134 and 133.
181. Ibid., 134.
182. Ibid., 136.
183. Marcet, *John Hopkins*, 'Poor's Rate', 101.
184. Ibid., 'Emigration', 89.
185. Ibid., 82.
186. Ibid., 97.
187. Ibid., 89. Marcet is far more positive about emigration in 1833 than in 1816. In *Conversations* she raises Malthusian qualifications concerning such a solution: 'Were emigration therefore allowed, instead of being checked, scarcely any would abandon their country but those who could not find a maintenance in it. But should emigration ever become so great as to leave the means of subsistence easy and plentiful to those who remain, it would naturally cease, and the facility of rearing children, and maintaining families, would soon fill up the vacancy in population.' See Marcet, *Conversations*, 132.
188. Marcet, *John Hopkins*, 'Corn Trade', 118. Malthus in his letter to Marcet 22 January 1833 raised only one criticism of *John Hopkins*: 'If I were obliged to find any fault, I should say that you have presented in rather too brilliant and unshaded colours the advantages which would accrue from the abolition of the Corn Laws, so as to excite expectations which cannot be realized.' See Polkinghorn, 'Unpublished Letter from Malthus': 845.
189. Ibid., 'Poor's Rate', 121.
190. *Edinburgh Review* XXXII (October 1819): 477 and 468. The reviewer was most likely Robert Torrens. See Shackleton, 'Two Early Female

Economists', 11–12. Jean Baptiste Say claimed Marcet was 'the only woman who has written on political economy and shown herself superior even to men'. See Thomson, *Adam Smith's Daughters*, 25.

191.   *Edinburgh Review* LVII (April 1833): 39.

192.   See above under *Hostile reception*, 23.

193.   Roberts, *Woman and the Hour*, Ch. 1, 10–25.

194.   Ibid., 22–3.

195.   Ibid., 23. John Ham made this claim in 'The Prudential Check – Marriage or Celibacy', *Tait's Edinburgh Magazine* 3 (June 1833): 318. This is the only source Roberts cites regarding this specific argument. More evidence would be needed to support her assertion that such fears were widespread among the middle class.

196.   Ibid., 23.

197.   Ibid.

198.   See Mitchell Dean, *The Constitution of Poverty: Toward a Genealogy of Liberal Governance* (London: Routledge, 1991) and Deborah Valenze, *The First Industrial Woman* (Oxford: Oxford University Press, 1995). Hereafter referred to as *Constitution of Poverty* and *First Industrial Woman* respectively. Roberts does not cite these authors.

199.   Dean, *Constitution of Poverty*, 104.

200.   Valenze, *First Industrial Woman*, 137. All phrases quoted are Valenze's.

201.   See n. 142 above.

202.   Shackleton, 'Two Early Female Economists': 11.

203.   Pichanick, *Harriet Martineau*, 51.

204.   Wheately, *Life and Work of Martineau*, 95.

205.   Quoted in Pichanick, *Harriet Martineau*, 69.

206.   Wheately, *Life and Work of Martineau*, 95.

207.   *Quarterly Review* LII (August–November 1834): 235.

208.   See n. 141 above.

209.   *Cobbett's Magazine* 1 (April 1833): 219.

210.   Webb, *Radical Victorian*, 118.

211.   Ibid., *The Quarterly Review* lambasted Martineau for her social contract theory in opposing slavery. See *Quarterly Review* XLIX (April 1833): 139–40.

212.   Martineau, *Autobiography*, 1: 236.

213.   Ibid.

214.   Ibid., 237.

215.   Ibid., 373–4. See also her disparaging remarks about 'the express "blue assemblies" of such pedants as Lady Mary Shepherd'. Ibid., 370–72.

216.   If *Fraser's Magazine* is any indication, however, age was not relevant. Of Martineau's Malthusian ideas, the magazine commented that 'it was indeed a wonder that such themes should occupy the pen of any lady, old or young, without a disgust nearly approaching to horror.' See *Fraser's Magazine* 8 (November 1833): 576.

Figure 3. Unknown artist, *James (Bronterre) O'Brien*, stipple engraving, date unknown, National Portrait Gallery, London, NPG D5374

Figure 4.   Auguste Hervieu, *Robert Owen*, 7.6 cm × 5.1 cm (3 in × 2 in), watercolour, 1829, National Portrait Gallery, London, NPG 2507

Figure 5.   Samuel Drummond, *Francis Place*, 91.4 cm × 71.4 cm (50 in ×
28¹⁄₈ in), oil on canvas, 1833, National Portrait Gallery, London, NPG 1959

Figure 6.   Unknown artist, *Richard Carlile* 'on his liberation after six years imprisonment in Dorchester Gaol', lithograph 29.2 cm × 18.4 cm (11½ in × 7¼ in), 1825, National Portrait Gallery, London, NPG D8083

CHAPTER THREE

Cobbett against the Parson

I have, during my life, detested many men; but never any one so much as you. Your book on Population contains matter more offensive to my feelings even than that of the Dungeon-Bill. It could have sprung from no mind not capable of dictating acts of greater cruelty than any recorded in the history of the massacre of St. Bartholomew. Priests have, in all ages, been remarkable for cool and deliberate and unrelenting cruelty; but it seems to have been reserved for the Church of England to produce one who has a just claim to the atrocious pre-eminence. No assemblage of words can give an appropriate designation of you; and, therefore, as being the single word which best suits the character of such a man, I call you Parson, which, amongst other meanings, includes that of Boroughmonger Tool ... . Your principles are almost all false; and your reasoning, in almost every instance, is the same. But, it is not my intention to waste my time on your abstract matter. I shall come, at once, to your practical result; to your recommendation to the Boroughmongers to pass laws to *punish the poor for marrying*.

(William Cobbett in an open letter to Malthus, 8 May 1819)[1]

George Bernard Shaw, renowned for his own scathing wit, once declared Karl Marx, John Ruskin and William Cobbett the three masters of nineteenth-century invective.[2] Cobbett certainly deserves inclusion among such an august trio and was unsparing in his often highly personal attacks on individuals and institutions. No single figure was more the butt of such venom than Thomas Robert Malthus. Cobbett labelled Malthus 'that impudent and illiterate Parson', the 'check-population parson', the 'blundering parson' and the 'muddy-headed Parson all through'.[3] He was nothing short of 'a monster in human shape' who expressed 'barbarous thoughts' and made 'diabolical' assertions – a 'political pimp' who deserved 'the severest punishment that outraged laws can inflict'.[4] Like Marx after him, Cobbett accused Malthus of plagiarism: the parson was merely a 'humble' follower of Daniel Defoe who had attacked poor relief in the reign of Queen Anne.[5]

It was not only Malthus himself who received such harsh condemnation but also anyone who espoused his ideas or attempted to implement them. 'MALTHUS and his tribe of insolent followers' and 'nasty disciples', were described by Cobbett as the 'Scotch Crew' engaged in 'the pestilent Scotch *feelosofee*'.[6] The fact that Malthus hardly qualified as a Scot – his great-grandfather on his mother's side was born in Scotland but moved to England where he became Apothecary to

George I and George II – did not in the least deter Cobbett from using such labels.[7] After all, *The Edinburgh Review* and Lord Chancellor Brougham espoused Malthusian ideas and were Scottish enough. Brougham, who praised Malthus when speaking in favour of the New Poor Law in the House of Lords, Cobbett summed up thus: 'He is the weazel, he is the indigestion, he is the nightmare, he is the deadly malady of the ministry'.[8] Brougham personified the 'Scotch monsters of the school of Parson MALTHUS' and the 'desperate, and half-mad, and half-drunken and inordinately greedy Scotchmen'.[9] Indeed, anyone who supported checking the population of labourers or who argued in favour of the New Poor Law became 'bawling hare-brained creatures' who were, moreover, 'the most cowardly, the very basest, the most scandalously base, reptiles that were ever warmed into life by the rays of the sun'.[10]

Cobbett, however, levelled a more specific charge at the 'parson' and his followers, one which many others before him had made and which Malthus himself, as early as 1807 in his *Letter to Whitbread,* had described with some anguish, as 'accusations of "hardness of heart"'.[11] He labelled Malthus the 'Callous Parson, hardened Parson' and referred to the 'execrable principles of the ... hard-hearted MALTHUS'.[12] Not only were his 'doctrines false' but his recommendations were 'unjust and cruel'.[13] Lord Brougham had 'openly and loudly declared himself to be a disciple of the merciless MALTHUS'.[14] Other Malthusian adherents he brandished as 'hardened ruffians, who can talk so calmly about the *"thinning of the population"*' or 'hard-hearted and blasphemous wretches who deny the right of the poor; who with the brutal ... Parson MALTHUS, would tell the destitute working man, that "he has no claim upon the community for even the smallest portion of food"'.[15]

The relevance of Malthus

Such vitriolic denunciations have led some historians such as Gertrude Himmelfarb to conclude that Cobbett 'personalized' his own relations not only to the 'System' as a whole but to individuals he disagreed with. Malthus thus became a bitter enemy.[16] J. R. Poynter has taken a more extreme position, arguing that Cobbett's opposition to Malthus was 'emotional rather than intellectual'. Thus Cobbett 'was not really a contributor to the Malthusian debate: he was simply anti-Malthusian.'[17] But here Poynter may be guilty of the fault he attributes to Cobbett. Although Cobbett certainly viewed his world in highly personal and emotive terms, to argue that he was devoid of substantial argument against Malthus does him a severe injustice.

of *right* to the smallest portion of food'?[28] Cobbett quoted this statement time and time again. If, as Malthus claimed, the poor could find no vacant cover at nature's mighty feast, then Cobbett argued that rather than perish they should force their way in and seize from her guests whatever provisions they deemed necessary. From this perspective Malthus became fundamental to much of Cobbett's social and political theory. As against the natural laws of Malthus's political economy, Cobbett's law of nature posited the right to subsistence as opposed to the inevitability of starvation.

If one accepts greater prominence for Malthus in Cobbett's thought, such a perspective gains even greater importance in the wider context of this work as a whole. As John Klancher has remarked, Cobbett emerged as 'England's most widely read radical author' and 'the most powerful single writer-publisher of the nineteenth century'.[29] Although it may be impossible to determine exactly how readers received him or to gauge precisely the nature and extent of his influence, there is no doubt that the sales and readership of his works were impressive and that he gained a substantial working-class audience.[30] In November 1816 Cobbett published a two-pence version of his 'Address to Journeymen and Labourers' which originally appeared in his *Political Register* of 2 November 1816 costing a shilling and a half-pence. He sold 20,000 copies within a fortnight and 200,000 copies within a year. Sales of these publications entitled *Two-Penny Trash* eventually reached 20,000–30,000 weekly.[31] Klancher estimates that the earliest two-pence editions reached a readership of between 150,000 and 200,000.[32] If such figures are anywhere near the mark, Cobbett outsold all other newspapers, periodicals or political tracts. Even after 1819, when the price was forced up to sixpence by the Six Acts and sales dwindled, circulation far outpaced *The Times* or even the more popular and cheaper unstamped press of the early 1830s.[33] Cobbett's popularity peaked in the tumultuous years of 1816–19 and 1830–34, but it is significant that in the 1820s, when radical audiences dwindled, Cobbett's *Political Register* survived unlike most other radical journals.[34] His books published in the 1820s, moreover, sold extremely well.[35]

Cobbett, like Harriet Martineau, was very conscious of his audience and was determined, moreover, that his works reached the non-literate and semi-literate. If modern readers of Cobbett find him repetitious in the extreme, that is because his reiteration of themes was thoroughly deliberate. In *The Poor Man's Friend* he justified repeating his arguments that the people of England were better off in the past:

> And, though I have done it on one or two former occasions, it is necessary to do it again here; for, those who may read now, may not have read before; and, besides, *boys* are every day rising up to the *age*

of thought; and in young men in particular, it is becoming to think seriously of these things, and to *ponder on the means of delivering their country*, their parents, and all those whom they love, from this state of increasing hunger, disgusting rags, misery, disgrace, and infamy.[36]

In one of his last books, *Legacy to Labourers* (1834), he justified restating his arguments against the New Poor Law thus:

Often as I have disproved these assertions; often as I have shown that the increased amount of poor-rates has not been so great, nor any thing like so great, as the increased amount of rent and taxes: often as I have shown that the inevitable tendency of the Bill is, to bring down the farmers and labourers of England to the state of those in Ireland; often as I have shown these things, I must show them again here; because I intend this little book to go into every parish in this whole kingdom; and to be in all the industrious classes (who alone give strength to the country, and who furnish the rich with all their riches), the *young man's best, most useful and most faithful companion*.[37]

In the latter part of 1834, Cobbett wrote a series of letters from Ireland to Charles Marshall, one of his labourers in the parish of Ash, England. He published these in the *Political Register* with the main purpose of revealing the depths of Irish misery in the absence of an Old Poor Law modelled on that of Elizabeth I. Charles Marshall was illiterate. Cobbett, however, was not in the least deterred about spreading his word:

Now, Marshall, I address this letter to you, because you are the most able and the most skilful of my labourers, though all of you are able and good. You cannot read it, I know; but, Mr DEAN will read it to you; and he will, some evening, get you all together, and read it, twice over, to you all. I will cause it to be printed on a slip of paper, and cause copies of it to be sent into all the parishes round about our own.'[38]

In spite of Cobbett's intention to reach a wide audience even among the unread, it is no easy task to determine how deeply his writings penetrated the consciousness of the labouring class and informed their conceptual framework. Ian Dyck is convinced that 'he enjoyed a formidable influence in the countryside', particularly during and after the 1830 Labourer's Revolt.[39] The *Political Register* (now selling at 7d. in its stamped version) he claims was widely circulated in rural alehouses and political clubs, not to mention the cheaper unstamped *Two-Penny Trash* which one Gloucestershire magistrate said was 'read in every country pothouse'.[40] The authorities were certainly convinced that Cobbett was inciting the masses to riot. At his prolonged state trial for seditious libel in 1831 he was accused of inflaming the 'minds of the labourers' and for encouraging 'acts of violent riot and … the burning and destruction of

I also beg leave to point out to the particular attention of the reader, the letter, signed A.O. upon the important subject of the *poor*, in the writer of which excellent letter, the check-population philosopher, Mr. Malthus, has met with a formidable opponent, who will, I confidently hope, continue on till he has completely put down the hard-hearted doctrine of this misanthropic economist.[54]

On 21 March 1807 Cobbett further denounced Malthusianism for attempting to curtail the population of the labouring poor.[55] It is ironic, of course, that Malthus himself also opposed Whitbread's bill although on very different grounds. Whitbread's proposal to build cottages for the poor at parish expense and to let them at whatever rent they could afford, Malthus argued, would only encourage early marriage, overpopulation and further misery.[56]

Once convinced of the error of Malthus's views, Cobbett launched a total critique of his premises. To be sure, like most writers, Cobbett contradicted himself upon occasion. In 1808, for example, he still appeared to accept some of Malthus's assumptions: 'Now, I think, it is a principle acknowledged upon all sides, that wherever there is subsistence there will be a *proportionate population*, or, to use the words of MR. MALTHUS (with whom I disagree as to the *checking of population*), population always treads close upon the heels of subsistence'.[57] By 1831, however, such principles became the subject of biting satire. In his play *Surplus Population: A Comedy in Three Acts*, Sir Gripe Grindum of Grindum Hall – the lecherous and miserly landlord of the village of Nestbed possessing an income of £40,000 per year – plays host to the Malthusian philosopher Squire Thimble who is working on an essay entitled 'Remedy Against Breeding'. On his first morning Thimble receives the following letter from Sir Gripe:

My dear Thimble, you know that our great master, Parson Malthus, lays it down, that population always treads closely upon the heels of subsistence. Acting upon this principle and fully agreeing with you, that the country is ruined by surplus population, I deem it a duty to my beloved country for the happiness and honour of which I have so long been toiling and making so many sacrifices, to suffer no subsistence to be in my house beyond a bare sufficiency to keep body and soul together. I have, therefore, told Farmer Stiles to send this to you to-morrow morning, and provide you with bed, board, &c., and I will call on you at his house about breakfast time.[58]

Cobbett never wavered after 1808 in his conviction that Malthus's arithmetic and geometric ratios were unfounded. Population, therefore, could never outstrip subsistence. In his comic play just cited, Last, the village shoemaker – who speaks throughout on behalf of Cobbett – is asked by Squire Thimble if he knows 'that there is, in nature, a tendency in every country, for the people to increase faster than the food that they usually live on.' Last replies: 'I do not only not know that fact, but I know that, besides its being contrary to reason and experience, it is next to blasphemy to assert it.'[59]

Cobbett's argument against Malthus's theory of imbalance between the food supply and population was based on the assumption that labourers produced more than enough food for their *own* subsistence (my emphasis). In 1824, referring to rural workers, he claimed: 'The more there are of them, the more food their labour will produce. The increase of produce must keep pace with the increase of mouths; for mouths never come without hands.' He could not, moreover 'see how any mischief is to arise from an increase of the people, provided that each mouth has a *pair of hands* belonging to it'.[60] During one of his rural rides down the Valley of the Avon in Wiltshire during 1826, he remarked:

> Now look at this Valley of Avon. Here the people raise nearly *twenty times as much food and clothing as they consume,* They raise five times as much, even according to my scale, of living. They have been doing this for many, many years. They have been doing it *for several generations.* Where, then, is their NATURAL TENDENCY *to increase beyond the means of sustenance for them?*[61]

In 1831 he presented statistical evidence (now technically known as the land-labour ratio) to the effect that there were on average for England and Wales as a whole '*forty-three acres of land to every single able labourer in agriculture*'. Even in the county of Bedford with virtually no wasteland there were still twenty-three acres per adult able-bodied labourer.[62]

Cobbett also vehemently opposed Malthus's contention that the Poor Laws of England created population growth by encouraging early marriage among labourers. Malthus, of course, justified abolishing the Old Poor Law on such grounds. Cobbett claimed, however, that an 'overflow of population in England, chiefly on account of the poor rates' was nothing but a 'lie'.[63] Recognizing the fact that the Elizabethan Poor Law had been in existence for over two hundred years, Cobbett addressed Malthus directly:

> You say that this population is increased by the poor rates. Can you tell me how it happens that it has not gone on increasing from the same cause, ever since the poor rates began to exist? Can you tell me that? Can you tell me why the poor rates should have begun to produce this effect only of late years? You can tell me no such a thing. You can give no reason why the increase should not have been going on from the time that the poor rates were first enacted. You can give no reason, why this increase should not have been regularly going on. In short, if it have been going on of late years, and going on from this cause; it must have *always* been going on.[64]

He furthermore denied that the poor deliberately married earlier in order to receive relief. In his comedy *Surplus Population,* the farm labourer Dick Hazle – much to Squire Thimble's chagrin – is anxious to marry Betsey Birch who is a mere eighteen years of age. He is reticent to do so, however, and says the following to his master, farmer Stiles, who urges him to follow through on the wedding banns: 'You need not tell me that, master; but we be so poor; and, suppose me to fall sick, I'd rather die than see her begging a morsel of bread from the flint-hearted hired overseer.'[65] Stiles then advances Dick five pounds and offers the couple lodging at his farm for a month or two. Dick is elated and decides to marry the next day.

Cobbett also used the case of Ireland to contradict Malthus. He was loathe even for a moment to admit Malthusian notions that the population of Ireland was rapidly increasing and that the Irish married very early. Accepting such suppositions, however, for the sake of argument but realizing that Ireland had no Poor Law he launched the following attack:

> This affair of Ireland is a puzzler for PARSON MALTHUS and his school. It was plain sailing with the hardened fellow, when he had only to assail English labourers. When he had merely to assert, that a 'redundant population' sprang out of the poor rates. He could dispose of those who took *poor rates.* He could even *draw up the Act of Parliament* for putting a stop to the evil of a redundant population, which proceeded from a people that bred too fast because they got relief and were made somewhat comfortable. But the Parson does not know what to do with those who breed too fast from an *exactly opposite cause.* He does not know what the devil to do with those who breed too fast because they are half naked and half starved! ... What, Parson, do precisely the same effects now-a-days come from precisely opposite causes! You should pray heartily, Parson that these Irish may all go to the devil; for thither, to a certainty, they have blown your system.[66]

Cobbett found it puzzling as well that in 'Ireland there are no *poor rates,* and there they marry earlier than they do in England.'[67]

If Cobbett denied Malthus's ratios and refused to accept that the Poor Laws facilitated population growth, he pushed his argument to the extreme by claiming that no overall population increase had occurred either in England or in Ireland for the past five hundred years. Far more likely, he argued, population had declined. Any assertion that population was increasing was nothing short of a 'great national lie'[68] propagated by Malthus and his followers and used by governments to suit their own purposes. Of the 'lies' of the '*anti-breeders*' or '*surplus population-mongers*' he remarked:

> What the great liars aim at is this: to make the people believe, that an

increase of population is certain proof of the prosperity of the nation; that prosperity is a proof of excellently good Government; and that, of course, this Government is *excellently good*! No wonder that all the Governments of Europe, and of America, too, should be seized with this fit of lying. They all seem to be trying to outlie and outbrag each other. The French say that their population has monstrously increased within the last thirty years; the Dutch, the Prussians, the Russians, the Austrians, the Pope and even the Turk say the same; so that here is the most wonderful thing that ever was heard of since the creation of the world: all these nations are wonderfully increasing in population: their people, therefore, are *all prosperous*; and the Turks and all, have excellently good Governments! No, no.[69]

Even more grating was the application of this 'monstrous lie' to Ireland: 'Is that people *prosperous*? Is that miserable race of men in a state for the Government to boast of? Is the Government of Ireland *excellently good*?'[70]

Historians have severely underestimated the amount of energy Cobbett expended in attempting to disprove England's 'most glorious lie' and the varieties of argument he presented in defence of his position.[71] From 1819 to his death in 1835, Cobbett constantly harped on this theme. Although prepared to admit that some parts of England were more populous than formerly – Lancashire, part of Yorkshire and the four counties bordering the great WEN of London – he never wavered in his conviction that the '*kingdom in general*' experienced no population increase and, if anything, a decline.[72] Even though his arguments were often contorted and illogical, the sheer volume of material on this issue attests to the importance of Malthus in Cobbett's social analysis. George Spater's contention that the subject of population change was a mere 'crotchet' in Cobbett's writings needs serious reconsideration.[73] After all, to deny population increase was to invalidate notions that labourers were prosperous as well as to remove the justification for refusing them relief and controlling their numbers.

Cobbett's first argument against population growth was presented in his 1819 critique entitled 'TO PARSON MALTHUS' and involved an attack on the accuracy of the 1801 and 1811 *Censuses of England and Wales*. In his second instalment of 'TO PARSON MALTHUS' in 1823 he incorporated the 1821 Census.[74] Even common-sense reasoning, he argued, would lead one to doubt census returns which claimed the population of England and Wales had increased from eight million in 1801 to eleven million in 1821:

> But, *upon the face of the thing*: without going into any enquiry about it: without any argument or any fact, is it not monstrous to attempt to make us believe that a population of eight millions has swelled up

to eleven millions in the course of twenty years, one half of which years have been years of *war*, and the other half years of *distress*, and, during the whole of which, there has been emigration going on from this country to the United States of America, and no emigration from other countries to this? Is it a thing to be believed, though upon the oaths of fifty thousand return-makers?[75]

Not content to rest his case on such reasoning, Cobbett conducted a detailed, if very convoluted and confusing, analysis attempting to prove that the 1801 and 1811 returns were deliberately falsified. The 1801 Census divided the population into three categories: persons employed in agriculture; persons employed in trade, handicraft and manufacture; and all other persons. The 1811 returns also presented a similar tripartite division of the population but now based this not on persons but on families in each category. Cobbett argued that this shift in definition and the figures provided in each classification were conscious attempts to disguise demographic reality. He angrily concluded:

> Now, Boroughmongers and Parsons, take your choice: was the first return a lie; or was the second a lie? Both. It has all been a lie from the beginning to the end. It is a mere fabrication to delude, deceive, cajole and cheat the nation and the world; and the money expended to propagate the cheat ought to be, every farthing of it, refunded by the cheaters, and given back to those Labouring Classes, from whence the greatest part of it was taken, and to whose detestation I now leave you, Parson Malthus, and your foolish insolent performance.[76]

Cobbett also presented forward and backward projections of the English and Welsh population to prove the census returns were false. In 1823 Cobbett reasoned that if the 1811 and 1821 Censuses were true then 'two more centuries must see the English people swarming like the lice in Egypt; and three centuries back (four centuries after the churches were built) there could have been only a single Adam and Eve turned down to breed!'[77] In 1824 Cobbett actually provided statistical projections of the future population of England and Wales. Based on an increase of roughly three million between 1801 and 1821 according to the census returns of those years, he predicted the following population totals: 1841 (15 million); 1861 (20 million); 1881 (27 million); 1901 (36 million); 2000 (102 million). Although failing to provide the reader with the exact basis upon which he extrapolated, he clearly found such estimates incredulous, cynically commenting: 'Thus a most jovial crew will Old England have, at last!'[78]

Cobbett, in addition, attacked the census returns at a micro-demographic level. In February 1824 he focused his attention on the village of Botley in Hampshire where he had formerly farmed, informing his readers that he knew 'every living creature in that parish'.[79] He accused the census takers of 'gross misrepresentation ... as to the occupations of its inhabitants'.[80] In the 1821 Census, he argued, the trade, manufactures, and handicrafts had been deliberately inflated at the expense of the numbers employed in agriculture. In Cobbett's view Botley was 'a purely agricultural village.' Except for two men who brought coal from Southampton, all the people of Botley were employed in agriculture, even the tailor and shoemaker – who made clothes and shoes for the farmer and labourer. Cobbett argued, in essence, that all crafts and professions – blacksmiths, wheelwrights, the school mistress, and even the two doctors – belonged to agriculture since they serviced agricultural production and labour. In short, he challenged the entire basis of occupational definition in the 1821 Census and accused the government of operating in the 'manufacturing interest'. [81]

Having discredited the census in terms of its occupational breakdown, Cobbett turned to the total number of inhabitants of Botley given in the census returns of 1801 (600), 1811 (624), and 1821 (690) and claimed they had been falsified by the Reverend Richard Baker to create the impression of a 'famously increasing population'.[82] The Reverend, according to Cobbett, had publicly declared in a letter to The Times dated 28 July 1818 that the parish of Botley contained 400 people, yet had signed the census return of 1811 certifying a population of 624. Even more disturbingly he had authorized a population of 690 for 1821. Cobbett further claimed that he and the 'Reverend' had taken their own unofficial census in 1806 arriving at a true total of 400 persons. Reminding Baker of 'the good old maxim, that a liar ought to have a good memory', Cobbett claimed that the Reverend in his letter of 1818 had remembered the 1806 figure but had forgotten what he had certified in 1811. Such deception concerning Botley was 'a pretty fair sample', moreover, of what was occurring nation-wide. 'This population affair', he remarked, 'is a most shocking humbug, from beginning to end.'[83]

If Cobbett was intent on destroying the credibility of the census in order to deny any recent increase in numbers, he was equally determined to prove that population levels in the past were much higher than the present. In the absence of official census figures prior to 1801, he utilized a variety of methods to confirm his contention. One was to argue that estimates of former populations in the literature available to him were grossly deflated. He vehemently contested, for example, Wilmot Horton's statement (derived from David Hume) that the population of Elizabethan England and Wales was a mere 900,000 – comprising 450,000 males, 300,000 of which were adults. Cobbett produced his own estimates arguing for the presence of at least 450,000 adult males, concluding that Horton was a 'brazen liar' and a 'monstrous fool'.[84] He likewise disputed George Chalmers' figure of 2,092,978 for England and

Wales in 1377 consisting of 523,243 able-bodied adult males. In this case, he cited Hume approvingly. How could Wat Tyler (according to Hume) have assembled 100,000 men (one-fifth of all the able-bodied men in the Kingdom) on Blackheath during the Peasants' Revolt of 1381? Medieval Canterbury moreover, frequently hosted (again, according to Hume) 100,000 pilgrims. Cobbett assumed that 50,000 of these were males and found it absolutely incredulous that 'more than a tenth of all the able-bodied men of England and Wales were frequently assembled at one and the same place, in one city, in an extreme corner of the island, to kneel at the tombs of one single saint.' 'Monstrous lie!', Cobbett thundered.[85]

His favourite argument, however, involved what Charles H. Kegel has nicely labelled his 'church capacity theory'. Cobbett first presented this in his second address 'To Parson Malthus' in the *Political Register* of 1823.[86] He reasoned that given the sheer size and large capacities of existing churches that were frequently empty and located in parishes with tiny numbers of inhabitants, population must have declined from the medieval period. Utilizing Parliamentary Returns of 1818 which gave an account of the benefices, population and the state of churches and chapels, he stated: 'In this Return we find several churches, several scores and hundreds of good fat benefices where there is now, in some places, "*scarcely any population at all*".' [87] At the local level, he found five parishes in Dorset with six churches and a chapel servicing a total of only 810 parishioners – one place of worship, on average, for roughly 115 persons. Addressing Malthus directly, Cobbett remarked: 'Now is it to be believed Parson, that these churches were built for the use of a population like this?'[88]

Cobbett, moreover, undertook detailed calculations regarding the size and capacity of churches to prove they could hold far more than existing populations. He described the church at Sharncut in Wiltshire which had only eight parishioners, as follows:

> The church is sixty feet long, and, on an average twenty-eight feet wide; so that the area of it contains one thousand six hundred and eighty square feet; or, one hundred and eighty-eight square yards! I found in the church eleven pews that would contain, that were made to contain, eighty-two people; and, these do not occupy a third part of the area of the church; and thus, more than two hundred persons, at the least, might be accommodated, with perfect convenience in this church.[89]

Overall, he estimated, the churches of England could hold 'four, five, or ten times the number of their present parishioners' and then repeatedly asked the obvious question:

> What should men have built such large churches *for*? .... And what

motive could there have been for putting together such large quantities of stone and mortar, and to make walls four feet thick and towers and steeple, if there had not been *people* to fill the buildings? And, how could the *labour* have been performed?[90]

Cobbett also applied this argument to Ireland. Referring to a House of Commons Committee Report that stated the population in 1695 to be 1,034,102, Cobbett indignantly replied, again raising the issue of labour supply:

> We must content ourselves with expressing our surprise. Ireland had, long before the Dutch King ever set his foot in England, about twenty Bishopricks and Archbishopricks; between thirty and forty Deans; together with Prebendaries, and all other dignitaries of a great church. She had many noble cathedrals; and I believe UPWARDS OF SIX THOUSAND PARISH CHURCHES! These facts are wholly undeniable. Mr. STANLEY, during the debate on Mr. HUME'S celebrated motion about the Irish church, said that the Irish were, when the Protestant church was first introduced, '*a bigoted illiterate people, possessing all the virtues and all the vices of savages.*' So, it was only *one million* of these '*savages,*' who built the cathedrals and the churches of Ireland, who reared all these noble edifices. [91]

Cobbett repeated his church capacity argument time and time again especially in his *Rural Rides*. While travelling through the Vale of Avon in Wiltshire in 1826, he noted, 'you plainly see all the traces of a great ancient population. The churches are almost all large, and built in the best manner .... Nothing can more clearly show than this, that all, as far as buildings and population are concerned, has been long upon the decline and decay.'[92] Kegel points out that Cobbett in his *Rural Rides*

> ... fashioned what amounted almost to a formula. As he rode from village to village, city to city, he counted the cathedrals and churches in the area. Then he repeated the inevitable question, 'What, I ask, for about the thousandth time I ask it; what were these twenty churches built for?' Always he was ready with the answer, that 'this country must, at the time of the Norman conquest, have literally *swarmed* with people.'[93]

In *Surplus Population*, Last the village shoemaker perhaps best sums up the author's views. When told by Squire Thimble that he 'must know ... that the people of this country have greatly increased in number', Last replies: 'I neither know nor believe it; for I see churches, built hundreds of years ago, with scarcely any parishioners; I see many of them quite tumbled down; and I know that they never would have been built, if there had not been people to go to them.'[94] The frequency with which Cobbett repeated this argument suggests that he considered it one of his strongest refutations of the Malthusian position. Indeed, when summarizing his arguments on the subject of population in 1831, he ranked his church capacity theory first among nine of the salient 'facts' he had advanced.[95]

In addition, Cobbett applied his capacity theory to the secular realm. During his travels through Wiltshire in 1826 he noted the decline in the number of manor houses: 'Every parish had its manor house, in the first place; and then there were, down this valley, twenty-one others; so that in this distance of about thirty miles there stood FIFTY MANSION HOUSES. Where are they now? I believe there are but EIGHT, that are but poorly kept up.' No longer could one observe 'once populous and gay villages and hamlets'.[96] Referring to a tour through Dorsetshire and Wiltshire in 1822, Cobbett drew on different types of evidence:

> On the outskirts of almost all the villages, you find still remaining, *small enclosures of land*, each of which has manifestly had its house formerly. They are generally in pasture at this time; but, if you look attentively at the ground, you will see unevenesses which show you that here are the relics of the foundations of houses; while, if you look at the fences you will see gooseberry, currant, or raspberry bushes, making their appearance here and there. In the middle of such little plots of ground, you frequently see old pear trees or apple trees, or the stumps of them remaining. All these are so many proofs of a greatly diminished, and of still diminishing population.[97]

Finally, he argued that since much more land was farmed in former times, population obviously must have declined. Maintaining that his forefathers cultivated 'millions of acres' more than at present he asked: 'Why should they have performed this prodigious labour if they had not had mouths to eat the corn? And how could they have performed such labour without numerous hands?' Summing up his case he concluded: 'The modern writings on the subject of ancient population are mere romances, or they have been put forth with a view of paying court to the government of the day.'[98]

If Cobbett denied the possibility of population outpacing the food supply, if he rejected the contention that the Poor Laws encouraged population increase, if he repudiated the very notion of an augmentation of the numbers of people living in England and Ireland, how then did he explain the poverty which so apparently abounded in the countryside among the labouring class? Such misery was obviously not a Malthusian positive check against a surplus population. Nor was it the fault of the poor themselves. Although Cobbett was prepared to admit that at times individuals were responsible for their own poverty – some men were 'reduced to poverty by their vices, by idleness, by gaming, by drinking, by squandering' – nevertheless, 'the far greater part' were poor because of factors beyond their control.[99] He defined the poor as those 'persons who, from age, infirmity, helplessness, or from want of the means of gaining any thing by labour, become destitute of a sufficiency of food, or of raiment, and are in danger of perishing if they be not relieved'.[100] He chastised those who blamed the poor for their poverty and insisted that increased poor-rates were not the result of 'idleness, drunkeness, and *profligacy*'.[101] As if uttering a universal law, he stated: 'Poverty, in some degree, is the lot of mankind; but if we take a survey of the state of nations, we shall find, that a very small portion of it really arises from any fault in the poor themselves.'[102]

Cobbett likewise refused to accept the Malthusian premise that the Poor Laws themselves created poverty by rendering the poor lazy and improvident. To be sure, certain practices such as overseers employing men to dig and carry gravel could degrade the labourer.[103] In no way, however, did such poor law policies cause poverty. Referring to the steep rise in expenditure on the poor, Cobbett attacked Malthus directly: 'Anyone but a mud-headed parson, or a perverse knave, would have looked about him for causes of the increase other than the practice of giving parish relief.'[104] Besides, he contended, the Poor Laws had existed for over two hundred years in England without producing such miserable conditions among the lower orders: 'They have existed,' moreover, 'in America from its first settlement, without ever having produced any such effect.'[105] Furthermore, Ireland had no Poor Laws and found itself in an unparalleled state of wretchedness.[106]

Rejecting notions of individual fault exacerbated by the provision of poor relief, Cobbett found the true causes of poverty most immediately in low real wages and unemployment. In 1824 he chastised *The Times* for publishing an article claiming rural labourers were 'tolerably at ease, in full employment'. Such statements were an 'insult to the public'. He set the record straight: 'The wretched state of the people in all parts of the kingdom is notorious. The wages of the day-labouring man do not afford him a sufficiency to give him bread alone, leaving every thing else out of the question.'[107] He presented statistics comparing wages with the prices of various essential commodities and argued that between 1760 and 1809 prices increased far more rapidly than wages to the point that real wages were cut in half.[108] Moreover many labourers were, without any fault of their own, 'unable to find work'.[109]

Cobbett inquired deeper and concluded that 'enormous taxes, co-operating with the paper-money' were the fundamental factors producing 'the *low wages* and the *want of employment*'.[110] Indeed, in Cobbett's anti-Malthusian analysis, taxes and not population increase lay at the very core of his explanation of poverty. As Spater points out, the weight of taxation increasingly fell on consumer goods following the repeal of the income tax in 1816. In 1817 Cobbett estimated that a common day-labourer earning 18 pounds a year (7 shillings per week) paid 10 pounds, or more than half his wages, in taxes on the items he consumed.[111] Such commodity taxes – on shoes, salt, beer, malt, hops, tea, sugar, candles, soap, paper, coffee, spirits, window glass, bricks, tiles and tobacco among others – amounted to more than one-half of what labourers paid for the article itself.[112] The working people, moreover, paid out of their wages the lion's share of the 52 million pounds in overall taxes collected by the government in 1835. Cobbett berated 'the beastly Malthusian philosophers' for maintaining such an iniquitous taxation system.[113]

Such a burden thrust on the backs of labour, Cobbett claimed, was responsible for increasing levels of wretchedness. In 1822 he argued for a direct correlation between poverty and taxation: 'It is *the taxes*; and this is shewn as clearly as daylight in the fact, that the poor rates have increased in precisely the same proportion that the taxes have increased.'[114] In 1835 he supported his contention with statistics matching poor rates and government taxes between the reign of James II and in 1833, again asserting that increasing levels of poor expenditure stemmed not from 'idle … vagabonds', nor from any defect in the Poor Laws or their administration, but from taxes.[115] Such onerous financial exactions, furthermore, severely affected the ability of farmers to pay rents, thus accentuating the problem of low wages and unemployment.[116] Cobbett concluded that Malthus 'who, seeing the alarming increase of pauperism, seems not to have looked at the *real cause*, the *taxes*, but to cast about him for some means of checking the increase of the *breed*'.[117]

Although the subject of taxation remained uppermost in Cobbett's mind, two other closely related issues – paper money and the national debt – also loomed large. The 'infernal Pitt system of paper-money' which greatly expanded the currency supply had led to high prices robbing the labourer of his wages and making paupers of the people of England.[118] Even though he praised Peel's bill of 1819, which facilitated a reversion to metal currency to replace the paper money issued to finance the Napoleonic War, Cobbett was far from convinced such a measure would solve the problem of poverty. Although the reduction in the quantity of paper money would lower the prices of farm produce and provide some benefit to labourers, the high level of taxes mitigated against any real gains. Farmers, moreover, faced with low prices for their crops yet paying the same nominal amount in rent and taxes would have to produce two or three times as many bushels of wheat to cover such costs. Vast numbers would be forced to lower their wage payments. Many would be completely ruined thus forcing up unemployment.[119] Furthermore, as long as the huge national debt remained (which stood at £700 million in 1815, with interest alone at £30 million per annum), the vexatious problem of high taxation would continue to devastate labourer and farmer alike.[120]

Cobbett, of course, had to explain why the national debt and resulting taxation had increased to such enormous levels. His reply to this question – the government's careless and absolutely wasteful expenditure – became a recurring theme in his writings especially in the 1820s and 1830s. Poverty was not a result, as Malthus contended, of the reckless breeding of the lower orders but rather a result of the reckless financial waste promulgated by those in power. Military expenditure, both in war and peace, ranked high on Cobbett's list. The huge debts incurred in defeating Napoleon were a 'curse entailed upon the country on account of the late wars against the liberties of the French people'.[121] Even more grating was the fact that through 'the means of paper-money and loans, the labouring classes were made to pay the whole of the expenses of the war'.[122] In addition, the cost of maintaining a standing army in time of peace, especially when used to quell public discontent, was totally unjustified.[123]

He was even more disturbed by the vast amounts paid out in pensions, sinecures, grants and allowances to the 'idle' classes, both religious and secular. The introduction of a married clergy during the Reformation had 'absolutely created an order for the procreation of dependants on the state ... bringing into the world thousands of persons annually who have no fortunes of their own, and who must be, somehow or other, maintained by burdens imposed upon the people'.[124] Huge numbers of places, commissions, sinecures and pensions were thus found for such individuals. Cobbett carped at the £100 per annum Malthus received 'for doing nothing' as the non-resident rector of Walesby in Lincolnshire, labelling him 'a nasty-pensioned monster'.[125] In the two decades prior to 1824, moreover, he claimed that over £1,500,000 had been 'voted by parliament out of the taxes for the "relief of the poor clergy of the Church of England"', while the bishops wallowed in luxury, appropriating the endowments of the lesser clerics.[126]

In the secular realm, military expenditure took precedence. Cobbett complained bitterly of gross financial waste:

> This Dead Weight is unquestionably, a thing such as the world never saw before. Here not only a tribe of pensioned naval and military officers, commissaries, quarter-masters, pursers, and God knows what besides; not only these, but their wives and children are to be pensioned, after the death of the heroes themselves. Nor does it signify, it seems, whether the hero was married, before he became part of the Dead Weight, or since. Upon the death of the man, the pension is to begin with the wife and a pension for each child; so that, if there be a large family of children, the family, in many cases, *actually gains by the death of the father*! Was such a thing as this

ever before heard of in the world? Any man that is going to die has nothing to do but to marry a girl to give her a pension for life to be paid out of the sweat of the people.[127]

The nobility and aristocracy, of course, took a huge share of such largesse. Referring to a parliamentary report of 1808, Cobbett claimed 'there were several hundreds of persons belonging to noble families who received pensions, or the amount of sinecures, out of taxes raised upon the people; that there were whole families maintained in this manner ... without any, even the smallest, pretence of their ever having rendered any service to the country.'[128] The aristocracy, he asserted, swallowed up millions in pensions, sinecures, allowances and grants. Expenditure on the 'Dead Weight' as a whole (amounting to between six and seven million pounds a year) exceeded that expended on relief of the poor, not even mentioning the usurious and non-productive profits of stockbrokers and stock-jobbers.[129]

He was aware, of course, that other important and often long-term factors contributed to increasing poverty levels. Enclosures had caused 'grievous injury' to the common people and produced such 'ruin and misery ... enough to wring the heart of any man of feeling'. He berated the 'Malthus's' and 'Scotch Economists' for having no proposals to counteract such devastation.[130] Likewise, the Game Laws had become so onerous that Cobbett in the early 1830s proposed removing all additions to these statutes enacted since 1760.[131] Cobbett equally condemned the more recent Corn Laws. Promulgated by 'rapacious landlords' and misguided farmers, they increased the cost of the labourer's food and were 'most oppressive in themselves'. Besides, such tariffs against the importation of wheat would not solve any problems, even with respect to the farmers, given the high levels of taxation.[132]

Cobbett returned time and time again to the subject of taxes when discussing the causes of poverty. In the end, he produced a class analysis based on exploitation and the labour theory of value:

> That the people are now divided into two very distinct classes, *tax-payers*, and *tax-receivers* (or, as they are properly enough called, *tax-eaters*); that whatever the former are compelled to give to the latter can never again be of any benefit to those former; and that, in short, what a man pays in taxes is just so much of *loss* to him, and of loss *for ever*, exactly as much so as if it were tossed into the sea.

> That, therefore, the tradesman, farmer, or other person, who receives none of the taxes, works to maintain the placemen, pensioners, sinecure people, grantees, the soldiers, the sailors, the half-pay people, and the like, with all their wives and families; that those live at their ease on the fruit of his labour; and that, thus, he is made to be poor; he and his family are *kept down*, while the tax-eaters and their families are raised up and kept above them.[133]

Labourers, however, were reduced to the lowest circumstances: 'As to the labouring classes, hunger, and rags, and filth, are now become their uniform and inevitable lot. No toil, no frugality, can save them from these; their toil is greater, and their food less, than those of the slaves in any part of the world that I have ever seen or ever heard of.'[134]

As early as 1821 Cobbett maintained:

> All property has its origin in labour. Labour itself is property; the root of all other property ... the produce of his labour would of itself produce a sufficiency of every thing needful for himself and family. The labouring classes must always form nine tenths of a people; and, what a shame it must be, what an imputation on the rulers, if nine tenths of the people be worthy of the name of poor! It is impossible that such a thing can be, unless there be an unfair and unjust distribution of the profits of labour. Labour produces every thing that is good upon the earth; it is the cause of every thing that men enjoy of worldly possessions; when, therefore, the strong and the young engage in labour and cannot obtain from it a sufficiency to keep them out of the ranks of the poor, there must be something greatly amiss in the management of the community.[135]

He later referred to the surplus created by labour and asked:

> What, then, is to be done with this over-produce! Who is to have it? Is it to go to pensioners, placemen, tax-gatherers, dead-weight people, soldiers, gendarmerie, police-people, and in short, to whole millions who do not work at all? Is this a cause of 'national wealth'? Is a nation made *rich* by taking the food and clothing from those who create them, and giving them to those who do nothing of any use?[136]

The 'Scotch *feelosofers*', he argued, had misunderstood the concept of '*national wealth*'.[137] Poverty, then, was not produced by Malthusian surplus population but rather by a system that unduly appropriated the surplus value of labour. Misery was produced not by individual improvidence and moral laxity but by unjust and exploitative institutions.

The rejection of Malthusian solutions

If Cobbett bitterly disputed Malthus's analysis of the causes of poverty, he just as viciously condemned the parson's solutions. Malthus, of course, proposed the preventive check of moral restraint as the ideal way out of the vice and misery generated by population increase outpacing growth in the food supply. The lower orders, he argued, should delay marriage – practising celibacy in the meantime – until they could support their children. Cobbett's attacks on this concept were at least as vitriolic as his denunciations of other Malthusian concepts. Thus Charles Kegel's contention that Cobbett's arguments were 'less intense' on this matter needs re-examination.[138]

In an open letter to Lord Lowick in 1831 he castigated Malthus while praising Godwin:

> I pray you to mark this, my Lord; MALTHUS was just their man. He found out a cause for the misery other than the taxes; and, SCOTCHMAN to the back-bone, he found out that the cause was the misconduct of the working people themselves, in marrying too young and having too many children! It is quite impossible for words to express the indignation due to this blasphemous doctrine. MALTHUS, of course, became a great favourite with the tax-eating rich, not ten of whom, I dare say, ever read the able and excellent production of Mr. GODWIN.[139]

The entire scheme to delay marriage among the labouring classes was 'dreadful', containing 'an equal portion of folly with the addition of a very large portion of insolent cruelty'.[140] Numerous 'nasty, beastly publications', moreover, were spreading such proposals regarding 'checking the surplus population'.[141]

The lower orders, furthermore, were reduced to the level of brute animals 'as live-stock upon a farm'.[142] Cobbett, indeed, became almost Swiftian in his critique. Addressing the labouring classes, he satirically suggested that more extreme measures than mere moral restraint might be needed to truly satisfy the Malthusians: 'What would they have you do? As some have called you the *swinish multitude*, would it be much wonder if they were to propose to serve you as families of young pigs are served? Or, if they were to bring forward the measure of Pharaoh, who ordered the midwives to kill all the male children of the Israelites?'[143] Squire Thimble, in *Surplus Population*, suggests the authorities should 'import a shipload of arsenic' to cut back the surplus population.[144] Cobbett even recommended castration and sterilization as ultimate remedies. Legislation 'to be of any effect must go further, and make England as famed for *singers* as Italy. He must, at once, declare the labourers to be *live-stock*, and authorize those operations upon them, of which male and female pigs are compelled to submit; and, in that case, I think, PARSON MALTHUS might with propriety be made operator general.'[145] At times he contended that if the poor were not quite brought down to the status of animals they had nevertheless become 'a *distinct race* amongst human beings, as wolves and asses are amongst four-footed animals'.[146]

Before proceeding to the content of Cobbett's opposition to moral restraint certain important issues need clarification. At numerous points, not unlike many other contemporary critics, he misread or deliberately misinterpreted Malthus. He failed to acknowledge, for example, the concept of prudential restraint – delay of marriage with occasional lapses in abstinence – that Malthus thought was a more realistic prescription in a less than perfect world. This, in itself, is not surprising. Even modern historians such as Charles Kegel have perpetuated such misinterpretations.[147] To be sure, Cobbett was correct in emphasizing Malthus's concern regarding early marriages, encouraged by poor relief, generating large numbers of offspring. In *Surplus Population*, for example, Betsey Birch, at eighteen years of age, intends to marry Dick Hazle. When asked by Squire Thimble how many children her mother had Betsey shocks him by replying: 'Only seventeen, Sir …. Seventeen now alive, Sir; she lost two and had two still born.'[148]

Cobbett's contention, however, that Malthus advocated prohibition of marriage and breeding of children by laws – 'that is to say by *force*' – specifically against early unions among the poor is inaccurate.[149] Malthus did advocate *voluntary* moral restraint and did propose laws gradually abolishing poor relief in order to facilitate the delay of nuptials (my emphasis). But he stopped short of direct punitive laws against marriage:

> After the public notice which I have proposed had been given, and the system of poor laws had ceased with regard to the rising generation, if any man chose to marry, without a prospect of being able to support a family, he should have the most perfect liberty to do so. Though to marry, in this case, is in my opinion clearly an immoral act, yet it is not one which society can justly take upon itself to prevent or punish; because the punishment provided for it by the laws of nature falls directly and most severely upon the individual who commits the act, and, through him, only more remotely and feebly on the society.[150]

Malthus, moreover, never condoned birth control within or outside marriage. Nor did he prescribe abortion as a means of family limitation. Cobbett misread the parson on both these issues. With regard to the villagers of Nestbed, Squire Thimble, for example, states that he aims 'first to persuade them not to marry, and next to teach them how to avoid having live children'.[151] Sir Gripe Grindum later claims that Thimble 'has openly advised women to procure abortion, which is murder'.[152]

Cobbett's most often used argument against moral restraint reverted back to the class analysis he employed in delineating the causes of poverty. Malthus and his disciples, he claimed, talked a lot about 'checking the breeding of labourers' but said 'not a word against the prolific *dead-weight* to whom they GIVE A PREMIUM FOR BREEDING'.[153] Why, he asked metaphorically, should the tax-eating 'drones' living off the 'honey' of the labouring 'bees' and receiving pensions and allowances which constituted a '*high premium* for increasing the population' not endure the moral restraint urged upon the labouring poor? Why, in other words, should not the disposition to marry among the *'idle'* classes be checked?[154] The 'cruel and insolent' Malthusians allowed the children of Lords and Ladies money granted in trust out of the taxes while unjustly denying relief and restricting the families of labourers and journeymen. 'Thousands upon thousands of pairs of this Dead Weight', he fulminated, were 'all busily engaged in breeding gentlemen and ladies; and all, while Malthus is wanting to put a check upon the breeding of the labouring classes; all receiving a *premium for breeding*.'[155] The families of army and navy officers likewise came under attack, as did the poor clergy, who, receiving relief out of the taxes, 'marry and have children without any attempt at hindrance'.[156]

Religion was also enlisted in the attack: the very concept of moral restraint was contrary to the laws of God. Malthus, by ignoring the biblical injunction 'Be ye fruitful and multiply', was propagating 'aetheistical' ideas tantamount to 'doctrines of the devils'.[157] As a parson, moreover, who had sworn to the articles of the Church of England, he completely denied the article that reprobated 'the doctrine of abstaining from *marriage*, as being Hostile to the word of God'.[158] In addition, he violated the very intent of the following words uttered at the Churching of women:

> Lo, children and the fruit of the womb, are an *heritage and gift that cometh of the Lord*. – Like as the arrows in the hand of the giant: even so are the young children. – *Happy is the man that hath his quiver full of them: they shall not be ashamed when they speak with their enemies in the gate*.[159]

If Malthus defied the laws of God, so too did he negate the laws of nature derived directly from the Supreme Being. The 'very first of nature's laws', Cobbett asserted, 'written in our passions, desires and propensities; written even in the organization of our bodies ... compel the two sexes to hold that sort of intercourse, which produces children.'[160] Any restraint on these passions through delay of marriage, moreover, deprived the labourer of his fundamental rights: 'To tell a man that he loses his claim to relief in consequence of his having children; is to tell him that he has no right to love; and to tell him that he has no *right to live*; that he has no right to carry a heart in his bosom, and no right to breathe the air!'[161]

He also forcefully argued that marriage, in harmony with natural law, should be based on love and affection rather than the Malthusian instrumentality operative under conditions of moral restraint. 'Marrying for the sake of money' was not only 'despicable' and 'disgraceful' but at best mere 'bargain and sale' and at worst 'a species of legal prostitution'.[162] The kinds of emotions Betsey Birch experienced when anticipating her marriage to Dick Hazle in *Surplus Population* were the proper basis for taking wedding vows: 'Oh, lor! I wish 'twas over; for my heart does beat so, and sink so, that I can hardly stand.'[163] Besides, Cobbett claimed, the passions between labouring couples was 'the greatest of all the compensations for the inevitable cares, troubles, hardships, and sorrows of life' that the married state might bring.[164] Even 'vulgar rich men' who undertook 'provident marriages' rather than ones based on love would have no counterbalance against the calamities that might befall them if poverty, as it frequently did, came their way 'in spite of the best-laid plans.'[165] Affection was so important to the marital union that he strongly advised couples who had promised marriage to each other to break off if either one liked another person better. Emphasizing passion over pure expediency he also listed beauty as a characteristic desirable in a wife but at the same time stressed that 'real' lovers should not be 'so smitten as to be bereft of reason'.[166]

Cobbett also placed great emphasis on the necessity of affection between parents and children. 'There are', he claimed, 'very few women who are not replete with maternal love.' Nevertheless, he felt it necessary to advise young men never to marry 'a girl who is not fond of children'.[167] Husbands, he asserted, were highly capable of displaying fondness for children: 'Those that did not were severely lacking.' He claimed he 'never knew a man that was good for much who had a dislike to little children'. Such behaviour, moreover, 'argues no effeminacy in a man, but as far as my observation has gone, the contrary'.[168] Affection thus became the basis of a happy family life even with many children in reduced circumstances. Mrs. Birch, Betsey's mother in *Surplus Population*, perhaps best sums up the author's views. When asked by Sir Gripe Grindum about her children she replies:

> Twelve boys and five girls, Sir, and though I say it, as good children they be as any in the parish, and, thanks be to God, not a day's sickness have we had in the house since their poor father died, and that was three years ago last Friday as ever was; and they be so dutiful to me, and comes so kindly to see me every Sunday, when they do their best to make up for the loss of their poor father, who, poor soul, used, when he came home from his work, to have four or five of them upon his knees at once. Oh, Sir, never was there such a father.[169]

If Cobbett denied moral restraint on philosophical and prescriptive grounds, perhaps his strongest arguments against Malthus were more pragmatic in content. Moral restraint simply would not work. Indeed, the parson himself would have been the first to agree that the passion between the sexes was a fundamental natural law. Malthus was, nevertheless, convinced by 1803 that such instincts could be tempered by reason and economic necessity. Cobbett vehemently disagreed. Attacking James Scarlett's Malthusian proposals to deny poor relief in order to delay marriage among the labouring classes, he remarked that Scarlett 'could not stifle the fire of youth: he cannot still the emotions of the heart; he cannot arrest the progress of the propensity of those emotions.'[170] In addition, rural labourers themselves would denounce any inducements to postpone wedding vows:

> For, as to preaching the Malthusian doctrine of restraint to the country girls, only let the *nasty feelosofers* go and state the doctrine to them IN PLAIN TERMS; let them state the unnatural, the beastly, the nasty ideas to them IN PLAIN UNVARNISHED LANGUAGE; let them do this, and see how soon their heads will be tied up in their aprons, and their filthy brains knocked out against the posts of the cow-cribs ![171]

Cobbett supported his contention by inquiring into the Protestant abolition of Catholic celibacy among priests. The foundation of this policy, he claimed, lay in the realization that unmarried clergy would and must be guilty of '*criminal intercourse*': that they could not, without marrying, 'preserve their purity'. If it were '*impossible*' for such educated men who had taken the most solemn vows of chastity to deny their sexual gratification, 'what hypocrites are those who now pretend, that mere '*moral restraint*' is, under prohibition to marry, of sufficient force to preserve the innocence of farmer's men and maids!'[172]

There was also the point that the imposition of moral restraint would virtually condemn the poor to live out their lives in an unmarried state. Dr Charles Hall supplied this argument:

> But who are the poor men that are to *wait before they marry*, and to *what time are they to wait*? I answer, that not this or that individual, but none of the labourers, or any of the common mechanics, can rear a family without the greater part of them perishing for want, *even with the interest of all the money they can possibly have saved during the time they are single.* – Are they, therefore, *never to marry?*[173]

The consequence, Cobbett argued, would destroy the very basis of existence:

> We all know that the greatest of all earthly blessings are found in the married state. Without woman, what is man? A poor, solitary, misanthropic creature; a rough, uncouth, a hard, unfeeling, and almost brutal being. Take from the heart the passion of love, and life is not worth having: youth has nothing to enjoy, and age nothing to remember with delight.[174]

Disastrous social consequences would follow given the passion between sexes outside of marriage. Babies born out of wedlock – 'love-children' as country girls called them – would produce a huge rise in illegitimacy and

deprive infants 'of the care and protection due from parents'.[175] Family
and community would be swept away in a flood of vice never imagined
by Malthus:

> No, adopt this impious doctrine, pass a law to put it in force, and all
> the bands of society are broken. Stigmatize marriage, and
> promiscuous intercourse is warranted and encouraged by law. To
> stay the current of the natural and amiable passions is to war against
> nature and against God. If the terms of the gratification be changed
> from the obligations of marriage to the voluntary offerings of
> affections or caprice, the indulgence can only be the more frequent
> and followed by effects more calamitous. From a community of
> fathers, mothers and families of children, this kingdom so long and
> so justly famed for kind husbands, virtuous wives, affectionate
> parents and dutiful children, will become one great brothel of
> unfeeling paramours, shameless prostitutes, and miserable homeless
> bastards.[176]

And all this for naught. The prevalent notion that checking improvident
marriages would cause a decline in the poor rates to farmers, thus easing
the burden of rent payments to landlords was totally misguided. The
prevalence of high taxes continued to ensure that their means of paying
rent would be severely curtailed.[177] Likewise, Cobbett maintained, moral
restraint imposed on the poor certainly would not solve the problem of
population increase that was a Malthusian illusion in the first place. In
any case, the entire solution was directed at the wrong class. It was the
idle and non-productive tax-eaters that constituted the real problem.

Malthus, of course, contended that voluntary moral restraint aimed at
reducing population growth would only be feasible under conditions of
strong negative and positive inducements for labourers to delay
marriage. With respect to the former, he recommended a gradual yet
total abolition of the Old Poor Law thus suspending outdoor relief,
especially in the form of allowances to children. He categorically denied
that the poor had any right to relief. Improvident labourers who married
early and could not support their offspring were thus doomed to starve
by the laws of nature. Fear of such consequences would encourage
prudential behaviour. From a positive perspective, he proposed state-
funded parish education to promote greater rationality, foresight and
independence. He also urged the poor to make greater use of Benefit
Clubs and Savings Banks to ensure adequate self-support in married life.
The poor, in short, were fully responsible for their own well-being.
Government was no longer under any obligation to provide a cushion
against destitution.[178]

As expected, Cobbett reacted vehemently to all such proposals,
devoting most of his energy to the issue of the Poor Laws. Although he
eventually adopted a passionate and unqualified stance in support of the

Old Poor Law, he was far from consistent on this issue. In his Tory phase he articulated Malthus's view that the Old Poor Law, and the allowance system in particular, 'humbled, debased, and enslaved' labourers, reducing them to paupers.[179] Even following his conversion to anti-Malthusian views in 1807 and his increasingly vocal defence of the right to relief after 1816 he remained highly critical of certain aspects of Poor Law policy. In July 1808 he claimed that allowances in aid of wages, for example, subjected labour to a state of dependency with the 'mind and character which belong to the pauper state'.[180] In September 1819 he argued that such relief was merely a method of lowering wages; especially for single men.[181] In the mid-1820s he veered more sharply towards a 'social control' view of the Old Poor Law. The original legislation of Elizabeth in 1601, he contended, was 'a measure of absolute necessity'. He further asserted: 'All the racks, all the law-martial of this cruel reign could not have kept down the people without this Act, the authors of which seem to have been ashamed to state the grounds of it, for it has no preamble whatever.'[182] In the late 1820s he attacked recent and degrading practices employed by parish authorities – the roundsman system, labour auctions and demeaning parish-sponsored work projects.[183]

By 1834, however, the tune had changed. The Old Poor Law was now 'that law, which has so long been the greatest glory of England.'[184] Referring to the people, he stated that

> an Act of Parliament was passed in the 43rd year of ELIZABETH, providing effectually for their relief, by parochial rates, and by the appointment of overseers to superintend the collection and distribution of those rates; and this law continued in force; and a happy and kind people lived under it for nearly two hundred years, till a 'reformed Parliament' met.[185]

Far from pauperizing, humiliating and controlling labour, poor relief (the allowance system included) became an exemplar of the moral economy in action where the higher orders benevolently recognized their obligations to satisfy the need for, indeed the right to, subsistence among their less fortunate brethren.

Ian Dyck quite rightly emphasizes that this absolute praise of the Old Poor Law at this juncture was a necessary strategy given the imminent passage of the New Poor Law – a measure which promised to end allowances without raising wages thus reducing labourers to even greater misery.[186] Yet Cobbett bestowed equally favourable epithets well before 1834. In 1821, for example, he referred to that 'wise, humane, and just code, called the poor-laws of England'.[187] In *The Poor Man's Friend*, first published in instalments in 1826 and 1827, he was far more effusive:

So good, so benignant, so wise, so foreseeing, and so effectual, is this, the very best of all our good old laws! This law, or rather code of laws, distinguishes England from all the other countries in the world, *except the United States of America*, where, while hundreds of other English statutes have been abolished, this law has always remained in full force, this great law of mercy and humanity, which says, that *no human being that treads English ground shall perish for want of food and raiment*. For such poor persons as are *unable to work* the law provides food and clothing; and it commands that *work* shall be provided for such as are able to work, and cannot *otherwise get employment*. This law was passed more than *two hundred years ago*.[188]

It is significant that both these statements were made in the context of threats to abolish the Old Poor Law. In 1821 James Scarlett had put forth a bill in the House of Commons to abolish relief to the able bodied. In *The Poor Man's Friend* Cobbett expressed his concern about the very survival of the Old Poor Law. He followed the lengthy passage quoted above with the following statement: 'Many attempts have been made to *chip it away*, and some have been made to destroy it altogether; but it still exists, and every man who does not wish to see general desolation take place, will do his best to cause it to be duly and conscientiously executed.'[189] Although often critical of and not totally consistent in his views on the Old Poor Law, he was clearly prepared to defend it without reservation against Malthusian assaults more than a decade prior to the Poor Law Amendment Act of 1834. He based his defence on the conviction that the poor had not only a moral but also a legal right to relief. From 1816 onwards (far earlier than some historians have thought) Cobbett consistently argued for this principle, developing increasingly more sophisticated arguments that culminated in perhaps his most lucid work entitled *Legacy to Labourers* in 1834.[190]

His basic premise was that poverty was not only inevitable in society but also necessary. 'That there shall be', he said, 'some poor; that some part of a populous community shall be *helpless*, whether from old age, infancy or infirmity, is the lot of mankind.'[191] Citing Scripture he claimed that 'the poor shall never cease from out of the land', adding that 'ailments', 'losses' and 'untoward circumstances of any sort' could create want, 'the impoverishing effects of which no human industry, care or foresight could have prevented'.[192]

Such misery, moreover, was essential to the functioning of society as a whole. The '*fear of poverty*', said Cobbett, 'was absolutely necessary … to induce men to perform all the various functions necessary to their support in civil society, and not less necessary to the existence of civil society itself.'[193] Such fear, furthermore, created 'the virtues of abstinence, sobriety, care, frugality, industry, and even honesty and amiable manners and acquirement of talent'.[194] In a God-given society based on inequality where some lived at ease and others laboured, extreme poverty would not only 'create industry' but also 'excite emulation' and the desire 'to get upwards in riches and fame'.[195]

Malthus no doubt would have agreed with such assumptions. He would certainly have disputed, however, the conclusions that Cobbett drew. If poverty was inevitable and necessary, Cobbett argued, then all who were indigent had a universal right to relief. In his *Address To Journeymen and Labourers* in 1816, he claimed that the 'unfortunate journeymen and labourers and their families have a *right*, they have a *just claim*, to relief from the purses of the rich.'[196] Later he asserted 'no man shall starve while there is food in the land.'[197] Even in the rare cases where the poor were to blame for their condition, they were entitled to such aid: 'Poverty is not a crime, and though it sometimes arises from faults, it is not, even in that case to be visited by punishment beyond that which it brings with itself.'[198]

Cobbett justified such claims by first appealing to the law of nature and the law of God. With regard to the former, he revoked Malthus's natural laws of population and political economy in favour of his own natural law of the right to subsistence. If Malthus argued that the poor had no place at nature's feast, Cobbett replied, to the contrary, that all labourers had a natural right 'to a sufficiency of food and raiment'. In his *Legacy to Labourers* (1834) he asserted: 'NATURAL JUSTICE, without any law either of God or man, would dictate to those who possess the necessaries of life, to give (if they have more than absolutely necessary to supply their own wants) some portion of them to prevent others from perishing.'[199] With typical exuberance he chastised Malthus's attitude towards the poor: 'He told us that for such persons "there was no seat at nature's board." Monster! did nature bid him, then, have a pension of a hundred pounds a year for doing nothing; and that pension too wrung from the sweat of the labouring people?'[200]

Scripture as well as nature sanctioned the right to relief. 'If the Priest', Cobbett asked in his sermon on *The Rights of the Poor* (1822), 'refer us to the Bible for proof of his claim to a share of the produce of the earth, shall not the poor also refer to the same Bible for proof of the justice of their claim?'[201] Later in this piece he commented: '*Obedience* and *fidelity* in servants God strictly enjoins, but the compensation for these is not to consist of garbage, rags and beds of straw: out of that which arises from his labour the servant is to share, not only in all things needful unto him, but in all the pleasures springing from the same source.'[202] In his *Legacy to Labourers* he cites lengthy passages from Deuteronomy, Isaiah and Job to illustrate the 'innumerable commands of God, to take care of the poor' and the 'most dreadful denunciations on those who withhold relief from the poor'. The laws of the medieval church, moreover, were in harmony with the laws of God: 'All the numerous religious establishments, abbeys, priories, friaries, nunneries, hospitals, and even the parish churches themselves, were founded in the name of, and dedicated to *"the service of God, and the care of the poor"*; and I defy all the MALTHUSES and BROUGHAMS upon the face of the earth to deny this fact.'[203]

The attack then proceeds to the very foundations of market economy. Malthus, of course, had argued that 'self-love' and not 'benevolence' would become, through the inevitable laws of nature, the guiding principle of society – 'the main-spring of the great machine'.[204] Cobbett countered with the notion of the moral economy. 'The labourer', he asserted 'is merely one of the links in the chain of society.' The rich were merely the 'more fortunate brethren of a numerous family' and should act 'justly, mildly and tenderly towards the poor'.[205] He despised, moreover, the notion of 'labour as an article of merchandise' to be purchased as cheaply in the market as possible: 'We are not justified, upon any principle of morality, to give less for anything than we ourselves believe the thing to be worth.' He reminded those who persisted in treating labour as a 'commodity' that the labourer had 'his right too; his rights of nature; his right to a sufficiency of food and of raiment'.[206] Cobbett prided himself on the example he set by showing 'mercy towards the poor' in his own economic practices.[207]

The right to relief, in addition, was legally sanctioned by the 'social compact', that agreement which all men accepted upon entering civil society. Cobbett neatly summarized the movement out of a state of nature – where no private property existed and only the law of self-preservation and self-enjoyment prevailed – in the following terms:

> In the process of time, no matter from what cause, men made amongst themselves a compact, or an agreement, to divide the land and its products in such a manner that each should have a share to his own exclusive use, and that each man should be protected in the exclusive enjoyment of his share by the united power of the rest; and, in order to insure the due and certain application of this united power, the whole of the people agreed to be bound by regulations, called laws. Thus arose civil society; thus arose property; thus arose the words mine and thine. One man became possessed of more good things than another, because he was more industrious, more skilful, more careful, or more frugal: so that labour, of one sort or another, was the basis of all property.[208]

Such laws, however, were designed to ensure '*the good of the whole*' and the 'mutual *benefit* and *protection* of all' and, given inherent inequalities, were premised on the assumption 'that no human being in the community was to be without the means of effectual relief in case of want.' It 'could not', said Cobbett, 'be a part of the social compact, that any part of the people then existing were to be bereft of food and of raiment and of the means of obtaining them by their labour.'[209]

This case did not rest on such general appeals to historical precedent. Indeed, he presented in great detail a history of England going back to the Conquest and beyond, arguing for a public commitment to the right of the poor to relief. In the process he radicalized historical discourse. The Norman Conquest, according to Cobbett, disrupted the natural transition from the state of nature to civil society by making the King 'as legal chief of the people ... the superior lord over all the estates in the kingdom'. It was in him that 'the ultimate property of all lands resides'. Holding the land in trust for the entire country, the monarch sat on the throne 'for the benefit of the whole nation' thus meeting the obligations of the social compact in securing the right to life and consequently the right to relief for all subjects.[210]

Drawing on the works of Blackstone and Coke, Cobbett further argued that landowners were thus tenants of the King. Although entitled to the use of such lands and the profits deriving from them, they by no means possessed absolute ownership or dominion over them. In particular, their access to such property had to be consistent with the well-being of society at large. 'All men', he insisted, 'hold their lands subject to such restraints with regard to the use of them, as are consistent with the good of the community at large.'[211] Therefore, landlords could not 'rightfully use the lands so as to cause the natives to perish of hunger or of cold'.[212] Even though the King had been deprived of his medieval services and revenues from the estates during the Cromwellian interregnum and the Restoration, he was still 'the lord paramount of them all' and Parliament could 'at any time pass an act to bring him back to the right of the former revenue out of them'.[213]

The legal right to relief, however, had even older roots in the pre-Norman era. The Bible, Cobbett argued, specified that tithes should be exacted on land, one-third of such revenue to provide for the relief of the destitute. These tithes in aid of the poor were retained after the Conquest and further legitimated by both canon and statute law. Monasteries 'were charged with a share of the maintenance of the poor and helpless' and also served as hospitals for the sick.[214] The Reformation, under Henry VIII, whereby all tithes and monastic lands were transferred to the King and doled out to individuals, constituted an outright 'robbery of the poor' and produced universal misery until passage of the Elizabethan Poor Law.[215] The provisions of this law, however, merely accorded to the poor what had always rightfully belonged to them:

> You will perceive, that this Act of Elizabeth provided no *gift* to the
> poor: it only gave them, in another shape, that which the Christian

religion, and the law of the land, had given them before: it only exacted from the land that which the land was charged with, at the time of the Norman conquest; and which, indeed, it had always been charged with, from the time that England was first called England. The *poor-rates* were no more than a *compensation* for what had been withheld from the people by the injustice of the Protestant clergy and the landlords: it was only giving them, under another name, under another form, and in another manner, that which they had before received out of the tithes, and out of the rents of the Abbey-lands, and to which they had a much older, and a much clearer title, than any man had, or has, to his landed estate.[216]

'The poor rates', as Himmelfarb points out, 'became what the tithes had been, a legal charge upon property, and poor relief became a legal charge upon property, and the poor law became a legal claim upon the rates. The poor law was thus a form of property, the property of the poor.'[217]

Cobbett, furthermore, drew on the works of 'great and wise men' – Blackstone, Paley, Hale and Montesquieu – to prove that the poor had a universal legal right to relief. In *Legacy to Labourers* he summed up his entire argument:

> Thus, then, according to the principles of natural justice, according to the practice of men, in a state of nature, and without any law whatever, either of God or of man, to guide them; according to the express and incessantly reiterated commands of God, in both the Testaments; and according to the laws of England, Canon-law, Common-law, Statute-law, laws made by Protestants, as well as laws made by Catholics, right to relief in the destitute is acknowledged; universally acknowledged; the practice upon this principle has been unvarying; and our Poor-law has really and truly been the glory of the country, and the admiration of the world.[218]

Given Cobbett's detailed justification for the right to relief, his venomous criticism of the New Poor Law is not in the least surprising. Indeed, in the last months of his life he fought almost single-mindedly to prevent the passage of the Poor Law Amendment Act and to revoke it once passed. Supporters of the Act argued that its intent was merely to return to the original principles of Elizabeth by removing abuses such as Speenhamland. Cobbett disagreed: what it signified was the wholesale denial of the right to relief and thus a complete violation of the ancient entitlements of the English people. Malthus and his disciples again came under intense attack. The 'monster Malthus', his chief disciple Lord Brougham and his hirelings such as 'Mother Martineau' had convinced the landlords of England to deny the legal right to relief and thus dispossess the poor.[219] The Whig government which introduced the New Poor Law, Cobbett labelled the 'coarser-food Ministry': a group of 'pensioned and sinecured reptiles' under the influence of Malthusian 'Scotch villains'.[220]

Cobbett, of course, was aware that the Poor Law Amendment Act did not deny relief entirely. Indoor relief in the workhouse, however, was tantamount to denying civil rights for the poor. John Locke had argued that condemning individuals to death or slavery was a denial of the basic right to life which no civil law could rescind since this would mean a return to the state of nature. Cobbett pointed out that the conditions under which relief was offered within the house did exactly that. In his *Legacy to Labourers* he stated his case:

> Thus, then, if the Government give power to Commissioners, to make it as 'IRKSOME' as possible to the destitute to obtain relief: if it be not to be obtained without close imprisonment in a workhouse, at a great distance from the house of the poor person; if the necessitous man be compelled to submit to wear a workhouse-dress; if he be wholly separated from his wife, night and day; if their children be wholly separated from them both; if they be cut off from all communication of every sort with friends outside of the prison; if no one can possibly come to claim their bodies, if they should die; and if, in case of death, a hired overseer, brought from a distance, have the power to dispose of their bodies for dissection: if all this be so, have we not before us the very case, which Mr LOCKE supposes; have we not before us that, which amounts to offering a man death or slavery?[221]

Cobbett, in addition, raised more pragmatic objections to the New Poor Law. He was totally sceptical of the evidence collected by the Poor Law commissioners in their *Rural and Town Queries* circulated throughout England in 1832, the replies to which supposedly confirmed the proposition that the Old Poor Law created the very poverty it set out to relieve. Cobbett, who examined the evidence in considerable detail, was the only contemporary who anticipated modern historians by arguing that the opinions expressed by 'gentlemen, noblemen, magistrates, clergy, experienced farmers and parish officers ... taken as a mass, are directly in the teeth of the opinions and recommendations of the poor-law fellows'.[222] In particular, he pointed out that of 1717 persons who agreed that agricultural capital was diminishing, only 159 blamed the Poor Laws or their administration for the decrease. Contrary to the contentions of the Poor Law commissioners, the poor rates were not ruining farmer and labourer alike. In fact there was 'no *real ground* for the passing of this bill'. [223] The Poor Law Amendment Bill, moreover, was rushed through the House of Commons and thus members had no time to read, let alone fully reflect, on the evidence even had they wished to do so.[224]

In addition, the centralized structure of the New Poor Law would subject 'thirteen thousand parishes to the absolute will of three commissioners, stuck up in London' with no restrictions on their powers of refusing relief.[225] And all this would 'screw' the labourers of England down to the level of the potato-eating Irish and ruin farmers, tradesman and mechanics alike! What the farmer saved in poor rates and wages would merely be transferred to landlords in the form of higher rents. The New Poor Law, Cobbett contended, was deliberately introduced for the benefit of the estate owners. With characteristic vigour he lashed out:

> All men are now satisfied that the object is, to lower rates, and, more particularly, to lower wages; and *to put the difference into the pockets of the landlords*. There is not a man in his senses who does not believe that the main object is this, and of course, to bring the English labourers down to live upon the base food, and to be clad in the miserable rags, which are the lot of the wretched people of Ireland, where a good and honest labourer, as good and as true as any in the world, works for sixpence a day, and sometimes for twopence. This is the object of the inventors of the scheme, or they must have been both drunk and mad at the same time, and both in an excessive degree.[226]

Passage of this legislation, Cobbett warned, would have even more dire consequences. Denial of the legal right to relief would mean an end to the social compact and a return to a state of nature where all duties and obligations to state and society would be nullified.

Cobbett developed this theory well before the more lucid presentation based on the civil rights of the poor in his *Legacy to Labourers*. In his address 'To PARSON MALTHUS' in 1819 he maintained:

> And, if a contingency arise, in which men, without the commission of any crime on their part, are unable, by moderate labour that they do perform, or are willing to perform, or by contributions from those who have food, to obtain food sufficient for themselves and their women and children, there is no longer *benefit* and *protection* to the whole; the social compact is at an end and men have a right, thenceforward, to act agreeably to the laws of nature.[227]

In *The Poor Man's Friend* he claimed that if 'society ... neglected to secure the legal means of preserving the life of the indigent and wretched; then the society itself, in so far as that wretched person was concerned, ceased to have a legal existence' and 'then the law of nature ... returns in its full force.'[228] He was convinced, of course, that ultimate responsibility for such a situation lay with Malthus and his disciples.

With the social compact dissolved, allegiance to sovereign and country would no longer exist, including the obligation to perform military service in defence of the realm or to pay taxes. In *Legacy to Labourers* Cobbett became incensed at the notion that labourers should be left to starve and at the same time be required to take up arms:

> However, the duty of rendering this service to the State must now rest upon the militia-man's claim, in case of need, to share in the fruits of the land; for, if that ground be wanting, how are we to

denominate the act of compelling him to perform such duty, on pain of suffering *flogging*, or *death*? What! tell him, in the words of MALTHUS and BROUGHAM (for BROUGHAM applauds all the sentiments of MALTHUS); tell him, that he has, in case of his utmost extremity, 'no claim upon the community for even the smallest portion of food;' and tell him, the next moment, that it is his duty to come forth and venture his life in defence of that community: tell him, that he has no claim whatsoever on the fruits of the land, even to save his life; and tell him, the next minute, that it is his duty to hazard that life in defence of that land!

Why, words are useless in such a case: the bare pronouncing of them makes the blood fry in one's veins: vengeful feelings rush forward and choke the voice of indignant abhorrence.[229]

Likewise, citizens would no longer be bound to pay taxes. The right of the state to tax was based on a recognition of the legal right of the poor to relief. 'This is the ground', he claimed, 'upon which you tax him; and what becomes of this ground if, in case of his hard necessity, you tender him '*a coarser sort of diet*', a workhouse dress, a cutting off from wife, children, and friends, and a dissection of his body at death; if, in short, your protection amounts, as Mr. Locke calls it, to an offer of death or slavery?'[230]

The most dangerous consequence, however, of the dissolution of the social compact and a return to the state of nature concerned the issue of property rights. If Malthus advocated that the poor be left to the '*punishment of nature*', Cobbett argued, they should also be '*rewarded by nature*'. [231] Far from being doomed to starve, as the 'audacious and merciless Malthus' recommended, the poor

> ... would ask nothing better than to be left to the law of nature; that law which knows nothing about buying food or anything else; that law which bids the hungry and the naked take food and raiment wherever you find it best and nearest at hand; that law which awards all possessions to the strongest; that law the operations of which would clear out the London meat-markets and the drapers and jewellers shops in about half an hour.[232]

In *The Poor Man's Friend*, Cobbett again employed detailed legal arguments to prove that the 'people would, according to the opinions of the greatest lawyers, have a right to take food and raiment sufficient to preserve them from perishing; and that such taking would be neither felony nor larceny' even if it took place against the will of individual property owners.[233]

Cobbett, of course, did not desire such an outcome. Until the actual passage of the Poor Law Amendment Act he held out hope that relief to the poor would be maintained. Neither had he advocated the use of violence in redressing the grievances of labourers. In *The Poor Man's Friend* he referred to the demise of property rights in the state of nature in the following terms:

> As long as our humane and excellent *Poor-Laws* shall be duly executed, we never can be exposed to this dreadful alternative; but, to hear what the law says on the subject, and to discuss that subject; these are necessary, in order to show the excellence of our own Poor-laws, to induce the people to appeal to and rely upon them, and to induce the Overseers and the Magistrates promptly to obey them, in order that, in the perilous times that are apparently approaching, we may, at any rate, avoid those violences, which must add to the misery already existing.[234]

Even after the Swing riots of 1830–31 he stated: 'In the whole body of the industrious and working people of England, there was scarcely a single man to be found, that had ever entertained the slightest thought of envying his richer neighbour, of wishing to share in his property, of wishing to see all men pulled down to a level.'[235]

Gertrude Himmelfarb maintains that Cobbett 'never wavered in this conviction'. Ian Dyck disagrees. He argues that the enactment of the New Poor Law in 1834 ended whatever trust Cobbett had placed in the English elite, erasing the last vertical tether in a horizontal rural society. This conclusion drove him to advocate a violent redistribution of property. Dyck cites a letter to John Oldfield, an old and trusted friend, written in June 1835, where Cobbett wrote: 'before the pressing of the Poor-Law Bill, I wished to avoid [a] convulsive termination. I now do not wish it to be avoided.' In April 1834 he wrote to John Fielden 'it is revolution all together.'[236]

Other public statements by Cobbett would appear to substantiate Dyck's conclusion. In the *Political Register* of 18 October 1834, for example, Cobbett angrily asserted that the 'Poor-law Bill has laid all bare; has ripped up every thing, and has given us but this one choice: JUSTICE to the industrious class by one means or another.' The Whig government, he claimed,

> could not have contrived anything to surpass this poor-law project, which in its very nature, *un-fixes the minds of all men with regard to the rights of property*; which rouses all the indignant, all the angry feelings of the millions of the community; and directs those feelings against those *orders which depend wholly* on *extraneous support*; which possess a showy power, but which have at bottom no power at all, if once it be disputed by the millions.[237]

In his *Legacy to Labourers* published in late 1834 Cobbett spoke in terms of class struggle:

> And, I shall now come to what is the main thing of all; that is to say,

to show, that, if you maintain that the poor have *no right*, no *legal right*, to relief, you loosen all the ligaments of property; and begin that career, which must end in a contest for property between the poor and the rich: you loosen all the bonds of allegiance; you get rid of all its duties; you proclaim that *might*, and not *right*, is to prevail; and, in short, you do all in your power to break up the social compact: to produce confusion; and to leave to chance a settlement anew.[238]

To be sure, Cobbett did urge that the New Poor Law be repealed 'while yet there be time' but admitted that he had not 'the smallest hope' of this coming to pass.[239]

Cobbett totally rejected Malthus's negative inducement to promote moral restraint and population control through abolition of the Old Poor Law. The parson's positive proposals regarding education and Savings Banks received the same treatment. Although not averse to teaching poor children to read, Cobbett argued there were more urgent priorities. 'The "expansion of the mind"', he said, 'is very well; but, really, the thing which presses most, at this time, is, the getting of something to expand the body a little more: a little more bread, bacon, and beer; and, when these are secured, a little "expansion of the mind" may do *vary weele*.'[240] Any such learning, however, must be based on *'true notions'*.[241] Government-sponsored educational schemes of the type Malthus advocated would merely distract the minds of labourers from the true causes of their poverty and lull them into a blind and passive acceptance of their misery. The tracts of the Society for the Diffusion of Useful Knowledge, supported by Lord Brougham, preached Malthusian lies.[242] It was on such grounds that Cobbett opposed the educational clauses in Whitbread's Bill of 1807 that advocated a national network of parish schools. Likewise, he fought the bill of 1833 that proposed government support for schools under the control of religious organizations.[243] The last thing Cobbett wanted labourers to learn was that they should seek their reward in the next world. The Bible clearly had more important lessons to teach.

Self-help schemes supposedly designed to render the poor independent also came under attack. Such *'wheedling* measures' – the Savings Banks, Parish Funds and Friendly Societies – answered no useful purpose. 'Indeed', he claimed, 'is it not monstrous, to talk of collecting *funds* from the *surplus* of a nation of *paupers*?'[244] He severely criticized George Rose's Act, passed in 1817, which established Savings Banks for labourers, the funds to be deposited with the Bank of England in order to reduce the National Debt. This Act, Cobbett contended, was merely a clever means of getting the poor to pay off the National Debt. Even more galling was the fact that George Rose and his son George Henry received pensions and sinecures amounting to nearly twelve thousand pounds a year from the public purse, a great part of this sum, Cobbett complained, paid by taxes on the labouring people.[245]

There was, of course, another possible solution to the problem of surplus population; namely, government-funded emigration. Cobbett, like some modern historians after him, misread Malthus on this issue. Although many supported such policies, Malthus himself never wholeheartedly considered emigration to be an adequate remedy for overpopulation simply because the places left vacant by those who departed would rapidly be filled up by increasing numbers of poor encouraged by the Old Poor Law to marry early and produce large families. He certainly rejected any form of compulsory emigration. Cobbett, as did many contemporary critics of Malthus, attributed to him ideas that he never espoused. In his *Rural Rides*, for example, he claimed to expose 'the folly, the stupidity, the inanity, the presumption, the insufferable emptiness and insolence and barbarity, of those numerous wretches who have now the audacity to propose to *transport* the people of England, upon the principle of the monster MALTHUS'.[246]

Both men opposed emigration although for very different reasons. Since no population increase had occurred in England, Cobbett argued, and since surplus population was therefore non-existent, schemes of emigration were completely unjustified. Besides, he contended, proposals to encourage labourers to emigrate to foreign countries were laden with the same class bias as was the advocacy of moral restraint. In his *Address To the Journeymen and Labourers* in 1816, Cobbett pointed out that no one ever proposed 'to *encourage* the Sinecure Placemen and Pensioners to emigrate; yet, surely, you who help to maintain them by the taxes which you pay, have as good a right to remain in the country as they have! You have fathers and mothers and sisters and brothers and children and friends as well as they.'[247] Indeed, by 1834, Cobbett was arguing, 'one of the great principles of natural justice is that every man has a right *to be* in the country where he was born.'[248]

Cobbett wrote *The Emigrant's Guide* in 1829 where he offered practical advice to those about to emigrate voluntarily and published a series of letters from emigrants to the United States who had bettered their lot. Cobbett did not demand that labourers abandon their rights or agree to forced emigration. He preferred that labourers remain in England but claimed that 'things have now taken that turn, and they present such a prospect for the future that I ... think it advisable for many good people to emigrate.' As Ian Dyck points out, Cobbett was at this stage by no means in favour of a violent uprising and 'thought it his duty to suggest alternative courses to insurrection, which by 1828 he knew to be imminent'.[249] Cobbett, however, continued to oppose government-directed schemes for emigration after 1829. In 1830, for example, he opposed Wilmot Horton's proposal to send 'English people to that miserable heap of rocks, called *Nova Scotia*!'.[250] He similarly opposed Lord Howick's Bill in 1831, which proposed mortgaging the poor rates to sponsor the emigration of English labourers to New South Wales.[251] In 1834 he opposed the appointment of commissioners under an Act to establish a new colony in Botany Bay.[252]

Given Cobbett's absolute rejection of Malthusian, or what he conceived to be Malthusian, remedies to the problem of poverty, and given his analysis of the root causes of such misery, his own solutions are predictable. In the 1820s Cobbett advocated repeal of '*the malt-tax*, and *those other taxes*, which take, even from the pauper, one half of what the parish gives him to keep the breath warm in his body'.[253] Such action in combination with the abolition of paper money would lower prices and thus increase the level of real wages. To be effective these measures had to be accompanied by a 'very large' reduction in the interest paid on the national debt.[254] This in turn could only be achieved by severe cuts in wasteful government expenditures: discharge of the standing army; abolition of all sinecures, places and pensions; elimination of relief to the poor clergy of England, Scotland and Ireland; withdrawal of grants to build roads and canals in Scotland, and the elimination of salaries to assistant overseers of the poor. He even opposed a grant to the British Museum, asking why working people's taxes should go to an institution open only between the hours of ten and three, and closed on Sundays, the sole day on which workers could use it.[255]

This economic solution, however, rested ultimately on parliamentary reform and, in particular, the extension of the franchise. In 1816 he proposed that every adult male who paid '*direct taxes*' should vote in annual elections. He did not exclude payers of indirect taxes (that is, consumer goods) lightly, but argued that only those who were formally assessed taxes and rates could be kept track of on voting lists.[256] By 1830 Cobbett, using the rule of consent embedded in the social compact, contended that no man should subject himself to rules and laws in the making of which he had no say. He now advocated universal adult male suffrage, excluding only criminals and the insane. As Himmelfarb points out, the implications of such a proposition were radical indeed, for Cobbett was asserting that even those males in receipt of poor relief were entitled to the franchise. The legal right to relief could not preclude other rights to which Englishmen were entitled–especially the right to vote.[257]

Following the passage of the New Poor Law in 1834 Cobbett no longer talked the language of political reform but rather the language of property redistribution. Prior to this date he was prepared to concede that although taxes on consumer goods needed to be abolished, a general tax payable on all property, personal as well as real, could be enacted to defray the interest on the national debt. Under the social compact where the people had a right, in case of need, to demand a share of the produce of the land, they too were bound 'to contribute from the fruit of their labour'. Abrogation of the Old Poor Law, however, absolved labourers of any such duty. The national debt now became 'a real, a bona fide, a tangible mortgage' on the estates of the landowners and thus their sole responsibility.[258] Failure to act on his proposed measures, Cobbett warned, would mean that 'the proprietorship of the land must change hands as if by an act of general confiscation, and a new granting of all the lands from the crown.'[259]

Significance and impact

The foregoing analysis reveals that Cobbett's critique of the 'parson' was far more than an emotional reaction based on a simple anti-Malthusianism. To be sure, Cobbett's violent outbursts tend to give such an impression. He often revealed an unparalleled personal animosity to individuals and groups, once angrily commenting that '*college* gentlemen ... always have ... the insolence to think themselves our *betters*', despite 'our superior talents'. All authors – 'Damn them' – are so 'full of college conceit ... that I would sooner have dealings with an old lecherous woman that would be tearing open my cod-piece fifty times a day!'[260] Many critics, perhaps deafened by such noise, have failed to recognize Cobbett's important contributions to political theory and so too have they misjudged the depth and seriousness of his attack on Malthus and underestimated the central place that Malthusian thought occupied in his overall analysis.[261] Malthus, of course, played no direct role in the passage of the New Poor Law. Cobbett was right, however, in perceiving that the core principles of the Poor Law Amendment Act were fundamentally Malthusian. If the denial of outdoor relief and reliance solely on workhouses shattered the social contract and drove men back to a state of nature, then Malthus and his followers were clearly to blame. Cobbett, perhaps more than any other individual, recognized that Malthus had shaped the entire debate on poverty in early nineteenth-century England. His shift, in the final analysis, to revolutionary radicalism cannot be explained, moreover, without reference to his anti-Malthusianism.

Cobbett brought a wealth of theoretical and empirical evidence to bear against Malthus. Although his arguments disputing the British census and his 'church capacity' thesis were dubious, other areas of his critique must carry greater weight. His close analysis of the evidence presented in the *Rural and Town Queries*, for example, exposed the shoddy basis upon which the Poor Law Commissioners of 1834 justified their conclusions. His proposition that denial of the legal right to relief violated the civil rights of the poor was a highly original adaptation of Lockean theory. His argument that the right of the poor to relief conferred the right to suffrage was equally original. In fact, such a right to those in receipt of relief was not granted in England until 1918.[262] Moreover, Cobbett, in his arguments against moral restraint, had seized on one of the central contradictions in Malthus. If 'the passions between the sexes is necessary and will remain nearly in its present state', as Malthus contended,[263] how could such a law of nature, asked Cobbett, simply be reversed by Poor Law policy or educational reform? If even educated priests found celibacy difficult, could one then expect the illiterate poor to engage in such behaviour? Cobbett was unaware of, or chose to ignore, the fact that Malthus had admitted as much. Indeed, his introduction of 'prudential restraint' – delay of marriage with occasional lapses into the vice of premarital intercourse – was an admission by Malthus that moral restraint was unfeasible. Cobbett, nevertheless, believed that such lapses would be far more than intermittent and would produce prostitution and illegitimacy on a vast scale.

Characteristically, Malthus never replied directly to Cobbett's criticisms. Although he never articulated why, it is probable that he lumped Cobbett with the critics he so denigrated in the Appendix to the 1806 edition of his *Essay*, those critics whose writings were 'so full of illiberal declamation, and so entirely destitute of argument, as to be evidently beneath notice'.[264] Or perhaps his comments regarding Godwin in 1825 were even more applicable to Cobbett:

> Since the last edition of this work was published an answer from Mr. Godwin has appeared, but the character of it both as to matter and manner is such that I am quite sure every candid and competent inquirer after truth will agree with me in thinking that it does not require a reply. To return abusive declamation in kind would be as unedifying to the reader as it would be disagreeable to me, and to argue seriously with one who denies the most glaring and best attested facts ... would evidently be quite vain with regard to the writer himself, and must be totally uncalled for by any of his readers whose authority could avail in the establishment of truth.[265]

Since he died on 29 December, 1834 Malthus probably did not see Cobbett's most important work, *Legacy to Labourers*, published just before.

That does not mean that one cannot, by inference, detect indirect references to his arch-enemy. In the 1817 edition of the *Essay*, Malthus did 'not hesitate to assert that, if the government and constitution of the country were in all other respects as perfect as the wildest visionary thinks he could make them, if parliaments were annual, suffrage universal, wars, taxes and pensions unknown, and the civil list fifteen hundred a year, the great body of the community might still be a collection of paupers.'[266] The Poor Laws, he argued, would continue to encourage rapid population growth thus creating greater misery for the poor. Later in the 1817 edition of his *Essay*, Malthus referred to the post-1815 depression and stated the following:

> But it must be allowed that full advantage has been taken by the popular orators and writers of a crisis that has given them so much power. Partly from ignorance, and partly from design, everything that could tend to enlighten the labouring classes as to the real nature of their situation, and encourage them to bear an unavoidable pressure with patience, has been either sedulously kept out of their view, or clamourously reprobated.[267]

The main issue is not whether or how Malthus replied to Cobbett. A close reading of his *Essay* makes it clear that he rejected all of Cobbett's arguments including the proposal for universal suffrage which Malthus claimed would result in 'a general disappointment of the people' and lead to every sort of experiment in government, till the career of change was stopped by a military despotism.'[268] What is important is the degree to which Cobbett influenced the labouring classes and fuelled discontent against Malthusian ideas. Malthus certainly thought that such 'popular' writers had great influence. That the lower orders, he said, 'should listen much more readily and willingly to those who confidently promise immediate relief, rather than to those who can only tell them unpalatable truths, is by no means surprising'.[269]

In 1819 Cobbett was certain he had made a substantial impact:

> When this Poor-Law Reform was begun, the design was to put in force the recommendations of PARSON MALTHUS; and, I verily believe, that, if I had never addressed the people on the subject, and explained to them the nature of their rights, and shewed them the cause of their poverty, we should long before now, have seen new laws for punishing bastardy, and laws, at the same time, to prevent marriage.[270]

Whether this was the case is no doubt debatable. By the early 1830s, however, it is clear that in spite of Cobbett's intense efforts to oppose the New Poor Law, in spite of the massive circulation of his works and in spite of the substantial influence his ideas had on the wider unstamped press, the tide of Malthusian thinking was moving irreversibly against him. Although he no doubt fuelled an increasing detestation of Malthus, such sentiments had minimal impact in the House of Commons. The New Poor Law was enacted with hardly a whimper of opposition. Lying on his deathbed in June 1835, Cobbett had lost his battle with the 'parson' who had died less than six months before. Ironically, the two arch-antagonists in the bitterly disputed transition to early capitalism had left the stage together.

Endnotes

1. William Cobbett, *Political Register* 34 (8 May 1819): 1019–21 (hereafter cited as *PR*).
2. Charles H. Kegel, 'William Cobbett and Malthusianism', *Journal of the History of Ideas* 19 (June 1958): 348 n. 3 (hereafter cited as 'Cobbett').
3. *PR* 35 (11 September 1819): 99; *PR* 47 (16 August 1823): 427; *PR* 72 (9 April 1831): 71, and *PR* 34 (8 May 1819): 1024. To gain a sense of why Cobbett despised 'parsons' to the degree he did, see *Legacy to Parsons: Cobbett's Legacy to Parsons; or, Have the Clergy of the Established Church an Equitable Right to the Tithes, or to Any Other Thing Called Church Property, Greater Than the Dissenters Have to the Same?* (London: William Cobbett 1835). Cobbett claimed that the Church of England was the only church in the world in which the poor were 'treated in a manner different from the rich' (114).
4. William Cobbett, *Cobbett's Legacy to Labourers; Or, What is the Right Which Lords, Baronets and Squires have to the Lands of England?*, 3rd edn. (London: William Cobbett, 1835), 121. Originally published in 1834 (hereafter cited as *Legacy to Labourers*); William Cobbett, *Advice to Young Men and (Incidentally) to Young Women in the Middle and Higher Ranks of Life* (London: Peter Davies, 1926), 320, para. 340. Originally published in 1830 (hereafter cited as *Advice*); *PR* 59 (16 September 1826): 740; William Cobbett, *Surplus Population: A Comedy in Three Acts*, *PR* 72 (28 May 1831): 509 (hereafter cited as *Surplus Population*); and *PR* 34 (8 May 1819): 1022.
5. William Cobbett, *A History of the Protestant 'Reformation' in England and Ireland* (London: R. and T. Washborne, 1900), para. 476. Originally published 1824–27 (hereafter cited as *Protestant Reformation*).
6. *PR* 34 (27 March 1819): 853; *PR* 59 (16 September 1826): 740; *PR* 72 (9 April 1831): 65 and 77.
7. Patricia James, *Population Malthus: His Life and Times* (London: Routledge and Kegan Paul, 1979). See the family tree of Malthus following p.xv (hereafter cited as *Malthus*).
8. Cited in *Cobbett in Ireland: A Warning to England*, ed. Dennis Knight (London: Lawrence and Wishart, 1984), 180 from *PR* (8 November 1834). Hereafter cited as *Cobbett In Ireland*. This work contains an excellent selection of articles Cobbett wrote for his *Political Register* while in Ireland during late 1834.
9. Ibid., 64 from *PR* (4 October 1834).
10. Ibid., 137 from *PR* (25 October 1834) and *PR* 59 (16 September 1826): 742–3.
11. Malthus claimed to be 'unmoved' by such accusations when based on ignorance or malice. When made by the MP Samuel Whitbread, however, he admitted to being pained by the fact. Whitbread he regarded as 'an enlightened and distinguished member of the British Senate'. See James, *Malthus*, 137.

12. *PR* 34 (8 May 1819): 1039 and Cobbett, *Legacy to Labourers*, 41.

13. *PR* 46 (12 April 1823): 69.

14. Knight, *Cobbett in Ireland*, 243 from *PR* (22 November 1834).

15. William Cobbett, *The Poor Man's Friend; or, Essays on the Rights and Duties of the Poor* (London: William Cobbett, 1829), para. 35. Originally published 1826–27 (hereafter cited as *Poor Man's Friend*). See also Cobbett, *Legacy to Labourers*, 132.

16. Gertrude Himmelfarb, *The Idea of Poverty: England in the Early Industrial Age* (London and Boston, MA: Faber and Faber, 1984), 225 (hereafter cited as *The Idea of Poverty*).

17. J. R. Poynter, *Society and Pauperism: English Ideas on Poor Relief, 1795–1834* (London: Routledge and Kegan Paul, 1969), 175–6 (hereafter cited as *Society and Pauperism*).

18. For an assessment of this debate see James P. Huzel, 'The Labourer and the Poor Law, 1750–1850' in *The Agrarian History of England and Wales 1750–1850*, vol. VI, ed. G. E. Mingay (Cambridge: Cambridge University Press, 1986), 755–810. See also George Boyer, *An Economic History of the English Poor Law 1750–1850* (Cambridge: Cambridge University Press, 1990). For Cobbett's use of this evidence that was published with the *Poor Law Report* of 1834 see Knight, *Cobbett in Ireland*, 136 from *PR* (25 October 1834) and Cobbett, *Legacy to Labourers*, 17–19.

19. Leonara Natrass, *William Cobbett: The Politics of Style* (Cambridge: Cambridge University Press, 1995), 158 (hereafter cited as *Cobbett*). For Cobbett's final statement on these issues see Cobbett, *Legacy to Labourers*.

20. Herman Ausubel, 'William Cobbett and Malthusianism', *Journal of the History of Ideas* 13 (1952): 250–56. (hereafter cited as 'Cobbett'). Ausubel, in addition, does not examine other important aspects of Cobbett's reaction to Malthusianism – emigration, the Corn Laws and education.

21. Kegel, 'Cobbett': 354–5.

22. Karl W. Schweizer and John W. Osborne, *Cobbett in His Times* (Leicester: Leicester University Press, 1990).

23. George Spater, *William Cobbett: The Poor Man's Friend*, 2 vols. (Cambridge: Cambridge University Press, 1982) (hereafter cited as *William Cobbett*) and Anthony Burton, *William Cobbett: Englishman: A Biography* (London: Aurum Press, 1997). Spater, however, does have a brief discussion of Cobbett and Malthus in an Appendix.

24. Ian Dyck, *William Cobbett and Rural Popular Culture* (Cambridge: Cambridge University Press, 1992) 209, 37 and 102–4 (hereafter cited as *Cobbett and Popular Culture*). See also Himmelfarb, *The Idea of Poverty*, 207–29. Himmelfarb does make frequent reference to Malthus in her chapter on Cobbett especially in the context of the New Poor Law, property rights and civil rights. She does not deal with many of the other criticisms Cobbett levelled at Malthus but this was not her purpose.

25. Ibid., 210.

26. For a discussion of Malthus's role in the New Poor Law see Chapter 1 above. For the argument that the New Poor Law was fundamentally Malthusian see Mitchell Dean, *The Constitution of Poverty: Toward a Genealogy of Liberal Governance* (London: Routledge, 1991), 104.

27. Dyck, *Cobbett and Popular Culture*, 208–9 and Himmelfarb, *The Idea of Poverty*, 212.

28.   *T. R. Malthus, An Essay on the Principle of Population: or a View of its past and present Effects on Human Happiness; with an inquiry into our Prospects, respecting the future Removal or Mitigation of the Evils which it occasions: The version published in 1803, with the variora of 1806, 1807, 1817, and 1826*, 2 vols, ed. Patricia James (Cambridge: Cambridge University Press, 1989), I: 374. His statement is contained in the 1803 edition (hereafter cited as *Malthus Variora).*

29.   Jon P. Klancher, *The Making of English Reading Audiences, 1790–1832* (Madison: The University of Wisconsin Press, 1987), 129 and 48 (hereafter cited as *English Reading Audiences).*

30.   Himmelfarb, *The Idea of Poverty*, 223 and 226.

31.   Patricia Hollis, *The Pauper Press: A Study in Working-Class Radicalism of the 1830s* (Oxford: Oxford University Press, 1970), 95 (hereafter cited as *Pauper Press*). Himmelfarb is right to stress that estimates of the sales of Cobbett's works are often based on Cobbett's own figures and therefore must be treated with caution. His sales, she contends, were nevertheless impressive. See Himmelfarb, *The Idea of Poverty*, 226. R. K. Webb is certain that 40,000–50,000 copies of the *Address to Journeymen and Labourers* were sold by the end of November 1816 (that is, within a month). See R. K. Webb, *The British Working Class Reader 1790–1848: Literacy and Social Tension* (London: George Allen and Unwin Ltd., 1955), 50 (hereafter cited as *Working Class Reader*). Richard D. Altick estimates 200,000 copies sold within two months. See Richard D. Altick, *The English Common Reader: A Social History of the Mass Reading Public 1800–1900* (Chicago, IL: The University of Chicago Press, 1957), 381 (hereafter cited as *Common Reader).*

32.   Klancher, *English Reading Audiences*, 101. Klancher assumes, of course, that there were multiple readers for each sale. Hollis suggests that the readership of radical papers 'far exceeded sales, perhaps by twenty times'. See Hollis, *Pauper Press,* 119. In addition, such publications were read aloud to the illiterate.

33.   Himmelfarb, *The Idea of Poverty*, 224. The Six Acts of 1819 tightened up the definition of a newspaper thus forcing many cheap radical papers 'either to conform to the requirements of a newspaper, carry a four penny stamp, and, like *The Times*, retail at sevenpence, or conform to the requirements of a pamphlet, and appear only monthly at an enlarged size or at a price above sixpence' thus raising the cost above what many of the working class could afford. See Hollis, *Pauper Press*, 97–8.

34.   Klancher, *English Reading Audiences*, 101.

35.   Cobbett's *Twelve Sermons* originally published in 1821–22 sold 211,000 copies by 1828. His *History of the Protestant Reformation* first issued in instalments between 1824 and 1827 sold 40,000 per number. A total of 700,000 copies of individual numbers had been issued by 1828. Such sales were comparable with the individual numbers sold of Dickens's *Pickwick Papers* (40,000 copies) and *Nicholas Nickleby* (50,000) in the late 1830s. See Altick, *Common Reader*, Appendix B, 381–2.

36.   Cobbett, *Poor Man's Friend*, para. 91.

37.   Cobbett, *Legacy to Labourers*, 9.

38.   Knight, *Cobbett in Ireland*, 45 from *PR* (22 September 1834).

39.   Dyck, *Cobbett and Popular Culture*, 170.

40.   Ibid., 169. Cobbett revived *Two-Penny Trash* in July 1830.

41. Ibid. See also Spater, *William Cobbett*, 2: 476–81 for details of Cobbett's trial. A hung jury led to Cobbett walking away a free man.

42. Dyck, *Cobbett and Popular Culture*, 167–8.

43. Ibid., 103. The play, however, was performed in Cobbett's own parish of Ash in Surrey on 27 March 1835 prior to being banned. In the same year Cobbett republished the play as *Surplus Population and the Poor Law Bill*. Cobbett also anticipated writing another play entitled *Bastards in High Life*. See Spater, *William Cobbett*, 2: 602 n. 4 and *PR* 88 (6 June 1835): 592–7.

44. Martineau's *Illustrations of Political Economy* (1832–34) sold 10,000 copies per month. Cobbett's *Political Register* in 1829 had a circulation of about 3,400 per week (about 13,600 a month). The estimate by Spater is based on the number of newspaper stamps purchased and more than likely underestimates total circulation. In the eighteen months ending in June 30, 1833, 1600 copies per week of the *PR* were sold but again this is an underestimate. See Spater, 2: 617 n. 54.

45. Hollis, *Pauper Press*, 203.

46. Himmelfarb, *The Idea of Poverty*, 212 n.

47. Dyck, *Cobbett and Popular Culture*, 103. See *PR* (11 June 1831): 650–51.

48. Ausubel, 'Cobbett': 250–51, cited from *PR* (16 February 1805). See also *PR* 6 (8 December 1804): 878 where Cobbett assents to the Malthusian principle of 'want and misery without which population never is or can be checked'.

49. Ausubel, 'Cobbett': 251, cited from *PR* (18 January 1806) See also *PR* 6 (8 December 1804): 869 where Cobbett agrees with Malthus that population tends to increase faster than the food supply.

50. George Spater argues that Cobbett's conversion to reform was as rapid as his previous shift in 1792 from Tom Paine to reactionary anti-Jacobinism. Himmelfarb and Kegel also contend that such a conversion took place in 1806–07. Dyck, however, claims that Cobbett's 'arrival at radicalism was a slow and painstaking process that simply cannot be characterized as opportunistic or arbitrary'. This change was rooted in a set of experiences of which the Poor Law was only one, albeit an important one, among others such as popular rural sports, the Napoleonic invasion fright and the common land of Hampshire. See Spater, *William Cobbett*, 1: 195, Himmelfarb, *The Idea of Poverty*, 209; Kegel, 'Cobbett': 350 n. 11; and Dyck, *Cobbett and Popular Culture*, 19–20.

51. *PR* 39 (19 May 1821): 437.

52. See Ausubel, 'Cobbett': 251, Poynter, *Society and Pauperism*, 210–11; and Dyck, *Cobbett and Popular Culture*, 36–7.

53. Cited in Dyck, *Cobbett and Popular Culture*, 37.

54. *PR* 11 (14 March 1807): 397. For Hazlitt's other two letters see *PR* 11 (16 May 1807): 883–95 and *PR* 11 (23 May 1807): 935–42. These letters eventually led to Hazlitt's book – *Reply to the Essay on Population* (1807).

55. See Ausubel, 'Cobbett': 251 and *PR* (21 March 1807).

56. Charles Kegel, although he does not mention Whitbread's Bill as a factor in Cobbett's conversion, suggests that Cobbett's reading of William Spence's *Britain Independent of Commerce* was an important influence. Kegel states: 'Spence argued that agrarian prosperity was the only solid base for the nation's economy and that the new commercial and factory

interests were in direct conflict with agrarianism. Poverty was caused not by the inability of the farmer to produce necessary subsistence from the soil, but by the disproportionate number of non-farmers, which the new commercial economy had called into being.' So excited did Cobbett become about this argument that he published several articles on it in the *PR*. See Kegel, 'Cobbett': 350 n. 11.

57.   *PR* 13 (23 April 1808): 646.
58.   Cobbett, *Surplus Population*, 494–95. Squire Thimble was most likely an amalgam of Malthus and the pro-Malthusian Francis Place. Cobbett detested Place for circulating handbills advocating contraception within marriage. See Peter Fryer, *The Birth Controllers* (London: Secker and Warburg, 1965), 81. See also Spater, *William Cobbett*, 2: 602 n. 4.
59.   Ibid., 498.
60.   *PR* 51 (3 July 1824): 22 and *PR* 52 (16 October 1824): 144. See also Cobbett, *Surplus Population*, 498 where Farmer Stiles says to Squire Thimble that 'God never sends mouths without sending meat.'
61.   *PR* 59 (16 September 1826): Cobbett's tours through rural England were first published in instalments in his *Political Register* and later as *Rural Rides* (London: William Cobbett, 1830). The edition used in this work is *Rural Rides*, ed. George Woodcock (Harmondsworth: Penguin Books, 1967).
62.   *PR* 72 (9 April 1831): 72–3. Cobbett also gives ratios for Devon, Lincoln, Norfolk and Kent.
63.   *PR* 50 (26 June 1824): 799.
64.   *PR* 46 (12 April 1823): 70. See also *PR* 50 (26 June 1824): 801–802.
65.   Cobbett, *Surplus Population*, 494.
66.   *PR* 51 (3 July 1824): 2 and 14–15.
67.   *PR* 50 (26 June 1824): 799. Malthus argued that the cause of early marriage and population increase in Ireland was reliance on the potato as the staple crop. See James, *Malthus Variora*, I: 291–7 from the 1803 *Essay*.
68.   The argument was first made in Cobbett's second address 'To Parson Malthus' in *PR* 46 (12 April 1823): 93.
69.   *PR* 69 (13 March 1830): 350 and *PR* 49 (14 February 1824) 398–9.
70.   *PR* 49 (14 February 1824): 399–400.
71.   See Cobbett's piece entitled 'MOST GLORIOUS LIE' in *PR* 69 (13 March 1830): 349. George Spater and Charles H. Kegel make only brief reference to Cobbett's arguments on population. Ausubel makes no reference at all.
72.   See *PR* 46 (12 April 1823): 72 for Cobbett's admission of regional population increase. The great Wen of London also comprised the surrounding counties of Kent, Berkshire, Surrey and Hampshire.
73.   Spater, *William Cobbett*, 2: 442.
74.   *PR* 34 (8 May 1819): 1044–7 and *PR* 46 (12 April 1823): 104–13. See also *PR* 52 (16 October 1824): 129–37.
75.   *PR* 46 (12 April 1823): 101.
76.   The quotation is from *PR* 34 (8 May 1819): 1047. For Cobbett's detailed arguments against the validity of the census returns see n. 74 above. Cobbett's arguments are confusing because he attempts to relate the number of *persons* in each category in 1801 with the number of *families* in 1811 (my emphasis) to calculate estimates of family size in each group. The figures he arrives at, he concludes, are ludicrous – for example, a family size of 2.3 for the labouring and trading classes including lodgers in

1811. He does not distinguish between family and household size. In addition, his calculations relating *persons* in 1801 to *families* in 1811 do not take into account changes from 1801 to 1811 in how each occupational category was defined. Cobbett, however, was right to question the accuracy of the census returns. Malthus, contrary to Cobbett, concluded that the Censuses of 1801, 1811 and 1821 underestimated the population. See James, *Malthus Variora*, I: 276–80 from the 1826 edition of Malthus's *Essay*. For modern discussion of census accuracy see E. A. Wrigley and R. S. Schofield, *The Population History of England and Wales 1541-1871: A Reconstruction* (Cambridge, MA: Harvard University Press, 1981). They conclude that the 1801 population was an overestimate although not significant. The many errors in the early English censuses, they argue, tended to cancel one another out (126). For their English population totals see Table 7.8, 208–209 (hereafter cited as *Population History*).

77. *PR* 46 (12 April 1823): 112.
78. *PR* 52 (16 October 1824): 137.
79. *PR* 49 (7 February 1824): 338. Cobbett purchased Botley House in 1805 and farmed in the parish of Botley until his 1817 departure for America.
80. *PR* 49 (14 February 1824): 400.
81. *PR* 49 (7 February 1824): 338–42. In this piece Cobbett was addressing the King's Speech given on 3 February 1824 which he criticized for elevating the manufacturing and commercial interest above that of agriculture. *The Morning Chronicle* newspaper had utilized the 1821 Census to prove this. For Cobbett's bias against commerce and manufacturing and his support for agriculture see Dyck, *Cobbett and Popular Culture*, 48–9, 51–3, and 199–200. Malthus, before 1817, ironically shared Cobbett's bias but for very different reasons.
82. *PR* 49 (14 February 1824): 402. Cobbett had been feuding with the Revd Baker since 1807 and had been attacked by him in the letter to *The Times* referred to in the text below. See Spater, *William Cobbett*, 2: 358–9. Thus Cobbett's attack on Revd Baker clearly bears the imprint of a personal vendetta.
83. *PR* 49 (7 February 1824): 341 and *PR* 49 (14 February 1824): 401–408. For another argument Cobbett used in denying population increase see *PR* 72 (9 April 1831): 72 where he uses census figures from 1821 to calculate the average size of parishes. Of 11,703 parishes in England and Wales he calculated that 300 had an average population of less than 150 persons.
84. *PR* 69 (13 March 1830): 350–52. Hume had written *Of the Populousness of Antient Nations* in 1764. Cobbett based his estimates for the higher orders on Spellman writing 'early in the reign of James I'. He does not, however, provide sources for his detailed estimates of adult males in the lower status groups. See also *PR* 72 (9 April 1831): 64 where Cobbett repeats this argument. Cobbett was right in this case. Wrigley and Schofield, *Population History*, 209 give a population total for England in 1601 of 4,109,981.
85. Cobbett, *Protestant Reformation*, 376–7, para. 453. See also Kegel, 'Cobbett': 353. Wrigley and Scholfield accept J. C. Russell's 1948 estimate of a population total for England and Wales in 1377 of 2,232,000. See Wrigley and Schofield, *Population History*, 566. George Chalmer's estimate that Cobbett disputed was thus quite close to modern estimates.

86. *PR* 46 (12 April 1823): 72–92. This second address to Malthus has been rarely used by historians.
87. Ibid., 72–3.
88. Ibid., 73. See also 74 where he presents similar evidence for Wiltshire.
89. Kegel, 'Cobbett': 353 n. 28 from *Rural Rides*.
90. Ibid., 353 from Cobbett's *Protestant Reformation*.
91. *PR* 52 (16 October 1824): 141.
92. *PR* 59 (16 September 1826): 731.
93. Kegel, 'Cobbett': 353. See also Cobbett, *Protestant Reformation*, 375–6, para. 453 and Cobbett, *Advice*, 56–7, para. 52.
94. Cobbett, *Surplus Population*, 499. Cobbett's church capacity argument fails, of course, to take account of the rise of non-conformity, internal migration and the rise of 'open' parishes.
95. *PR* 72 (9 April 1831): 72–3. The list given here is a good summary by Cobbett of his arguments on population.
96. *PR* 59 (16 September 1826): 732.
97. *PR* 46 (12 April 1823): 80.
98. Cobbett, *Protestant Reformation*, 376 para. 451.
99. Cobbett, *Advice*, 321 para. 341.
100. Cobbett, *Poor Man's Friend*, para. 37.
101. *PR* 41 (2 March 1822): 548.
102. William Cobbett, 'The Rights of the Poor' in William Cobbett, *Twelve Sermons* (London: William Cobbett, 1828), 74 (hereafter cited as 'Rights of the Poor'). The *Sermons* were originally published in 1821–22. The new edition of 1828 was used in this study.
103. *PR* 49 (14 February 1824): 393.
104. *PR* 34 (8 May 1819): 1040–41.
105. *PR* 35 (11 September 1819): 116.
106. Knight, *Cobbett in Ireland*, 46 from *PR* (22 September 1834) and Ibid., 93 from *PR* (18 October 1834). See also Cobbett, *Protestant Reformation*, 275, para.334.
107. *PR* 49 (14 February 1824): 389 and 392. *The Times* published the article on 31 January 1824.
108. *PR* 39 (19 May 1821): 450–51. The basket of commodities comprised in each year: flour, bread, bacon, butcher's meat, cheese, malt, butter, sugar, soap, candles and shoes. See also Cobbett, *Protestant Reformation*, 399, para. 475 where he refers to 'the giving of low wages compared with the price of food and raiment'. See also Dyck, *Cobbett and Popular Culture*, 29–30 and 34–5.
109. *PR* 31 (2 November 1816): 564. See also Spater, *William Cobbett*, 2: 340, 342–3.
110. Cobbett, *Poor Man's Friend*, para. 39.
111. *PR* 32 (4 January 1817): 23. See also *PR* 41 (2 February 1822): 283 where Cobbett estimated that two-fifths to one-half of wages went to taxes on consumer goods. Spater suggests taxes on a farm labouring income for a man and wife earning £20 to £30 yearly amounted to £8. See Spater, *William Cobbett*, 2: 411. Thus Cobbett probably exaggerated the proportion paid in taxes.
112. For Cobbett's complete list of items taxed see *PR* 31 (2 November 1816): 561–2.
113. Cobbett, *Legacy to Labourers*, 15–16. Cobbett earlier maintained that

overall taxes collected had increased from 16 million pounds in 1792 to 53 million pounds in 1822. See *PR* 41 (2 February 1822): 283. Spater estimates 17 million pounds in 1790 increasing to 58 million in 1821. The largest item of cost, he contends, was the interest on the debt amounting to 32 million pounds (or 55%) in 1821. See Spater, *William Cobbett*, 2: 410. Thus Cobbett's estimates most likely were not far off.

114.   *PR* 41 (2 March 1822): 548.
115.   Cobbett, *Legacy to Labourers*, 12–13. Cobbett presented the following table:

	Poor Rates £	Govt. Taxes £
Reign of James II	160,000	1,300,000
1776	1,496,906	8,000,000
1789	2,250,000	16,000,000
1833	6,700,000	52,000,000

116.   *PR* 41 (2 March 1822): 548. Farmers, Cobbett pointed out, were also being ruined by low prices. Low prices, however, did not benefit labourers because of high taxation. See Knight, *Cobbett in Ireland*, 232 from *PR* (18 October 1834).
117.   *PR* 32 (4 January 1817): 27.
118.   William Cobbett, *The Emigrant's Guide: in Ten Letters*, new edn, (London: William Cobbett, 1830), 14, para. 6. This work was originally published in 1829 (hereafter cited as *Emigrant's Guide*). See also *PR* 46 (12 April 1823): 66.
119.   For Cobbett's discussion of these issues see *PR* 39 (19 May 1821): 464 and 467; Cobbett, *Emigrant's Guide*, 14–15, para. 6; *PR* 41 (2 March 1822): 549; and Knight, *Cobbett in Ireland*, 232 from *PR* (22 November 1834). See also Spater, *William Cobbett*, 2: 410–13.
120.   Spater, *William Cobbett*, 2: 340 and 413. Spater contends that Cobbett firmly believed that the debt was too large to be paid off. Financial failure would result, leading eventually to parliamentary reform, ibid., 2: 413–14.
121.   *PR* 47 (16 August 1823): 424–5. Spater estimates the wars against Napoleon cost England more than £1,000 million. He comments: 'And what, Cobbett asked, had been accomplished for these millions of pounds and the thousands of lives that had been lost? The Bourbon dynasty – always hated in England, and one of the most tyrannous and corrupt in Europe – had been restored.' Spater, *William Cobbett*, 2: 340.
122.   *PR* 47 (16 August 1823): 425.
123.   *PR* 39 (19 May 1821): 465. See also *PR* 42 (8 June 1822): 590 where Cobbett also objected to expenditure on military academies, barracks, arsenals and depots.
124.   Cobbett, *Protestant Reformation*, 94, para. 127.
125.   Knight, *Cobbett in Ireland*, 103 from *PR* (18 October 1834). See also Ausubel, 'Cobbett': 252. Cobbett, in fact, underestimated the value of Malthus's living at Walesby. Patricia James values it at £300 per annum rising to £440 per annum by 1831. Malthus held the living from 1803 until his death in 1834. Out of this income Malthus, being non-resident, paid a curate £70 to £80 per annum, See James, *Malthus*, 102.
126.   Cobbett, *Protestant Reformation*, 94, para. 127; Cobbett, *Emigrant's Guide*, 9, para. 3; and Knight, *Cobbett in Ireland*, 102 from *PR* (18 October 1834).

127. *PR* 47 (16 August 1823): 426.
128. Cobbett, *Emigrant's Guide*, 12, para. 3.
129. Knight, *Cobbett in Ireland*, 102 from *PR* (18 October 1834); Cobbett, *Legacy to Labourers*, 14; and *PR* 47 (16 August 1823): 426.
130. *PR* 52 (16 October 1824): 149 and 147. Cobbett later cheered on the Otmoor fence – throwers in the fight against enclosure of their commons. See Dyck, *Cobbett and Popular Culture*, 155.
131. Ibid., 188.
132. For Cobbett's opposition to the Corn Laws see Cobbett, *Poor Man's Friend*, para. 128; Dyck, *Cobbett and Popular Culture*, 68; and Spater, *William Cobbett*, 2: 412. Cobbett also viewed the Settlement Laws and the Combination Acts as contributors to poverty. See Spater, *William Cobbett*, 2: 541 and Dyck, *Cobbett and Popular Culture*, 130 respectively.
133. Cobbett, *Emigrant's Guide*, 7–8, para. 3. See also Dyck, *Cobbett and Popular Culture*, 12 for Cobbett's theory of exploitation and the labour theory of value. For the degree to which the distinction between town and country cut across class analysis in Cobbett's ideology see Dyck's discussion in ibid., 47.
134. Cobbett, *Emigrant's Guide*, 7, para. 3.
135. Cobbett, 'Rights of the Poor': 84–5. Dyck argues that Cobbett's vertical perspective on rural society began to crumble gradually from 1807–08 onwards. See Dyck, *Cobbett and Popular Culture*, 60.
136. *PR* 59 (16 September 1826): 735.
137. Ibid., 734.
138. Kegel, 'Cobbett': 355–6. Kegel claims that Cobbett, as the father of fourteen children, 'was well aware of the humour implicit in the moral restraint concept.' (356). In fact, Cobbett was very serious in his attacks on this Malthusian idea.
139. *PR* 72 (9 April 1831): 71.
140. *PR* 32 (4 January 1817): 26 and 24.
141. Cobbett, *Poor Man's Friend*, para. 89.
142. Cited in Kegel, 'Cobbett': 355.
143. *PR* 31 (2 November 1816): 562–3. Jonathan Swift's *Modest Proposal for Preventing the Children of Poor People from being a Burden to their Parents or the Country* (1729) satirically proposed that Irish babies should be fattened until they were a year old to make food for the rich. He offered culinary suggestions as to how they might best be served up. See James, *Malthus*, 454–5.
144. Cobbett, *Surplus Population*, 496. Malthus, of course, never suggested killing off the population and he opposed infanticide.
145. *PR* 39 (19 May 1821): 477. Malthus, of course, never advocated such procedures.
146. *PR* 32 (4 January 1817): 27.
147. See Kegel, 'Cobbett': 354 and 356 where he accepts without qualification that Malthus advocated premature and improvident marriages be prohibited by law and that he accepted birth control.
148. Cobbett, *Surplus Population*, 496.
149. William Cobbett, 'The Sin of Forbidding Marriage' in William Cobbett, *Twelve Sermons* (London: William Cobbett, 1828), 199 (hereafter cited as 'Marriage').

150. James, *Malthus Variora*, II: 140 from the 1803 *Essay*.
151. Cobbett, *Surplus Population*, 503. See also Kegel, 'Cobbett': 356. Francis Place, however, did advocate birth control within marriage. Thus Cobbett did not misread Place on this issue.
152. Ibid., 505.
153. *PR* 52 (16 October 1824): 151 and *PR* 59 (16 September 1826): 741.
154. *PR* 72 (9 April 1831): 73 and Cobbett, 'Marriage': 201.
155. *PR* 31 (2 November 1816): 564 and *PR* 47 (16 August 1823): 427.
156. *PR* 32 (4 January 1817): 30. Cobbett also argued that rather than restrict the population of one particular class it might be more advisable to impose moral restraint upon harsh and cruel individuals who, by producing 'their like', endangered the 'hearts and minds and souls of a whole community.' See Cobbett, 'Marriage': 208.
157. Ibid., 199 and 208.
158. *PR* 32 (4 January 1817): 29.
159. Ibid., 29.
160. *PR* 31 (2 November 1816): 563 and *PR* 34 (8 May 1819): 1024–5.
161. Cobbett, 'Marriage': 203. Dyck aptly describes Cobbett as a 'sexual populist'. It should be remembered, however, that Cobbett, of course, never sanctioned premarital intercourse or birth control. See Dyck, *Cobbett and Popular Culture*, 103.
162. Cobbett, *Advice*, 94, para. 86; and 92, para. 84.
163. Cobbett, *Surplus Population*, 495.
164. Cobbett, *Advice*, 92, para. 84.
165. Ibid., 93, para. 85.
166. Ibid., 139, para. 137; 96, para. 89; and 95, para. 95. Cobbett used the terms 'love' and 'affection' interchangeably. In addition to beauty, the other ideal qualities of a wife were chastity, sobriety, industry, frugality, cleanliness, knowledge of domestic affairs and good temper. As Leonore Natrass points out Cobbett advised male labourers to choose a 'sober girl in the country sense of the word, meaning steadiness, seriousness, carefulness, scrupulous propriety of conduct', Natrass, *Cobbett*, 189. Thus Cobbett did not advocate marriages based merely on blind passion. Delaying marriage for purely economic reasons, however, was totally unjustified.
167. Cobbett, *Advice*, 175, para. 179.
168. Ibid., 175, paras. 179 and 180.
169. Cobbett, *Surplus Population*, 501.
170. *PR* 39 (19 May 1821): 477. James Scarlett, MP, later Lord Abinger, introduced bills to abolish the Old Poor Law in 1821 and 1822.
171. *PR* 72 (9 April 1831): 79. Ian Dyck has pointed out to me that Cobbett disdained the 'culture of restraint', quite apart from its demographic consequences. 'He deplored', comments Dyck, 'moderation in all aspects of living (and even for that matter in his politics, as revealed when he asked so-called "moderate reformers" whether they would like "moderate chastity" in their wives'. Correspondence from Ian Dyck, 12 May 1998.
172. Cobbett, 'Marriage': 211–12. Again, I should stress that Cobbett clearly had not read Malthus thoroughly enough or chose not to recognize the latter's concept of 'prudential restraint' – delay of marriage with lapses in abstinence. Malthus admitted that this would be a more realistic scenario. See Chapter 1.

173. *PR* 32 (4 January 1817): 28. Cobbett was citing Charles Hall, *The Effects of Civilization on the People* (1805).

174. Cobbett, 'Marriage': 200.

175. *PR* 39 (19 May 1821): 477 and Cobbett, 'Marriage': 201.

176. Cobbett, 'Marriage': 212.

177. *PR* 41 (2 March 1822): 548.

178. See Chapter 1.

179. Quoted by Himmelfarb, *The Idea of Poverty*, 218 from *PR* (8 February 1806).

180. Ibid., from *PR* (16 July 1808).

181. *PR* 35 (11 September 1819): See also Spater, *William Cobbett*, 1: 200 for Cobbett's claim that the Speenhamland system lowered wages.

182. Cobbett, *Protestant Reformation*, 397, para. 472.

183. See Cobbett, *Emigrant's Guide*, 10–12, para. 3. Cobbett drew on a report from a Committee on the Poor Laws presented to the House of Commons in 1828. Under the roundsman system labourers would have to do the rounds of farmers to seek work before receiving allowances.

184. Knight, *Cobbett in Ireland*, 46 from *PR* (27 September 1834).

185. Cobbett, *Legacy to Labourers*, 115. See also Cobbett, *Poor Man's Friend*, para. 52 where he contends that the Act of Elizabeth represented 'benevolence towards the people'.

186. Dyck, *Cobbett and Popular Culture*, 205. See also Himmelfarb, *The Idea of Poverty*, 218 where she suggests Cobbett became a 'great defender of the old poor law' only in the early 1830s.

187. *PR* 39 (19 May 1821): 471.

188. Cobbett, *Poor Man's Friend*, para. 43.

189. Ibid.

190. See Himmelfarb, *The Idea of Poverty*, 218 where she cites Cobbett's *Advice* (1830) implying that Cobbett's notion of the right to relief originated in the early 1830s.

191. *PR* 34 (27 March 1819): 844. See also Cobbett, *Protestant Reformation*, 271, para. 331 and Cobbett, *Poor Man's Friend*, para. 90.

192. Cobbett, *Advice,* 322–3, para. 342 and Cobbett, 'Rights of the Poor': 71.

193. Cobbett, 'Rights of the Poor': 70.

194. Cobbett, *Advice*, 323, para. 343.

195. Cobbett, 'Marriage': 204; Cobbett, *Legacy to Labourers*, 102; and Cobbett, *Advice*, 323, para. 343. See also Cobbett, *Advice,* 333, para. 353 where he argues that God created inequalities of talent, industry, perseverance and the capacity to labour.

196. *PR* 31 (2 November 1816): 560. See also Cobbett, 'Marriage': 201. Malthus, although he never addressed Cobbett directly, argued that relief destroyed the very virtues Cobbett was trying to promote.

197. Cobbett, *Poor Man's Friend*, para. 34.

198. Cobbett, *Advice,* 322, para. 342. But see Cobbett, 'Marriage': 203 where he argues that relief be given only in case of '*unavoidable* misfortune' (my emphasis). Cobbett appears to have changed his mind by 1830.

199. Cobbett, *Legacy to Labourers*, 100. See also Cobbett, 'Rights of the Poor': 89 and Himmelfarb, *The Idea of Poverty*, 210.

200. Knight, *Cobbett in Ireland*, 103 from *PR* (18 October 1834).

201. Cobbett, 'Rights of the Poor': 80.

202. Ibid., 92.

203. Cobbett, *Legacy to Labourers*, 102, 104, and 109.
204. *An Essay on the Principle of Population: Thomas Robert Malthus*, ed. Philip Appleman (New York: W.W. Norton, 1976), 75 from the 1798 *Essay*.
205. Cobbett, 'Rights of the Poor': 84 and 82. Cobbett also argued that such behaviour would be in the interest of the wealthier members of society in preventing disturbances among the lower orders.
206. Ibid., 88–89.
207. Cobbett, *Advice*, 165, para. 170. Cobbett was justified in making this claim. As Dyck points out, he paid his labourers wages at 20 per cent above the average rates in his district and provided them with sickness benefits and allowances in old age. He also paid substantial amounts in poor rates, none of which went to his own workers. See Dyck, *Cobbett and Popular Culture*, 139.
208. Cobbett, *Advice*, 315, para. 333.
209. *PR* 39 (19 May 1821): 444; *PR* 34 (8 May 1819): 1028; Cobbett, 'Rights of the Poor': 77, and Cobbett, 'Marriage': 201–202.
210. Cobbett, *Legacy to Labourers*, 67–8. See also Himmelfarb, *The Idea of Poverty*, 210–11 for an excellent summation of Cobbett's historical argument. For his radicalization of historical discourse see Natrass, *Cobbett*, 158.
211. Cobbett, *Legacy to Labourers*, 80.
212. Ibid., 99.
213. Ibid., 63–4 and 53–6.
214. *PR* 34 (27 March 1819): 845 and Cobbett *Protestant Reformation*, 99, para. 133. For Cobbett's defence of monasteries against Hume's views see ibid., 95–101, paras. 130–35. See also *PR* 39 (19 May 1821): 444–7; Cobbett, *Poor Man's Friend*, paras. 50–52; and Cobbett, *Legacy to Labourers*, 109–14. Cobbett sometimes asserted that one-quarter of tithes were allotted to the poor.
215. *PR* 34 (8 May 1819): 1036 and Cobbett, *Protestant Reformation*, 268, para. 326.
216. Cobbett, *Legacy to Labourers*, 116.
217. Himmelfarb, *The Idea of Poverty*, 211.
218. Cobbett, *Legacy to Labourers*, 116–17.
219. Ibid., 121, 111 and 100. See also Knight, *Cobbett in Ireland*, 117 from *PR* (18 October 1834), and 129 from *PR* (25 October 1834).
220. Knight, *Cobbett in Ireland*, 252 and 247 from *PR* (29 November 1834).
221. Cobbett, *Legacy to Labourers*, 123. Cobbett commented frequently on the evils of dissection referring to the Anatomy Act of 1832 which he called the 'Dead-Body Bill' (see ibid., 33). For an excellent treatment of this subject in the context of poverty see Ruth Richardson, *Death, Dissection, and the Destitute* (London: Routledge and Kegan Paul, 1987).
222. Knight, *Cobbett in Ireland*, 136 from *PR* (25 October 1834). For modern historians employing this source see n. 18 above.
223. Cobbett, *Legacy to Labourers*, 17–19.
224. Knight, *Cobbett in Ireland*, 109 from *PR* (18 October 1834). Cobbett also contended that the majority of the house 'were committed by their votes long before they could possibly see the evidence'. See Cobbett, *Legacy to Labourers*, 19.
225. Cobbett, *Legacy to Labourers*, 8 and 24.

226. Knight, *Cobbett in Ireland*, 138 from *PR* (25 October 1834) and also ibid., 94 and 107 from *PR* (18 October 1834) and Cobbett, *Legacy to Labourers*, 28.

227. *PR* 34 (8 May 1819): 1029–30. See also *PR* 35 (11 September 1819): 115 where Cobbett makes a similar statement.

228. Cobbett, *Poor Man's Friend*, para. 48. See also *Advice*, 315, para. 334.

229. Cobbett, *Legacy to Labourers*, 130. See also Knight, *Cobbett in Ireland*, 117 from *PR* (18 October 1834); *PR* 34 (8 May 1819): 1042; *PR* 34 (27 March 1819): 854–5; and Cobbett, *Poor Man's Friend*, para. 87 where Cobbett asks 'but, how can MALTHUS and his silly and *nasty* disciples; how can those who want to abolish the poor rates or to prevent the poor from marrying; how can this at once stupid and conceited tribe look the labouring man in the face, while they call upon him to take up arms, to risk his life, in defence of the land?'

230. Cobbett, *Legacy to Labourers*, 131.

231. *PR* 34 (8 May 1819): 1032.

232. Cobbett, *Advice*, 320–21, para. 340.

233. Cobbett, *Poor Man's Friend*, para. 44. For Cobbett's detailed arguments see ibid., paras. 44–85.

234. Ibid., para. 36.

235. Quoted in Himmelfarb, *The Idea of Poverty*, 214–15 from Cobbett's *Tour in Scotland* (1833). Cobbett toured Scotland in October and November 1832. See Spater, *William Cobbett*, 2: 504–505.

236. Himmelfarb, *The Idea of Poverty*, 214 and Dyck, *Cobbett and Popular Culture*, 208–209. John Fielden was Cobbett's fellow MP for Oldham.

237. Knight, *Cobbett in Ireland*, 105 and 117 from *PR* (18 October 1834).

238. Cobbett, *Legacy to Labourers*, 124.

239. Knight, *Cobbett in Ireland*, 136 from *PR* (25 October 1834) and 226 from *PR* (15 November 1834).

240. Quoted in Spater, *William Cobbett*, 2: Appendix 1, 541. See also ibid., 1: 203.

241. Ibid.

242. Cobbett, *Legacy to Labourers*, 11. See also Dyck, *Cobbett and Popular Culture*, 94.

243. Dyck, *Cobbett and Popular Culture*, 36–7 and Himmelfarb, *The Idea of Poverty*, 221.

244. *PR* 35 (11 September 1819): 120. See also Cobbett, *Protestant Reformation*, 91, para. 126 where he attacks the Hampshire Friendly Society. For Malthus's support of Savings Banks see James, *Malthus Variora*, I: 376 and II: 182–3 and 191. Malthus also corresponded with Bewicke Bridge on the subject of Savings Banks and managed such banks in London and Hertford. See the letter from Bewicke Bridge to Malthus, 2 April 1817, *T. R. Malthus: The Unpublished Papers in the Collection of Kanto Gakuen University*, vol. I, eds John Pullen and Trevor Hughes Parry (Cambridge: Cambridge University Press, 1997), 89–90 and 89 n. 96.

245. Poynter, *Society and Pauperism*, 293–4 and *PR* 32 (4 January 1817): 30–31.

246. Cobbett, *Rural Rides*, 298 in the Valley of the Avon in Wiltshire, 28 August 1826. For Malthus's views on emigration see Ch 1. For modern misinterpretation of Malthus see Kegel, 'Cobbett': 354. Sir Francis Burdett, Edward Gibbon Wakefield and Wilmot Horton were among

those strongly in favour of emigration. For Cobbett's critique of Burdett see *PR* 51 (3 July 1824).

247. *PR* 31 (2 November 1816): 565.

248. Cobbett, *Legacy to Labourers*, 82. Cobbett again cites Blackstone to prove his case.

249. Cobbett, *Emigrant's Guide*, 6 and Dyck, *Cobbett and Popular Culture*, 156.

250. *PR*. 69 (13 March 1830): 351.

251. *PR* 72 (9 April 1831): 66.

252. Knight, *Cobbett in Ireland*, 221 from *PR* (15 November 1834).

253. Cobbett, *Poor Man's Friend*, 89.

254. *PR* 41 (2 February 1822): 288. For Cobbett's recommendation to abolish paper money see *PR* 34 (27 March 1819): 843.

255. *PR* 41 (2 February 1822): 288; *PR* 31 (2 November 1816): 560; *PR* 39 (19 May 1821): 442–3, and Cobbett, *Poor Man's Friend*, para. 110. See also Spater, *William Cobbett*, 2: Appendix 1, 540 regarding the British Museum.

256. *PR* 31 (2 November 1816): 565-66. Cobbett claimed that with 'no *list* of taxpayers in the hands of *any* person, mere menial servants, vagrants, pick-pockets and scamps of all sorts might not only come to poll, but they might poll in several parishes or places on one and the same day', ibid., 566. Once a reformed parliament had been elected, Cobbett proposed that indirect taxes could be replaced by a small direct tax 'upon every master of a house, however low his situation', ibid., 566–7.

257. Cobbett, *Advice*, 316–17, paras. 336–7. See also Himmelfarb, *The Idea of Poverty*, 219.

258. Knight, *Cobbett in Ireland*, 127–8 from *PR* (25 October 1834).

259. Ibid., 226 from *PR* (15 November 1834).

260. Cited in *Canadian State Trials: Law, Politics, and Security Measures, 1608–1837*, vol. I, eds F. Murray Greenwood and Barry Wright (Toronto: University of Toronto Press, 1996), 5.

261. See Dyck, *Cobbett and Popular Culture*, 214 where he criticizes the tendency on the Left to argue that Cobbett was 'shallow on political theory'. Cobbett, Dyck argues, wrote 'widely and thoughtfully on political theory', ibid.

262. Himmelfarb, *The Idea of Poverty*, 219.

263. See Chapter 1.

264. James, *Malthus Variora*, II: 204 from the 1806 *Essay*. David Ricardo, however, did attack Cobbett directly labelling him as a 'mischievous scoundrel'. See Poynter, *Society and Pauperism*, 240.

265. Ibid., 252. Malthus was referring to William Godwin's *Of Population* (1820).

266. James, *Malthus Variora*, I: 374 from the 1817 *Essay*.

267. Ibid., II: 135. James suggests that Cobbett could well have been one of the popular writers Malthus had in mind.

268. Ibid., II: 135 from the 1817 *Essay*.

269. Ibid.

270. *PR* 35 (11 September 1819): 111.

CHAPTER FOUR

The radical working-class press against the Malthusian crew

Friend Brougham,

I have long had some odd sayings of thine in my mind, for which I have been more than half inclined to give thee a sound rating; but I have forborne out of mere charity as there appeared no great chance of thy ever being able to reduce them to practice. Since thou hast enlisted under the orders of Serjeant Scarlett, as a volunteer in his crusade against the poor, thou mayst be able to do some mischief, and therefore it is my duty to stop thee, if I can. Thee and Malthus may be very good men, for ought I know to the contrary; but I must tell thee and him, that the principles he lays down, and which thou hast ventured, rather late, to adopt, are detestable, and abominable; and as proceeding from *married men*, deserve even a worse epithet, than I shall give them. The direct tendency and the *only effect* of your joint doctrines, since you have gone into partnership with him to share the odium, is to establish *polygamy* and *concubinage* among *the rich—prostitution* to the most frightful extent amongst the poor. The Devil himself could not have invented a better method of establishing his reign upon earth, than by the introduction of such a system, *if the poor would suffer it to be reduced to practice*:—which they would not—for nature would cry out against it, and nerve the hands of all her children to resist its baneful influence! I shudder at the coldness of the feelings which could suggest a plan, only calculated to fill the land with *promiscuous debauchery!*—and, at the contempt for the well-being of God's creatures, which an accidental elevation above the common ills of mortality seems in most instances to produce. Is it not enough that a system which makes all honor, all importance, all respectability, depend upon the *acquisition of wealth* alone, no matter how acquired, sufficiently horrible; but that every natural enjoyment, even the society of woman, shall be denied to the wretched beings the system makes poor by its demands, and then insults with poverty!

(T. J. Wooler opposing moral restraint in *The Black Dwarf*, 13 June 1821).[1]

... on the continent, the women used some means of preventing conceptions, which were uniformly successful. Mr. Owen set out for Paris to discover the process. He consulted the most eminent physicians and assured himself of what was the common practice among their women, that the female was always prepared to absorb the semen and its influence by a small piece of sponge, at the time of coition, and not allow it to impregnate the genital vessels. The matter is most simple and most clear: it strikes us with physical and philosophical reasons, in a moment, why it must succeed, and why it is the only means that will succeed. It shocks the mind of a woman, at first thought, that never dreamt of such a thing; but once practised, all prejudice flies and gratification must be the consequence. To weak and sickly females, to those to whom pregnancy and parturition are dangerous, and who never produce living or healthy children, the discovery is a real blessing. And it is a real blessing in all other cases, where children are not desired. It will become the very bulwark of love and wisdom, of beauty, health, and happiness.

(Richard Carlile, advocating contraception in 'WHAT IS LOVE?', *The Republican*, 6 May 1825)[2]

Thomas Wooler and Richard Carlile represent polar views regarding Malthus in the radical working-class press of the 1820s and 1830s. Wooler, editor of *The Black Dwarf* (1817–24), strongly supported Cobbett's critique of the 'parson'. He rejected the notion that population was outstripping the food supply and thus vehemently opposed the need to restrict population growth, especially through moral restraint imposed on the poor. Like Cobbett, he argued that delay in the age at marriage would only promote promiscuity among the poor. Richard Carlile, editor of *The Republican* (1819–26) and numerous other papers, vigorously disagreed with Cobbett. He eventually accepted the notion of over-population but rejected the Malthusian checks of misery, vice or moral restraint. Despite the admonitions of Francis Place, in 1825 he published 'What is Love?', publicly declaring his support for preventing conception by use of the sponge.[3] Both Wooler and Cobbett vehemently opposed voluntary birth control. Such 'experiments', argued Wooler, would 'end in the grossest abominations!'. Cobbett was typically far more caustic. Of Carlile he claimed:

> At last ... a man is found to put his name to a publication ... openly and avowedly teaching young women to be prostitutes before they are married, and in a way *so as not to prevent their future marriage*, to which publication is prefixed, most appropriately, the figures of a man and woman in a state of *perfect nakedness*, the instructions being conveyed in terms so filthy, so disgusting, so beastly as to shock the mind of even the lewdest of men and women.

Carlile was 'nearly a madman' and a 'poor half-mad tool, of *the enemies of reform*'.[4]

Such heated disagreements reflect the degree to which Cobbett's well publicized views on Malthus and his opposition to Malthusian solutions regarding the problem of poverty were by no means adopted wholesale by the working-class press. Patricia Hollis may be correct in asserting that 'most' of the unstamped press of the 1830s consulted Cobbett.[5] To consult, however, is not necessarily to accept. Important papers such as *The Destructive* (1833–34) edited by Henry Hetherington and James Bronterre O'Brien opposed Cobbett. Others, especially *The Crisis* (1832–34) and *The New Moral World* (1834–37), edited by Robert Owen, developed ideologies markedly different from Cobbett. Even papers such as *The Poor Man's Guardian* (1831–35) – edited by Henry Hetherington and Bronterre O'Brien – which often bestowed great praise upon Cobbett, nevertheless disagreed with him on fundamental issues as did *The Black Dwarf* earlier on. Other papers published prior to the unstamped press of the 1830s such as Carlile's *Republican* condemned Cobbett or, like *The Economist* (1821), edited by George Mudie, proposed Owenite cooperative ideas. Although Gertrude Himmelfarb is right to assert that Cobbett's notion of poor relief as a form of property – the denial of which eliminated all rights to property – was 'heard again and again' in the 1830s,[6] some important papers ignored both Cobbett and the New Poor Law.

This chapter will analyse the reaction to Malthus in the working class press between 1817 and the passage of the New Poor Law in 1834 and its immediate aftermath with particular emphasis on the extent to which Cobbett's anti-Malthusianism was superceded by new and analytically more powerful critiques of the principle of population. Both Patricia Hollis and Gertrude Himmelfarb make a distinction between an 'old ideology' represented by Cobbett and his adherents and an emerging 'new ideology' reflected especially in the writings of Bronterre O'Brien. In the 'old analysis', as Hollis terms it, poverty resulted from exactions on the labourer after he received his wages, particularly in the form of taxation. Such exactions were used to support corrupt institutions such as the government and the Church of England.[7] The true villains, then, were 'the tax collectors, pensioners, and parasites of the Old Corruption'.[8]

In the 'new analysis', the root causes of poverty stemmed from the fraudulent expropriation of property by landlords conspiring with capitalists leading to the transfer of wealth from labouring producers to a '*monied monopoly*' and to a monopolization of political power and law making. As Hollis points out, 'the heaviest exactions were taken from the working man in the economic process itself, before he received his wages.'[9] The new villains thus became the middle-class capitalists united with the aristocratic landowning class.[10] Himmelfarb argues that 'the real novelty' of this new ideology 'came from the simultaneous redefinition of poverty and the redefinition of the radical enterprise, the first making poverty a function of property and political equality, the second making radicalism a function of class and class struggle'.[11]

Both Hollis and Himmefarb agree that impressive as the new ideology was, it never fully displaced the old. Nor did the new analysis become 'the dominant radical ideology, still less the dominant working-class ideology'.[12] The new clearly overlapped the old. The old rhetoric intermingled with the discourse of the new. Can the same be said when dealing more specifically with the critique of Malthus? Were Cobbett's arguments against the 'parson' eclipsed by an anti-Malthusianism rooted in the context of the new ideology? Or did his persistent fulminations against Malthus prevail in spite of a working-class press increasingly imbued with newer forms of analysis? Furthermore, is such a dichotomy between old and new even relevant given that the most radical case against Malthus – the advocacy of birth control – was made by Carlile, a Painite republican who, in spite of his strenuous objections to Cobbett, railed against excessive taxation and the corruption of church and state without offering a deeper critique of political economy?

The pauper press

The following analysis cannot possibly encompass the hundreds of newspapers and periodicals constituting the working class press.[13] The discussion instead will focus on approximately two dozen of the most important papers spanning the period 1817–36. These papers not only had wide circulation but also represent a broad spectrum of the most influential radical thinkers.[14] The majority of these papers were published unstamped between 1830 and 1836. The stamp tax was a product of one of the Six Acts passed in the aftermath of Peterloo in 1819. The tax intended to wipe out radical penny and twopenny papers such as Cobbett's *Political Register* and imposed a 4d. newspaper duty on all periodicals that appeared more frequently than every 26 days. Most papers in the 1820s complied with the law and suffered declining circulation, like the *Political Register* or, as in the case of *The Black Dwarf* in 1824, ceased publication. The unrest of the 1830s and the revival of popular radicalism, however, led to the creation of numerous unstamped illegal papers intent on spreading the radical message with the deliberate aim of defying the 'taxes on knowledge'.[15]

Eleven of the papers examined reflect the views of the three most influential editors and publishers of the 1820s and 1830s. Richard Carlile's activities as a publicist of the old ideology stemming from Tom Paine spanned two decades. With Cobbett, he dominated the 1820s producing *The Republican* between 1819 and 1826 and *The Lion* in 1828–29. His widespread influence continued in the pages of *The Cosmopolite* (1832–33) and *The Gauntlet* (1833–34).

Henry Hetherington and Bronterre O'Brien, representatives of the new ideology and the frontal assault on political economy, were also prominent in the 1830s. Hetherington, often employing O'Brien as editor, published *Penny Papers For The People* (1830–31), *The Poor Man's Guardian* (1831–35), *The Destructive* (1833), *The People's Conservative and Trade Union Gazette* (1833–34) and the *Twopenny Dispatch* (1834–36). With James Lorymer as editor, Hetherington also circulated *The Radical* (1832–33) and *The Republican* (1832–33).

In addition to the newspapers of these major figures in the radical movement other important publications, whose editors propounded a variety of opinions, were selected. Thomas Wooler's *The Black Dwarf* (1817–24) and John Wade's *The Gorgon* (1818–19) reflected the old analysis. Both, with some reservations, adhered closely to many of Cobbett's views. William Carpenter, although later adopting moderate views, expressed the new ideology in his *Political Letters and Pamphlets* (1830–1831), the first significant illegal newspaper of the 1830s. He became sub-editor of John Bell's *The True Sun* (1832–36), the only stamped paper to adopt the causes of the unstamped. Bell also edited *The New Political Register* (1835).

Three moderate papers advocating factory reforms were also analysed: John Watson's and James Cleave's *The Working Man's Friend* (1832–33), John Doherty's *Poor Man's Advocate* (1832–33) and James Morrison's *The Pioneer* (1833–34). Owenite ideology was represented in George Mudie's *The Economist* (1821) and two publications by Robert Owen, *The Crisis* (1832–34) and *The New Moral World* (1834–1837). In addition, *The Political Penny Magazine* (1836), published specifically in opposition to the New Poor Law, was utilized.[16]

The above group of newspapers by no means constitutes a rigorous 'sample' of the working-class radical press in the 1820s and 1830s. Nor does it represent a body of unified and cohesive thought. Not only did individuals like Carlile and Carpenter alter their views over time but also the 'pauper press' experienced intense internal quarrels. Carlile feuded bitterly with Wooler, Hetherington, Carpenter, Watson and trade unionists in general. O'Brien adamantly disagreed with Owen and Morrison, both of whom refused to accept universal suffrage as the solution to working-class ills. Hetherington even fell out with O'Brien upon occasion. Most radicals, of course, took issue with Cobbett on one matter or another.[17] This selection of radical opinion, nevertheless, should provide sufficient scope to assess the reaction to Malthusian thought, divided as that reaction might be.

Echoes of Cobbett against Malthus

The influence of Cobbett's ideas on the working-class press in the 1820s and especially in the 1830s immediately before and after the passage of the New Poor Law is undeniable. Radical papers praised him directly. They heaped invective on Malthus in rhetoric sometimes reminiscent of Cobbett's acerbic attacks. Most editors rejected Malthus's ratios and the notion that poverty was caused by surplus population. In analysing the true causes of poverty, many reiterated Cobbett's arguments by focusing on taxation and old corruption. They similarly drew on his work in their rejection of Malthus's solutions, especially moral restraint and the denial of the right to relief. Their own proposals to alleviate poverty often closely paralleled Cobbett's prescriptions.

In February 1820 *The Black Dwarf* supported Cobbett's bid for election in Coventry by publishing a letter from his seconder Richard Taylor who referred to him as 'a zealous, enlightened and eminent patriot' and 'the intrepid champion of liberty'. Taylor predicted that Cobbett would soon achieve retribution against the 'insignificant reptiles' and 'yelping curs' who fostered tyranny and corruption.[18] Six months later the same paper praised him for his strength of mind, 'energy of character' and 'most prudent' advice. He was, moreover, a realist: 'Things impress themselves upon his mind as they really are' and he was not prone 'to mispresent things to others'.[19]

Adulation of Cobbett extended into the 1830s. William Carpenter's *Political Letters and Pamphlets* in early January 1831 defended him against attacks made by *The Courier* and denied that his lectures had precipitated incendiarism in Sussex. Carpenter later claimed that Cobbett would lay 'open to the world, the real condition of the English people'.[20] *The Poor Man's Advocate* described him 'as that first, ablest, and undeviating ADVOCATE of *the people.*'[21] *The Political Penny Magazine*, defending the right to poor relief, claimed that Cobbett's *Legacy to Labourers* had 'forever set the *principle* to rest'.[22]

Even *The Poor Man's Guardian*, which at times strongly opposed Cobbett, lauded his achievements. Not only did it reprint many of his pieces from the *Political Register*, it also published many pro-Cobbett letters to the editor.[23] *Legacy to Labourers* received high praise and the last issue of the *Political Register* was described as 'one of the noblest monuments of his unrivalled pen'.[24] Cobbett was 'the unflinching champion' of the 'strong common-sense school' and 'notwithstanding his multifarious inconsistencies' he played 'a deep game that cannot fail ultimately to benefit the people'.[25] Henry Hetherington, moreover, sold Cobbett's books and pamphlets and supported his election as MP for Oldham in 1832.[26]

More surprising was Carlile's support of Cobbett in the 1830s. In *The Republican* (1819–26) Carlile had lashed out against Cobbett on political and religious matters and especially on the issue of birth control.

In *The Gauntlet* published in 1833 and 1834, however, he whole-heartedly supported Cobbett's advocacy of reduced taxation both in principle and detail: 'I entirely agree with that admirable speech of Mr. Cobbett's on this subject, which you will find in this number of *The Gauntlet*.'[27] Carlile endorsed Cobbett's recommendation that taxes be reduced from 50 million pounds to 10 million.[28]

If many working-class newspapers were prepared to extol Cobbett in general, they were even more willing, in specific terms, to uphold his denunciation of Malthus and his supporters, although rarely achieving the invective of the master. All papers examined, with the exception of those edited by Carlile consistently opposed Malthus throughout the 1820s and especially in the early 1830s. Some, like *The Poor Man's Guardian* in November 1834, published articles from the *Political Register* where Cobbett inveighed against the 'pottering, dabbling, patching, pinching, muddling, poking ... Malthusian crew'.[29] In March 1834, it praised *Cobbett's Magazine* for presenting 'a bulwark of practical experience against the theoretical wisdom of the Scotch "feelosofers"'.[30]

Many newspapers, like Cobbett, argued that Malthus was simply wrong. *The Economist* in 1821 claimed that Malthus's 'errors' were 'of a much more fatal description than those of Dr. Smith'.[31] Prior to the passage of the New Poor Law in 1834, *The True Sun* described Malthusian philosophy as 'a narrow view of the relations which ought to connect together the various portions of society' which was fundamentally 'fallacious'.[32] Robert Owen in *The Crisis* referred to the concept of overpopulation and claimed that Malthus's 'great powers of mind had ... been paralyzed at an early period of life by this erroneous idea'.[33]

Irony and satire, techniques often employed by Cobbett, were invoked to discredit Malthus. *Political Letters and Pamphlets* on 4 February 1831 printed the following tidbit: 'AN ANTI-MALTHUSIAN – A young woman, named Fanny Fowler was last week sentenced to six months imprisonment in Abingdon House of Correction for bastardy, it being her *fifteenth* transgression.'[34] A month later it ran an extract from John Minter Morgan's *Revolt of the Bees* (1826) where a journeyman weaver describes the following experience:

> A few days afterwards, while standing at the window of my apartment, which is an attic at the lower end of St. Martin's Court, I was surprised to see a procession pass along the Strand to take water at Hungerford Stairs. They proved to be the Political Economists themselves, with a numerous body of emigrants. The cavalcade was preceded by a gentleman in black, his hat was slouched over his eyes, and the brim, which was somewhat broad, appeared to have been once fastened up in a clerical shape, but the loops had given way, and

left it doubtful whether the wearer was still a clergyman or not: he held in his hand a large manuscript which he was perpetually altering; and I have since been informed by those who stood near, that the words 'Principle of Population' was conspicuous, and that there was an astonishing number of corrections; his countenance was melancholy, and betrayed symptoms of disappointment, -

> 'With broken lyre and cheek serenely pale,
> Lo, sad Alcaeus wanders down the vale.'

The Political Economists followed him at some distance, but with reluctant step; for they now regarded him as the author of all their calamities, although in the zenith of his fame they attended constantly at his levees, and repeated his decisions to the wondering multitude, as the oracles of wisdom: little dreaming into what a labyrinth of error he would lead them.[35]

As a protest against the passage of the New Poor Law, *The Poor Man's Guardian* quoted a description of the frontispiece to a pamphlet entitled *England's Passing Bell*, or the *Obsequies of National Holiness, National Liberty, and National Honour*:

> On the right of the picture is the Bishop of London scourging a poor young woman with the cat-o'-nine-tails, while a still-born infant lies at her feet, the father of which, with a star on his breast, stands laughing at her. In his left hand the Bishop holds a scroll inscribed 'The Malthusian Plan.' In the middle of the picture, in the distance, is a large new Workhouse, with the date 1834.[36]

As the above commentary suggests, the castigation of Malthus most often included, as in Cobbett's diatribes, all who espoused his ideas. They were stereotyped as 'Scotch philosophers', 'the Class of Population Regulators', 'grinders of the poor' and members of the 'bloody-minded set'.[37] Lord Chancellor Henry Brougham was the most frequent target, variously described as 'a noisy echo of the Malthusian system', as 'bewildered by these unnatural and impracticable theories of Mr. Malthus' and as a 'besotten Whig, whose whole life has been one continued scene of hypocrisy'.[38] Harriet Martineau, 'the anti-propagation lady', was put in the same camp as was that 'tyrannical and heartless fellow Chadwick'.[39] *The True Sun* also included the political economist John Ramsay McCulloch: 'Let but the poor attempt to secure higher wages for their labour – and straightway the terrors of McCulloch's and Malthus's philosophy are suspended over their devoted heads!'[40]

It is no surprise, moreover, that the working-class press closely paralleled Cobbett by denouncing Malthusians as heartless and inhumane. *The Gorgon* described them as 'frozen-hearted philosophers'.[41] *The Poor Man's Guardian* in February 1835 referred to 'the hard-hearted fabrications of the Whigs "who propagated" the bitter first fruits of the principles of the defunct Malthus.' A few months later it printed a public letter from Robert Owen to Lord Brougham. Mr. Malthus, Owen claimed, had produced more hard-heartedness among the wealthy and non-producers, than, perhaps, any individual that has yet lived.[42]

Nor is it any wonder that criticism of Malthus was often based on gross misinterpretations of his work. *The Black Dwarf* accused Malthus of deliberately wishing to 'thin the population' and 'kill off' the poor, especially the very young: 'When Malthus contends that the children of those who cannot provide for them have no right to subsistence, how far is he from the commendation of *infanticide*!'[43] *The People's Conservative and Trade Union Gazette* typically misread Malthus on the issue of emigration: 'The over population men of all kinds would be glad if half the working classes were to emigrate, or were banished, or were dead, or were anything but what they are and where they are.'[44]

Although echoing much of Cobbett's hostility to Malthusians, the working-class press only rarely achieved his level of invective. Perhaps *The Political Penny Magazine*, which frequently cited Cobbett, came closest to his scathing rhetoric. On 3 September 1836, almost two years after Malthus died, it exclaimed:

> I know perfectly well that dead Malthus and outcast Brougham have shown both by precept and practice that there *may* be wretches so utterly destitute of all the nobler and better feelings of our nature, as to be able to resist the behests of Holy Writ, and the small still pleadings, of which even their black and bile-filled souls must, surely, be sometimes conscious. Parson Malthus and the infidel Brougham (apt editor and Illustrator of the theological work of the Deist Paley!) perfectly well know that among the most terribly eloquent passages of the Old Testament are its denunciations of those who oppress the poor, and send the hungry away unfed .... The scriptures might, in the judgment of these blackhearted and man-hating wretches, do perfectly well to quote *against* the poor. 'Servants obey your masters' is a text which Parson Malthus (if not permanently non-resident) would make zealous application in his pulpit and which livid Brougham, if not too drunk, would babble upon with great unction, in that stye of hereditary swine, the House of Lords .... Scripture, humanity and law, say the poor have a *right* to be supported; the base Whig liars, (for even the fellow Malthus must have been a Whig in his heart), and the filthy rubbish they chose to call Political Economy, say the contrary.[45]

In terms of specific anti-Malthusian content, the vast majority of the working-class press agreed with many of Cobbett's detailed criticisms of the 'Parson'. Although none of the editors accepted his dubious argument that population had not increased but in fact had declined, they were almost unanimous in their rejection of Malthus's ratios whereby population increase outstripped the food supply. T. J. Wooler in *The*

Black Dwarf consistently claimed that 'population has *never* pressed against the means of subsistence.'[46] Indeed, there was 'room for *additional millions* upon our island'.[47] The amount of food could be increased five-fold and even Ireland could provide for another million people.[48] There was no proof, he claimed, of the incapacity of the earth to provide adequate subsistence; the globe, in fact, was only half-cultivated.[49] Other papers of the 1820s expressed similar sentiments. *The Economist*, for example, asserted that England was 'capable of sustaining several times the number of her present population' and was confident that each man could produce 'more than can be consumed by twenty individuals'.[50]

The working-class press of the 1830s, especially the unstamped, was even more adamant on this issue. *The Poor Man's Guardian* denied the notion of 'surplus population'[51] and stated that Great Britain and Ireland could sustain five times their population. Cobbett, the paper contended, had offered conclusive proof:

> The land is, 'in quantity and quality, superabundant.' Mr. Cobbett has frequently shown, that instead of surplus population, the land is not half cultivated, for want of hands in parts of the country. He has calculated the produce of particular parishes with all the precision of figures, and comparing the produce with the mouths to consume it, he has shown that, even with the present limited cultivation, there is food enough, and more than enough for the population.[52]

Political Letters and Pamphlets argued that 'Nature extends population and the means for their support together' while *Penny Papers for the People* claimed that 'Political Economists, bound to the truth by the uncompromising rigidity of figures, unanimously confess, that were the population treble its present number, England could support them.'[53] Robert Owen concurred with such views. In *The Crisis* he rejected the concept of 'over-population': 'society now has the means of bringing into existence ten or twenty times more in amount of the necessities and comforts of life than the present population of the world requires.'[54] Great Britain, he asserted in *The New Moral World*, has the most ample materials 'to provide happiness … forever to her whole population'.[55]

Like Cobbett, the working-class press also rejected the Malthusian view that the Old Poor Law created the very poverty it set out to relieve and strongly denied that destitution was the fault of the poor themselves. *The Gorgon*, for example, refused to accept that 'the poor-rate has created the very evil it was intended to cure.'[56] More specifically, the paper disputed the contention that provisions for the poor promoted population increase by encouraging early and improvident marriages.[57] Nor, according to *The Black Dwarf*, did the poor laws lower 'the price of labour any more than it will raise the price of produce.'[58] *The True Sun*, moreover, argued that 'idleness, improvidence, and vice' were not products of poor relief. The 'labouring classes in England' were, in fact, 'the most industrious and ingenious in the world'.[59]

If the Old Poor Law was not responsible for poverty, neither were the poor themselves. 'The English poor, taken as a body', exclaimed *The Black Dwarf*, 'are not drunken or indolent.'[60] The distress of the poorer classes, asserted *The Poor Man's Guardian*, lay not in their 'want of industry' and certainly not in themselves. The 'industry of Englishmen, after all, was proverbial over the world'.[61]

What then were the true causes of indigence? Having ruled out 'surplus population', the working-class press by and large accepted the 'old ideology' of Cobbett's analysis. Even radicals like O'Brien in *The Poor Man's Guardian* who moved towards a 'new ideology' still gave at least secondary focus to many of the factors raised by Cobbett, especially regarding the legal rights of the poor. In other words, if low wages and unemployment were the root causes of poverty, such conditions were produced by excessive taxation, corruption and nepotism among the pensioned elite, wasteful and reckless government expenditure, a host of oppressive laws and fundamental inequalities in the distribution of resources and power.

As with Cobbett, the burden of taxation was frequently cited as the primary cause of destitution. *The Black Dwarf* ran headers such as 'The Tax Payers against the Tax Eaters!' and 'TAXATION THE "ROOT OF ALL EVIL"'.[62] 'The tax-gatherer', it claimed, 'is a more frightful monster than any wild beast of the desert.' Taxation was a 'cruel and ruinous system' constituting outright 'public robbery'.[63] *The Gorgon* and *Political Letters* were convinced that the enormous taxes placed on the labouring people were responsible for increased pauperism, crime and 'the consequent misery of thousands of our fellow men'.[64] *The True Sun* claimed that 'intolerable taxes' robbed the poor of their earnings and *The Radical* had as its motto: 'TAXATION WITHOUT REPRESENTATION IS TYRANNY AND OUGHT TO BE RESISTED.'[65] Even Richard Carlile, who disagreed vehemently with Cobbett's solutions, accepted the premise that taxation bred 'distress, disease, and death, by starvation'.[66]

Although editors of the working-class press gave less emphasis than Cobbett to the disastrous effects of paper money, they rallied to his side in condemning the huge national debt – a product of wasteful expenditure – which perpetuated an increasingly enormous tax burden.[67] *The Black Dwarf* predicted that the increasing debt would 'swallow up all the resources of the country!'. The National Debt, moreover, was *'taken from the labour of the people'*.[68] *The Gorgon* referred to the 'detested' paper money and the Debt that ate at 'the substance of the poor'.[69] *Political Letters*, in a lengthy editorial devoted entirely to the national debt, deemed it 'a ponderous and extensive evil'.[70] Even *The Poor Man's Guardian*, which refused to view taxation as the root cause of distress, emphasized the debt problem.[71]

Unanimous, moreover, was the condemnation of unjustified expenditure – a dominant theme in Cobbett's writings. Since the costs of the French wars were largely responsible for the huge debt, papers from T. J. Wooler's *The Black Dwarf* in the late 1810s to Hetherington's *The Poor Man's Guardian* and Robert Owen's *The New Moral World* of the 1830s vociferously opposed further wars and the maintenance of a standing army. Such policies served to prop up 'despotism in all corners of the earth' and led to millions of labourers being 'murdered'.[72] Owen argued that 'the human race must remain in a state of slavery and misery' if permanent military or naval institutions were retained.[73]

A litany of financial abuses concerning military, religious and political pensions was universally highlighted. Such attacks on 'old corruption' permeated the pages of even *The Poor Man's Guardian*. References to 'high-fed priests', 'fat sinecurists' and a 'spendthrift' monarchy abounded.[74] Detailed lists of those holding sinecures or receiving pensions and the amounts they received were published. *Political Letters* calculated that over 2.5 million pounds were expended annually, while *The Poor Man's Guardian* estimated that First Lord of the Treasury, Earl Grey, and his relatives received nearly 171,892 pounds per annum.[75] Richard Carlile perhaps best summed it up in an open letter to the same Lord Grey (now Prime Minister) in *The Gauntlet* in 1834:

> There remains an abused royalty, a prostituted church, a pensioned, placed, and pampered aristocracy, and a people pained with the labour to live after providing your revenue. You have professed to meddle with everything – you have improved nothing. This is the correct general view of your administration, and, after such a view, details are but repetitions.[76]

The aristocracy – those 'noble paupers' and 'haughty idlers' living off the 'fat emoluments of office' were the 'real beggars' of the nation.[77] Carlile enthusiastically reprinted in *The Gauntlet* the following poem:

WHAT IS A PEER?

What is a Peer? – An useless thing –
A costly TOY to please a King –
A BAUBLE near the throne;
A lump of animated clay –
A gaudy pageant of the day –
AN INCUBUS – A DRONE.

What is a Peer? – A nation's curse –
A PAUPER on the public purse –
Corruption's own jackal;

A haughty domineering blade –
A CUCKOLD at a masquerade –
A DANDY at a ball.
Ye butterflies whom Kings create –
Ye caterpillars of the State, –
Know that your time is near;
Enlightened France will lead the van,
To overthrow your worthless clan:
This moral learn – that GOD made MAN,
But never made a PEER.[78]

The Black Dwarf likewise labelled the aristocracy as un-masculine:

> They are no longer Englishmen, but 'DANDIES!' There is a sublime
> epithet for them. There is a name for immortality to consecrate! This
> new race of demi-gods, it is asserted, eat, drink, and sleep much like
> other men; but they wear stays, and drink GOD save the King, in
> dandy punch. Their gender is not yet ascertained, but as their
> principal ambition seems to be *to* look *as pretty as women*, it would
> be most uncharitable to call them *men*. One of them the other day
> dropped his glove, and seemed quite astonished that one of the
> passing male brutes did not pick it up for her, or him. And indeed it
> was quite shocking to see the poor thing distressed in attempting to
> stoop for it itself.[79]

So effete, corrupt and incompetent were such individuals that Wooler in
the same piece satirically suggested that the ladies of the realm take
charge of government, giving the wash-tubs, ironing boards and
scrubbing brushes to former placemen.[80]

In addition to financial issues, the working-class press reiterated
Cobbett's arguments against a whole set of oppressive laws designed to
foster increased destitution. Enclosure acts were referred to by *The Black
Dwarf* as 'Bills of Famine' and constituted a 'monstrous injustice'.[81] *The
Poor Man's Guardian* produced statistics relating increasing enclosures
to rising Poor Rates.[82] The Corn Bill was labelled the 'Starvation Law' –
a monopoly that benefited parsons and especially landlords by raising the
price of bread.[83] The Game Laws likewise were condemned. Of the new
Game Bill of 1831, *The Poor Man's Guardian* remarked: 'an act more
aristocratic in its principles ... never received the sanction of legislature
... what good does it do the poor?'[84]

In the broadest sense, the working-class press denied Malthus's
contention that poverty was a result of the natural laws of population
and instead focused on institutional factors concerning the distribution
of resources and income. 'That there is wretchedness we know,' said *The
Black Dwarf*, 'but it arises from the great mass of society being deprived
of a considerable proportion of what they produce, to maintain those
who produce nothing.'[85] Reiterating the old ideology of Cobbett, the
editor found the roots of such inequality:

> Something, however, totally independent of the *means* of *producing* subsistence, prevents the distribution of it in a due proportion, as the recompense of labour. What is this something? No more, or less, than a *despotic government*, and a *rapacious church establishment*! Where the few have the power to accumulate wealth, by compelling the labourer to toil without being adequately rewarded, it matters but little as to the relative number of the labourers.[86]

The familiar rhetoric of the worker deprived of the fruits of his labour permeated editorial commentary throughout the 1820s and 1830s. The '*true source*' of poverty among workers, argued *The Black Dwarf*, was 'the deprivation of the due reward of their labour ... by the privileged classes'.[87] *Political Letters*, in an open letter to Sir Robert Peel, contended that a 'monopoly of power' deprived the people of the 'fruit of their labour'.[88] According to *The Gauntlet*, the aristocracy 'make such laws as rob the people of the fair produce of their labour.'[89] Even *The Poor Man's Guardian*, which viewed property distribution as the fundamental cause of poverty and regarded Cobbett's emphasis on taxes, paper money and sinecures as mere symptoms, continued to employ the old discourse: 'All the poor require is, to be allowed to keep the fruits of their own industry or to exchange them for others upon equitable terms.'[90]

If the working-class press rejected Malthus's premises concerning the origins of poverty its editors likewise consistently opposed his solutions. As in Cobbett's analysis, they universally condemned the concept of moral restraint. *The Black Dwarf* opposed any attempts to delay or 'put a stop to marriage':

> Mr. Malthus thinks the poor have no right to marry. Mr. Scarlett thinks they ought to give security for the maintenance for all the little beings they may help to bring into the world. And Mr. Brougham thinks it is as bad to produce children without being able to maintain them, as to enter a shop, and order goods without the means of payment!!! This is no mere tavern wit, but grave senatorial recommendation; and Mr. Scarlett actually produced part of a system, which when completed, was to confine the procreative faculties of the poor within certain limits to be *by law established*. By some fortunate chance for the poor country lads and lasses, Mr. Malthus has not yet had the satisfaction of seeing his system acted upon.[91]

Such measures, moreover, were unnecessary since 'population has *never* pressed against the means of subsistence.'[92] *The Gorgon* regarded abstention from matrimony and procreation as 'strange doctrines' propagated by Malthus and his followers.[93] *The Poor Man's Guardian* quoted Voltaire's *Philosophical Dictionary* against Malthus and in favour of marriage: 'Marriage renders men more virtuous and wise.'[94] *The Working Man's Friend* opposed any scheme that sought 'to intimidate the young men from forming matrimonial ties'.[95] Robert Owen could not believe that anyone would 'attribute merit to *barenness*, and demerit to men and women for being *prolific*, except ... Mr Malthus, and his ardent, but inexperienced disciples'.[96]

Moral restraint, moreover, was laden with class bias against the poor. Employing one of Cobbett's favourite metaphors, *The Black Dwarf* suggested, 'the political economist should rather dispose of the drones who sat without working, than check the multiplication of the working bees, in order that more honey may be left to the drones.' [97] *The Poor Man's Guardian* published a letter to the editor that argued that it was the 'idlers' that increased population and not the actual producers.[98]

The working-class press rarely argued that moral restraint was contrary to the biblical injunction to be fruitful and multiply. More common was the argument that delay of marriage while remaining celibate was contrary to natural law. Such action, argued *The Black Dwarf*, would violate 'the natural principle which dictates the sexual appetite' and thus 'counteract the laws of nature'.[99] 'To dream of stopping or diminishing the intercourse of the sexes by law,' claimed *The Poor Man's Guardian*, 'we hold to be the height of madness. Legislators might as well try to hush the tempest, or silence the thunder.'[100] Robert Owen contended that man had a natural aversion 'to whatever prevents him from propagating the species'. 'Marriages late in life', he maintained, 'are unnatural ... and directly opposed to the well-being and happiness of individuals and society.'[101] Moral restraint, then, simply would not work. The social repercussions, moreover, would be disastrous. *The Black Dwarf* predicted increased levels of prostitution and 'promiscuous debauchery', while *The Crisis* foresaw more 'disease, discontent, crime, and misery'.[102]

Malthus, of course, advocated total abolition of the Old Poor Law and denied the poor any legal right to relief. Such negative measures, he believed, would facilitate moral restraint since labourers with no parish support for their children would delay marriage fearing utter destitution. Although some working-class papers came to defend the Old Poor Law and condemn the New much later than Cobbett – *The Poor Man's Guardian*, for example, did so only in May 1834, mere months before the New Poor Law's final passage in August 1834 – most, with the exception of Carlile's *The Republican*, rigorously defended the right to relief throughout the 1820s and early 1830s and staunchly urged repeal of the new enactment after 1834.

To be sure, aspects of the Old Poor Law could be extremely degrading, especially parish road work often done in gangs. As *The Gorgon* pointed out, however, weekly allowances were absolutely necessary to prevent 'human beings perishing of hunger'. John Wade, its editor, urged paupers 'to demand it with the air of men asking for their right'.[103] In tones reminiscent of Cobbett, *Political Letters* spoke of 'the humane provisions of the 43rd. Elizabeth' and John Bell (former editor of *The True Sun*) in *The New Political Register* proclaimed 'that the principle of the Poor Laws of Elizabeth is, beyond comparison, the finest and most important principle which any system of society has ever exhibited.'[104]

The defence of the right to relief drew directly on Cobbett's arguments. 'Mr. Cobbett'. claimed *The Black Dwarf*, 'justly remarks that it is no shame for a man to receive parish relief. It is his *right*, if he needs it; and it is more than his right if those of whom he seeks support, profit by the system which makes and keeps him poor.'[105] Such right constituted 'a principle of nature'. No one should be excluded from nature's feast. 'I see,' said *The Black Dwarf*, 'the general table sufficiently spread; and I *wish* all who are forcibly excluded from the feast, would try their strength with those who would shut them out.'[106] *The Pioneer* published an extract from Richard Oastler's pamphlet entitled *A Few Words to the Friends and Enemies of the Trades' Unions* that invoked the metaphor in far more caustic tones:

> Some even pretend that Nature has not provided enough for all. If she were really neglectful, the shortest way, and a far more humane one than the present, would have been to have made a law, that every accoucheur and midwife should be sworn to strangle every third child born in the land, of rich or poor, of high or low! Start not, mothers! There is no need for such a law. Nature's table has bountifully provided for them all. It is only the capitalists who libel her, and say we are too many. But if this were true, and Nature had ceased to care for her own productions (the bare assertion is preposterous, and a libel on Nature's God!) it would be more merciful, and far more just, to execute this bloody Pharaohian law on every class, than, as we now do, at the bidding of Malthus, employ the rich to drive the poor from Nature's abundantly provided table, until starvation shuts them in the grave, or banishes them from their native soil, to enrich, by their sweat and their dust, the lands of savage tribes! We profess to be wise, and to have discovered folly in Nature's laws. Our pride blinds us, our excessive love of gold hardens us, and we are fast pushing onwards to our own destruction.[107]

Oastler's appeal to 'Nature's God' mirrored earlier pronouncements by *The Black* Dwarf: 'it was not Elizabeth, but GOD himself, who gave rights as irrevocable to the POOR as to the RICH!'[108]

It was Cobbett's argument, however – that poor relief was, in fact, the property of the poor – that most frequently appeared in the working-class press. *The Gorgon*, for example, defended the Old Poor Law thus:

> They wish to do away with the poor's-rate altogether; to rob the poor of their property. We say *their property*, because the poor-rates

are their property, to which they have as good a claim as the holders of any other species of property whatever. They are no voluntary gift, but a legal and established claim upon all the real property of the kingdom, and for which they can, if required, produce the *title deeds*. They have as much right to them as the parson to his tithes, a fundholder to his dividend, or an aristocrat to his rent, and while we can wield a pen or wag a tongue we will let them know it.[109]

The True Sun time and time again reiterated this theme: 'The Poor Laws are the real *Magna Charta* of the labouring classes. The Poor Laws secure to the labouring classes a conditional mortgage over all the land of England. The Poor Laws constitute, therefore, to the poor, a right of property.'[110] In the opinion of *The Working Man's Friend*, 'private property and a poor law are correlative principles.'[111]

Although the working-class press did not present anywhere near the detailed history that Cobbett produced in justifying the right to relief, many editors did reiterate his thesis concerning Henry VIII's plunder of the poor. The Poor Law of Elizabeth, so the argument ran, was fundamentally a restoration of the rights of the poor that were 'annihilated' by Henry VIII's sequestration of church property and abolition of religious houses, institutions which had relieved the poor through the exaction of tithes.[112] *The Poor Man's Guardian* perhaps summed it up best:

> The right of these poor people to parish relief is of more than two centuries standing. It was given them in exchange for their share of the church property, of which the Reformation had despoiled them. It was their 'vested interest,' in the most enlarged sense of those words, for it was not only guaranteed by the law of the land, but also by those of justice, humanity, and sound religion. Yet, of this most sacred of all sacred properties have the poor been despoiled by the capitalists.[113]

In addition, Cobbett's notion of a social compact originating well before the Reformation was employed. *The True Sun*, for example, referred to the 'patrimonial interest' that the poor had in the soil of England, an interest 'which the lapse of centuries has rendered sacred'. More specifically it claimed:

> If a legal provision for the poor be 'a mischievous arrangement,' the institution of property must be a mischievous arrangement. If the consciousness that has for ages supported the English poor – the consciousness that under the social compact they possessed a guarantee against starvation, be mischievous in its influences on society, the stronger consciousness of independence which belongs to the wealthy must, on the very same principles, be denounced as incomparably more mischievous.[114]

Given such a vociferous defence of the right to relief, it is no surprise that the working-class press unanimously opposed any threats to the legal guarantee of subsistence for the poor. The focus of such opposition, of course, centered on the New Poor Law. Even *The Poor Man's Guardian*, which tended to view the Poor Law as secondary to the central issues of universal male suffrage and unfair property distribution, eventually gave absolute precedence to the repeal of the 'NEW POOR LAW BILL'. Although Gertrude Himmelfarb may be correct in asserting that *The Poor Man's Guardian* believed that no institutional forms of relief could address the root causes of poverty, she underestimates the degree to which this influential newspaper defended the Old Poor Law and opposed the New.[115] In October 1835, O'Brien, the editor, made his position very clear indeed:

> ... the horrible Starvation Act admits of no delay. At the moment we write, human beings are dying, and human hearts are breaking, and agricultural produce is probably blazing all over the country, in consequence of that murderous enactment. The repeal of that enactment should, therefore, be the uppermost thought with every human being who pretends to the name of Reformer, or the name of man. Ardently as we desire Universal Suffrage, we should postpone it for this. To repeal the Poor Law Act is to arrest the arm of death. All considerations should, therefore, be secondary to it in the order of the time.[116]

O'Brien, moreover, made frequent and direct reference to Cobbett and especially praised his hard work 'on behalf of the poor and humanity' and against 'the miscalled Poor Laws Amendment Bill' for which 'he has our best thanks.'[117] Numerous extracts from the *Political Register* were reprinted under the heading 'SCRAPS FROM COBBETT'. *Legacy to Labourers* was reviewed in glowing terms and referred to as an 'excellent little book' containing solid reasonings and 'a mass of valuable information on the Poor-Laws Amendment Bill'.[118]

The Poor Man's Guardian claimed that with the exception of the Whig *Morning Chronicle*, the entire public press both stamped and unstamped (including *The Times)* had opposed the New Poor Law and 'the bitter first-fruits of the principles of the defunct Malthus'.[119] *The True Sun*, months before the passage of the New Poor Law argued that it violated 'the spirit of the poor man's charter' and 'the right of property in the poor'. The Poor Laws Amendment Bill, said the editor John Bell, was 'one of the grossest frauds which even the Whigs have attempted upon the poor'. If the 'Malthusian Poor Law Bill' was carried into law it would 'impose upon this country a worse than Egyptian bondage'.[120] Robert Owen in *The New Moral World* decried the theories of Malthus and labelled the Poor Law Bill a 'measure that will prove the greatest mistake that ... a political economist could have imagined'.[121] Hetherington's *Twopenny Dispatch* referred to the 'arbitrary, brutal, pauper-starving Whig Bastile law' which was 'more infernal in its operation than hell itself'.[122] *The Political Penny Magazine* urged the repeal of the 'Poor Law Tyranny Bill' claiming that this 'infamous and atrocious' law 'grinded, subdued, and robbed the poor'. It published a poem entitled 'THE DEVIL'S VISIT TO ENGLAND':

> He went where the workhouses built for the poor
> Show what our free people of England endure –
> The souls that are born to be saved
> Where thousands are starved upon three-pence a day
> That one man may have thousands a year for his pay
> The devil almost could have saved
> To think that the Whigs had invented this curse
> If hell is damned bad this is thousand times worse.[123]

Like Cobbett, the working-class press focused much of its opposition on the introduction of new workhouses – the 'gaols' constructed under the 'English Starvation and Bastile Bill'.[124] Of particular concern beyond the harsh discipline and cruelty involved – cases regarding the maltreatment of pregnant women were presented in detail – was the separation of husband, wife and children. *The Working Man's Friend* chastised *The Morning Chronicle* for advocating that married couples live separately in the workhouse.[125] *The Poor Man's Guardian* approvingly published a letter to the editor by J. Sekots who described the plight of a man, his wife and four children:

> Then they must go into the poorhouse, where the husband becomes a single man, for the Christian overseers set the marriage law at defiance. A virtuous wife is sent to sleep with prostitutes; the man is set to work on the mill all day, and locked up in the men's room at night; and the children are sent to another part of the house, away from their parents; and if the man and his wife are seen talking together in private, the woman is put into the straw-room and the man into the black-hole, and kept on bread and water during the pleasure of the governor ... .[126]

The Times was praised for its stance against the 'Starvation Law' and especially for its opposition to 'the separation of male from female and of child from adult, without the least reference to the ties of relationship, whether by marriage or by blood'.[127] *The Poor Man's Guardian* also argued that segregation of husband and wife was calculated to deter husbands from entering the workhouse and instead induce them 'to prefer any degree of tyranny from the masters, to such a horrible alternative', concluding that 'a viler crew never wielded power than the present Malthusian Ministers.'[128]

The working-class press likewise opposed the authority allocated to the Poor Law Commissioners in London. *The People's Conservative and Trades Union Gazette* disparagingly referred to a 'central board of bashaws with £1000 a year each'.[129] *The True Sun* cited a speech by Lord

Wynford in the House of Lords objecting to the right of Commissioners to examine all property titles in any particular parish they wished. Such 'extraordinary' powers, moreover, were not 'subjected to any real responsibility' in the manner in which they were exercised.[130]

Cobbett, of course, had predicted grave outcomes upon reform or abolition of the Old Poor Law. Similar arguments appeared in the wider working-class press. *The Poor Man's Advocate* in January of 1832, for example, spoke of the dissolution of the social compact and a return to the state of nature:

> Society was formed and laws were instituted, for the protection of the weak against the oppressions of the strong. But if society and those laws do not afford that protection, the ends of the institution are not obtained, and we return to our natural state of freedom and equality, when every individual is at liberty to procure for himself as much of the goods of the earth as he can.[131]

As early as 1821, in opposition to Scarlett's Poor Law Bill, *The Black Dwarf* claimed that if the poor were denied relief they would simply take what they needed:

> THE POOR WILL BE FED, in *some way* or other:–and were they refused the miserable pittance they now receive, they would HELP THEMSELVES with a less sparing hand. You may say they would have *no right* to do this – you may tell them it would be *illegal* to do this – but they would still do it, and feel satisfied they had a right, upon which none of their fellow-creatures had authority to sit in judgment![132]

All military duties to the state, moreover, would cease. Referring to the legal right to relief, *The Black Dwarf* stated:

> They only say, that in a state of society, those who cannot obtain labour, and those who cannot perform it, shall be provided with the bare means of subsistence. This is all the laws say—and these laws only recognize a principle of nature, a precept of reason, and what you must admit to be a divine commandment. The gift of life carries with it the right to live. It is not rational, that men who are bound to obey the laws, and defend the interests of society, should be refused the means of enabling them to discharge the obligations which society imposes. Shall society possess the right of saying to the hardy peasant, or the patient artisan— 'You shall be torn from your families, to fight our battles in our day of danger; but we will not, in your hours of distress, allow you bread to moisten with your tears!'[133]

In addition, abnegation of the rights of the poor would lead to violent uprisings against the property of the rich. 'Touch the poor laws in England,' threatened *The Black Dwarf*, 'and you formally declare war against the *existence* of a great proportion of society ... . The repeal of the poor-laws would be celebrated by an illumination in which half the barns and granaries in the kingdom, would blaze in terrific refulgence.' Nothing short of 'a revolution, or a state worse than revolution' would result.[134]

The True Sun, opposing the New Poor Law, claimed to go far beyond *The Times*, 'admirable' as was that establishment paper's stance: 'If the Whigs and Tories shall presume to violate the right of property in the poor, let them not shrink from the natural consequences.' Such natural consequences entailed a general uprising of the poor beginning in the southern counties of Kent and Sussex, which would 'be found strong enough to excite alarm in the breasts even of those who are not inclined to start at shadows'.[135]

The editors of the working-class press, then, clearly rejected Malthus's hypothesis that abolition of the Old Poor Law would foster moral restraint and increasing providence and individual responsibility among the poor. They likewise mirrored Cobbett's opposition to Malthusian arguments that stressed education and Savings Banks as positive inducements to such prudential values. Although at times misreading Cobbett – he did not, as some believed, oppose teaching poor children to read – they were in total agreement that education which merely promoted servility among the poor was thoroughly debilitating. Bronterre O'Brien in *The Destructive* gave the best summation:

> Some simpletons talk of knowledge making the working classes more obedient, more dutiful—better servants, better subjects and so on, which means making them more subservient slaves and more conducive to the wealth and gratification of idlers of all descriptions. But such knowledge is trash; the only knowledge which is of service to the working people is that which makes them more dissatisfied, and makes them worse slaves. This is the knowledge which we shall give them.[136]

Lord Brougham and the publications of the Society for the Diffusion of Useful Knowledge came under particular attack. *The Penny Magazine* and *Saturday Magazine*, for example, promoted 'poisonous doctrines' and 'sophistries … in favour of property' intent on 'reconciling the poor (in the name of religion!) to hunger and servitude'.[137]

Savings Banks, moreover, harmed rather than benefited the poor. *The Poor Man's Guardian* reported a speech by William Pare at a meeting of the Cooperative Conference on 23 April 1832, where he argued that the banks loaned the deposits of labourers to manufacturers who used such capital to depress wages and raise prices.[138] The savings of the poor also ended up in the 'hands of idle and unproductive fundholders'.[139] The working classes, claimed *The Poor Man's Guardian*, should 'devote their funds to their own purposes, instead of placing them as in the Savings' Banks, at the disposal of bad government'.[140]

With rare exception, the working-class press also opposed emigration as a solution to the Malthusian dilemma. Malthus was often inaccurately labelled as an unqualified supporter of emigration. 'The political economists, with a Christian clergyman at their head,' said William Carson in a speech quoted in *The Poor Man's Guardian*, 'wish what they term the surplus population of the country to transport themselves to distant shores and foreign climes.'[141] Much of the anti-emigration sentiment, however, was directed not at Malthus himself but at outspoken advocates of the out-migration of the poor such as Wilmot Horton and George Poulett Scrope, MP, who favoured systematic colonization abroad. Like Cobbett, Hetherington's *Penny Papers for the People* opposed Lord Howick's emigration bill in 1831 and argued that even political economists were agreed that England could support treble its population.[142] William Carpenter in *Political Letters* voiced similar arguments denying the existence of surplus population and thus any necessity for government-sponsored emigration, as did Robert Owen in *The Crisis*.[143]

Proposals to remove the poor from England, moreover, were opposed on the basis of class bias. *Political Letters* approvingly published a letter to Wilmot Horton from William Pare who employed a familiar Cobbett metaphor:

> There remains one matter in this scheme of emigration, which I do not feel warranted in passing over in silence. I mean the project for sending from the country the *able-bodied* LABOURERS. If a beehive were to become over-populated, think you that the inhabitants would drive away the *working* bees! Would not their attention be rather directed to the getting rid of the *drones*,—of those who idly consumed the sweets of the industrious, and who created not one jot or tittle.[144]

The Poor Man's Guardian printed letters in a debate between Jeremy Dewhurst, chairman of the Handloom Weaver's Central Committee, whom the editors supported, and George Poulett Scrope. Dewhurst claimed he would consent to emigration under only one condition:

> That condition is, that the surplus population (as political economists say) shall be submitted to a general ballot of all classes and professions – peers, commoners, clergy and people, capitalists and paupers, and there shall be no release, no hire of substitutes, but actual and identical transportation. And, forasmuch as we are informed by you, that labour without capital would be 'worse off than ever,' we annex to our bargain this condition – that for every draught of labourers there shall be a draught of capitalists, and that Mr. George Poulett Scrope, and John Poulett Thomson, his brother, shall go with the first batch, and take their capital to spend upon our labour.[145]

The working-class press, however, at times admitted that given the deplorable conditions under which the poor laboured, individuals might have no choice but to leave their country of birth. 'Seriously speaking,' asserted *The Black Dwarf*, 'the attractions of liberty, and independence are so powerful when opposed to the horrors of dependence and slavery, that man would traverse the globe in search of them.'[146] Well aware of what *Political Letters* called the 'HORRORS OF EMIGRATION' – case-studies of which were frequently published especially regarding Van Diemen's Land and Canada – editors were often prepared to offer advice for those intent on leaving.[147] *The Black Dwarf*, in fact, praised Cobbett for his 'most prudent' counsel to those embarking for America while stressing the fact that he did not recommend emigration.[148] *The Poor Man's Guardian* took a similar position. Advertising a book entitled *RARE NEWS FOR LABOURERS*; or *Advice to Emigrants*, it presented the following brief review:

> Of this little work we can only say that it contains the best, because the plainest and most useful information to Emigrants that we have seen. Persons wishing to obtain information respecting leaving the land of their nativity, and the course which they should pursue, will not regret the purchase of this little neat and useful book.—Mind, *we* do *not* say 'leave the land of your fathers,' but if you will go, here is advice you *ought* to possess.[149]

Having rejected the solutions of Malthus, both negative and positive, the working-class press advocated their own remedies for poverty that often paralleled Cobbett's proposals. The repeal of taxes especially on consumption goods loomed large in such discussions. Stressing high taxes as a fundamental cause of distress, *The Black Dwarf*, in typical Cobbett fashion, used the headline 'The Tax Payers against the Tax Eaters!' and argued that taxation, not poor relief, should be reduced.[150] *Penny Papers for the People* specifically advocated the removal of taxes on malt and soap.[151] *The Poor Man's Guardian* called for the 'immediate repeal of all the taxes which directly or indirectly fall upon the poor man' and placed second among seventeen 'NATIONAL OBJECTS OF THE PRODUCTIVE CLASSES' the following item: 'An abolition of all other customs, duties, and taxes, national, county, and parochial'.[152]

Ironically it was Richard Carlile who most passionately sought to reduce taxation. In the 1820s he had vehemently opposed Cobbett on the issues of republicanism, birth control and religion. By the early 1830s, he acknowledged that Cobbett's idea of reducing total tax revenues from fifty million pounds a year to ten million was a worthy and necessary goal.[153] In *The Gauntlet* he called on all men and women fourteen years of age and above to enroll as volunteers pledged to reduce taxation to ten million a year. A roll of volunteers would be published creating a 'moral congregation of the public' which would 'shew the strength of the people' and 'make the present government feel its weakness and its wickedness'. Such volunteers, moreover, would form a core of 'sturdy reformers', ready to take whatever action necessary, even physical force, to achieve change.[154]

Reduced taxation, of course, was closely allied with cuts in wasteful government expenditure and elimination of the national debt. *The Poor Man's Guardian*, in a list of policies parliamentary candidates concerned about the 'popular interest' should support, included the following: 'The *Abolition of all Sinecures, the Extinction of Pensions*, not merited by public services, and the exclusion of pensioners from the House of Commons, are changes which justice and the sufferings of the poor, imperiously dictate.'[155] The same paper proposed to extinguish the national debt by purchasing 'the interests of the present holders of stock at present value in the market 'and letting them receive their dividends until they had drawn their full amount. 'This', continued the editor O'Brien, 'would leave them at ease for some 20 and odd years, during which they might train themselves and their families for an honester and more useful course of life. But at the expiration of this time, we should hear no more of national debts, except as matters of history.'[156]

Like Cobbett, much of the working-class press – even though they may have disagreed with him about the root causes of poverty – placed great emphasis on universal male suffrage as a major if not *the* solution to England's ills (my emphasis). T. J. Wooler in *The Black Dwarf* ran a headline in 1822 which read: 'UNIVERSAL SUFFRAGE, AN ESSEN-TIAL PART OF RADICAL REFORM'.[157] The 'system', argued Wooler, 'could never be reformed until *the poor chuse their own law makers*, instead of their being *chosen for them by the rich*.'[158] The notion that reducing population would eliminate the evils affecting labour was 'entirely chimerical'. The labourer, he maintained, must attain 'actual possession of his political rights'.[159] John Wade in *The Gorgon* defended universal suffrage on the Benthamite grounds of 'the greatest good, to the greatest number of individuals'.[160] The 'whole gist and marrow' of the issue was the 'expedience and practical benefits' that would result from such a system of representation.[161] Economic and social inequality, he argued, stemmed from 'the exclusion of the people from a just share in their government'.[162] In *The Republican*, Richard Carlile approvingly printed an essay entitled 'THE PEOPLE, THE FOUNTAIN OF AUTHORITY' which contended that legitimate political authority 'must be derived from the whole community' since the people constitute the natural source of all power.'[163]

Papers of the 1830s expressed similar sentiments. Carlile continued to advocate for universal suffrage in *The Gauntlet*. 'I am', he declared, 'a radical reformer of the House of Commons. It should be the choice of the whole people.' He further claimed, 'the right of the people to appoint the legislator admits of no right of abridgement.'[164] *Political Letters and Pamphlets* advocated 'the full and fair representation of *THE WHOLE PEOPLE*' which would secure 'the national and individual dignity of the people, in a more just division of wealth, and of the enjoyments of society'.[165] *The True Sun* argued that no changes should be made to the Old Poor Law until 'the labouring classes shall be fairly represented in Parliament – till, in short, universal suffrage shall be established.'[166] Following Cobbett's reasoning, John Bell, the editor, contended that the Poor Laws constituted 'to the poor, a right of property' and thus 'the same right to the elective franchise which the rich possess'.[167]

It was *The Poor Man's Guardian*, however, which became the staunchest advocate of political equality. In the absence of 'Universal Suffrage and Vote by Ballot, and No-Property Qualifications', all other solutions 'will end in smoke, at least so far as the interests of the working millions are concerned'.[168] Such political reform, it claimed, was 'the only remedy ... we deem worthy of the attention of the working classes'.[169] Cobbett on his election as MP for Oldham in 1832 was given high praise for his consistent support of universal suffrage and described as 'the labourer's best friend – the unrivalled advocate of useful reform, and equal rights for all classes'.[170] Political power, *The Poor Man's Guardian* argued, would provide '*a voice in making the laws*' and was '*absolutely essential to the working classes, if they would emancipate themselves from their present deplorable state of poverty and slavery*'.[171] Such power would confer '*equal rights and equal laws for all*':

> By equal rights, we mean not simply Universal Suffrage, as Mr. Owen seems to think, but the equal right of every individual to a full participation in all the advantages of the State, according to the value of his services. This would include not only education, preferment, freedom of opinion, etc., etc., but also his due share of the national wealth. Now, Universal Suffrage is but a single step towards this end; but, being the first and most important step, we always speak of it as a *sine qua non*.[172]

Robert Owen, of course, totally rejected universal suffrage in favour of voluntary cooperation, education and moral reform. 'The North Americans,' he claimed, 'have Universal Suffrage, and their evils, in proportion to their means, are similar to those of other nations.'[173] *The Poor Man's Guardian* objected vehemently to Owen's position and much of its defence of Universal Suffrage was directed against the Owenites. Owen's cooperative communities were utopian designs unachievable until 'the poor shall possess themselves of political power'.[174] The people of the United States, although failing to move from universal suffrage towards equal rights and equal laws, nevertheless were 'tolerably comfortable', had 'good wages' and 'were they to lose their political rights, they would soon sink into the condition of our own labourers.'[175]

Cobbett clearly had an immense influence on the anti-Malthusianism of the working-class press throughout the 1820s and early 1830s. His works were directly cited, praised and also frequently reprinted, especially pieces from his *Political Register*. Even when not mentioned by name his arguments and often his metaphors permeated editorial discourse. Yet while retaining much of his old ideology, editors – particularly of the unstamped papers between 1830 and 1834 – moved in new directions developing a more sophisticated and innovative critique of Malthus's thought. In the process, many of Cobbett's assumptions and conclusions were openly and often forcefully attacked.

Beyond the master of invective: the new ideology

If Cobbett was frequently praised, he was often damned. His departure to New York in late March 1817, for example, provoked outrage in *The Black Dwarf*. T. J. Wooler called such flight an 'evident dereliction of duty', an act of 'desertion' based on fear and cowardice.[176] Cobbett, in typical fashion, labelled Wooler's attack on him a personal vendetta. He had previously insisted that Wooler be fired as a printer of his *Political Register* in London 'on account of his dilatoriness, his inaccuracies, and his slovenliness, arising from his drunkenness and dissolute life'. Wooler, he claimed, was merely seeking revenge.[177]

Richard Carlile in *The Republican*, castigated Cobbett in more general terms:

> Mr. Cobbett is a freebooter in politics, and in other matters, and feeling this to be right, he sees no gain but in the principles and practices of a freebooter. He is in himself an *all in all*, a self-elected, universal sovereign in the political world, a freebooter warring with all who do not pay him political homage and tribute and ask his protection. A man that cannot endure a political competitor, and, under all these ideas of self-sufficiency and self-importance, void of all sound political principles or good principles of any kind, and incessantly making political blunders by contradicting positively today the most positive assertions of yesterday; a man, who, though laborious, as a writer, never could take a large view of any subject, and who never was right, on any political subject.[178]

Cobbett responded by branding Carlile a 'monster' and a 'beast'.[179]

Although deeming the language 'rather rough' and 'too severe', *The Poor Man's Guardian* nevertheless reprinted from *The Man* the following castigation of Cobbett:

Such is the doctrine of that shuffling trickster, Cobbett, of whom Broughton (when a man) very justly said, 'he is consistent in nothing but in being inconsistent.' In the language of the adage, 'he measures other men's corn by his own bushel;' hence his opposition to the education of the people – finding that in proportion as he himself acquires knowledge, the more artifice, knavery, and deceit, he is enabled to practise. By these means did he doff the buckskins and quarter-jacks with which he delved in the royal gardens at Kew, and by these means has he seated himself in the den of St. Stephen, to flatter royalty, and hoodwink the king-gull'd million. However, he will probably fulfil in his own person his prophecy on his brother fungus Burdett, 'he will live to stink in the nose of the nation.'[180]

There were two fundamental ways in which significant sectors of the working-class press moved beyond Cobbett's anti-Malthusian analysis. Although most editors accepted Cobbett's denunciation of the 'principle of population' – that surplus population was the fundamental cause of poverty – many disagreed with his conclusions regarding the origins of mass destitution. They developed what Hollis and Himmelfarb respectively term a 'new ideology' or a 'new radicalism'. The causes of immiseration were now rooted in the unequal distribution of property, class domination by capitalists, and an erroneous theory of political economy promulgated by the likes of Malthus and McCulloch. The solution now lay in the redistribution of property ideally through the peaceful attainment of political equality. Failing this, many were prepared to sanction violent revolution. Not surprisingly, however, the working-class press did not speak with a unified voice. Robert Owen, a persistent critic of Malthus, proposed a vision of a new cooperative society achieved through the gradual non-violent means of moral reform and education. Political change through the creation of universal suffrage he deemed irrelevant.

The second and, in principle at least, more damaging assault on Malthusianism was the advocacy of voluntary birth control which Cobbett vehemently denounced. To be sure, those who endorsed such practices agreed with Cobbett in condemning 'moral restraint' as a viable means of curbing population growth. Unlike Cobbett, however, they accepted Malthus's argument that overpopulation bred poverty. Given the necessity of restricting family size, they were prepared to support various means of preventing conception. Many, like Robert Owen, no doubt favoured contraception but were wary of making their views public. Others, like Henry Hetherington and James Watson, advertised and sold Robert Dale Owen's *Moral Physiology* (1831) and Charles Knowlton's *Fruits of Philosophy* (1832), works dealing specifically with birth control. J. S. Mill published articles anonymously in the working-class press during the 1820s. Francis Place did likewise and, in addition, circulated thousands of anonymous handbills in working-class London and the industrial north of England. The most outspoken on the subject was Richard Carlile who provoked Cobbett's wrath by publishing 'What is Love?' on 6 May 1825 in *The Republican* and in the following year revised and reprinted the essay as a book entitled *Every Woman's Book; or What is Love?*

As Gertrude Himmelfarb has rightly remarked, writers such as Bronterre O'Brien in *The Poor Man's Guardian* argued that Cobbett's analysis of the origins of poverty – excessive taxation, paper money, sinecures – mistook causes for what, in fact, were mere symptoms.[181] What, *The Poor Man's Guardian* asked, was the 'main cause' of 'all the evils of society?'. The answer was clear indeed: 'Why, it is property and property only. They all spring from distinctions arising in some way out of property.'[182] Property was defined as:

> The right which one man claims to seize (by force or fraud) the fruits of another's labour, without giving him an equivalent in exchange. This is the secret of all the crimes on earth. This is the original sin of the world. This is the father of all superstitions. This is the monster which sharpens the soldier's bayonet against his own brother, and knots the cat-'o-nine-tails against the soldier's back. Yes, brother reformers, *'property'* is the great destroyer.[183]

Mere tampering with symptoms would not solve anything: 'Now, we have a hundred times shown that a mere reduction, or transfer of taxes, if unaccompanied by other far more important changes, would not in the smallest degree benefit the working classes, under the present system of servitude.'[184]

Property, moreover, was the basis of an exploitative class system. Cobbett, of course, after the passage of the New Poor Law, increasingly adopted an analysis based on class conflict. His rhetoric, however, which focused on a potential struggle between rich and poor, was still imbedded in the old ideology. O'Brien in *The Poor Man's Guardian* had clearly moved towards a far more sophisticated class interpretation:

> Now, since all wealth is the produce of industry, and as the privileged fraction produce nothing themselves, it is plain that they must live on the labours of the rest. But how is this to be done, since everybody thinks it enough to work for himself. It is done partly by *fraud* and partly by *force*. The 'property' people having all the law-making to themselves, make and maintain fraudulent institutions, by which they contrive (under false pretences) to transfer the wealth of the producers to themselves. All our institutions relating to *land* and *money* are of this kind. These institutions enable certain individuals, called '*landlords*', to monopolize the soil, to the exclusion of the rest of society, who are thereby defrauded of their just and natural inheritance. To secure themselves in this monopoly, the landlords unite with another band of conspirators called '*capitalists*', and from

this union proceeds a *monied monopoly*, which is (if possible) a thousand times more baneful than the monopoly in land. From these two master monopolies proceed a thousand others, all working in the same way, and all tending to the same end – namely, the absorption of the annual produce of the country into the hands of the monopolists. One portion is absorbed under the name of *rent*. Another under that of *tithes*, a third under that of *taxes*, a fourth under that of *tolls*, a fifth under that of *law expenses*, a sixth under that of *interest*, a seventh (which is by far the greatest) under that of *profits*, and so on with *commissions, agencies, brokerage* etc. to the end of the chapter. These and the like are the pretences under which the useful classes are plundered for the benefit of the useless.[185]

Although O'Brien seems to imply a calculated conspiracy, he nevertheless spoke in terms of a 'system' which left 'no alternative, but to victimize or be victimized'. Unlike Cobbett he was reluctant to blame individuals. 'We do not', he claimed, 'accuse the monied capitalist of intentional robbery.' Their 'spoliations of the industrious classes' occurred not from 'sinister design' but from 'the silent operation of causes over which they have no control under the existing arrangements of society'.[186] Arguing against the tactic of assassination, he contended that individual rulers were the tools of 'classes that uphold them in power'. 'The slavery of states', he argued, was 'the work of classes, not individuals'.[187]

The new emphasis on property and class exploitation was part of a wider assault on political economy that went far beyond Cobbett. Patricia Hollis points out that although the unstamped press was rife with hostile references to political economy, the main attacks came from William Carpenter in *Political Letters* and from Hetherington and O'Brien in *The Poor Man's Guardian* and *The Destructive*.[188] The former published a series of letters from the Owenite William Pare against Wilmot Horton's pro-emigration arguments.[189] O'Brien consistently critiqued Malthus and increasingly attacked J. R. McCulloch who, by the 1830s, had become highly influential among political economists.[190]

Such writers questioned a number of core principles agreed upon by Malthus and his followers. Carpenter, for example, reiterated Robert Owen's theme of the evils inherent in self-interested competition. He published articles by George Mudie, former editor of the Owenite *Economist*. The fundamental error of society, Mudie argued, was that '*the interest of each individual has been placed, in direct opposition to the interest of other individuals, and to the interest of society.*'[191] Owen, himself, had no doubts on this issue. In *The Crisis* he addressed workers directly: 'By the individual competitive system, which involves you in the ignorance and distress which you have experienced, you have been compelled to become a population of inconsistent, wretched, irrational creatures.'[192] *The Poor Man's Guardian*, on a list entitled 'PROGRESS OF CIVILIZATION. NATIONAL OBJECTS OF THE PRODUCTIVE CLASSES', entered the following: 'Arrangements to be adopted, as soon as practicable, to put an end to individual and national competition and contest, now unnecessary, and producing innumerable grievous evils to all classes'.[193]

In addition, the commodification of labour was severely censured. William Pare, for example, claimed that in Owenite cooperative communities labour would no longer be offered for hire and would cease to be '*a purchasable commodity*'.[194] The utilization of machinery, he claimed, would then become beneficial.[195] *The Poor Man's Guardian* cited a speech given by James Watson to the National Union of the Working Classes where he decried the reduction of labour 'to the standard of a marketable commodity'.[196] O'Brien attacked Brougham by claiming that 'his whole superstructure of argument (if such wretched sophistry can be called argument) is based upon the Ricardo-dogma that "*labour is a marketable commodity*", a dogma which we have shewn ... to be a most impudently false assumption, disguised under the form of an abstraction.'[197]

O'Brien, moreover, clashed head-on with the principles of political economy in arguing that the separation of politics from economics was fundamentally erroneous. Even though political economists were prepared to sanction state intervention in education (Smith, Malthus, McCulloch), communications (Smith, McCulloch), and certain health measures (McCulloch), they nevertheless viewed the political realm as distinct from the economic. Even before O'Brien became editor, *The Poor Man's Guardian* had clearly stated: 'From government all good proceeds – and from the government, all the evils that afflict the human race emanate. There is no power except that of government, that can extensively effect the social state of man.'[198] As Hollis points out, O'Brien went on to develop a double critique of society, which viewed politics and economics as inseparable. Class domination occurred because the rich made the laws. Such power over legislation led to economic hegemony. Workers were doubly oppressed: politically in being denied the vote, economically in being denied the produce of their labour. As O'Brien said of the capitalists:

> By the law they can make wrong right, and right wrong – they can make bad money good money and *vice versa*, they can make blasphemy religion and religion blasphemy. They can even draught off one section of the people to slaughter the other .... The law, then, being our chief enemy, we should spare no efforts to obtain a mastery over it ... for without a power over the *law* we see no means of controlling the land and currency.[199]

'seized upon the monopoly of law-making thus depriving six-sevenths of the population 'of acquiring anything beyond a bare subsistence'.[208] Property 'fairly acquired' represented 'labour done' or 'services rendered', proceeded from 'honest sources' and did not sacrifice 'any other man's right and privileges'. Such property, he maintained, should be protected.[209] O'Brien then asked how property should be reformed:

> Is it by destroying it, or ordaining that that there shall be no property? By no means. – This is Mr. Owen's doctrine, but not ours. Mr. Owen believes that the evils alluded to are inseparable from any or every institution of property. We think differently. We believe them to arise only from bad institutions of property, – institutions which give to one man a property in what does really and ought to belong to another man. The object of all institutions should be to make every individual in the state contribute (in service of some kind) as much to society as he takes from it. If he produces 5*l*. worth of wealth of any kind, he ought to get 5*l*., or an equivalent in other produce ... in short, that in all cases, he should get an equivalent for his labour, but in no case be permitted to get a property, or profit out of other people's labour without yielding a fair equivalent. If our institutions were formed with a view to these objects, there would be no accumulations in individual hands. None would be rich; because in such a state there would be neither the means nor the motives for amassing; and none would be poor, because the labour of each would be more than sufficient to supply his wants, and even surround him with luxuries.[210]

In the same issue (28 March 1835) of *The Poor Man's Guardian,* O'Brien proposed specific changes to land and the capital employed in commerce and manufacturing. After a twenty-year period of compensation to the landlords, the 'whole soil of the country' would be appropriated to the 'whole people'. All income from land would flow to the nation – now the 'sole landlord' – and be used to increase the comforts of the whole population.' Capitalist proprietors would be likewise compensated. Their firms would then be democratized. Profits that previously enriched only the owner of the enterprise would now be apportioned among all employees, 'each member receiving a share proportional to his services'.[211]

As Himmelfarb aptly remarks, *The Poor Man's Guardian* did not reconcile its differential treatment of land that was to be nationalized and capitalist enterprise, which retained private ownership.[212] Nor did O'Brien explain the apparent contradiction between his desire to protect legitimate private property and his proposal to expropriate all land on behalf of the state. He nevertheless was convinced that such 'reform' would constitute a 'direct blow at the principle of *unjust* accumulation':

> We say, *unjust* accumulation, for there can be no just objection to any man accumulating the fruits of his own earnings. All that is

> required is, – that he take no interest for the loan of such
> accumulations, and that the laws shall prevent any such disposal or
> bequest of them as would create a race of idlers, calling themselves
> an 'aristocracy,' and lording it over their more industrious
> brethren.[213]

The application of similar policies to church property, the national debt
and all other 'vested interests' would ensure that within two decades
'every man might start fair, in the field of competition or co-operation as
they thought fit, and be in full condition to receive the full equivalent for
their services to society.'[214] If O'Brien opposed competition under
conditions of unjust accumulation he sanctioned its spirit under
conditions of equality.[215]

To envision a new society is one thing: to create it is another. Most
radicals advocated peaceful means towards political and economic
reform: working-class support for model parliamentary candidates;
consumer boycotts of goods such as alcohol, tea, coffee and tobacco;
withdrawal of funds from Savings Banks, and non-payment of taxes.[216]
Much of the working-class press rejected physical force on principle,
among them Robert Owen's *The Crisis* and *New Moral World*, James
Morrison's *The Pioneer*, John Wade's *Gorgon* and William Carpenter's
Political Letters (at least after the 1830–31 agricultural labourers'
uprising). Cobbett, in the main, agreed with such strategies. Only when
the repeal of the New Poor Law seemed beyond reach did he reluctantly
speak of violent 'revolution'. Even then he did so mostly in private letters
with little specificity.

A small number of unstamped papers, however, explicitly and
menacingly sanctioned violence well before the passage of the New Poor
Law. Richard Carlile in *The Gauntlet*, for example, proposed the
following resolution:

> That, so long as any kind of tyrannical rule is exercised over us, so
> long as the Government is not what it ought to be, or whenever it
> shall deviate from that which it ought to be, we will severally and
> individually provide for ourselves and learn the use of the best
> possible weapons, as arms, and make it a moral duty to be prepared,
> with arms and ammunition, to resist all tyranny that may be
> attempted upon us.[217]

In *The Cosmopolite*, he informed his readers 'it is an armed people only
that a tyrannical government fears.'[218] James Lorymer, editor of *The
Radical* and numerous other journals claimed that the oppressed had
never redressed their grievances 'by any other means than intimidation,
menaces, and coercion'.[219] He later became an active 'physical force'
Chartist at the end of the 1830s.

Even though O'Brien denounced such views and advocated nonviolent change through 'law' rather than 'force',[220] he was capable of employing extremely threatening rhetoric: 'We had rather see our countrymen up to their ears in blood, than see them die by inches, the despised outcast victims of your cannibal legislation.'[221] Prior to O'Brien's editorship, which began in November 1832, *The Poor Man's Guardian* promoted all-out war: 'Such is the horrible policy of our oppressors, – and such are the enemies of God and man, against whom we have sworn eternal war, – "war to the knife," – war that shall have no limit but the establishment of eternal truth and justice on the ruins of oligarchy, usurpation, and robbery.'[222]

In April 1832 it published extensive extracts from Colonel Frances Macerone's *Defensive Instructions for the People* which offered detailed tactics on the defence of villages and towns, the strategies of street fighting, the use of small arms and ammunition, the effectiveness of moveable barricades and the manufacture of explosives, combustibles and burning acids. Said Macerone, former Aide-de-camp to the King of Naples:

> It is essential for a free people to be armed. To hope that liberty and justice can be preserved with all the means of power and coercion, existing in the hands of the governing minority, is an infantine delusion! In the United States, every man has his rifle, and knows well how to use it. An armed people cannot be subdued by any faction. They require no paid army to *protect* them; and none can coerce them. ARM, THEN, OH, BRITISH PEOPLE, AND YOU WILL BE SAFE!'[223]

Beyond the master of invective: birth control

If the new ideology represented one broad assault on Malthusianism that went beyond Cobbett, a second, more specific and potentially more devastating critique, went even further: the covert or outright promotion of voluntary birth control to prevent conception. Malthus, of course, rejected such 'promiscuous intercourse' on both moral and economic grounds. 'Indeed,' he claimed, 'I should always particularly reprobate any artificial and unnatural modes of checking population, both on account of their immorality and their tendency to remove a necessary stimulus to industry.'[224] Cobbett, for once, was in agreement at least on moral grounds. He abusively described Richard Carlile – the most public advocate of birth control in the 1820s and the author of 'What is Love?' – as 'the tool of an execrable wretch in London, who is probably, and most likely the tool of other execrable wretches, that must finally be dragged forth to light.'[225]

Angus McLaren rightly stresses that the potential use of contraception struck at the heart of Malthusian doctrine. This solution allowed individuals, such as Frances Place, J. S. Mill and Richard Carlile, to approve of Malthus's premises regarding overpopulation as the cause of poverty while offering a panacea that would eliminate the necessity of self-denial, whether in the form of moral restraint or the responsibility of the male breadwinner to support a family in the absence of state welfare. Malthus's concern that birth control would lead to under-population was echoed by McCulloch who contended 'few, compara-tively, among the poorer classes, would be inclined to burden themselves with the task of providing for a family.'[226] Such a situation, as Malthus argued, would undermine the stimulus so necessary to goad the naturally lethargic labourer to acquire 'habits of industry, economy and prudence'.[227] McCulloch predicted 'society would gradually sink into apathy and languor.'[228]

Such fears proved unfounded. Those who condemned birth control formed a decisive majority of early nineteenth-century public opinion. The minority who condoned such practices often expressed their views only in private letters. David Ricardo, for example, wrote to Francis Place, approving of the passage in his *Illustrations and Proofs of the Principle of Population* that sanctioned contraception. In a letter to Malthus the next day, however, he spoke more cautiously: 'Place speaks of ... preventives to an excess population – he does not dwell upon it, but I have a little doubt whether it is right even to mention it.'[229]

Place himself suffered widespread public condemnation for nearly two decades once it was discovered that he had written and circulated birth control handbills in the 1820s. He was frequently condemned in print. Many declined introductions to him. The Society for Promoting Useful Knowledge would not allow him to write tracts for workers claiming 'thy ought to recollect what Mr Place had written respecting Population and to take care not to identify the Society with him.'[230] Carlile's first wife Jane warned her husband that Place was 'a black villain' who 'wants to bring you into a deep disgrace'.[231]

Jane Carlile, moreover, would not even read her husband's book and despised anyone who sympathized with his views on birth control. Richard met with widespread public disapproval. At a lecture in Bath he was shouted down and chased out of town while *Every Woman's Book; or What is Love?* was publicly burnt.[232] Many women in the towns of Bristol, Coventry, Bolton and Glasgow opposed him.[233] The well-known radical Mary Fildes of Manchester, a courageous participant at Peterloo, mistakenly associated birth control with 'the doctrines of the cold-blooded Malthus' and denied Carlile's claims that she was a convert to his cause and was secretly promoting it.[234] When Place's anonymous handbills were delivered to her with a request to distribute them, she refused, claiming the contents were 'a disgrace to human nature'.[235]

Although certain influential sectors of the radical press, most notably *The Poor Man's Guardian*, remained silent on the issue, others joined Cobbett and the chorus of wider public opinion in condemning the propagation of birth control. J. T. Wooler in *The Black Dwarf* provided the most extensive critique. Between September and December 1823 he published and replied to Place's anonymous handbills as well as letters by Place and J. S. Mill signed only 'AZ' and 'AM' respectively. He thus launched England's first public debate on contraception. Wooler firmly rejected the limitation of births on economic, political and moral grounds.

As a confirmed anti-Malthusian, Wooler argued that birth control, like moral restraint, was simply unnecessary. In response to J. S. Mill, he claimed it was 'capable of proof, that the produce of this country could be increased, at least five-fold including the cultivation of wastes; – and, with these advantages, destroyed or prohibited by a bad system, it certainly appears to be shunning the great question, to talk of the redundancy of population, and the necessity of checking it.'[236] Referring to Malthus's metaphor of the feast he saw 'the general table sufficiently spread' and wished 'all who are forcibly excluded from the feast, would try their strength with those who would shut them out'.[237] He chastised Malthus for wishing 'to get rid of the children of the poor, and of the poor themselves, except just what number may be requisite for the production of subsistence for the rich',[238] and argued 'child-bearing was not the evil of all others to be avoided.'[239]

Wooler, speaking of the poor, reasserted the old ideology that 'the *true source* of their poverty' was 'the deprivation of the due reward of their labour by the excessive demand for enjoyment at their expense, by the privileged classes'.[240] Such economic inequality, moreover, was based on the denial of the suffrage, allowing the rich to create laws in their own interest. His solutions closely paralleled Cobbett's proposals for economic and political reform – lower taxes, elimination of sinecures and wasteful expenditure and 'political rights' for labourers.[241] 'To attempt,' argued Wooler, 'to counteract these evils by diminishing the population by any artificial means is entirely chimerical.'[242]

Population pressure, moreover, would encourage reform:

> No impression will ever by made upon the fears of our borough lords, but the numbers and determination of the people. The natural remedy for such a corrupt state of things, is the INCREASE of population, even to the extreme of pressure against the means of subsistence; for it is the nature of the multitude to bear with oppression, and want, as long as their animal necessities will permit

them; and it is only by reducing them to a state bordering on despair, that they will ever be induced to avenge their wrongs, or to claim their rights.[243]

Birth control, in addition, might result in too few children being born. Wooler unwittingly echoed Malthus's and McCulloch's fears concerning underpopulation: 'We do not see how the exact quantity of children should be born, to keep up, what some of our political economists would call, the exact ratio between mouths, and the means of keeping them employed.' Childbirth should not be tampered with but rather should be 'very safely left to that Providence which has spread so beautiful a table for all his creatures'.[244]

Wooler also strongly objected to birth control on moral grounds. Such practices, he condemned as counteracting the laws of nature and destroying the very moral basis of society, an argument commonly made by anti-birth-controllers:

> Nature abhors such expedients: and true policy consists in a strict accordance with the precepts of nature. Let the circulators of these handbills remember that they are at the same time taking away from illicit intercourse the great preventive to that vice in the dread of the consequences: – and thus conferring a premium on the destruction of female morals; and encouraging the most extended scale of prostitution. But this is not all. – They are preparing the way for further experiments which may end in the grossest abominations; and extend the infamous practices which have so shamefully disgraced so many *ornaments of the church*, and *pillars of the state.*[245]

What experiments and abominations Wooler had in mind were not specified. A few months later, however, he did express a fear that infanticide might be the next step: 'Those who should familiarize themselves with the remedy proposed, might pass from prevention to destruction – from the dread of having too many future competitors to the annihilation of present rivals.'[246]

Other radical papers denounced birth control as immoral. *The Trades' Newspaper and Mechanics' Weekly Journal* referred to the birth controllers as the 'Muirheads of the day', alluding to John Grossett Muirhead's forthcoming trial for indecent assault on a male youth. With moral indignation, the editor John Robertson exclaimed:

> Extensive as has been the importation of foreign vices since the peace, manliness of feeling is still the pride and boast of Englishmen. We only wish that the public indignation would extend a little farther; and include in its vengeance the advocates and eulogists of certain practices for regulating the population of the country, which, though represented as the fruits of *soundest political economy*, are, in fact, as detestably wicked as any that the reports alluded to have revealed.[247]

Robertson, much like Wooler, described Place's proposal as 'prospectively murderous at least' and unnecessary since 'there can be no more mouths in the land, than Providence has, for some good purpose, sent there.'[248]

Most vituperative in its attack was *The Bull Dog*, a short lived weekly (only four issues were published) founded in the summer of 1826 with the singular purpose of annihilating Place and Carlile in both literary and political terms. Its editor, William Thomas Haley, a former shopman of Carlile's, impugned Place, Carlile and Bentham as 'a gang of persons determinately and brutally bent on the destruction of all loyal, religious, and moral feelings, in the lower and middle classes of this our great and happy land'.[249] Carlile, he fulminated, was a 'Beast,' who had authored 'that most foul and detestable publication that had issued from the press, even in the present age of sublimated bestiality'.[250] Place was 'a reptile' living 'for lust and appetite alone' and 'unfit for human fellowship':

> You, Sir, are ...a nasty old man ... . You are the author of ... a most foul and devilish attempt, at corrupting the youth of both sexes in this country; an attempt at no less than making CATAMITES of the male portion of the youth, and of the females, PROSTITUTES.[251]

Those who favoured birth control varied immensely in the degree to which they were prepared to publicly support the practice either in deeds or words. If almost all leading utilitarians concealed their views on the matter, so too did the socialist Robert Owen.[252] His role in the birth control movement remains indefinite. J. F. C. Harrison contends that Owen was involved from 1823 onward and that Owenites in general were champions of feminism, divorce and birth control.[253] D. E. C. Eversley and David Martin take a similar view.[254] In the 1820s Place circulated the story, later repeated by Carlile, that Owen had visited France in 1818 and brought back specimens of a birth-control device known as the sponge. Rumours prevailed that he encouraged its use at his model community at New Lanark.[255]

McClaren, however, stresses Owen's anti-Malthusianism and his denial of the necessity of limiting population. Contraception, McClaren contends, had no place in his ideal society.[256] Fryer points out that in 1827 Owen denied introducing the sponge to England. Furthermore, no reliable evidence exists that it was ever employed as a contraceptive technique at New Lanark.[257] Although Fryer concedes that Owen had an interest in contraception, he refuses to include him as a pioneer of birth control. Indeed, it would be fallacious to assume that just because his son Robert Dale Owen openly advocated birth control, the father must have done likewise.[258]

Dudley Miles maintains that Owen did indeed bring several sponges back to England in 1818, two of which he gave to Francis Place who had persuaded him to search for contraceptive information in France. He is convinced, however, that Owen took no interest in birth control after 1818. His concern in 1818, moreover, was based not on an attempt to find a solution to Malthusianism, which he had rejected by this date, but rather on his secret advocacy of free love and his desire to eliminate the fear of pregnancy.[259]

Regardless of the ambiguity concerning Robert Owen's views and actions, one thing is certain. At no point did he publicly advocate birth control. *The Crisis* and *The New Moral World,* which he edited in the early 1830s, did not raise the issue. Admittedly, *The Crisis* did advertise Robert Dale Owen's pro-birth-control *Moral Physiology* but only after Robert Dale himself had taken over effective editorship of the paper from his father.[260] Similarly, *The Economist,* an Owenite journal edited by George Mudie in the 1820s, did not discuss contraception. On the contrary, each of these publications was replete with anti-Malthusian commentary decrying the need to limit the population. Owenites were convinced that their new society would ensure an abundance of all resources for an expanding population. It is highly significant, moreover, that Robert Owen warned his son of the dangers of publishing an English edition of *Moral Physiology* that first appeared in the United States in 1831. Robert Dale ignored his father's advice and was publicly censured. At a debate in Bristol in 1841, for example, Robert Dale Owen's opponent, John Brindley, described *Moral Physiology* as an obscene book, 'too beastly to be named'. The chairman, presented with a passage to peruse quickly , refused 'for common decency's sake' to permit it to be read aloud.[261]

Other radicals refused to make their views public but, unlike Robert Owen, were prepared to publish and use the working-class press to advertise and sell birth-control tracts. James Watson is a case in point. With John Cleave he launched the *Working Man's Friend* in December 1832. Two months earlier, he had published the first unauthorized edition of Robert Dale Owen's *Moral Physiology* and eventually became the foremost publisher of birth-control works in the 1830s and 1840s.[262] Although he ran advertisements for Owen's book in *The Working Man's Friend*, no editorials or commentary were directed to the issue of contraception.

Henry Hetherington, publisher of *The Poor Man's Guardian* and *The Destructive,* similarly carried no discussion of birth control in his papers. His editor, Bronterre O'Brien, was firmly opposed to such practices. He was a confirmed anti-Malthusian who denied the necessity of limiting population growth and never forgave Hetherington, Watson and Cleave for selling the works of Owen, Knowlton and Carlile. This clash between owner and editor no doubt explains *The Poor Man's Guardian's* editorial silence on the subject. Hetherington, nevertheless, did publish lists of the periodicals and books available for purchase at his warehouse in central London. Included were Robert Dale Owen's *Moral Physiology* and Charles Knowlton's *Fruits of Philosophy*.[263]

Numerous ads, moreover, for these works appeared in *The Poor Man's Guardian* often supplemented with explicit pro-birth-control commentary. A typical advertisement for *Moral Physiology* contained the following:

> This work is one of the first importance; not only as furnishing a plain and explicit reply to the Malthusian Doctrine, 'that population must always press upon subsistence,' but also as supplying to every father and mother of a family, the knowledge by which, without injury to health, or violence to the moral feelings, any further increase which is not desired may be prevented; more especially in cases where the health of the mother, or the diminished income of the father imperatively advise no further addition to the number of offspring.[264]

At times both *Moral Physiology* and *Fruits of Philosophy* were advertised together with nearly the same text.[265] The anti-Malthusian message was clearly intended to conform to *The Poor Man's Guardian*'s consistent denial of the notion of surplus population while allowing for family limitation that rejected Malthus's moral restraint. Such a contradictory argument probably reflects a compromise between O'Brien and Hetherington.

Francis Place and John Stuart Mill were prepared to go much further. Both published anonymous pro-birth-control letters in *The Black Dwarf* and circulated handbills written by the former. In February 1822, Place published his book entitled *Illustrations and Proofs of the Principle of Population*, where he advocated birth control but held back on any mention of actual contraceptive methods. At this stage, moreover, he still had some faith that increasing delay of marriage through moral restraint could also aid in reducing surplus population.[266] It was not until *The Black Dwarf* anonymously published his handbill and letter to the editor in September and November 1823 respectively, that details regarding techniques of family limitation were made known to a wider public. By this point, Place had totally rejected moral restraint as an option.

The handbill entitled 'To the Married of Both Sexes' began with the Malthusian assumption that excess population is the root cause of poverty:

> To those who constitute the great mass of the community, whose daily bread is alone procured by daily labour, a large family is almost always the cause of ruin both of parents and children; reducing the parents to cheerless, hopeless, and irremediable poverty; depriving the children of those physical, moral, and mental helps which are

necessary to enable them to live in comfort, and turning them out at
an early age to prey upon the world, or to become the world's
prey.[267]

In his letter Place expanded on this theme arguing that 'there is an actual
surplus of labour in the country.' He supported the conclusion of
Malthus's *Essay* that population growth outstripped subsistence and
produced starvation thus necessitating a limitation of numbers.[268]

Given that population must be reduced, however, Place rejected all of
Malthus's checks. 'The idea of diminishing the actual number of people
in existence' – misery in Malthusian terms – he found 'a repugnant and
painful contemplation'.[269] Moral restraint or any measures to prevent
marriages he now considered 'an interference with the happiness of
mankind'. It would be 'unjust', he argued, to subject the poor to 'so vast
a measure of privation':

> The real and indispensable necessity which a poor man has for a
> wife, renders marriage the only state of existence which can make life
> productive of any comfort or any enjoyment. Worn down with toil,
> he needs an assistant to prepare his scanty refreshment, and relieve
> him of those domestic duties which it would be out of his power to
> discharge; and how is he to obtain this succour?—he cannot pay a
> fellow creature for yielding him the comfort he requires – he cannot
> execute them himself – he must therefore procure gratuitous
> assistance, and this is only to be done by marrying, whereby he
> provides a companion as well as a help, and ensures an identity of
> interest.[270]

Place married at nineteen and fathered fifteen children. As Dudley Miles
suggests, he no doubt came to realize the hypocrisy of preaching to others
what he could not do himself.[271]

The only viable solution, Place concluded, was birth control within
marriage, the techniques of which he graphically spelled out in his
handbill. Although mention was made of withdrawal, he clearly
favoured the use of the sponge because it 'depends on the female':

> It consists in a piece of sponge, about an inch square, being placed in
> the vagina previous to coition, and afterwards withdrawn by means
> of a double twisted thread, or bobbin, attached to it. No injurious
> consequences can in any way result from its use, neither does it
> diminish the enjoyment of either party. The sponge should, as a
> matter of preference, be used rather damp, and when convenient a
> little warm. It is almost superfluous to add, that there may be more
> pieces than one, and that they should be washed after being used.[272]

This method, he claimed, had been used successfully, and was
recommended by eminent physicians in cases where pregnancy had 'been
found injurious to the health of delicate women'.[273] Place thus added
medical reasons in justification of contraceptive use.

The benefits of family limitation for the working people would be immense. Fewer workers would raise wages and lead to 'the gradual extirpation of poverty' and a more equal distribution of wealth. 'The temptation', argued Place, 'to theft, to fraud, abuse of trust, to drink to excess, (as far as the desire of assuaging a sense of wretchedness goes) would all diminish. ...' Better diet and clothing would produce 'augmented vigour' and health in the common people. Increased leisure would allow the worker 'to acquire instruction, and to inform himself on those subjects most important to himself and his fellow creatures'. Such 'dissemination of knowledge' would be the 'grand engine' of political reform towards universal suffrage.[274]

Against those who feared that the supply of workers would decline far below levels of demand, Place argued for a 'universal propensity and desire to possess offspring'. Assuming 'every working man to be at liberty to have children or not, according to his choice, the very instant when he could afford to maintain a child, he would desire it; so prevalent and so powerful are the feelings which prompt the wish for descendants, for heirs, for the personal happiness connected with the possession of offspring.' High wage rates, moreover, would make having children 'profitable'. Their earnings would ensure a 'comfortable subsistence' for the entire family.[275]

Moral as well as economic benefits would ensue. Contrary to those who argued that birth control, by lessening the fear of pregnancy, would destroy female chastity and vastly increase prostitution, Place contended that contraceptive use among the married 'would operate to diminish the whole amount of unchastity prevalent in society'. With the knowledge that you need have only as many children as you wish, earlier marriage would take place among males and females. The 'youthful passions of men' would thus be contained within the 'healthy gratification' of marriage, lessening the overall numbers of females being seduced as well as the demand for prostitutes. The proportion of unmarried women would decrease, again reducing the numbers at risk of losing their virginity or becoming unwed mothers. In addition, Place argued, communities composed 'chiefly of married persons' would have a greater chance of promoting 'decorous conduct' and that 'love of morality most essential to their ... interests'.[276]

Place was insistent, moreover, that birth control was not in '*violation of the laws of nature*'. Employing the utilitarian criterion 'that whatever tends to promote human happiness is justified in the performance', he argued that 'omitting into the world annually several thousands of beings for whom a comfortable subsistence cannot be found, ought not to be stigmatized as an outrage upon the benevolent intentions of Providence'. Besides, human society did not find it repugnant to interfere in animal life by castrating various species to prevent procreation or to create docility. Human disease, moreover, was a process of nature and yet society did not censure cures for such ailments. The laws of nature, Place asserted, are rendered 'nugatory whenever their infringement is more agreeable than their inviolability'. Surely the removal of 'a mass of positive misery' by the use of contraceptives was not an unjustifiable interference with the 'assumed designs of Providence.'[277]

John Stuart Mill's pro-birth-control arguments are likewise contained in anonymous letters to *The Black Dwarf*. Like Place, he was also prepared to circulate handbills and was arrested in the early 1820s for tossing leaflets in areas of London where servant girls could retrieve them.[278] His commitment to contraception rested on foundations similar to those of Place. The causes of poverty were Malthusian in nature – an excess of population over the means of subsistence and employment. A reduction in the size of working-class families would lead to higher wages, full employment and the elimination of destitution. Well-fed and well-clothed workers with more leisure time would be better able to obtain instruction, rid themselves of apathy and thus achieve emancipation 'from the double yoke of priestcraft and reverence for superiors'. In summary, Mill contended, 'if the superstitions of the nursery are discarded, we may hope ere long to see the English people well paid, well instructed and eventually well governed.'[279]

On moral issues Mill advanced new arguments against the anti-birth-controllers. Replying to Wooler's fear that the prevention of births was a step towards murdering infants he asserted: 'As to infanticide, I leave you to judge, whether a parent, who has a larger family than it is possible to maintain, or a parent who has only a small family, is most likely to be tempted to destroy a child.' Contraception, in any case, had no relationship to committing murder.[280]

Mill was even more insistent than Place in maintaining that birth control was not contrary to the laws of nature. Providence, he argued, sends rain and yet we protect ourselves from it. 'To check population', he contended, 'is not more unnatural than to make use of an umbrella.'[281] Like Place, Mill appealed to principles of utility: 'It is a law of nature, that sexual intercourse, if not artificially prevented, occasions the generation of children. But it is also a law of nature, that man shall seek happiness.'[282] Replying to Wooler in his second anonymous letter, he neatly summed up his views:

> By checking population, no pain is inflicted, no alarm excited, no security infringed. It cannot, therefore, on any principles, be termed immoral; and if the above arguments be correct – if it tends to elevate the working people from poverty and ignorance to affluence and instruction, I am compelled to regard it as highly moral and virtuous;

> nor can I agree with you in treating as 'heartless,' the desire of seeing so inestimable a benefit conferred upon mankind; unless, indeed, the word heartless, be one of the engines of a sentimental cant, invented to discourage all steady pursuit of the general happiness of mankind.[283]

As much as Place and Mill aired the issues surrounding birth control in the working-class press, they did so anonymously. It was Richard Carlile who made the boldest and most shocking contribution to the public debate. In early May 1825, writing from Dorchester Gaol where he was imprisoned for six years on charges of blasphemy, he published under his own name and in his own paper, *The Republican*, an essay entitled 'What is Love?' which not only advocated contraception but did so on the grounds of free love.[284] Carlile had initially opposed such measures on the conventional grounds that they were unnatural and would lead to a vastly increased sexual promiscuity among women. By the end of 1824, however, he became an increasingly ardent convert to the cause of birth control.

'What is Love?' clearly owed a debt to the views of Francis Place who was largely responsible for his conversion.[285] Carlile, in fact, included one of Place's handbills entitled 'To the Married of Both Sexes of the Working People' in the essay and praised the sponge as the most viable means of contraception: 'The matter is most simple and most clear; it strikes us with physical and philosophical reasons, in a moment, why it must succeed, and why it is the only means that will succeed. It shocks the mind of a woman, at first thought, that never dreamt of such a thing; but once practiced, all prejudice flies. ...'[286]

In his justification for birth control, however, he courageously – some would say recklessly – departed from all other advocates. Under the mistaken physiological assumption that both men and women produced semen, Carlile argued that 'genuine love' was 'nothing but the passion to secrete semen in a natural way'.[287] Such love must be freely expressed by both males and females to produce health and beauty and avoid illness: 'It will admit of no ... delay. It must be gratified or its victim pines and dies. ... What a dreadful thing it is that health and beauty cannot be encouraged and extended, that love cannot be enjoyed, without the danger of a conception, when that conception is not desired.'[288] Use of the sponge, Carlile contended, would remove 'all dread from the necessary practice of intercourse between the sexes' and ensure 'the happiness of the unmarried female'.[289] Such women, moreover, should be free to initiate such activity:

> Why should not the female state her passion to the male, as well as the male to the female? What impropriety can there be in it? What bad effect can it produce? Is it immodest? Why is it immodest? Is it

not virtuous? Why is it not virtuous? I claim equality for the female and give her the right to make advances in all the affairs of genuine love. I hate the hypocrisy, the cruelty, that would stifle or disguise a virtuous passion, whether in the male or in the female. Young women, assume an equality, plead your passions where you feel them and to those to whom it may apply.[290]

By linking birth control with sexual freedom and advocating its use for unmarried females, Carlile had ruined any possibility that such practices would gain popular approval. Place had discussed his own support for free love, albeit in a distant future, with Carlile in September 1824 but was determined, as a matter of tactics, to keep his views secret. His public statements thus recommended contraception only for the married and consistently stressed that earlier marriage would ensue, resulting in a marked reduction in sexual promiscuity. As Dudley Miles points out, Place made 'a very serious mistake' in raising the subject with Carlile who was, to say the least, a loose cannon with no inclination to keep his views private no matter how far they defied public opinion. Indeed, Place tried frantically to persuade him not to publish 'What is Love?' but clearly to no avail.[291]

For not only was Carlile convinced of the merits of free love, he also viewed the issue of birth control as a vehicle to further his assault on Christianity against which he consistently fulminated in *The Republican*. As the country's leading atheist, his essay heaped invective on traditional beliefs. 'Religion', he argued, 'makes every thing like itself, turns every thing into hypocrisy, defaces every thing that is moral and good: at least, this has been the character of the Christian Religion founded by that loveless cripple Saint Paul. Love has not, in reality, existed or been able to hold up its head and high pretensions since the predominance of that religion.'[292] The entire era of Christianity was 'degrading' and 'unnatural'.[293] Worst of all, according to Carlile:

> Religion being founded in gross error must have been a great destroyer of beauty; must have greatly deteriorated the healthy character and fine structure of the human body. It has been a mental disease that has turned love into a fancied sin and made it commit dreadful ravages as a disease brought on from the want of due seminal secretions, even where secret indulgence has been obtained, a dread of discovery has caused an equally distressing mental distraction. Religion is an unnatural vice, and can only be properly classed with sodomy and bestiality. It never ought to inhabit the mind of any person; but to a young person, with signs of health, it is a rankling poison.[294]

Given Carlile's emphasis on free love, Malthusian justifications for birth control so prevalent in the writings of Place and J. S. Mill clearly became a secondary concern. His essay, at times, did posit a link between excess numbers and poverty. The results of unwanted pregnancies, for example, he analysed as follows:

> Again, see what an evil arises from bastard children, from deserted children, from half-starved and diseased children, and even where the parents are most industrious and most virtuous, from a half-starved, naked, and badly housed family, from families crowded into one room, for whose health a large house and garden is essential. All these matters are a tax upon love, a perpetual tax upon human pleasure, upon health, a tax that turns beauty into shriveled ugliness, and that defaces the noble attitude of mankind, that makes the condition of mankind worse than that of the cattle of the field.[295]

Such references, however, were rare. Even here greater emphasis is given to the negative effects on love, health and beauty rather than to poverty *per se*.

Carlile, in August 1826, admitted publicly that he had never read Malthus although he eventually became familiar with his doctrines through the writings and influence of Francis Place.[296] His reluctance to present a more explicit defence of birth control in terms of surplus population most certainly stems from his ambivalence towards, rather than ignorance of, Malthusian principles. In May 1826 Carlile stated 'he always put the question of improved government before the check population system.'[297] In January 1828 he boldly exclaimed: 'I am not a Malthusian.' In typical fashion he underwent a conversion and declared later the same month: 'Upon the whole, we do not hesitate to hold up Mr. Malthus as the friend of the labouring man.' He further declared him a 'sound and radical reformer' and retracted 'all that I have ever expressed against Mr. Malthus ... save and except my disapprobation of his recommendation of abstinence from marriage'.[298] Carlile, at this point, was convinced that limiting population was the most important solution to the problem of poverty.

Several factors led him to this Malthusian conclusion. The sheer destitution he witnessed in his tours of the manufacturing areas of the Midlands and the North in the late 1820s indelibly impressed on his mind the consequences of uncontrolled fertility. In 1829 he accused the workers of Nottingham of the 'monstrous and brute-like habit in mankind to breed to the increase of unhappiness'.[299] The labourers of Bradford, Rochdale, Bolton, Manchester and Liverpool he chastised for 'excessive child-getting'.[300] In addition, the ideas of Francis Place were gaining an even stronger hold on Carlile's thinking, especially the notion that poverty could be combated by the effort of individuals. He also became more sympathetic to Malthusianism when he discovered that Malthus had expressed positive views on 'the passions between the sexes' albeit within the confines of marriage.[301] He quoted Malthus's 1803

Essay approvingly while at the same time stressing a crucial contradiction:

> After the desire of food, the most powerful and general of our desires is the passion between the sexes taken in an enlarged sense. Of the happiness spread over human life by the passion very few are unconscious. Virtuous love, exalted by friendship, seems to be that sort of mixture of sensual and intellectual enjoyment, particularly suited to the nature of man, and most powerfully calculated to awaken the sympathies of the soul and produce the most exquisite gratifications. Perhaps there is scarcely a man (or a woman) who has once experienced the delight of virtuous love, however great his intellectual pleasures may have been, who does not look back to that period as the sunny spot in his whole life, where his imagination loves most to bask, which he recollects and contemplates with the fondest regret, and which he would most wish to live over again.'
>
> In proof of his assertion he embodies the following passage from *Godwin's Political Justice*.
>
> 'It is' the symmetry of the person, 'the vivacity, the voluptuous softness of temper, the affectionate kindness of feeling, the imagination, and the wit' of woman, which excite the passion of love, and not the mere distinction of her being a female.
>
> How strange that a man who could feel thus truly, and write thus elegantly, and deliver himself thus eloquently on the subject of love, should persist in recommending abstinence from marriage amongst young people.[302]

If Carlile eventually came to accept Malthus's analysis of the causes of poverty only in early 1828, the reservation he expresses in the last sentence of the above quote indicates that he consistently rejected the solution of moral restraint. Even before he penned 'What is Love?' in May 1825 he had adopted this position. Indeed, the essay attacked Malthus directly regarding checks to population growth. Carlile copiously quoted from an appended supplement to *Fides Catholica* that used Malthus as a 'Philosophical defence' of Catholicism on the grounds that 'voluntary moral restraint' by priests and monks would 'arrest an undue increase of mankind'.[303] In typically anti-Christian fashion, Carlile set out to 'knock down this new argument for Roman Catholicism.' He universally rejected such Malthusian abstinence in favour of openly advocating contraception even if, in the process, he should 'again come into hostile contact with Mr. Cobbett'.[304] In addition, like Francis Place, he rejected the positive check of misery by 'removing ... the horrid inference of Malthus, that the superfluous numbers of mankind should be legislatively left to a natural destruction for want of food, whilst superfluous numbers of aristocrats riot upon the taxed labour of the labouring man.'[305]

The benefits of birth control Carlile summed up near the end of his essay:

1st. That no married couple shall have more children than they wish and can well maintain.

2nd. That no unhealthy woman shall bear children that cannot be reared, and which endangers her own life in the parturition: that ineffectual pregnancy shall never be suffered.

3rd. That there be no illegitimate children, where they are not desired by the mother.

4th. and finally. That sexual intercourse, where useful and desired, may be made a pleasure independent of the dread of a conception that blasts the prospects and happiness of the unmarried female.[306]

Carlile, unlike Place or Mill, did not stress higher wage levels, full employment or the elimination of mass poverty again reflecting his view, at this stage, that reducing population was not the *sole* solution to destitution (my emphasis). To be sure, the first and third of the beneficial effects listed do imply an improved standard of living. The strongest emphasis, however, is placed on female health and the sexual happiness of both married and unmarried women. Such factors were given prominence earlier in the essay where Carlile claimed that contraception 'will become the very bulwark of love and wisdom, of beauty, health, and happiness'.[307]

In February 1826 Carlile published his essay as a book entitled *Every Woman's Book or What is Love?* which went through four editions by the end of the year with total sales of 5,000 copies, a substantial number given its controversial message.[308] By the fourth edition, Carlile had made significant changes. Intent on employing more of his own ideas, he excluded Place's handbill. In addition, although still preferring the sponge because it gave women control, he discussed other means of contraception, especially withdrawal and the condom. In order to make his views more palatable, he qualified his strident advocacy of free love claiming he was against 'indiscriminate intercourse'. He also eased somewhat his caustic attacks on religion.[309]

True to his idiosyncratic style, however, Carlile proceeded to undo such gestures of moderation by suggesting that classical-style Temples of Venus be established 'where young people could appease their passions' under a form of worship akin to the Greeks and Romans.[310] The cross he referred to as the 'mathematical emblem of the Phallus'.[311] He also included a reference to the 'dildo', albeit as a form of 'unnatural gratification'.[312] The frontispiece of the book portrayed Adam and Eve in full-frontal nudity.

More important for our purposes, all references to Malthus were withdrawn from the book. Carlile gave no specific reasons for such editing. His ambiguity towards Malthusian theory, however, no doubt played an important role. Carlile was not yet convinced, as he later was in 1828, that over-breeding by the poor was *the* most important cause of poverty (my emphasis). Nor was he convinced that voluntary birth control independent of broader reforms in the political and economic realm – especially the reduction of taxation – constituted *the* major solution (my emphasis).

Malthus's reaction

Regardless of whether the radical press adhered to Cobbett's critique of the 'parson' or went beyond him, the arguments advanced against Malthus represent a substantial attempt to refute his principles. Yet Malthus never replied to this barrage of criticism, probably for the same reasons he refused to respond to Cobbett. Such 'abusive declamation' which 'denied the most glaring and attested facts', Malthus argued, was 'evidently beneath notice'. Specific references in his work to editors of the working-class press were almost non-existent. We do not know, of course, exactly how much, if any, of the working-class press Malthus actually read. There is no doubt, however, that he was aware of the ideas 'popular orators and writers' presented to the people and did criticize such concepts in general terms. Such radical notions, he argued, were 'extravagant demands' which served only to 'deceive' the labouring classes, 'to aggravate and encourage their discontents, and to raise unreasonable and extravagant expectations as to the relief expected from reform'. In addition, writers 'most extensively read among the common people' condemned the very 'line of conduct' that could 'improve the condition of the poor'. Their doctrines were 'grossly absurd' especially those that taught the poor to rely on the parish for subsistence, to marry early and disregard 'any degree of prudence in the affair of marriage', to avoid Savings Banks and to blame low wages on excessive taxation.[313]

Malthus did, however, make one important exception. In the 1817 edition of the *Essay*, he replaced his chapter on William Godwin with one refuting the theories of Robert Owen, entitled 'Of Systems of Equality'. Malthus claimed to have 'a very sincere respect' for Owen and referred to him as a 'friend to humanity' and 'a man of real benevolence'.[314] He especially praised Owen's attempts to procure an Act of Parliament limiting the hours of child labour in the cotton factories as well as his enlightened views on education.[315] Malthus, however, strongly opposed Owen's proposal for communal labour presented in his *A New View of Society* (1816) where the latter envisaged self-sufficient villages of two to three hundred families in which all labour would be performed for the wider good of the community.

Malthus's objections to Owen's ideal society are similar to earlier arguments made against Godwin and others. First, he argued, 'a state of equality' was unsuitable 'to the production of those stimulants to exertion which can alone overcome the natural indolence of man, and prompt him to the proper cultivation of the earth and the fabrication of those conveniences and comforts which are necessary to his happiness'.[316] He did admit that exceptions to this general rule could occur. The Moravians – a Protestant Episcopal sect that emigrated to Germany, England and North America from Bohemia in the Austro-Hungarian Empire – 'are known', said Malthus, 'to have had much of their property in common without occasioning the destruction of their industry'.[317]

The second argument, however, was universally applicable 'in every age and in every part of the world'.[318] A system of equality, Malthus contended, would eliminate any incentive to moral restraint. No one individual would 'think himself obliged to practice the duty of restraint more than another'.[319] Early marriage would lead to rapid population growth outstripping subsistence. Society would eventually be reduced to severe want and misery. Only the laws of property and succession – private property, that is, and its attendant inequalities – would provide an institutional framework conducive to marrying late or 'not at all'. Only such behaviour would keep population in line with the food for its support.[320]

Final reflections

The foregoing examination of the reaction of the radical press to Malthusian theory warrants several conclusions. If one argues along the lines of Hollis and Himmelfarb, that, in general terms, the 'new ideology' never fully eclipsed the 'old', neither did this occur with specific reference to the critique of Malthus. In many different ways, Cobbett's arguments against the 'parson' based on the old ideology of corruption and nepotism in state and church continued to hold sway well into the 1830s. His denial of the Malthusian notion that population growth would outstrip the means of subsistence was accepted by the vast majority of the working-class press as was his denunciation of moral restraint as a feasible solution to the pressing problems of poverty. His argument moreover, that poor relief was the property of the poor, was universally adopted by those opposing the introduction of the New Poor Law. As we have seen, even *The Poor Man's Guardian*, perhaps the best exemplar of the new radicalism, praised Cobbett's *Legacy to Labourers* (1834) and, for a time, elevated opposition to the Poor Law Amendment Bill above its major goal of universal male suffrage. Although rarely matching Cobbett's level of invective, the pauper press drew heavily on his rhetoric, frequently employing his metaphors. The 'drones' and 'bees' came up time and time again.

To be sure, O'Brien and others moved towards a much more class-based ideology that viewed poverty as a fundamental result of structural inequalities deeply rooted in the economic and political hegemony of a 'monied monopoly' of landlords and capitalists. If Malthus had mistaken the true causes of poverty, they could now readily be found in a system of class exploitation. Such an analysis, however, did not preclude reference to the old ideology of Cobbett and others. Indeed, frequent mention was made of unfair taxation, pensions and sinecures, wasteful government expenditure and a litany of oppressive laws.

In addition, as Himmelfarb has warned, one must avoid – tempting though it is – viewing O'Brien's ideology as 'a premature or incipient Marxism'.[321] The Poor Man's Guardian's classes were not Marx's class-conscious proletariat or his bourgeoisie with interests distinct from landlords. The older discourse of rich versus poor, of useful as against useless classes, was often employed. The centrality of universal male suffrage, moreover, was far from Marx's view that such political change was merely a first step in the process of revolution.[322] Nor did O'Brien wish to eliminate private property in the manufacturing sector.

To further complicate matters, the 'old ideology' at times moved so close to the 'new' as to blur any clear-cut distinction. Cobbett, for example, supported universal male suffrage. Near the end of his life, when all hopes of defeating the New Poor Law Bill were dashed, he began to speak in terms approximating a class struggle that would lead to a violent redistribution of property. As early as 1821, Thomas Wooler, editor of The Black Dwarf who by and large supported Cobbett, threatened violent revolution against property owners if the Old Poor Law was repealed. Carlile in The Gauntlet and The Cosmopolite, and James Lorymer in The Radical openly advocated armed insurrection against tyrannical government.

One must remember as well that, in terms of circulation, press representing the 'old ideology' clearly predominated over the 'new'. In 1832 and 1833, papers representing the latter had estimated sales of 25,000 copies while the former appeared in a larger number of papers with substantially wider circulation. If The Poor Man's Guardian sold 16,000 copies at its peak, Cobbett's Political Register alone more than doubled this figure.[323]

The dichotomy is further confused by the fact that the most devastating critique of Malthus, at least in a theoretical sense, came not from the new radicalism of O'Brien but from Carlile who consistently denounced kings, priests and lords as enemies of the people and viewed unjust taxation as a fundamental cause of poverty. His public advocacy of birth control, whether justified on the grounds of free love or the elimination of poverty, threatened the very core of Malthusian principles at least in terms of the methods to be employed to reduce population. Artificial family limitation eliminated the need for moral restraint thus denying one of Malthus's most central assumptions, that is, that labourers were lethargic and thus in need of a stimulus to become industrious and prudent. Such habits, Malthus believed, would be promoted not only by the need to delay marriage but also by the necessity of the male breadwinner to support his family without recourse to Poor Law subsidies from the state.

In terms of anti-Malthusian popular opinion, then, it appears that the distinction between the 'old' and 'new' ideology is not a very useful one. Certainly the latter body of thought developed a more radical, though not dominant, perspective on the root causes of poverty. Overall, however, both views equally condemned the Malthusian theory of population growth threatening the food supply. Both equally condemned moral restraint as either necessary or effective. Those supporting birth control such as Place, Mill and Carlile accepted Malthus's view that the excessive supply of labour bred poverty but clearly denied his solution. Such thinking did not really fit either ideology, although Carlile, until his conversion to Malthusian overpopulation theory, drew heavily on older notions of radical thought.

What may one conclude about the wider impact of such popular opinion against Malthus? The radical press no doubt produced an increasing hatred of Malthus in the working class, thus fanning the flames produced by Cobbet. Carlile claimed he encountered immense hostility to Malthus among the working people of Lancashire when he was on a lecture tour in the late 1820s.[324] In practical terms, however, such public opinion had little effect. With Tories and Whigs in basic unity – Peel and Wellington siding with Lord Althorp and Brougham – the New Poor Law which had fuelled such anti-Malthusian sentiment was legislated into existence with little opposition in either the House of Commons or the Lords. Such a unified front testifies to the degree to which notions of the market economy had permeated the highest levels of the political spectrum and how deeply older notions of paternalism had been eroded among the landed elite. The tide of the new political economy laden with Malthusian assumptions was, it appears, unstoppable.

One should stress that this was the case even though *The Times*, much to the chagrin of Harriet Martineau and the Whigs who were promoting the new enactment, came out strongly against the New Poor Law in 1834 and led a vitriolic campaign against it which lasted a decade. For once, the most influential newspaper in England sided with Cobbett and the working-class press.

The reasons for such opposition were personal, commercial and ideological. Harriet Martineau in her *Autobiography* claimed that the editor of *The Times*, Thomas Barnes, was expressing a personal hatred of Lord Chancellor Brougham. Barnes also despised three members of the Royal Commission on the Poor Laws: the political economist Nassau Senior, the Benthamite William Coulson, and Blomfield, Bishop of London. In addition, John Walter, MP, the chief proprietor of *The Times*, had well-known reasons for his dislike of Edwin Chadwick, one of the principal architects of the New Poor Law. The latter, in his preliminary report on the Poor Laws, had criticized Walter for misusing parish funds. As justice of the peace in Berkshire, Walter had decided appeals in favour of pauper claimants thus involving parishes in expensive litigation. Martineau also claimed that opposition of the country justices to the new measure was an important factor. The potential loss of this important sector of its readership led to a vote among proprietors of *The Times* which went in favour of humouring the country justices and opposing the new bill.[325]

Ideological motivations, however, were even more important. Both Walters and Barns believed parishes had the obligation to provide outdoor relief, especially to raise wages and to relieve temporary distress although they opposed the allowance system.[326] Both vehemently disagreed with the principle of less eligibility and, in particular, the workhouses that turned paupers into criminals housed in prisons.[327] Both condemned the dictatorial powers of the Poor Law Commissioners – the 'Three Tyrants of Somerset House' – whose centralized powers concerning Poor Law policy superceded the authority of resident magistrates and were not answerable to parliament.[328]

In more general terms, Barnes opposed 'the new fangled science of political economy' branding its proponents as 'heartless theorists'.[329] Such theories, moreover, were mired in a system 'where no meaning passes for philosophy, and captious ratiocination is mistaken for profound reason'.[330] Although the bulk of *The Times*'s increasing invective was directed at Brougham during and after the passage of the New Poor Law Bill, he was viewed essentially as the mouthpiece of Malthus. On 24 July 1834, following Brougham's speech in the House of Lords that heaped praise on Malthus and castigated the Old Poor Law, Barnes reacted thus:

> It is indeed a thing to fright and scare the boldest pretender, the most reckless speculator, to find the head of the judicature of this country, the LORD HIGH CHANCELOR of England, denouncing the 43d of ELIZABETH as a *pernicious* statue; but it is a subject of far greater wonder and alarm to hear the gravest functionary of the realm revive and laud with profuse flattery the cold-blooded and cruel code of MALTHUS which has for years past been exploded from all civilized communities and spurned of all but the most flinty-hearted and the most wrong-headed of every class and clime.[331]

Employing Cobbett-like satire Barnes ended his editorial with the following:

> We published the other day Dean SWIFT'S 'Modest proposal for preventing the *Children* of poor People becoming a Burden to their Parents or the country.' It was exceedingly easy and simple, and not at all calculated to lead to litigation, which is the greatest defect in the present poor laws, – it was that the children of the poor should be *eaten*. The savages have an equally efficient mode of getting rid of the aged and infirm of their tribes. They *kill* them; which is, at least, more humane than painful and lingering death, whereas the tomahawk is as speedy as it is certain in its operation. Why not bring in a short bill combining these two plans – that of Dean SWIFT and that of the savages? One additional recommendation of such a measure is that there will be no necessity for the appointment of a *commission* to inquire into the scheme. Its merits are obvious at a glance. The general stock of the number of consumers being diminished by the consumption of the children, and by the removal of the aged and infirm, from the adoption of the simple and unexpensive process of the savages, all classes of the community must of necessity be benefited.[332]

If the powerful influence of *The Times* could not prevent passage of the New Poor Law or ensure repeal, one could hardly expect any greater success on the part of the working-class press that appealed to a disenfranchised readership with no political clout.

The other major assault on Malthus, of course, was the advocacy of birth control. In both ideological and practical terms such prescriptions for voluntary family limitation failed miserably and, if anything, served to seriously divide opinion in the working-class press. Carlile's *What is Love?* did achieve remarkable sales given its shocking content and he did gain some support among medical men, some women and individual freethinkers such as Thomas Marshall.[333] Carlile, however, greatly exaggerated his appeal when he stated that his contraceptive advice was widely supported by gentlemen and doctors and when he claimed: 'I know hundreds of well-informed and moral men and many virtuous women who agree with me on the utility of this book.'[334] The vast majority of public opinion along the entire political spectrum, including the radical press, opposed Carlile's views on birth control and found his justification on the grounds of free love abhorrent. As Angus McClaren has pointed out, even the medical profession condemned artificial means of family limitation well into the 1860s.[335] He further contends that although the relationship between feminism and birth control was highly complex, most feminists mistrusted artificial means of restricting births and few were prepared to publicly defend such practices until Annie Besant did so later in the nineteenth century.[336]

The actual limitation of births by the working classes, of course, did not occur on any mass scale until the late nineteenth and early twentieth centuries, although some groups such as textile workers were doing so as early as the 1850s. Such family limitation, however, is subject to two important qualifications. First, it is more likely that natural means – abstinence and coitus interruptus – were more frequently employed than artificial means. Secondly, such fertility control was not a response to intellectual discussions on the subject – innovative knowledge somehow trickling down the social scale – but rather a response to economic, social and cultural conditions.[337]

In terms of the early advocates of birth control – Place, Mill and Carlile – their writings, lectures and distribution of handbills failed to change reproductive practices among the working class. Nor did their efforts pose any threat to Malthusian ideology. Malthus, in rejecting birth control on moral grounds, placed himself firmly on the side of prevailing public opinion. Those openly advocating such practices, or whose anonymity was exposed, damaged themselves more than the man they sought to challenge and discredit.

Endnotes

1. *The Black Dwarf* 6, no. 24 (13 June 1821): 859–60. Volume, issue and page numbers, where relevant, and date are given for all periodicals cited.
2. *The Republican* 11, no. 18 (6 May 1825): 556. Robert Owen, in fact, denied that he imported the sponge to England contrary to rumours he had done so after a visit to France in 1818. See Peter Fryer, *The Birth Controllers* (London: Secker and Warburg, 1965), 45.
3. Ibid., 75
4. For the reaction of Wooler and Cobbett to voluntary contraception see ibid., 79–80 where Fryer cites *Black Dwarf* 11, no. 12 (17 September 1823) and Cobbett's *Political Register* (hereafter cited as *PR*) 3 (15 April 1826). Wooler's comments were directed against Francis Place who had circulated handbills advocating birth control.
5. See Patricia Hollis, *The Pauper Press: A Study in Working-Class Radicalism of the 1830s* (Oxford: Oxford University Press, 1970), 203 (hereafter cited as *Pauper Press*).
6. See Gertrude Himmelfarb, *The Idea of Poverty: England in the Early Industrial Age* (London and Boston, MA: Faber and Faber, 1984). Hereafter cited as *The Idea of Poverty*.
7. Hollis, *Pauper Press*, 222. See also Chapter VI, 203–209.
8. Himmelfarb, *The Idea of Poverty*, 250.
9. Hollis, *Pauper Press*, 222–3. The term 'monied monopoly' is O'Brien's.
10. Himmelfarb, *The Idea of Poverty*, 250.
11. Ibid., 250. Himmelfarb does not view this ideology as 'premature or incipient Marxism'.
12. Ibid., 251. See also Hollis, *Pauper Press*, 301.

13. For listings of this voluminous literature see Hollis, *Pauper Press*, 318–28. See also Joel H. Weiner, *The War of the Unstamped: The Movement to Repeal the British Newspaper Tax, 1830–1836* (Ithaca, NY and London: Cornell University Press, 1969), 281–5 (hereafter cited as *War of the Unstamped*).

14. All papers utilized are listed in Hollis, *Pauper* Press, 318–28 where editor(s), price, dates of circulation and political orientation are also provided.

15. For more detail on the stamp tax and its impact see Wiener, *War of the Unstamped*, 2–9, Hollis, *Pauper Press*, 3, 26–9, and Himmelfarb, *The Idea of Poverty*, 231–2. In 1836 the tax was reduced to a penny. It was finally abolished in the 1850s.

16. The editor of *The Political Penny Magazine* is unknown. For brief biographies of most of the radical thinkers mentioned above see Hollis, *Pauper Press*, 307–25 in her Appendix.

17. For divisions within radical thought see ibid., 147–55. Hollis argues that in spite of such disagreements cut-throat competition rarely occurred. Himmelfarb, although recognizing extreme diversity, nevertheless accepts the term 'radical' as an appropriate label: 'What was remarkable about this motley crew was not only the variety but the extent to which they overlapped and interlocked with each other, so that even the most discordant of them had enough in common to warrant that common label.' See Himmelfarb, *The Idea of Poverty*, 230.

18. *Black Dwarf* 4, no. 7 (23 February 1820). Cobbett's bid for election, of course, was unsuccessful.

19. Ibid. 5, no. 5 (2 August 1820): 166–7.

20. *Political Letters and Pamphlets*, no. 16 (7 January 1831): 2 and 14, and no. 22 (18 February 1831): 15.

21. *The Poor Man's Advocate*, no. 4 (11 February 1832): 251.

22. *Political Penny Magazine*, no. 1 (3 September 1836).

23. For reprintings see, for example, *The Poor Man's Guardian* 3, no. 181 (22 November 1834). Hereafter cited as *PMG*. See also *PMG* 4, no. 188 (10 January 1835): 389 and *PMG* 4, no. 212 (27 June 1835): 581. For letters to the editors see *PMG* 3, no. 127 (9 November 1833): 363 and *PMG* 3, no. 129 (23 November 1833): 378. All references to *The Poor Man's Guardian* are taken from *The Poor Man's Guardian* (London: H. Heatherington, 1831–35; reprint, 4 vols., London, Merlin Press, 1969) with volume and issue number, date and page number given.

24. *PMG* 4, no. 193 (14 February 1835): 431 and *PMG* 4, no. 228 (17 October 1835): 701.

25. *PMG* 3, no. 147 (29 March 1834): 64 and *PMG* 3, no. 185 (20 December 1834): 365.

26. Hetherington, of course, was a bookseller as well as newspaper publisher. For a list of Cobbett's books he sold see *PMG* 3, no. 148 (5 April 1834): 71. For his support of Cobbett as MP see *PMG* 2, no. 82 (29 December 1832): 661.

27. *The Gauntlet*, no. 7 (24 March 1833): 97.

28. *Gauntlet*, no. 9 (7 April 1833): 129.

29. *PMG* 3, no. 182 (29 November 1834): 340. The article in *PR* appeared on 22 November 1822.

30. *PMG* 3, no. 147 (29 March 1834): 64.

31.   *The Economist* 1, no. 3 (10 February 1821): 39.

32.   *The True Sun* (13 March 1834) and (17 March 1834).

33.   *Crisis* 4, no. 18 (9 August 1834): 137.

34.   *Political Letters*, no. 20 (4 February 1831): 12.

35.   *Political Letters*, no. 29 (2 April 1831): 5.

36.   *PMG* 3, no. 174 (4 October 1834): 277.

37.   See *Poor Man's Advocate*, no. 4 (11 February 1832): 25, *Black Dwarf* 11, no. 20 (12 November 1823): 661, and *PMG* 3, no. 184 (13 December 1834): 354, *Political Penny Magazine*, no. 1 (3 September 1836) respectively.

38.   See *True Sun* (22 July 1834), *New Moral World* 1, no. 9 (27 December 1834): 66 and *Political Penny Magazine*, no. 1 (3 September 1836) respectively.

39.   For Martineau see *PMG* 3, no. 167 (16 August 1834): 220. For Chadwick see *Political Penny Magazine*, no. 1 (3 September 1836).

40.   *True Sun* (14 April 1834).

41.   *The Gorgon*, no. 46 (17 April 1819): 378.

42.   See *PMG* 4, no. 194 (21 February 1835): 435 and *PMG* 4, no. 212 (27 June 1835): 579.

43.   See *Black Dwarf* 11, no. 20 (12 November 1823): 662 and *Black Dwarf* 11, no. 23 (3 December 1823): 780–81. Malthus of course, did not advocate such remedies. Only *The True Sun* (17 March 1834) was prepared to recognize the 'benevolence' of Malthus's purpose and 'the merit' of his 'conscientiousness'. His theory, nevertheless, was 'fallacious'.

44.   *People's Conservative and Trade Union Gazette* (19 April 1834). Malthus, of course, took a severely qualified view of emigration.

45.   *Political Penny Magazine*, no. 1 (3 September 1836).

46.   *Black Dwarf* 11, no. 20 (12 November 1823): 661.

47.   *Black Dwarf* 3, no. 1 (6 January 1819): 2.

48.   *Black Dwarf* 11, no. 23 (3 December 1823): 774 and *Black Dwarf* 11, no. 21 (19 November 1823): 698.

49.   *Black Dwarf* 11, no. 23 (3 December 1823): 783 and *Black Dwarf* 11, no. 20 (12 November 1823) 662.

50.   *Economist* 1, no. 1 (27 January 1821): 5 and 9.

51.   *PMG* 3, no. 146 (22 March 1834): 51 and *PMG* 2, no. 95 (30 March 1833): 98.

52.   *PMG* 4, no. 198 (21 March 1835): 465.

53.   *Political Letters*, no. 30 (16 April 1831): 6 and *Penny Papers for the People* (18 February 1831): 5.

54.   *The Crisis* 4, no. 18 (9 August 1834): 137.

55.   *The New Moral World* 1, no. 10 (3 January 1835): 77. Owen did admit, however, in 1827 that there were ultimate limits to the amount of population the earth could sustain. In a letter to the editor of the *Bolton Chronicle* he stated: 'While, on the contrary, the conviction on my mind is, that under an enlightened organization of society, founded on the known laws of our nature, population may be permitted to increase, according to its natural tendency; and every addition to its increase will bring with it the means to acquire more leisure for all, more wealth, more knowledge, and to multiply happiness in proportion to the numbers brought into existence, until the whole earth shall have been so well cultivated, that no greater product can be obtained from it .... Then, and then only, a stop

must be put to any further increase of mankind.' The letter was reprinted in Richard Carlile's *The Lion*, 1, no. 3 (18 January 1828): 87.

56. *Gorgon*, no. 3 (6 June 1818): 24.
57. See *Gorgon*, no. 48 (17 April 1819): 377 and *Gorgon*, no. 44 (20 March 1819): 350.
58. *Black Dwarf* 6, no. 22 (30 May 1821): 776.
59. *True Sun* (19 March 1834).
60. *Black Dwarf* 1, no. 18 (28 May 1817): 287.
61. *PMG* 2, no. 114 (10 August 1833): 254.
62. *Black Dwarf* 2, no. 11 (18 March 1818): 170 and *Black Dwarf* 8, no. 20 (15 May 1822): 705.
63. *Black Dwarf* 2, no. 13 (1 April 1818): 206 and *Black Dwarf* 3, no. 20 (19 May 1819): 318.
64. *Gorgon*, no 44, (20 March 1819): 350 and *Political Letters*, no. 2 (9 October 1830): 1.
65. *True Sun* (19 March 1834). *The Radical* was edited by Hetherington and Lorymer.
66. *Republican* 14, no. 14 (13 October 1826): 419. See also Carlile's statements in *The Gauntlet*, no. 23, (28 July 1833): 385 and no. 34 (29 September 1833): 529 where he claims the people were being 'robbed by taxation' and where he refers to taxation as 'tyranny'.
67. The issue of paper money was taken up, however, by *Black Dwarf*, *Gorgon*, *Republican* (Carlile) and *Political Letters*.
68. *Black Dwarf* 2, no. 13 (1 April 1818): 206 and *Black Dwarf* 8, no. 20 (15 May 1822): 709.
69. *Gorgon*, no. 29 (5 December 1818): 228.
70. *Political Letters*, no. 12 (9 December 1830): 1–3.
71. *PMG* 2, no. 98 (20 April 1833): 123.
72. See *Political Letters*, no. 3 (15 October 1830): 2 and *PMG* 3, no. 122 (5 October 1833): 318 respectively. The standing army was also used 'to keep down the poor by force'. *PMG* 3, no. 164 (26 July 1834): 194.
73. *New Moral World* 1, no. 10 (3 January 1835): 75.
74. See *The Pioneer* 1, no. 1 (5 July 1834): 429 and *The Working Man's Friend*, no. 31 (20 July 1833): 244.
75. See *Political Letters*, no. 11 (7 December 1830): 12 and *PMG* 2, no. 65 (8 September 1832): 526.
76. *Gauntlet*, no. 58 (16 March 1834): 913.
77. See *True Sun* (21 March 1834), *PMG* 1, no. 7 (20 August 1831): 51, *Gorgon*, no. 1 (23 May 1818): 3, and *Black Dwarf* 7, no. 10 (5 September 1821): 334.
78. *Gauntlet*, no. 1 (10 February 1833): 2.
79. *Black Dwarf* 2, no. 36 (9 September 1818): 573.
80. Ibid., 575.
81. *Black Dwarf* 3, no. 1 (6 January 1819): 5.
82. *PMG* 3, no. 164 (26 July 1834): 198.
83. See *Gorgon*, no. 29 (5 December 1818): 228 and *PMG* 4, no. 233 (21 November 1835): 748.
84. *PMG* 1, no. 23 (26 November 1831): 84.
85. *Black Dwarf* 11, no. 20 (12 November 1823): 662.
86. *Black Dwarf* 11, no. 21 (19 November 1823): 698.
87. *Black Dwarf* 11, no. 12 (17 September 1823): 2.

88. *Political Letters*, no. 3 (15 October 1830): 2.
89. *Gauntlet*, no. 1 (10 February 1833): 2.
90. *PMG* 2, no. 87 (2 February 1833): 33.
91. *Black Dwarf* 9, no. 12 (18 September 1822): 398. See also *Black Dwarf*, 11, no. 21 (19 November 1823): 703.
92. *Black Dwarf* 11, no. 20 (12 November 1823): 661.
93. *Gorgon*, no. 48 (17 April 1819): 378.
94. *PMG* 1, no. 47 (5 May 1832): 383.
95. *Working Man's Friend*, no. 32 (27 July 1833): 252.
96. *New Moral World* 1, no. 9 (27 December 1834): 66.
97. *Black Dwarf* 11, no. 12 (17 September 1823): 405.
98. *PMG* 3, no. 147 (29 March 1834): 60. The letter was from 'Political Corrector'.
99. *Black Dwarf* 11, no. 20 (12 November 1823): 663 and *Black Dwarf* 11, no. 21 (19 November 1823): 705. For arguments that moral restraint was contrary to biblical law see *Black Dwarf* 3, no. 47 (24 November 1819): 771 and *Political Penny Magazine*, no. 1 (3 September 1836).
100. *PMG* 3, no, 155 (24 May 1834): 124. The working-class press, like Cobbett, did not acknowledge Malthus's advocacy of prudential restraint.
101. See *New Moral World* 1, no. 10 (3 January 1835): 73 and *Crisis* 4, no. 18 (9 August 1834): 137.
102. See *Black Dwarf* 6, no. 24 (13 June 1821): 859 and *Crisis* 4, no. 18 (9 August 1834): 137.
103. *Gorgon*, no. 3 (6 June 1818): 24. For complaints against the Old Poor Law see *Political Letters*, no. 3 (15 October 1830): 1 and *Poor Man's Advocate*, no. 1 (21 January 1832): 10.
104. See *Political Letters*, no. 3 (15 October 1830): 5 and *The New Political Register* 1, no. 1 (17 October 1835).
105. *Black Dwarf* 3, no. 46 (17 November 1819): 750.
106. See *Black Dwarf* 6, no. 16 (18 April 1821): 538 and *Black Dwarf* 11, no. 23 (3 December 1823): 781.
107. *Pioneer* 1, no. 44 (5 July 1834): 432.
108. *Black Dwarf* 6, no. 22 (30 May 1821): 777.
109. *Gorgon*, no. 3 (16 June 1818): 18.
110. *True Sun* (8 May 1834). See also *True Sun* (19 March 1834), (24 February 1834), and (23 July 1834).
111. *Working Man's Friend*, no. 28 (29 June 1833): 217 quoting *The Monthly Repository*.
112. See *Black Dwarf* 6, no. 16 (18 April 1821): 542–3 and *Political Letters*, no. 3 (15 October 1830): 4.
113. *PMG* 3, no. 176 (18 October 1834): 290.
114. *True Sun* (18 April 1834) and (23 July 1834).
115. Himmelfarb, *The Idea of Poverty*, 244.
116. *PMG* 4, no. 230 (31 October 1835): 720–21.
117. *PMG* 4, no. 212 (27 June 1835): 581 and *PMG* 3, no. 173 (27 September 1834): 269. O'Brien, however, still criticized Cobbett for not publishing an unstamped paper and thus not directly defying the Stamp Act.
118. See, for example, *PMG* 4, no. 188 (10 January 1835): 389 and *PMG* 4, no. 212 (27 June 1835): 581. For the review of *Legacy to Labourers* see *PMG* 4, no. 193 (14 February 1835): 430.
119. *PMG* 4, no. 194 (21 February 1835): 435.

120. See *True Sun* (24 February 1834), (8 May 1834), and (14 May 1834). For reference to the 'Malthusian Poor Law Bill' see *True Sun* (13 September 1834).

121. *New Moral World* 1, no. 9 (27 December 1834): 65.

122. *Twopenny Dispatch* (9 July 1836).

123. *Political Penny Magazine*, no. 1 (3 September 1836) and no. 3 (17 September 1836).

124. See *True Sun* (13 October 1834) and *PMG* 4, no. 234 (28 November 1835): 754.

125. *Working Man's Friend*, no. 28 (29 June 1833): 217. For cases of cruel treatment see, for example, *PMG* 4, no. 238 (26 December 1835): 795–6.

126. *PMG* 3, no. 177 (October 1834): 302.

127. *PMG* 4, no. 215 (18 July 1835): 600. The *PMG* here is quoting *The Times*.

128. *PMG* 4, no. 207 (23 May 1835): 540 and *PMG* 4, no. 215 (18 July 1835): 600.

129. *People's Conservative* (3 May 1834). The term 'bashaw' is synonymous with a 'pasha' or Turkish military or naval or civil officer of high rank.

130. *True Sun* (25 July 1834) and *True Sun* (15 September 1834).

131. *Poor Man's Advocate*, no. 1 (21 January 1832): iv.

132. *Black Dwarf* 6, no. 16 (18 April 1821): 540.

133. *Black Dwarf* 6, no. 16 (18 April 1821): 539–40. See also J. Sekot's letter to the editor in *PMG* 3, no. 177 (25 October 1834): 302.

134. *Black Dwarf* 6, no. 16 (18 April 1821): 541. These statements were made in opposition to Scarlett's Poor Law Bill. See also *Black Dwarf* 6, no. 22 (30 May 1821): 774 where 'an *interminable* and *exterminating* warfare between rich and poor' was predicted.

135. See *True Sun* (8 May 1834), (15 September 1834) and (13 October 1834).

136. *The Destructive* (7 June 1834).

137. See *PMG* 1, no. 42 (31 March 1832): 334 and *PMG* 2, no. 86 (26 January 1833): 25 and *PMG* 2, no. 87 (2 February 1833): 33.

138. *PMG* 1, no. 47 (15 May 1832): 380.

139. *PMG* 3, no. 175 (11 October 1834): 283.

140. *PMG* 2, no. 101 (11 May 1833): 147.

141. *People's Conservative* (19 April 1834) where reference was made to 'over population men'.

142. *Penny Papers* (12 March 1831). The political economists referred to were not specified by name.

143. See *Political Letters*, no. 15 (31 December 1880): 2 and 3 and *Crisis* 4, no. 18 (9 August 1838): 137–8.

144. *Political Letters*, no. 29 (2 April 1833): 3.

145. *PMG* 4, no. 217 (1 August 1835): 621. See also *PMG* 1, no. 47 (5 May 1832): 380 and *PMG* 4, no. 128 (16 November 1833): 368.

146. *Black Dwarf* 2, no. 13 (1 April 1818): 207.

147. *Political Letters*, no. 29 (2 April 1831): 3. See also *PMG* 4, no. 128 (16 November 1833): 368 and *PMG* 4, no. 217 (15 August 1835): 634.

148. *Black Dwarf*, 5, no. 5 (2 August 1820): 167.

149. *PMG* 2, no. 54 (23 June 1832): 436.

150. *Black Dwarf* 2, no. 11 (18 March 1818): 171 and *Black Dwarf* 6, no. 22 (30 May 1820): 777.

151. *Penny Papers* (18 February 1831): 5.

152. *PMG* 1, no. 7 (20 August 1831): 51 and *PMG* 3, no. 140 (8 February 1834): 7.

153. Carlile opposed Cobbett in the pages of *The Republican* published from 1819 to 1826. For his support of Cobbett see *Gauntlet*, no. 9 (7 April 1833): 129.

154. See ibid and *Gauntlet*, no. 15 (19 May 1833): 226. Although the movement made little impact, Carlile did print the names of over 3,000 volunteers. Almost all vendors of the unstamped press enlisted themselves. See Hollis, *Pauper Press*, 276–7.

155. *PMG* 3, no. 182 (29 November 1834): 338.

156. *PMG* 4, no. 199 (28 March 1835): 475.

157. *Black Dwarf* 9, no. 7 (14 August 1822): 241.

158. *Black Dwarf* 9, no. 11, (11 September 1822): 385.

159. *Black Dwarf* 11, no. 23 (3 December 1823): 775.

160. *Gorgon*, no. 1 (23 May 1818): 5.

161. *Gorgon*, no. 1 (23 May 1818): 8.

162. *Gorgon*, no. 48 (17 April 1819): 379.

163. *Republican* 6, no. 19 (4 October 1822): 599.

164. *Gauntlet*, no. 25 (28 July 1833): 385 and no. 1 (10 February 1833): 1.

165. *Political Letters*, no. 2 (9 October 1830): 12.

166. *True Sun* (24 February 1834) and (12 July 1834).

167. *True Sun* (8 May 1834).

168. *PMG* 2, no. 66 (15 September 1832): 530.

169. *PMG* 2, no. 98 (20 April 1833): 121.

170. *PMG* 2, no. 82 (29 December 1832): 661.

171. *PMG* 4, no. 220 (22 August 1835): 639.

172. *PMG* 4, no. 198 (21 March 1835): 467.

173. *PMG* 4, no. 197 (14 March 1835): 460. Owen's comments were contained in a letter to the editor of the *PMG*.

174. *PMG* 4, no. 231 (7 November 1835): 730.

175. See *PMG* 4, no. 200 (4 April 1835): 481 and 4, no. 231 (7 November 1835): 730.

176. *Black Dwarf* 1, no. 40 (29 October 1817): 667–8.

177. *Black Dwarf* 2, no. 1 (7 January 1818). Cobbett claimed that the *Political Register* was not in his own hands at the time but that he insisted the printer (unknown to him at the time) be fired.

178. *Republican* 13, no. 7 (17 February 1826): 194.

179. *Republican* 14, no. 2 (21 July 1826): 62.

180. *PMG* 3, no. 122 (5 October 1833): 319. Burdett refers to Sir Francis Burdett with whom Cobbett had a falling-out.

181. See Himmelfarb, *The Idea of Poverty*, 234 and Chapter X entitled 'The Poor Man's Guardian: The "New Radicalism"', 230–52.

182. *PMG* 4, no. 199 (28 March 1835): 473. See also Himmelfarb, *The Idea of Poverty*, 249 where she quotes the 12 December 1835 edition of the *PMG*: 'Property, property – this is the subject of subjects.'

183. *PMG* 3, no. 164 (26 July 1834): 193.

184. *PMG* 4, no. 224 (19 September 1835): 681.

185. *PMG* 3, no. 164 (26 July 1834): 194. Also quoted in Hollis, *Pauper Press*, 222–3.

186. *PMG* 4, no. 198 (21 March 1835): 466. Although O'Brien referred to a 'system', he did not employ the term 'capitalism'.

187. *PMG* 4, no. 236 (12 December 1835): 778. Himmelfarb is careful to point out that the 'new ideology' should not be interpreted as a 'premature or incipient Marxism' especially given its reliance on universal suffrage as the ultimate solution. Marx, of course, argued in the *Manifesto of the Communist Party* that suffrage was merely 'the first step in the revolution'. The labour theory of value, moreover, pre-dated both Marx and *The Poor Man's Guardian* and went back at least to Locke as did the notion that government was a tool of the ruling classes. See *The Idea of Poverty*, 250–51 and 560n. and 65 and 67.

188. See Hollis, *Pauper Press*, 220 and especially her informative discussion of O'Brien's critique of political economy, 221–30.

189. For Pare's letters see *Political Letters*, no. 17 (13 January 1831): 1–2, no. 19 (28 January 1831): 3–4, no. 21 (12 February 1831): 1–3, and no. 29 (2 April 1831): 3–6.

190. For reference to J. R. McCulloch see, for example, *PMG* 2, no. 114 (10 August 1833): 254. It is significant that McCulloch is mentioned here along with Lord Brougham. Thus his association with Malthus remains prominent.

191. *Political Letters*, no. 8 (13 November 1830): 10. See also no. 29 (2 April 1831): 4 where William Pare quotes Robert Owen's *Report to the County of Lanark*.

192. *Crisis* 4, no. 19 (16 August 1834): 146.

193. *PMG* 3, no. 140 (8 February 1834): 7.

194. *Political Letters*, no. 19 (28 January 1831): 4. This statement is in Pare's second letter to Wilmot- Horton.

195. *Political Letters*, no. 26 (19 March 1831): 4.

196. *PMG* 1, no. 28 (24 December 1831): 220.

197. *PMG* 3, no. 133 (21 December 1833): 407.

198. *PMG* 1, no. 50 (26 May 1832): 402. Most of this statement is quoted in Hollis, *Pauper Press*, 247. My discussion here relies heavily on Hollis's section entitled 'Economics and Politics', Chapter VII, 246–53.

199. Quoted by Hollis, *Pauper Press*, 249 from *PMG* 3, no. 143 (1 March 1834): 25.

200. *PMG* 3, no. 129 (23 November 1833): 374. Also quoted in Hollis, *Pauper Press*, 249.

201. *Economist* 1, no. 1 (27 January 1821): 4. Mudie was a popularizer of Owenite ideas.

202. Himmelfarb, *Idea of Poverty*, 235.

203. *PMG* 3, no. 121 (28 September 1833): 309.

204. *PMG* 3, no. 125 (26 October 1833): 342.

205. *PMG* 3, no. 122 (5 October 1833): 318.

206. *PMG* 3, no. 121 (28 September 1833): 3

207. See Cobbett, *Legacy to Labourers*, 124 and *PR* (18 October 1834).

208. *PMG* 3, no. 129 (23 November 1833): 374.

209. *PMG* 3, no. 179 (8 November 1834): 314.

210. *PMG* 4, no. 199 (28 March 1835): 473–74.

211. *PMG* 4, no. 199 (28 March 1835): 474–5. It should be stressed that O'Brien's scheme to nationalize the land of England was by no means new. As early as 1775 Thomas Spence in *Rights of Man* had advocated such a policy. As Himmelfarb points out, Spence and his followers were only the more high profile of agrarian socialists calling for such radical measures. See Himmelfarb, *The Idea of Poverty*, 250.

212. Himmelfarb, *The Idea of Poverty*, 239–40.
213. *PMG* 4, no. 199 (28 March 1835): 475.
214. Quoted in Himmelfarb, *The Idea of Poverty*, 240 from *PMG* 4, no. 199 (28 March 1835): 475.
215. As Himmelfarb points out, O'Brien in this respect was opposed to Owenite principles which viewed competition *per se* as irrational and immoral. See Himmelfarb, *The Idea of Poverty*, 240.
216. See Hollis, *Pauper Press*, 253–8 for a more detailed discussion of such methods.
217. *Gauntlet*, no. 7 (24 March 1833): 98.
218. Cited by Wiener, *War of the Unstamped*, 218 from *Cosmopolite* (1 June 1833). Wiener underestimates Carlile's advocacy of physical force when he claims that Carlile 'refused steadfastly to endorse any action beyond "moral" resistance to tyranny'. Ibid, 214.
219. Cited in Wiener, *War of the Unstamped*, 216 from *Republican* (13 and 27 April 1834).
220. *PMG* 4, no. 231 (7 November 1835): 730.
221. Cited in Wiener, *War of the Unstamped*, 217 from *PMG* 2, no. 107 (22 June 1833): 197.
222. *PMG* 2, no. 67 (22 September 1832): 537.
223. *PMG* 1, no. 44 (11 April 1832): 346. For the extracts see 346–52.
224. T. R. Malthus, *An Essay on the Principle of Population: or a view of its past and present Effects on Human Happiness; with an inquiry into our Prospects, respecting the future Removal or Mitigation of the Evils which it occasions: The version published in 1803, with the variora of 1806, 1807, 1817, and 1826*, 2 vols, ed. Patricia James (Cambridge: Cambridge University Press, 1989), II: 235 from the Appendix to the 1817 edition (hereafter cited as *Malthus Variora* with vol. I or vol. II specified). For his reference to 'promiscuous intercourse' as degrading to the 'female character', see ibid., II: 97 from the 1803 edition.
225. Quoted in Fryer, *The Birth Controllers*, 80 from Cobbett's *PR* 3 (15 April 1826). The 'execrable wretch' referred to was no doubt Francis Place who had convinced Carlile to support birth control.
226. Quoted in Angus McClaren, *Birth Control in Nineteenth-Century England* (New York: Holmes and Meier, 1978), 50 (hereafter cited as *Birth Control*). For McClaren's discussion of this issue see 50–51. McCulloch's statement is from his *The Principles of Political Economy*.
227. James, *Malthus Variora*, II: 235 from the Appendix of the 1817 edition.
228. Quoted in McClaren, *Birth Control*, 50.
229. Ricardo's letters to Place on 9 September 1821 and to Malthus 10 September 1821 are quoted in Dudley Miles, *Francis Place: The Life of a Remarkable Radical 1771–1854* (New York: St Martin's Press, 1988), 149–50 (hereafter cited as *Francis Place*).
230. Quoted in Fryer, *The Birth Controllers*, 85.
231. Quoted in M. L. Bush, *What is Love? Richard Carlile's Philosophy of Sex* (London: Verso, 1998), 135 (hereafter cited as *What is Love?*).
232. See Fryer, *The Birth Controllers*, 84.
233. See Bush, *What is Love?*, 134.
234. Ibid. Fildes was injured at the 'Peterloo Massacre' on 16 August 1819 where the yeomanry marched on a crowd of 60,000 in Manchester killing eleven people and wounding 400. See Miles, *Francis Place*, 133.

235. *Black Dwarf* 11, no. 13 (24 September 1823): 463, Miles, *Francis Place*, 133. Fildes' comment is described by John Edward Taylor of the *Manchester Observer* in a letter to the editor dated 18 September 1823.
236. *Black Dwarf*, 11, no. 23 (3 December 1823): 774.
237. Ibid., 781.
238. Ibid.
239. *Black Dwarf*, 11, no. 12 (17 September 1823): 405.
240. Ibid., 410.
241. *Black Dwarf*, 11, no. 23 (3 December 1823): 775.
242. Ibid.
243. *Black Dwarf*, 11, no. 12 (17 September 1823): 409–10.
244. Ibid., 405.
245. *Black Dwarf* 11, no. 12 (17 September 1823): 410.
246. *Black Dwarf* 11, no. 23 (3 December 1823): 780. Wooler also argues here that Malthus in contending 'the children of those who cannot provide for them have no right to subsistence' was in fact, advocating '*infanticide*'.
247. Quoted in Fryer, *The Birth Controllers*, 81–2 upon which this paragraph is mostly based.
248. Quoted in Miles, *Francis Place*, 154. Miles also points out here that Robertson nursed a personal grudge against Place who defeated him in London Mechanics' Institute elections.
249. Quoted in Fryer, *The Birth Controllers*, 82.
250. Quoted in ibid., 82–3. Jeremy Bentham favoured birth control but concealed his opinions on the subject. See Miles, *Francis Place*, 149.
251. Fryer, *The Birth Controllers*, 83. I am indebted to Fryer for the contents of this paragraph. For more detail regarding Haley's dealings with Place and Carlile see Miles, *Francis Place*, 154.
252. For Utilitarians such as Jeremy Benthan see ibid., 149.
253. See John F. C. Harrison, *Quest for the New Moral World: Robert Owen and the Owenites in Britain and America* (New York: Charles Scribner's Sons, 1969), 62 and McClaren, *Birth Control*, 72.
254. McClaren, *Birth Control*, 72.
255. See Fryer, *The Birth Controllers*, 45.
256. McClaren, *Birth Control*, 73.
257. Fryer, *The Birth Controllers*, 45. See also p. 284 n. 5 where he cites a visitor to New Lanark who, in 1876, claimed that there were more illegitimate children in New Lanark than in any other parish in Scotland, thus indicating the absence of contraception.
258. Ibid., 45. See also McClaren, *Birth Control*, 72.
259. See Miles, *Francis Place*, 143 upon which this paragraph is based.
260. Ibid., 268 n. 11.
261. See Fryer, *The Birth Controllers*, 94–5. Owen's English edition was published in December 1832 although an unauthorized English edition was published in October 1832 by James Watson who soon after launched *The Working Man's Friend*.
262. See Miles, *Francis Place*, 155. Fryer claims that the October 1832 edition of *Moral Physiology* was full of mistakes and omissions. See Fryer, *The Birth Controllers*, 94.
263. For the clash between Hetherington and O'Brien see Hollis, *Pauper Press*, 231. For a list of Hetherington's periodicals and books for sale see *PMG* 3, no. 148 (5 April 1834): 71–2.

264. *PMG* 2, no. 96 (6 April 1833): 112. See also *PMG* 2, no. 69 (6 October 1832): 560, *PMG* 3, no. 128 (16 November 1833): 372, and *PMG* 4, no. 225 (26 September 1835): 686.
265. *PMG* 4, no. 206 (16 May 1835): 536. See also *PMG* 4, no. 208 (30 May 1835): 550 and *PMG* 4, no. 209 (6 June 1835): 558.
266. See Miles, *Francis Place*, 146–7. For Place's discussion see Francis Place, *Illustrations and Proofs of the Principle of Population* (London: Longmans, 1822; repr., London: Allen and Unwin, 1930), 138, 154–6, 39.
267. *Black Dwarf* 11, no. 12 (17 September 1823): 408–409. There were two other versions of the handbill: 'To the Married of Both Sexes of the Working People' and 'To the Married of Both Sexes in Genteel Life'.
268. For Place's reliance on James Mill see *Black Dwarf* 11, no. 20 (12 November 1823): 665–7. For his relationship with Mill see Miles, *Francis Place*, 97–8. For Mill's support of birth control see ibid., 143 and McClaren, *Birth Control*, 51. Place, however, did not refer directly to Malthus on overpopulation and preferred to cite his mentor James Mill who secretly favoured birth control. The anti-Malthusianism of *Black Dwarf* and the working-class press in general no doubt led Place, like many birth controllers, to distance himself from 'the parson'.
269. *Black Dwarf* 11, no. 20 (12 November 1823): 667.
270. Ibid.
271. Miles, *Francis Place*, 145. See also Donald Winch, *Riches and Poverty: An Intellectual History of Political Economy in Britain, 1750–1834* (Cambridge: Cambridge University Press, 1996), 283 (hereafter cited as *Riches and Poverty*).
272. *Black Dwarf* 11, no. 12 (17 September 1823): 408–409.
273. Ibid., 408.
274. All quotations in this paragraph are taken from Place's anonymous letter to *Black Dwarf*. See *Black Dwarf* 11, no. 20 (12 November 1823): 667.
275. All quotations from ibid., 676–7.
276. All quotations from ibid., 674.
277. For the arguments in this paragraph see ibid., 669–70.
278. See Miles, *Francis Place*, 149. Mill was released without being charged.
279. For Mill's arguments see *Black Dwarf* 11, no. 22 (27 November 1823): 749, 750, 752 and 775 and *Black Dwarf* 11, no. 24 (10 December 1823): 792 and 795. Mill does not refer to Malthus specifically nor to any other political economists.
280. *Black Dwarf* 11, no. 24 (10 December 1823): 797.
281. *Black Dwarf* 11, no. 22 (27 November 1823): 756.
282. Ibid.
283. *Black Dwarf* 11, no. 24 (10 December 1823): 798.
284. The essay appeared in *Republican* 11, no. 18 (6 May 1825): 545–69 and is reprinted in Bush, *What is Love?*, 55–80. All references to the essay in the following analysis are taken from Bush.
285. For Carlile's conversion under the influence of Francis Place see ibid., 22–3. See also Joel H. Wiener, *Radicalism and Free Thought in Nineteenth-Century Britain: The Life of Richard Carlile* (Westport, CT and London: Greenwood Press, 1983), 125 (hereafter cited as *Richard Carlile*).
286. Bush, *What is Love?*, 67.

287. Ibid., 59.
288. Ibid., 62–3.
289. Ibid., 75.
290. Ibid., 56.
291. For the contents of this paragraph I am indebted to Miles, *Francis Place*, 152–3. Place described Carlile as 'a single minded honest hearted fanatic'. See Wiener, *Richard Carlile*, ix.
292. Bush, *What is Love?*, 61.
293. Ibid., 68.
294. Ibid., 62. For a more detailed discussion of Carlile's hostility to traditional Christianity see Wiener, *Richard Carlile*, 130–36.
295. Bush, *What is Love?*, 63.
296. For Carlile's admission see McClaren, *Birth Control*, 76 n. 29. Place gave Carlile a copy of his *Illustrations and Proofs of the Principle of Population* shortly after it was published in 1822. Carlile thus acquired some familiarity with Malthus's ideas without having to read his work. Bush, *What is Love?*, 22. See also Wiener, *Richard Carlile*, 125 for Place's role in making Carlile aware of Malthus's theory. In 1828 Carlile admitted: 'Some years back, after Mr. Cobbett's assault, not knowing any thing of Mr. Malthus, but through that medium his name was associated in my bosom with something like abhorrent feeling.' See *The Lion*, 1, no. 3 (18 January 1828): 94. He is presumably referring to the period before 1822.
297. See Bush, *What is Love?*, 106.
298. Ibid., 107. For his retraction see *Lion* 1, no. 3 (18 January 1828): 95.
299. Bush, *What is Love?*, 107.
300. Ibid., 107.
301. Ibid., 108.
302. See *Lion* 1, no. 3 (18 January 1828): 94. Carlile also quoted Malthus approvingly on education. The fact that Carlile was aware of the changes Malthus had made in editions of the *Essay* after 1798 and 1803 suggests that by 1828 he had read Malthus thoroughly. Carlile also referred to his works on political economy. See ibid., 92.
303. Bush, *What is Love?*, 65–6.
304. Ibid., 66. Earlier in the essay Carlile completely misread Cobbett as being in favour of celibacy in general and labelled him 'the eulogist of Malthus'. Cobbett, of course, opposed moral restraint and never praised Malthus although he did firmly oppose contraception. See ibid., 63 and 66.
305. Ibid., 66.
306. Ibid., 75.
307. Ibid., 67.
308. As Bush points out, Carlile's book outsold Robert Dale Owen's *Moral Physiology* that sold only 1,500 copies in its first five months. See ibid., 139. For further details on sales of both the essay and the book see ibid., 49.
309. For Bush's discussion of these and other changes see ibid., 5–9.
310. Ibid., 101.
311. Ibid., 102.
312. Ibid., 109.
313. For Malthus's statements quoted in this paragraph see James *Malthus Variora*, II: 252, 204, 135 and 136 and I: 375–6. The comments referring to popular writers first appeared in the 1817 edition of the *Essay* and were

retained in 1826. At another point in the *Essay* he justified a national system of education on the grounds that 'an instructed and well-informed people would be much less likely to be led away by inflammatory writings, and much better able to detect the false declamation of interested and ambitious demagogues, than an ignorant people.' See ibid., II: 154. Malthus ignored many other important critics both inflammatory (Robert Southey and William Hazlitt) and moderate (Francis Place). See Winch, *Riches and Poverty*, 285 and 293–4. He did, however, critique Tom Paine, see James, *Malthus Variora*, II: 126–7.

314. Ibid., I: 334. Owen wished to reduce the workday to six hours for children. No child, moreover, should be employed until they were ten years of age.
315. Ibid., I: 335.
316. Ibid.
317. Ibid., I: 336.
318. Ibid.
319. Ibid.
320. Ibid., I: 337–8. Under a system of equality, laws could be introduced to enforce moral restraint. Such laws, Malthus thought, would be 'unnatural, immoral, or cruel in a high degree' and would not succeed, ibid., I: 338.
321. See Himmelfarb, *The Idea of Poverty*, 250.
322. Ibid., 251.
323. For these estimates see Hollis, *Pauper Press*, 301 and Himmelfarb, *The Idea of Poverty*, 251.
324. See his comment in *Lion* 1, no. 3 (18 January 1828): 94.
325. For the above details see ibid., 178. The reaction of *The Times* to the New Poor Law and to Malthusianism in general still awaits a full study, as does the Whig-owned *Morning Chronicle* that supported the New Poor Law.
326. See The Times, *The History of The Times: 'The Thunderer' in the Making 1785–1841* (London: The Times, 1935), 296 and Himmelfarb, *The Idea of Poverty*, 178.
327. See Nicholas C. Edsall, *The Anti-Poor Law Movement, 1833–1844* (Manchester: Manchester University Press, 1971), 18–19 and Himmelfarb, *The Idea of Poverty*, 179.
328. Ibid., 179. John Walter voted against the New Poor Law Bill in the House of Commons. See Anthony Brundage, *The Making of the New Poor Laws: The Politics of Inquiry, Enactment and Implementation* (New Brunswick, NJ: Rutgers University Press, 1978), 56.
329. The Times, *History of the Times*, 293.
330. *Times* (3 July 1834). The bill at this point had passed the House of Commons and had moved on to the House of Lords.
331. Ibid. *The Times*, of course, also attacked Martineau directly and published a letter to the editor claiming that 'among the many persons who have yet to answer for the gross misrepresentations which have been made on the subject of the relief given to the poor, no individual is more conspicuous than Miss Martineau.' See ibid. (28 August 1834).
332. Ibid. (3 July 1834).
333. Bush, *What is Love?*, 138–9. Marshall supported most of Carlile's principles, especially the notion that physical love was 'the gratification of a natural propensity'. See ibid., 137.
334. Ibid., 138.

335.   McClaren, *Birth Control*, 129.
336.   Ibid., 204, 203 and 207. Besant publicly declared her support for birth control and with Charles Bradlaugh was involved in the famous birth control trial that gained widespread publicity in the 1870s.
337.   See McClaren, *Birth Control*, 255. McClaren rightly disputes the trickle-down theory that family limitation somehow diffused from the middle classes down the social scale. The very fact that textile workers were limiting family size as early as 1850 – before classes above them – suggests that the working classes did not need to wait for middle-class advice on this matter.

Malthus. Even though her tales were purchased by the libraries of Mechanics's Institutes it is unlikely that her espousal of Malthusianism met with approval among adult working-men, given the influence of Owenite and other radical ideas especially in the 1820s and 1830s.[4] Cobbett and the pauper press denounced her in scathing terms as an outright Malthusian and hireling of Lord Brougham, labelling her the 'anti-propagation lady' and referring to the New Poor Law as 'the Mother Martineau Bill'. At the opposite end of the political spectrum, the *Quarterly Review and Fraser's Magazine,* representing Tory views, launched vicious attacks on her, especially in terms of gender. Martineau, the Malthusian messenger, was mercilessly shot down in these quarters. The fact that she had pronounced disagreements with Malthus did not register with her critics.

Why was she so severely savaged? Caroline Roberts argues that Martineau's advocacy of Malthusian delay of marriage through moral restraint 'challenged prevailing ideologies of the middle class' especially the 'domestic ideal' so critical 'to the division of the public and private spheres'.[5] Delay of marriage presumably would leave more single females unemployed and more likely to enter the public sphere. Roberts, however, cites only one critic who made this argument, hardly enough evidence to support the contention that such fears were general.[6] More important, it is clear that Malthus, rather than attacking the domestic ideal, wished to impose it upon the poor. The male head of the household, no longer entitled to poor relief, would become solely responsible for the support of his wife and children. Malthus thus advocated the 'breadwinner' model of family life. Moreover, he clearly supported the notion of separate spheres by positing, as Deborah Valenze points out, a distinct separation of 'mother-as-nurturer and father-as-provider'.[7] Indeed, there was much in Malthus that would appeal to, rather than alienate, a middle-class audience.

There are alternative explanations for the scorn and abuse heaped on Martineau. Like Malthus himself, her support of moral restraint was misinterpreted, especially by Tory critics, as advocating birth control *within* marriage – an unmentionable subject in the early nineteenth century (my emphasis). She was further misread as being anti-natal and anti-marriage, charges likewise made against Malthus. Even more important was her stance on the Poor Law and, in particular, her association with Lord Brougham who was condemned as a Malthusian promulgator of the 1834 Act. Both Tories and spokesmen for the working class vociferously opposed notions to abolish the Old Poor Law and deny the right to relief, views supported by Martineau in her *Illustrations of Political Economy.* Martineau further exposed herself to vitriolic criticism when she rejected abolition and declared her support

Conclusion

The major aim of this study has been to examine the popular transmission of Malthus's ideas during his lifetime and thus to remedy a significant oversight in the historiography of his thought and influence. My central conclusion substantiates a claim made by J. R. Poynter over three decades ago in his now-classic work entitled *Society and Pauperism*; namely, that 'Malthus's contribution to shaping opinion on pauperism was incomparable.'[1] I contend that such influence permeated far below the level of controversy among established political economists and other eminent writers or those with the legislative power to shape social policy. I have focused my discussion on three substantial bodies of popular work: Harriet Martineau's pro-Malthusian moral tales, William Cobbett's vast range of commentary critiquing Malthus and, finally, the most significant and influential newspapers of the pauper press which often drew heavily on Cobbett's arguments.

No doubt other sources would be worthy of analysis. The novels of Thomas Love Peacock such as *Headlong Hall* (1816) and *Melincourt* (1817) contain Malthusian characters as do those of Charles Dickens. At the level of direct working-class action, a re-examination of protest and riots against the New Poor Law – in both rural south and industrial north – might provide further insight.[2] A close perusal of surviving sermons could shed light on how Malthusian ideas were purveyed from the pulpit. More detailed research into the vast collection of early nineteenth-century government committees and reports, especially the volumes of evidence in the replies to the *Rural and Town Queries* of the *1843 Poor Law Report*, would reveal further evidence of Malthusian attitudes on the part of the clergy as well as parish officers and farmers who submitted responses.[3] It would be impossible to do justice to such sources in a single volume and, besides, much of this research would go beyond 1834 where the present work terminates. In any case, such material, with the exception of Dickens after 1834, did not have the wide readership and popular dissemination of the literature I have analysed. It remains to determine what lessons I can distil from my investigation.

Harriet Martineau was clearly intent on proselytizing the Malthusian cause to a mass audience. Given her astonishing level of sales, she no doubt gained many converts among the middle class and those with Whig propensities. With regard to the working class and conservative Tories, her project backfired and, if anything, fuelled the detestation of

for the New Poor Law. Even *The Times* turned against her on this issue. Her stance, of course, provoked the ire of the working-class press who viewed the New Poor Law as a Malthusian measure.

A further question stems from Roberts's interpretation. If Malthusian ideas were such a threat to middle-class ideology, why was Jane Marcet, who similarly advocated moral restraint in fictional format, spared the invective heaped on Martineau? Again the Poor Law is relevant. Marcet did not publicly support the New Poor Law and stayed out of the debate surrounding its passage. In addition, Martineau was prepared to attack entrenched interests such as slavery, colonial monopoly and privileged trading companies. Marcet kept clear of such controversial issues and maintained a much more conservative profile. I argue, as well, that Marcet's age, marital status and respectability could be important factors. In 1833, the year that *John Hopkins's Notions of Political Economy* was published, Marcet was sixty-four years of age and had been married for thirty-four years to an eminent medical doctor. In the same year Martineau was thirty-one years old and was never to marry. Marcet's lifestyle as a conventional and fashionable London woman possibly allowed her to discuss the delicate subject of moral restraint without censure.

William Cobbett, of course, was Malthus's most consistent and vociferous critic in the early nineteenth century. Although his attacks were often highly emotional and laden with personal invective, it is mistaken to consider his arguments as devoid of intellectual content. To be sure, some of his criticisms were illogical in the extreme. His denials, for example, that population had increased were based more on a paranoid view that the Censuses of England were deliberately rigged to suit the Malthusian purposes of government than on any solid statistical evidence. His church capacity theory – that is, if population indeed had increased why were the Anglican churches of England frequently empty? – completely ignored rural-urban migration but more important failed to recognize declining adherence to the Anglican religion and the growth of dissenting sects.

Yet in other important areas, particularly his defence of the right of the poor to relief, Cobbett's arguments must be taken seriously. Drawing on the works of Locke, Blackstone, Hall, Paley and Montesquieu he developed original theories of the social compact, natural law and the civil and property rights of the poor. The Old Poor Law, he argued, was the property of the poor. The legal right to relief was universal and sanctioned by natural law and the social compact. The New Poor Law, by confining individuals to the workhouse, violated the civil rights of the poor. In reaching such conclusions he also rewrote the history of England and radicalized its historical discourse.

That Cobbett advanced such arguments against Malthus is highly significant. Historians have paid scant attention to the role that anti-Malthusianism played in the development of his social and political ideology. The sheer energy he devoted to refuting the 'Parson' testifies to the centrality of Malthus in his thought. Upon passage of the New Poor Law, which he viewed as destroying the social compact, Cobbett advocated violent revolution. It was Malthus – who denied the universal legal right to relief – who drove society back to a state of nature thus justifying, in Cobbett's opinion, the forcible seizure of land and the means of subsistence. The New Poor Law, he argued, was a Malthusian measure which denied outdoor relief for the poor. His conversion to extreme radicalism at the end of his life can only be understood by reference to Malthus.

Cobbett's mass readership testifies to the widespread animosity to Malthus he promoted among the working class. Further evidence of his influence is provided by an examination of the pauper press. Cobbett received much personal praise and adulation in such papers. His arguments against Malthus and the New Poor Law and his advocacy of the legal right to relief were often repeated – with or without specific credit – especially his argument that such subsidies were the property of the poor. Malthus and his followers, especially Lord Brougham and Harriet Martineau, were mercilessly castigated although seldom with the forcefulness of Cobbett's venomous pen. Although much discord prevailed among the editors of the working-class press, they were virtually unified in their opposition to the Malthusian notion of surplus population. They likewise refused to accept moral restraint and abolition of the Old Poor Law as solutions to the problem of poverty, the roots of which could be found in Cobbett's old corruption: unfair taxation, a burgeoning national debt and wasteful government expenditure, especially on pensions and sinecures.

If many editors in the pauper press echoed what some historians refer to as Cobbett's 'old ideology', others promoted a 'new ideology' although both views were frequently intermingled and the distinction often blurred. The latter moved beyond Cobbett to a more sophisticated analysis which viewed class exploitation by capitalists and landlords as the prime source of poverty and vehemently denied that Malthusian natural law dictated inequality and the inevitability of the poor in society. Excessive taxation and other factors emphasized by Cobbett were now seen as symptoms of a far more deep-seated cause of destitution; namely, the power of a monied monopoly where capitalists and landlords united to create laws and institutions that plundered the workers and transferred wealth to themselves. Such analysis adamantly rejected Malthusian assumptions that surplus population was the cause of immiseration.

A minority strand of thought, quite separate from the 'new ideology', accepted Malthus's premise of overpopulation but proposed solutions that Cobbett, and indeed Malthus himself, vehemently opposed. Richard Carlile, Francis Place and J. S. Mill rejected the efficacy of moral restraint and advocated contraceptive birth control during intercourse. Although in theory this measure posed a dire threat to the very foundation of Malthus's principles, in practice such proposals could not upset the Malthisian edifice. The vast majority of English society – including the working class – equated this type of family limitation with obscenity and vice, and condemned such behaviour. Cobbett, who would have agreed with at least some of the tenets of the 'new ideology', such as universal adult male suffrage, defence of the Old Poor Law and even, in his later days, the necessity of violent revolution if all else failed, could never, on moral grounds, accept birth control as a viable option. So taboo was the subject that the few who condoned such practices expressed their opinions in private. Those who published their views did so anonymously or, as in the case of Francis Place in his *Illustrations and Proofs of the Principle of Population* (1822), dealt with the subject in non-specific terms and certainly did not dwell on it.[8]

The exception, of course, was the impetuous Richard Carlile, who, against the frantic urgings of Francis Place, published 'What is Love?' in 1825. Not only did he provide specific details concerning the sponge as the best method of contraception, he also advocated its use among both single and married women. As if this did not go far enough, he argued that the free expression of love would produce health and beauty and prevent illness. Intercourse between the sexes, he contended, was absolutely necessary to happiness. Females, moreover, should be free to initiate such activity. The use of the sponge would remove the fear of pregnancy and the birth of illegitimate children. Within marriage it would prevent unwanted births and raise the standard of living. In addition, sexual intercourse would become a pleasure independent of procreation. Having rejected Malthus's moral restraint, Carlile believed he had discovered the only viable solution to the Malthusian misery of excess numbers. By linking contraception to free love, however, he realized the worst fears of Place and destroyed any possibility that birth control would gain increasing acceptance. If society was hardly ready to receive the message of artificially limiting births even within marriage, it certainly was nowhere near accepting Carlile's ideas concerning sexual freedom. The backlash against his extreme views did incalculable harm to the cause of family limitation and certainly did not pose a serious challenge to Malthus in the public domain. Carlile's project, like Martineau's from a different direction, backfired even more completely.

The detestation of Malthus and his adherents by Cobbett and the working-class press has been clearly established in this study. There remains the task of explaining why such opposition reached the venomous levels it did and why it was so persistent. A further issue arises. Equally acerbic critiques of Malthusianism stemmed from conservative quarters: articles in the Tory *Quarterly Review* and the writings of early romantics, some of which adopted ultra-Tory views.[9] Did such attacks from such polar ends of the political spectrum share anything in common? Or were their assumptions fundamentally different?

A number of similarities stand out. Both radicals and conservatives opposed the tenets of political economy and viewed Malthus as the inhumane personifier of such ideas. Both refused to accept the Malthusian premise that a natural law of population was the fundamental cause of poverty and denied the existence of overpopulation. Nor was poverty the fault of the poor themselves. Destitution, they agreed, was rooted in faulty social institutions. Malthus's solutions, moreover, were likewise rejected. Moral restraint was either impractical or illogical. In addition, both sectors of opinion condemned Malthus's proposal to abolish the Old Poor Law and deny legal entitlement to relief, labelling him a hard-hearted enemy of the poor.[10] In 1807, Cobbett, the radical, published in his *Political Register* three lengthy letters by William Hazlitt, an admirer of the Lake Poets, castigating Malthus and defending the poor.[11]

Such common threads, however, mask significant differences. Winch maintains that the fundamental hatred of Malthus by the early Romantics was driven by their attempt to defend the Nature/Culture dichotomy. Malthus, they believed, confused the world of man with that discovered by Newton by proposing universal natural economic laws which governed the behaviour of human beings. Such 'naturalism', Winch argues, meant nothing less for Romantics than 'an abandonment of moral judgement' and 'could never be what it was for Malthus, a basis for improving such judgments.'[12] Radical critics were not concerned with such issues. Indeed, Cobbett proposed his own natural laws as against those of Malthus to justify the right to bear children and to defend the right to relief and subsistence among the poor.

If both conservatives and radicals, moreover, agreed on the general causes of poverty their specific arguments on this issue were very distinct. The early Romantic, Robert Southey, was the first to attribute the immiseration of the labouring poor to the rise of manufacturing. This system drew the lower orders of the countryside into the towns creating not only a mass of urban poor but also, even more important, a population increasingly subject to moral degeneration. The removal of rural labour from the paternal influences of village existence – especially the social mores and religious instruction provided by gentlemen and clergy – led to the burgeoning of an urban mob which, according to

Southey, was becoming increasingly capable of revolt and the destruction of class harmony.[13] Such moral decline, however, was not limited solely to the lower classes. The higher orders had failed to establish 'moral government' so imbued had they become, argued Coleridge, with the materialist notions of the commercial spirit.[14] The sources of misery were found not in the natural or physical laws of Malthus but in the collapse of moral acumen.

Cobbett, at times, exhibited ambivalence towards urban manufacturing and displayed nostalgia for an ideal rural past. Like radicals in the working-class press, however, he did not, in the final analysis, oppose manufacturing *per se* (my emphasis) but condemned the way it dispossessed workers of the fruits of their labour. In addition, writers on this end of the spectrum focused on the inequities inherent in political and social institutions rather than on questions of moral degeneration. The causes of poverty – especially for those espousing the new ideology – were rooted not in Malthusian surplus population but rather in political and economic control by an elite which fostered class exploitation.

Differing explanations of poverty, of course, led to diametrically opposed solutions. Romantics and conservative Tories sought to restore public order and a status quo based on the moral and educational precepts of the Church of England and the paternalism of a landed elite ruling in the interests of social harmony. To be sure, strong and judicious government would be necessary – a government prepared to tax and spend heavily in the national interest whether such expenditure be directed to controlling the press and punishing radical activity, to defence of the realm in war, to national education controlled by the Church of England, to public works, to land reclamation or to emigration abroad.[15] Needless to say any extension of the franchise, especially the Reform Bill of 1832, was viewed with immense alarm as were proposals for greater economic equality.[16]

Radicals developed markedly different solutions. Reform, involving greater political and economic equality was of the order and, failing that, violent revolution. Malthuianism was viewed as inimical to such reform. Although he belatedly and rather timidly supported the Reform Bill of 1832, Malthus was staunchly opposed to universal adult male suffrage.[17] His attacks on the Old Poor Law and especially his denial of the legal right to relief were viewed as removing any chance the poor might have to subsist, let alone achieve greater economic equality. His notion that individual behaviour rather than institutions was to blame for destitution infuriated the likes of Cobbett as well as editors and contributors to the working-class press.

Their intense hatred of Malthus perhaps runs deeper. Karl Max realized well after Malthus's death that to accept the Malthusian view as true would render revolution or even reform unnecessary. For if labourers were capable of adopting the prudential virtues advocated by Malthus then any argument that their situation was hopeless and in need of drastic institutional change would be seriously undermined. If, as Malthus argued, such prudence – especially the delay of marriage – allowed workers to appropriate some of the surplus they produced then the need for revolution or reform would be precluded.[18] Although Cobbett and other radicals never admitted such views, the sheer bitterness of their attacks on Malthus might be explained in such underlying terms.

In spite of profound differences there was one overriding feature that both conservative and radical critics had in common. Their detestation of Malthus led to flagrant misrepresentation of his ideas. There is no doubt that such distortion was often deliberate. Even the most cursory reading of the 1798 and 1803 editions of the *Essay* makes it clear that Cobbett and the working-class press misled their readers. At no point, for example, did Malthus oppose marriage or childbearing *per se* (my emphasis). Although he desired a delay in marriage, he never advocated laws specifying minimum ages at which men and women could first marry. Nor did he advocate birth control within marriage or sanction abortion as a means of limiting population. Charges that he advocated infanticide or wished death upon the poor in general were likewise totally unfounded.

Other misrepresentations more likely stem from the fact that Malthus's critics never bothered to read later editions of his *Essay* let alone his *Principles of Political Economy* (1820).[19] Cobbett and the pauper press, for example, continually berated Malthus for arguing in the 1803 *Essay* that there was no room for the poor at 'nature's mighty feast'. That he removed this infamous passage from all subsequent editions of the *Essay* was never commented upon by such critics. Likewise, the failure to consider Malthus's concept of 'prudential restraint' as opposed to 'moral restraint' – where he conceded that absolute celibacy before marriage was unrealistic – could be explained by the fact that Malthus made this distinction clear only in his 1806 *Essay*, although admittedly a close reading of the 1803 *Essay* would have revealed his changing position.

On certain interpretations, however, his popular critics should not be faulted. After all, one should not expect such individuals – given their passionate involvement in the ideological issues of the day – to be akin to modern scholars perusing all of his works to detect complex shifts in thought. Even modern writing is hardly immune from ideological bias or faulty interpretation.[20] To charge his contemporary critics, for example, with failing to realize that Malthus softened his position on abolition of

the Old Poor Law, altered his views on emigration, expressed reservations about his support of the Corn Laws or favoured moderate electoral reform would be unfair. The evidence for such transitions are contained either in his personal correspondence or sometimes buried in brief and often relatively obscure passages of his later work. Besides, there still remains considerable debate among historians as to the validity of some of these readings of Malthus's work.

Regardless of how deliberate was the misrepresentation of Malthus in the radical press, one thing is clear. Malthus never replied specifically to these critics just as he refused to reply to the vicious attacks by early Romantics such as Southey and Hazlitt.[21] 'Popular orators and writers', he argued, misled 'the labouring classes as to the real nature of their situation' and did so 'partly from ignorance and partly from design'. He had no interest, moreover, in returning 'abusive declaration in kind' or in arguing seriously with critics whose writings were 'so full of illiberal declamation and so entirely destitute of argument, as to be evidently beneath notice.'[22] In adopting this stance, Malthus ensured that no direct debate between him and writers in the pauper press occurred. The result was that the transmission of his ideas to a wider working-class audience remained one-sided and often laden with misinterpretation. His refusal, moreover, to support publicly Martineau's popular brand of Malthusianism left her highly vulnerable to the vitriolic attacks of both radicals and conservatives.[23]

Did Malthus's aloofness, however, really matter in practical terms? After all, his ideas prevailed where they counted most – at the level of the ruling elite and legislative bureaucrats who enacted the New Poor Law. Malthus made no contribution to the debate surrounding its passage, and the role he played – for that matter the role any intellectual played – is still subject to dispute. No doubt a complex set of factors was involved and much research is still needed. I contend that Malthus not only framed the parameters of the discourse on poverty for over three decades prior to 1834 but also indirectly influenced the core principles of the reformed Poor Law. Although not denying legal entitlement to relief, the New Poor Law nevertheless prohibited outdoor relief to able-bodied men and their families thus rendering the individual breadwinner totally responsible for the welfare of his wife and children – a central tenet in Malthus's thought. To be sure, the workhouse would be available but only as a last and desperate measure. Even here there were Malthusian overtones: the segregation by gender clearly intended to prevent procreation among the poor. The *1834 Poor Law Report*, moreover, was laden with Malthusian language stressing that the dire consequences of improvidence must be borne by individuals and their families and frequently reiterating a theme prominent in Malthus's early writings;

namely, that Poor Law allowances encouraged early marriage and large families. One should remember that in the 1820s, Malthus, at least in private, moved away from advocating a complete abolition of the Old Poor Law in favour of an 'improved administration of our actual laws' and an amelioration of the present system.'[24] In his last published work in 1830, entitled *A Summary View of the Principle of Population*, he conceded publicly that those in dire need might receive assistance. He was certainly amenable to a reformed Poor Law even though he never commented specifically on the 1834 Act itself.

Malthus's influence becomes even more significant when one considers how relatively easily the vast majority of the provisions in the Poor Law Amendment Act passed through the House of Lords and especially the House of Commons. Clearly, the landed elite, Tory as well as Whig, was prepared by 1834 to abnegate its paternal responsibility to the poor. The abandonment of such principles was a gradual process and the product of a wide range of social and economic forces eroding the moral economy. Nevertheless, the intellectual impact of Malthus must be given high priority. For it was Malthus who inspired the writings of clerics and liberal Tories such as Bishop John Bird Sumner and members of the 'Noetic' school at Oxford University, such as John Davison and Edward Coplestone. These thinkers not only developed his ideas in the post-1815 period but also successfully translated them to the Anglican Church, the landowning elite and the country gentry. Peter Mandler asserts that by 1830 such elites had become imbued with Christian versions of Political Economy and suffused with Malthusian ideas. By 1834, then, the vast majority of the Tory contingent in the House of Commons was prepared to accept a New Poor Law brought to Parliament by a Whig government.[25]

The Noetics, moreover, played a direct role in the provisions that were eventually contained in the 1834 Act. Not only did their updated versions of Malthusianism – especially their emphasis on less eligibility – provide the basic groundwork for such amendments but also their dominance on the Royal Commission on the Poor Law established in 1832 ensured their principles would hold sway. The core of the commission – Nassau Senior, William Sturges-Bourne, Bishop John Sumner, C. J. Blomfield and the Revd Henry Bishop were all connected to the Noetics.[26] Nassau Senior who, by 1832, had become a major economic adviser in high ministerial circles was an avowed Malthusian and drafted large sections of the *1834 Poor Law Report*. Prior to sitting on the commission he described Malthus as 'our most eminent living philosophical writer'.[27]

William Empson, a colleague and close friend of Malthus at East India College remarked in *The Edinburgh Review* in 1837, that 'the poor law

amendment bill ... would have been absolutely impossible, unless Mr. Malthus had stood in the gap for so many years, bearing the brunt of argument and obloquy, fearless of danger, regardless of every interest but the interests of truth.'[28] Would the New Poor Law have transpired without the intellectual contribution of Malthus? Such counterfactual questions, perhaps, are of limited use to historians. One might equally ask whether the 1834 Act would have occurred without the 'Swing' riots of 1830–31 which signalled the death knell of a paternalist society based on a reciprocal relationship between master and labourer. Or would such legislation have been enacted without the immediate agricultural crisis of 1830 which provoked the riots in the first place? No doubt these factors increased the urgency of administrative reform. Such questions remind us of the complexities involved in explanations of changing social policy. Clearly, Malthus's influence was but one among many. I would argue, nevertheless, that his writing was a necessary if not sufficient cause of the timing and shape of perhaps the most significant piece of nineteenth-century social legislation.

Karl Polanyi argued long ago that 'the social history of the nineteenth century was determined by the logic of the market system proper after it was released by the Poor Law Reform Act of 1834.'[29] The New Poor Law – which eliminated the interference of wage subsidies in the form of allowances thus creating a competitive market in labour – was a critical turning point in the creation of a market economy. Malthus played a much greater role in this process than did Smith or Ricardo and must be given his due weight in this fundamental transition.

Certainly his contemporary radical critics did not hesitate to do so. As much as they misrepresented Malthus's ideas, they had grasped the significance of Malthusianism in the creation of the New Poor Law and sensed the threat he posed to the interests of labour. Malthus, of course, argued that moral or prudential restraint would eventually benefit labourers by reducing their numbers and raising their wages. His critics believed such prescriptions to be futile. Some contended, perhaps rightly, that contraception was the only viable recourse.

Such popular opposition to Malthus was to no avail. Although nothing is inevitable in history, it appears that the forces, both long term and short, generating the rise of a fully-fledged market system were inexorable. The voices of Cobbett and the working class press, laden with a passion and hatred often heard in the pages above, remind us once again that the rise of early industrial capitalism was bitterly contested and testify to the centrality of Malthus who so frequently was the focus of attack. Although debate over his impact on the New Poor Law will no doubt continue, the permeation of his ideas into the deepest recesses of the popular press is undeniable. From this perspective he must rank, for ill or good, as one of the most significant thinkers of the early nineteenth century.

Endnotes

1. J. R. Poynter, *Society and Pauperism: English Ideas on Poor Relief, 1795–1834* (London: Routledge and Kegan Paul, 1969), 109.
2. For examination of such protest see Nicholas C. Edsall, *The Anti-Poor Law Movement, 1833–34* (Manchester: Manchester University Press, 1971), John Knott, *Popular Opposition to the 1834 Poor Law* (London: Croom Helm, 1986), *The English Poor Law, 1780–1930*, ed. M. E. Rose (New York: Barnes and Noble, 1971). These works make only brief reference to Malthus. A more thorough analysis of Malthusian content, however, might pay dividends.
3. See *Report from His Majesty's Commissioners for Inquiring into the Administration and Practical Application of the Poor Laws: Rural Queries and Town Queries*, vols XXXV–XXXVI (1834). For the main body of the report the most convenient source is *The Poor Law Report of 1834*, eds S. G. Checkland and E. O. A. Checkland (Harmondsworth: Penguin Books Inc., 1974).
4. For the influence of Robert Owen and radicals such as Thomas Rowe Edmonds and Thomas Hodgskin on the London Mechanics' Institute see J. F. C. Harrison, *Quest for the New Moral World: Robert Owen and the Owenites in Britain and America* (New York: Charles Scribner's Sons, 1969), 65–6.
5. Caroline Roberts, *The Woman and the Hour: Harriet Martineau and Victorian Ideologies* (Toronto: University of Toronto Press, 2002), 22–3.
6. Ibid., 23. The critic was John Ham writing in *Tait's Edinburgh Magazine*.
7. For the 'breadwinner' model see Mitchell Dean, *The Constitution of Poverty: Toward a Genealogy of Liberal Governance* (London: Routledge, 1991), 14 and 104. For Malthus's support of separate spheres see Deborah Valenze, *The First Industrial Woman* (Oxford: Oxford University Press, 1995), 137. The phrases quoted are Valenze's.
8. See Francis Place, *Illustrations and Proofs of the Principle of Population including an Examination of the Proposed Remedies of Mr. Malthus, and a Reply to the Objections of Mr. Godwin and Others* (London: Longmans, 1822), 176–7, 165.
9. I use the terms 'Tory', 'ultra-Tory' and 'conservative' loosely as meaning, in the broadest sense, support for a return to the status quo. The term 'radical' is also used loosely to mean those in favour of significant reforms that would benefit labour. For a discussion of the pitfalls of using such labels especially as definitive binary opposites (Whig/Tory) see Donald Winch, *Riches and Poverty: An Intellectual History of Political Economy in Britain, 1750–1834* (Cambridge: Cambridge University Press, 1996), 28–29. Hereafter cited as *Riches and Poverty*.
10. Winch argues, however, that the early Romantics, with the exception, perhaps, of Wordsworth eventually capitulated, at least privately, to a Malthusian view of the Old Poor Law. John Rickman was a crucial influence in this shift. See Winch, *Riches and Poverty*, 311–22.

References

Primary Sources

Writings, edited works and reprints

Carlile, Richard, *Every Woman's Book or What is Love?* 4th edn. London: R. Carlile, 1826.

Cobbett, William. *Advice to Young Men and (Incidentally) to Young Women in the Middle and Higher Ranks of Life*. London: William Cobbett, 1830.

———. *Cobbett in Ireland: A Warning to England*. Dennis Knight, ed. London: Lawrence and Wishart, 1984.

———. *Cobbett's Legacy to Labourers; Or, What is the Right Which Lords, Baronets and Squires have to the Lands of England?*. London: William Cobbett, 1834.

———. *The Emigrant's Guide: in Ten Letters*. new edn. London: William Cobbett, 1830. Originally published 1820.

———. *A History of the Protestant 'Reformation' in England and Ireland*. London: William Cobbett, 1824–27.

———. *Legacy to Parsons; or Have the Clergy of the Established Church an Equitable Right to the Tithes, or to Any Other Thing called Church Property, Greater Than Dissenters Have to the Same?*. London: William Cobbett, 1835.

———. *Political Register:* variously titled *Cobbett's Political Register, Annual Register, Cobbett's Weekly Political Register, Cobbett's Weekly Register*. 89 vols. London: William Cobbett, 1802–35.

———. *The Poor Man's Friend; or, Essays on the Rights and Duties of the Poor*. London: William Cobbett, 1826–27.

———. 'The Rights of the Poor' in *Twelve Sermons*. new edn. London: William Cobbett, 1828, 69–92.

———. *Rural Rides in the Counties of Surrey, Kent, Sussex, Hampshire, Wiltshire, Sommersetshire, Oxfordshire, Berkshire, Essex, Suffolk, Norfolk, and Hertfordhsire: With Economical and Political Observations Relating to Matters Applicable to, and Illustrated by the State of Those Counties Respectively*. London: William Cobbett, 1830 and George Woodcock, ed. Harmondsworth: Penguin Books, 1967.

———. 'The Sin of Forbidding Marriage' in *Twelve Sermons*. new edn. London: William Cobbett, 1828, 197–213.

————. *Surplus Population: And Poor-Law Bill. A Comedy in Three Acts*. London: William Cobbett, 1835.

————. *Twelve Sermons*. new edn. London: William Cobbett, 1828. Originally published 1821–22.

————. *Two-Penny Trash; or, Politics for the Poor*. London: William Cobbett, 1830–32.

Croker, John Wilson, and G. Poulett Scrope, 'Miss Martineau's *Monthly Novels*'. *Quarterly Review* XLIX (April 1833): 136–52.

Empson, William. '*Illustrations of Political Economy*: Mrs. Marcet – Miss Martineau'. *Edinburgh Review* LVII (April 1833): 1-39.

————. 'Life, Writing and Character of Mr. Malthus'. *Edinburgh Review* LXIV (January 1837): 469-506.

Ham, John. 'The Prudential Check – Marriage or Celibacy'. *Tait's Edinburgh Magazine* 3 (June 1833): 316–20.

Malthus, T. R. *Definitions in Political Economy, Preceded by an Inquiry into the Rules which Ought to Guide Political Economists in the Definition and Use of their Terms; with Remarks on the Deviation from these Rules in their Writings*. London: John Murray, 1827.

————. 'Depreciation of paper currency'. *The Edinburgh Review* XVII (February 1811): 339–72.

————. *An Essay on the Principle of Population, as it affects the Future Improvement of Society, with Remarks on the Speculations of Mr. Godwin, M. Condorcet, and Other Writers*. anonymous, London: J. J. Johnson, 1798; revised and enlarged as *An Essay on the Principle of Population: or a View of its past and present Effects on Human Happiness; with an Inquiry into our Prospects respecting the Removal or Mitigation of the Evils which it occasions*. 2 vols. London: J. J. Johnson, 1803; revised and enlarged again, London: J. J. Johnson 1806, 1807; revised and enlarged again, 3 vols. London: John Murray, 1826.

————. *Essay on the Principle of Population; and, A Summary View of the principle of population*. Anthony Flew, ed. Harmondsworth: Penguin, 1970.

————. *An Essay on the Principle of Population: Thomas Robert Malthus*. Phillip Appleman, ed. New York: W. W. Norton, 1976.

————. 'Godwin on Malthus'. *The Edinburgh Review* XXXV, no. lxx (July 1821): 362–77.

————. *The Grounds of an Opinion on the Policy of Restricting the Importation of Foreign Corn, Intended as an Appendix to 'Observations on the Corn Laws'*. London: John Murray, 1815.

————. 'High price of bullion'. *The Edinburgh Review* XXVLL (August 1811): 448–70.

————. *An Inquiry into the Nature and Progress of Rent and the Principles by which it is Regulated*. London: John Murray, 1815.

———. *Introduction to Malthus.* D. V. Glass, ed. London: Watts and Co., 1953.

———. *Letter to the Right Honorable Lord Grenville Occasioned by Some Observations of his Lordship on the East India Company's Establishment for the Education of Their Civil Servants.* London: J. Johnson, 1813.

———. *Letter to Samuel Whitbread, Esq., M. P. on his Proposed Bill for the Amendment of the Poor Laws.* London: J. Johnson and J. Hatchard, 1807.

———. *The Malthus Library Catalogue: The Personal Collection of Thomas Robert Malthus at Jesus College Cambridge.* Cambridge and New York: Pergamon Press, 1983.

———. 'On the meaning which is most usually and most correctly attached to the term "Value of a Commodity"'. *Transactions of the Royal Society of Literature* I, part 2 (1825–29): 74–81.

———. 'On the Measure of the Conditions Necessary to the Supply of Commodities'. *Transactions of the Royal Society of Literature* I, part 1 (1825–29): 171–80.

———. *The Measure of Value Stated and Illustrated, with an Application of it to the Alterations in the Value of the English Currency since 1790.* London: John Murray, 1823.

———. *Observations on the Effects of the Corn Laws, and of a Rise or Fall in the Price of Corn on the Agriculture and General Wealth of the Country.* London: J. Johnson, 1814.

———. *Occasional Papers of T. R. Malthus: On Ireland, Population, and Political Economy, from Contemporary Journals, written anonymously and hitherto uncollected.* Bernard Semmel, ed. New York: Burt Franklin, 1963.

———. *The Pamphlets of Thomas Robert Malthus.* Reprint, New York: Augustus M. Kelly, 1990.

———. 'Political Economy'. *The Quarterly Review* XXX, no. lx (January 1824): 297–334.

———. 'Population'. *Supplement to the Fourth, Fifth and Sixth Editions of the Encyclopaedia Britannica.* vol. 6. M. Napier, ed. London: Hurst Robinson, 1824, 307–33.

———. *The Principles of Political Economy Considered with a View to their Practical Application.* London: John Murray, 1820; revised and enlarged edn. London: William Pickering, 1836.

———. *Statements Respecting the East-India College with an Appeal to Facts, in Refutation of the Charges Lately Brought Against it in the Court of Proprietors.* London: John Murray, 1817.

———. *A Summary View of the Principle of Population.* London: John Murray, 1830.

———. 'Tooke on High and Low Prices'. *The Quarterly Review* XXIX, no. lx (April 1823): 214–39.

———. *The Travel Diaries of Thomas Robert Malthus*. Patricia James, ed. Cambridge: Cambridge University Press, 1966.

———. *T. R. Malthus, An Essay on the Principle of Population; or a View of its past and present Effects on Human Happiness; With an Inquiry into our Prospects respecting the future Removal or Mitigation of the Evils which it occasions: The version published in 1803, with the Variora of 1806, 1807, 1817, and 1826*. 2 vols. Patricia James, ed. Cambridge: Cambridge University Press, 1989.

———. *T. R. Malthus: Principles of Political Economy: Variorum Edition*. 2 vols. John Pullen, ed. Cambridge: Cambridge University Press, 1989.

———. *T. R. Malthus. The Unpublished Papers in the Collection of Kanto Gakuen University*. John Pullen and Trevor Hughes Parry, eds. vol. I. Cambridge: Cambridge University Press, 1997.

———. 'On the State of Ireland I'. *The Edinburgh Review* XIII (July 1808): 336–55.

———. 'On the State of Ireland II'. *The Edinburgh Review* XIV (April 1809): 151–70.

———. *The Works of Thomas Robert Malthus*. 8 vols. E. A. Wrigley and David Souden, eds. London: William Pickering, 1986.

Marcet, Jane. *Conversations on Political Economy; In Which the Elements of that Science are Familiarly Explained*. London: Longman, Hurst, Rees, Orme and Brown, 1816 and Philadelphia, PA: Moses Thomas, 1817.

———. *John Hopkins's Notions of Political Economy*. London: Longman, Hurst, Rees, Orme and Brown, 1833.

———. *Rich and Poor*. London: Longman, Brown, Green, and Longmans, 1851.

Martineau, Harriet. *Harriet Martineau's Autobiography*. 3 vols. London: Smith, Elder and Co., 1877.

———. *A History of England During the Thirty Years' Peace A. D. 1816-1846*. 4 vols. London: George Bell and Sons, 1877.

———. *Illustrations of Political Economy*. 9 vols. London: Charles Fox, 1834.

———. *Poor Laws and Paupers Illustrated*. 4 vols. London: Charles Fox, 1833–34.

Otter, William. 'Memoir of Robert Malthus' in *T. R. Malthus. The Principles of Political Economy Considered with a View to their Practical Application*. 2nd edn. London: William Pickering, 1836, xiii–liv.

Place, Francis. *Illustrations and Proofs of the Principle of Population including an Examination of the Proposed Remedies of Mr. Malthus, and a Reply to the Objections of Mr. Godwin and Others.* London: Longmans, 1822; repr., London: Allen and Unwin, 1930.

Journals, magazines and newspapers

The Black Dwarf; *The Bulldog*; *Cobbett's Magazine*; *The Cosmopolite*; *The Crisis*; *The Destructive*; *The Economist*; *The Edinburgh Review*; *Fraser's Magazine*; *The Gauntlet*; *The Gorgon*; *The Lion*; *The Monthly Magazine*; *The Monthly Repository*; *The Morning Chronicle*; *The New Monthly Review*; *The New Moral World*; *The New Political Register*; *Penny Papers for the People*; *The People's Conservative and Trade Union Gazette*; *The Pioneer*; *Political Letters and Pamphlets*; *The Political Penny Magazine*; *Political Register*; *The Poor Man's Advocate*; *The Poor Man's Guardian*; *The Quarterly Review*; *The Radical*; *The Republican*; *Tait's Edinburgh Magazine*; *The Times*; *The True Sun*; *Twopenny Dispatch*; *The Working Man's Friend.*

Government reports

Checkland, S. G. and E. A. Checkland, eds. *The Poor Law Report of 1834*. Harmondsworth: Penguin Books, 1974.

First, Second and Third Reports from the Select Committee on Emigration from the United Kingdom with Minutes of Evidence, Appendix and Index. Irish University Press Series of British Parliamentary Papers. Emigration 2, 1826–27.

Report from His Majesty's Commissioners for Inquiring into the Administration and Practical Application of the Poor Laws: Rural Queries and Town Queries. vols. XXXV–XXXVI, 1834.

Secondary sources

Altick, Richard D. *The English Common Reader: A Social History of the Mass Reading Public 1800–1900*. Chicago, IL: The University of Chicago Press, 1957.

Ausubel, Herman. 'William Cobbett and Malthusianism'. *Journal of the History of Ideas* 13 (1952): 250–56.

Beauchamp, Gorman. 'The Dystopian Theology of Parson Malthus'. *Humanitas* 13, no. 2 (2000): 54–71.

Bonar, James. *Malthus and His Work*. 2nd edn. London: Frank Cass, 1924.

Boner, Harold A. *Hungry Generations: The Nineteenth-Century Case Against Malthusianism*. New York: Russell and Russell, 1955.

Boyer, George. *An Economic History of the English Poor Law 1750–1850*. Cambridge: Cambridge University Press, 1990.

Brundage, Anthony. 'Debate: The Making of the New Poor Law Redivivus'. *Past and Present*, no. 127 (November 1990): 183–6.

———. *The English Poor Laws, 1700–1930*. New York: Palgrave, 2002.

———. *The Making of the New Poor Laws: The Politics of Inquiry, Enactment and Implementation*. New Brunswick, NJ: Rutgers University Press, 1978.

Burton, Anthony. *William Cobbett: Englishman: A Biography*. London: Aurum Press, 1977.

Bush, M. L. *What is Love? Richard Carlile's Philosophy of Sex*. London: Verso, 1998.

De Marchi, Neil. 'Introduction to Minisymposium: Malthus at 200'. in 'Minisymposium: Malthus at 200'. *History Of Political Economy* 30, no. 2 (Summer 1998): 289–91.

Dean, Mitchell. *The Constitution of Poverty: Toward a Genealogy of Liberal Governance*. London: Routledge, 1991.

Digby, Anne. 'Malthus and the Reform of the Poor Law' in J. Dupâquier, A. Fauve-Chamoux and E. Grebnik, eds. *Malthus Past and Present*. London: Academic Press, 1983, 97–109.

Dunkley, Peter. 'Paternalism, the Magistracy and Poor Relief in England, 1795–1834'. *International Review of Social History* XXIV, no. 3 (1979): 371–97.

———. 'Whigs and Paupers: The Reform of the English Poor Laws, 1830–1834'. *Journal of British Studies* XX, no. 2 (1981): 124–9.

Dupâquier, J., A. Fauve-Chamoux, and E. Grebnik, eds. *Malthus Past and Present,* London: Academic Press, 1983.

Dyck, Ian. *William Cobbett and Rural Popular Culture*. Cambridge: Cambridge University Press, 1992.

Edsall, Nicholas C. *The Anti-Poor Law Movement 1833–44*. Manchester: Manchester University Press, 1971.

Eversley, D. E. C. *Social Theories of Fertility and the Malthusian Debate*. Oxford: Clarendon Press, 1959.

Eastwood, David. 'Debate: The Making of the New Poor Law Redivivus'. *Past and Present*, no. 127 (November 1990): 186–94.

———. 'Rethinking the Debates on the Poor Law in Early Nineteenth-Century England'. *Utilitas* 6, no. 1 (May 1994): 97–116.

Fryer, Peter. *The Birth Controllers*. London: Secker and Warburg, 1965.

Gilbert, G. 'Economic Growth and the Poor in Malthus's *Essay on Population*'. *History of Political Economy* 12 (Spring 1980): 83–96.

Grampp, W. D. 'Malthus and his Contemporaries'. *History of Political Economy* 6 (Fall 1974): 18–40.

Greenwood, F. Murray and Barry Wright, eds. *Canadian State Trials*. Vol. 1, *Law, Politics, and Security Measures, 1608–1837*. Toronto: University of Toronto Press, 1996.

Harrison, John F. C. *Quest for the New Moral World: Robert Owen and the Owenites in Britain and America*. New York: Charles Scribner's Sons, 1969.

Hilton, Boyd. *The Age of Atonement: The Influence of Evangelicalism on Social and Economic Thought 1795–1865*. Oxford: Oxford University Press, 1988.

———. Review of *Riches and Poverty* by Donald Winch. *Times Literary Supplement* (16 August 1996): 9.

Himmelfarb, Gertrude, *The Idea of Poverty: England in the Early Industrial Age*. London and Boston, MA: Faber and Faber, 1984.

Hobsbawm, E. J. *Industry and Empire: An Economic History of Britain Since 1750*. London: Weidenfeld and Nicolson, 1968.

Hollander, Samuel. *The Economics of Thomas Robert Malthus*. Toronto: University of Toronto Press, 1997.

———. 'An Invited Comment on "Reappraisal of Malthus the Economist, 1933–97"' in 'Minisymposium: Malthus at 200'. *History of Political Economy* 30, no. 2 (Summer 1998): 335–41.

———. 'Malthus's Abandonment of Agricultural Protectionism: A Discovery in the History of Economic Thought'. *American Economic Review* 82 (June 1992): 650–59.

———. 'More on Malthus and Agricultural Protectionism'. *History of Political Economy* 27 (Fall 1995): 531–8.

Hollis, Patricia. *The Pauper Press: A Study in Working-Class Radicalism of the 1830s*. Oxford: Oxford University Press, 1970.

Hunter, Shelagh. *Harriet Martineau: The Poetics of Moralism*. Aldershot: Scolar Press, 1995.

Huzel, James P. 'The Demographic Impact of the Old Poor Law: More Reflexions on Malthus'. *Economic History Review* 2nd ser. XXXIII (August 1980): 367–81.

———. 'The Labourer and the Poor Law 1750–1850' in G. E. Mingay, ed. *The Agrarian History of England and Wales*. Vol. VI. Cambridge: Cambridge University Press, 1989, 755–810.

———. 'Malthus, the Poor Law, and Population in Early Nineteenth-Century England'. *Economic History Review* 2nd ser. XXII (December 1969): 420–52.

———. 'Parson Malthus and the Pelican Inn Protocol: A Reply to Professor Levine'. *Historical Methods*, no. 17 (Winter 1984): 25–7.

———. 'Thomas Robert Malthus (1766–1834)' in Gary Kelly and Edd

Applegate, eds. *British Reform Writers, 1789–1832. Dictionary of Literary Biography*. Vol. 158. Detroit, MI, Washington, DC and London: Bruccoli, Clark, Layman, 1996, 194–210.

James, Patricia. *Population Malthus: His Life and Times*. London: Routledge and Kegan Paul, 1979.

Kegel, Charles H. 'William Cobbett and Malthusianism'. *Journal of the History of Ideas* 19 (June 1958): 348–62.

Klancher, Jon P. *The Making of English Reading Audiences, 1790–1832*. Madison: University of Wisconsin Press, 1987.

Knott, John. *Popular Opposition to the 1834 Poor Law*. London: Croom Helm, 1986.

Le Mahieu, D. L. 'Malthus and the Theology of Scarcity'. *Journal of the History of Ideas* 40 (July–September 1979): 467–74.

Levine, David. 'Parson Malthus, Professor Huzel and the Pelican Inn Protocol'. *Historical Methods* no. 17 (Winter 1984): 21–4.

Logan, Deborah Anne. *The Hour and the Woman: Harriet Martineau's 'Somewhat Remarkable' Life*. DeKalb, IL: Northern Illinois University Press, 2002.

Mandler, Peter. 'Debate: The Making of the Old Poor Law Redivivus'. *Past and Present,* no. 127 (November 1990): 194–201.

———. 'The Making of the New Poor Law Redivivus'. *Past and Present*, no. 117 (November 1987): 131–57.

———. 'Tories and Paupers: Christian Political Economy and the Making of the New Poor Law'. *Historical Journal* 33, no. 1 (1990): 81–103.

Meek, Ronald, ed. *Marx and Engels on the Population Bomb*. Berkeley, CA: Ramparts Press, 1971.

Miles, Dudley. *Francis Place: The Life of a Remarkable Radical 1771–1854*. New York: St. Martin's Press, 1988.

McClaren, Angus. *Birth Conrol in Nineteenth-Century England*. New York: Holmes and Meirers Publishers, 1978.

McCleary, G. F. *The Malthusian Population Theory*. London: Faber and Faber, 1953.

Natrass, Leonara. *William Cobbett: The Politics of Style*. Cambridge: Cambridge University Press, 1995.

Petersen, William. *Malthus*. Cambridge, MA: Harvard University Press, 1979.

Pichanick, Valerie Kossew. *Harriet Martineau: The Woman and Her Work*. Ann Arbor: University of Michigan Press, 1980.

Polanyi, Karl. *The Great Transformation: The Political and Economic Origins of Our Time*, 2nd edn. Boston: Beacon Press, 2001.

Polkinghorn, Bette. 'Political Economy Disguised as Fanciful Fables'. *Eastern Economic Review* 8 (April 1982): 145–56.

————. 'An Unpublished Letter from Malthus to Jane Marcet, January 22, 1833'. *American Economic Review* 76 (September 1986): 845–7.

Poynter, J. R. *Society and Pauperism: English Ideas on Poor Relief, 1795–1834*. London: Routledge and Kegan Paul, 1969.

Pullen, John. 'The Last Sixty-Five Years of Malthus Scholarship' in 'Minisymposium: Malthus at 200'. *History of Political Economy* 30, no. 2 (Summer 1998): 343–52.

————. 'Malthus on Agricultural Protection: An Alternative View'. *History of Political Economy* 27 (Fall 1995): 517–29.

————. 'Malthus's Theological Ideas and Their Influence on his Principles of Population'. *History of Political Economy* 13, no. 1 (Spring 1981): 39–54.

————. 'Thomas Robert Malthus (1766–1834)'. *University of New England School of Economics Working Paper Series in Economics*, no. 2001–2002. (January 2001): 1–12.

Richardson, Ruth. *Death, Dissection and the Destitute*. London: Routledge and Kegan Paul, 1987.

Roberts, Caroline. *The Woman and the Hour: Harriet Martineau and Victorian Ideologies*. Toronto: University of Toronto Press, 2002.

Rose, M. E., ed. *The English Poor Law, 1780–1930*. New York: Barnes and Noble, 1971.

Ross, Eric B. *The Malthus Factor: Poverty, Politics and Population in Capitalist Development*. London and New York: Zed Books, 1998.

Sanders, Valerie. *Reason over Passion: Harriet Martineau and the Victorian Novel*. Brighton: Harvester Press, 1986.

Santurri, E. N. 'Theodicy and Social Policy in Malthus's Thought'. *Journal of the History of Ideas* 43 (April–June 1982): 315–20.

Schweizer, Karl W. and John W. Osborne. *Cobbett in his Times*. Leicester: Leicester University Press, 1990.

Shackleton, J. R. 'Two Early Female Economists: Jane Marcet and Harriet Martineau'. Research Working Paper, The Polytechnic of Central London, no. 35 (October 1988): 1–29.

Smith, Kenneth. *The Malthusian Controversy*. London: Routledge and Kegan Paul, 1951.

Spater, George. *William Cobbett: The Poor Man's Friend*. 2 vols. Cambridge: Cambridge University Press, 1992.

Spengler, J. J. 'Malthus's Total Population Theory: A Restatement and Reappraisal'. *Canadian Journal of Economics and Political Science* 11, no. 83 (1945): 234–64.

Thomas, Gillian. *Harriet Martineau*. Boston: Twayne Publishers, 1985.

————. 'Harriet Martineau' in William B. Thesing, ed. *Victorian Prose Writers Before 1867. Dictionary of Literary Biography*. vol. 55.

Detroit, MI, Washington, DC and London: Bruccoli, Clark, Layman, 1987, 168–75.

Thompson, E. P. *Customs in Common: Studies in Traditional Popular Culture*. New York: The New Press, 1993.

———. 'The Moral Economy of the English Crowd in the Eighteenth Century'. *Past and Present*, no. 50 (February 1971): 76–136.

Thomson, Dorothy Lampen. *Adam Smith's Daughters*. New York: Exposition Press, 1973.

The Times, *The History of the Times: 'The Thunderer' in the Making 1785–1841*. London: The Times, 1935.

Turner, Michael, ed. *Malthus and His Time*. London: Macmillan, 1986.

Valenze, Deborah. *The First Industrial Woman*. Oxford: Oxford University Press, 1995.

Waterman, A. M. C. 'Malthus as Theologian: The "First Essay" and the Relation between Political Economy and Christian Theology' in J. Dupâquier, A. Fauve-Chamoux and E. Grebnik, eds. *Malthus Past and Present*. London: Academic Press, 1983, 195–209.

———. 'Reappraisal of "Malthus the Economist 1933–97"' in 'Minisymposium: Malthus at 200'. *History of Political Economy* 30, no. 2 (Summer 1998): 293–334.

———. *Revolution, Economics and Religion: Christian Political Economy 1798–1833*. Cambridge: Cambridge University Press, 1991.

Webb, R. K. *The British Working Class Reader 1790–1848: Literacy and Social Tension*. London: George Allen and Unwin Ltd., 1955.

———. *Harriet Martineau: A Radical Victorian*. London: Heineman, 1960.

Wheately, Vera. *The Life and Work of Harriet Martineau*. London: Secker and Warburg, 1957.

Wiener, Joel. *Radicalism and Free Thought in Nineteenth-Century Britain: The Life of Richard Carlile*. Westport, CT and London: Greeenwood Press, 1983.

———. *The War of the Unstamped: The Movement to Repeal the British Newspaper Tax, 1830–1836*. Ithaca, NY: Cornell University Press, 1969.

Williamson, J. G. *Coping with City Growth during the Industrial Revolution*. Cambridge: Cambridge University Press, 1990.

Winch, Donald. *Malthus*. Oxford: Oxford University Press, 1987.

———. 'The Reappraisal of Malthus; A Comment' in 'Minisymposium: Malthus at 200'. *History of Political Economy* 30, no. 2 (Summer 1998): 353–63.

———. *Riches and Poverty: An Intellectual History of Political Economy in Britain 1750–1834*. Cambridge: Cambridge University Press, 1996.

Wood, John Cunningham, ed. *Thomas Robert Malthus: Critical Assessments*. 4 vols. London: Croom Helm, 1986.

Wrigley, E. A. and R. S. Schofield. *The Population History of England and Wales 1541–1871: A Reconstruction*. Cambridge, MA: Harvard University Press, 1981.

Index

References to illustrations are in **bold**

an **informa** business

ISBN 978-1-138-26302-4

9 781138 263024

Routledge
Taylor & Francis Group
www.routledge.com